W9-BDJ-540

100 HEADLINES THAT CHANGED THE WORLD

James Maloney

A Herman Graf book
Skyhorse Publishing

Copyright © 2012 Constable & Robinson Ltd

All Rights Reserved. No part of this book may be reproduced
in any manner without the express written consent of the publisher,
except in the case of brief excerpts in critical reviews or articles.
All inquiries should be addressed to Skyhorse Publishing,
307 West 36th Street, 11th Floor,
New York, NY 10018.

Skyhorse Publishing books may be purchased in bulk
at special discounts for sales promotion, corporate gifts,
fund-raising, or educational purposes.
Special editions can also be created to specifications.
For details, contact the Special Sales Department,
Skyhorse Publishing, 307 West 36th Street,
11th Floor, New York, NY 10018
or info@skyhorsepublishing.com.

www.skyhorsepublishing.com

ISBN 978 1 61608 371 7

Printed and bound in the UK

10 9 8 7 6 5 4 3 2 1

Library of Congress Cataloging-in-Publication Data available on file

DISCARD
FCPL discards materials
that are outdated and in poor condition.
In order to make room for current,
in-demand materials, underused materials
are offered for public sale.

100 HEADLINES
THAT CHANGED
THE WORLD

CONTENTS

INTRODUCTION

As a journalist as well as an author with a keen interest in history and a fascination with newspapers, I found compiling this book was an absolute joy for me. I soon realised that there was no shortage of headlines from which to choose. The problem was what to leave out. This wealth of riches meant that some momentous events did not find their way into the pages of this book.

I had been very aware from the outset that my final choice of *100 Headlines* would cause disagreement, incredulity and possibly some anger amongst readers. How could such-and-such be left out? Why has *that* been included? Did that really *change* the world? It would be impossible to please all, perhaps even the majority, so in the end I have just had to please myself.

I could quite easily have filled the book with war and conflict or natural disasters, murder or scientific discoveries. All have been plentiful over the years. But I have striven to bring variety, and so we have tragedies co-existing with medical breakthroughs, heroic feats, political disasters and wonderful inventions.

Sadly, there have been all too many tragedies in history. I have had to be highly selective in choosing which to include. My criterion has not been solely based on the number of deaths or injuries in an incident. Nor have I adhered doggedly to global impact. I have endeavoured to bring together a selection of headlines that caused shock, disbelief and a considerable amount of emotional outpouring at the time of their happening. And so we have the likes of the 1958 Munich air disaster, which tore apart the young Manchester United football team – the most exciting team of the era – or the devastating Boxing Day tsunami of 2004, which saw the loss of over 200,000 lives. General Custer's last stand finds a place, as do the First and Second World Wars. And so on.

The main theme of the book is that headlines – or events – should have changed the world. Some of the chosen headlines clearly did change the world, while others may have had a less obvious impact. Ultimately the choice is subjective. It could also be argued that everything and anything changes the world to some degree.

This is a book of headlines, the stories behind them and the impact they would have on the future of the world. I have delved into the world's newspaper archives and found some remarkable articles on famous events such as the sinking of the *Titanic*, the assassination of Abraham Lincoln and the serial murders of Jack the Ripper. But some things I imagined I might include I had to abandon because I was unable to find a headline. These are mostly inventions, scientific discoveries and medical advances that were not fully appreciated at the time and so, outside of scientific, medical and other specialist publications, they received little or no attention in mainstream newspapers. For some I have managed to find a later headline with which to write a retrospective piece. This I did with the advent of Microsoft, for example, by including it under a headline announcing Bill Gates's departure from the company he set up.

The Internet, social networking sites and 24-hour TV and radio news have changed the way we hear the news. But in this book, many of the headlines you see were the main source of information at the time. News travelled at a slower pace in decades past and so major events were often not reported in newspapers until days – sometimes weeks – later.

Old newspapers' front pages were very different from today's. Many of them had classified adverts on the front and the news stories, however major, were 'buried' inside in small columns easily overlooked in the 'wall of print'.

While it is true that newspaper readership has declined as the electronic media have flourished, the printed word still carries great impact. Newspapers are both fascinating social documents of the time and records of history. There is nothing like seeing and holding an old newspaper in your hands, knowing that the very paper itself was there when the event actually happened – be it the first man to set foot on the moon or the Russian revolution of 1917. It feels like living history.

Newspapers have been around in one form or another for hundreds of years. The ancient Romans can probably lay claim to distributing the first form of public news in the form of bulletins carved in metal or stone and prominently displayed for all to read. In 59 BC Julius Caesar informed the public about social, political and military events with information written on large white boards and placed in prominent places. In 8th-century China, hand-written newsheets were distributed. And in 1556 the Venetian government published *Notizie scritte*, for which readers paid a small coin, or 'gazzetta', hence the popular newspaper name of *Gazette*.

But the newspaper as we might recognise it did not begin to appear until the 17th century as printing presses became more widespread and newspapers appeared more regularly.

The arrival of the telegraph in 1844 meant that information could be relayed much more quickly. This enabled newspapers to be more timely and relevant in reporting distant events. They became the most important means of communication and, as more and more national and local newspapers appeared, the headlines became increasingly bigger and more attention-grabbing in an attempt to entice people to buy them. *100 Headlines That Changed The World* features some of the most memorable banner headlines with the stories behind the headlines retold in as concise a form as possible to put the headline in context and explain how these stories from the past helped to shape the world that we live in today.

PENNY POSTAGE PICTURES

(*Liverpool Standard*, 12 May 1840)

THE PENNY BLACK was the world's first adhesive postage stamp used in a public postal system. It was issued in Britain on 1 May 1840, for official use from 6 May, and it marked a turning point in social history.

Prior to 1840, the post service was too expensive for most people to use. The cost of sending a single letter could equate to a working man's daily wage, or more. Postage was charged by the number of sheets of paper used and the distance travelled. And it was paid by the recipient. But all Members of Parliament and Lords had the right to frank and receive a number of letters free.

The expense meant it was difficult for family or friends living long distances apart to communicate with each other. Sending letters was, therefore, a privilege of the wealthy, but to save money it became common practice to cram as many words as possible onto both sides of a sheet of paper. There was no such thing as an envelope. Letters were simply folded and sealed with wax. There were no pillar boxes, so it would have to be taken to a post office. If the addressee lived in a remote area they might never receive the letter. And the recipient of a costly letter could simply refuse delivery.

GUMMED LABELS

All of this began to cause some concern to the government in the 1830s. Some maintain that James Chalmers, a bookseller and printer from Dundee, first came up with the idea of pre-paid gummed labels. But it was Rowland Hill, a teacher turned civil servant from Kidderminster, Worcestershire, who is widely credited with the invention of the adhesive stamp and the basis of the modern postal system.

BROKEN HEARTED

Hill, so the story goes, was inspired to begin planning a whole new postal system when he came across a sobbing young woman, broken hearted because she had no money and could not afford to pay for a letter that had been sent to her by her fiancé.

In 1835, Hill embarked on a study of the existing postal system and, two years later, he produced a pamphlet called 'Post Office Reform: Its Importance and Practicability.' The mainstay of Hill's reform proposals was a penny post, which meant that any letter weighing less than half an ounce (14 grams) could be sent anywhere in Britain for one penny.

The Postmaster General, Lord Lichfield, was startled by such a radical concept and commented, 'Of all the wild and visionary schemes which I ever heard of, it is the most extravagant.' But merchants and reformers backed Hill, seeing the benefit of allowing the common man to be able to afford to send letters.

Hill's pre-paid system advocated the use of stamped 'covers' consisting of 'a bit of paper just large enough to bear the stamp, and covered at the back with a glutinous wash'. This was to eventually become the Penny Black. He also suggested the use of envelopes.

CONTROLLER OF STAMPS

Hill appointed his older brother, Edwin, as the first Controller of Stamps, a position he would retain for the next 32 years. Edwin also invented a machine for making envelopes. The covers (stamps) were designed by artist William Mulready, based on an engraved head of the reigning monarch, Queen Victoria, as a young woman. The black background included the word 'POSTAGE' at the top of the stamp and 'ONE PENNY' at the bottom, along with flourishes around the borders and ornamental stars. Stamps would be printed in sheets of 240 that could be cut by the postmaster or postmistress using scissors or a knife.

But the rather sombre design was disliked by some and the

Liverpool Standard newspaper in a lengthy article headlined, 'Penny Postage Pictures' criticised the stamp, describing, 'little bits of stuff like sticking plaster, with a dirty looking bust of Her Majesty, for dabbing on the back of a letter.' It added, 'Perhaps Rowland Hill, Esq. or the artist W. Mulready, Esq. R.A. can explain, but for our part, we give up the attempt in despair.'

The Penny Postage Bill was passed by Parliament on 17 August 1839, whereby prepayment would become the standard for sending letters and the basic cost would be a one-penny stamp.

The Penny Black first went on sale on 1 May 1840, although they were only valid for postage from 6 May 1840. It was followed a day later by the Two Penny Blue. This new postal system became an instant success with a huge increase in people sending letters, which provided lucrative revenue.

RED INK PROBLEMS

But the Penny Black was in use for a little over a year. The red cancellation mark that was used on the stamp was found to be hard to see on a black background and the red ink was easy to remove, making it possible to re-use stamps after they had been cancelled.

In 1841, it was determined that black ink was more robust and so the Treasury switched to the Penny Red and issued post offices with cancellation devices with black ink.

By the end of 1840, more than 160 million letters had been sent in Britain and by the turn of the century, the figure had rocketed to 2.3 billion.

STAMPS SPREAD WORLDWIDE

The use of an envelope brought added privacy to letter writing, which encouraged people to write more confidential messages, including 'love letters'.

Adhesive postage stamps were gradually introduced throughout the world. The head of the reigning monarch has featured on British stamps ever since. Because the Penny Black and Two Penny Blue were the world's first postage stamps, they did not name their country of origin and British stamps are still the only ones in the world that carry on this tradition. •

GOLD MINE FOUND

(*Californian*, 15 March 1848)

RUMOURS OF GOLD in California had existed for years but it wasn't until gold was discovered at Sutter's Mill that the Gold Rush began. People from all over the United States and from around the world made their way to this sleepy backwater and changed the face of California for all time.

On 4 January 1848, James Marshall, who was building a sawmill for Swiss emigrant John Sutter in Sacramento, found what he thought might be gold along by the river. He took it back to show Sutter and tests showed that it was, indeed, gold.

Worried that the find would bring an onrush of prospectors to his land and that his own workforce would desert him, Sutter asked his workers to stay quiet about the find. But word soon got out.

When this local newspaper report relayed the story of the find at Sutter's Mill, hordes of gold-hunting

Californians began to make their way to the area. And after major newspapers began to report the find, President James Polk, speaking to Congress on 5 December 1848, confirmed that gold had been discovered in California. It was then that 'gold fever' broke out in earnest.

MINER FORTY-NINERS

By 1849 the rush was on. Many miners or 'forty-niners', as they were nicknamed after the year of their arrival, expected to find rivers overflowing with gold and were unprepared for the gruelling necessity for panning and digging.

Gold was found throughout much of California and made some rich, but many went away with little or nothing at all. As more and more people arrived, those with an entrepreneurial flare gave up the hunt for gold and, instead, used their skills as carpenters, traders, builders and teachers, to service the mining industry

ANGER AT FOREIGNERS

As gold became increasingly more difficult to find, anger and fighting broke out. Americans became incensed that foreigners were raping their lands and drove them out of mining camps so that they had to set up camps of their own.

California had become a possession of the U.S. following the war with Mexico but was not a formal territory. It was a pretty lawless place and anyone who found gold was quickly surrounded by others. Thieves, thugs and conmen found their own 'shortcut' ways of getting their hands on the treasure.

Claim laws had to be set on which pieces of land individuals were allowed to mine. And camps set up claims officers to patrol mines and settle disputes.

Gradually, California was being transformed. Towns and cities were chartered and roads and houses and stores built. A state constitution was drawn up, elections were held and representatives sent to Washington, D.C., to negotiate the adoption of California as a state.

POPULATION EXPLOSION

Before the gold rush, California was largely inhabited by missionaries and Native Americans – a total of about 2,000 people. By late 1849 its population had grown to 15,000, and by 1853 there were over 300,000 people living there.

When silver was discovered in Nevada in 1859, the miners headed there and the California Gold Rush came to an end

Many of the communities that had been built – full of shacks, shops and saloons – became 'ghost towns.' But, by this time, California had a growing economy of farming and commerce with many staying on to take advantage of the rich agricultural land and business opportunities.

CALIFORNIAN DREAM

Roads, schools, churches, railways and civic organisations were

11

created throughout the land. On 9 September 1850 California became part of the United States of America. The phrase 'Californian Dream' was used to describe the varied opportunities to flourish and prosper in this new golden state.

The population quickly expanded, especially with the coming of the trans-continental railroad link in 1869, and today more people live in California than in any other state.

They still hunt for, gold, too with tourists and hobbyists panning gravel in streams across the state and there are almost 25,000 official active gold mining claims. Despite the high price of gold, however, the meagre amounts that are extracted today are not likely to bring on another bout of gold rush fever. ●

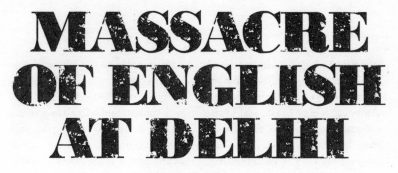

MASSACRE OF ENGLISH AT DELHI

(*Daily Telegraph*, 29 June 1857)

A REBELLION WITHIN the Indian Army caught the British government by surprise when it escalated across the country and gained the support of thousands of citizens.

Britain, as the colonial power, was used to acquiescence amongst Indian troops and had failed fully to appreciate the warning signs over the years that all was not well. And when the troops finally took a stand, there was shock and outrage at what was seen as a betrayal.

The *Daily Telegraph* reported how from Calcutta to Lahore the troops of the Bengal Presidency were in 'open or undisguised mutiny'.

Variously described as 'The Indian Mutiny', 'The Great Rebellion', 'The Sepoy Uprising' or 'India's First War of Independence', it was a result of mounting tension among Indian troops over unfair treatment from European officers.

It began on 10 May 1857 when sepoys (native Indian soldiers) of the British East India Company's army, in the town of Meerut, shot their British officers and marched on Delhi. Word of the uprising quickly spread and other sepoys rebelled in different parts of India.

THE SEPOY SOLDIERS

The background to the rebellion was a series of incidents which led to mounting grievances, resentment and anger. The sepoys were a combination of Hindu and Muslim soldiers who made up the bulk of the army in the East India Company (which effectively governed India).

The forces were divided into three Presidency armies – the Bombay, the Madras and the Bengal.

There had been some early resentment amongst the soldiers when the army's campaign to annex more land forced them to serve in distant areas such as Burma in the Anglo-Burmese Wars of 1856. There were more grievances when, under the General Service Act, new recruits would no longer receive a pension on retirement. Another cause of friction was the increasing number of European officers in the battalions, which made promotion for the rank and file increasingly slow and difficult. The Bengal Presidency had extra cause to feel bitter because they were paid less than Bombay and Madras.

NEW CARTRIDGES

The final spark which ignited this seething pressure can of resentment was the issue of new paper cartridges to use with the new Enfield rifles. The cartridges came pre-greased and to load the rifle, sepoys had to bite the cartridge open to release the powder. But the tallow used to grease the paper was believed to be made with cow and pig fat, upsetting the religious sensibilities of both Hindus and Muslims.

On 26 February 1857 the 19th Bengal Native Infantry (BNI) refused to use the cartridges and their angry colonel confronted them on the parade ground, backed with artillery. But after some negotiation, the artillery was taken away and the next morning's parade was cancelled.

LONE REBEL COURT-MARTIALLED

A month later, a 29-year-old sepoy of the BNI named Mangal Pandey told his colleagues he was going to rebel against his commanders. On hearing of his intent, Sergeant-Major James Hewson went to investigate, only to have Pandey shoot at him.

Pandey had failed to incite others to join him in the rebellion but they showed their support in refusing orders to arrest him – save for one man, Shaikh Paltu, who managed to restrain him.

Pandey was court-martialled on 6 April and hanged two days later. The regiment was disbanded and stripped of its uniforms for its failure to act.

On 24 April, all apart from five of the 90 men of the 3rd Bengal Light Cavalry at Meerut refused to accept the cartridges. Retribution was severe. On 9 May, 85 men were court martialled and most were sentenced to ten years' imprisonment with hard labour.

The entire garrison was put on parade to witness the men being stripped of their uniforms and placed in shackles. As they were marched off to jail, some of them chided their comrades for their lack of support.

There was some protest in the city amongst civilians, with fires started in several of the buildings.

OFFICERS KILLED

The following day, the 3rd Cavalry, broke into revolt. Officers were killed when they tried to curtail them. Then European civilians' quarters were attacked with 50 Europeans killed, including soldiers, four male civilians, eight women and eight children.

The sepoys freed their 85 imprisoned comrades from jail, along with 800 other prisoners, and marched towards Delhi in the evening.

With other rebellions breaking out across India, garrisons were beleaguered for several months before the British could send reinforcement troops.

Early on 11 May the 3rd Cavalry reached Delhi and called for Emperor Bahadur Shah in his palace, to acknowledge and lead them, which he later did. Meanwhile, the house of the Chief Magistrate was destroyed and European officials and their families were killed by sepoys or other crowds of rioters.

Panicking British officers felt they could trust no one and opened fire on their own sepoys, managing to turn some potentially faithful men into enemies.

SIEGE OF DELHI

It wasn't until the beginning of July that British troops arrived on the outskirts of Delhi and established a base on the ridge to the north of the city. Heavy artillery rained down on the rebels in what became known as 'The Siege of Delhi' and by mid-September the city had been retaken. Bahadur Shah was arrested and many Indian citizens and sepoys were killed in retaliation.

A shocking incident had taken place in June when rebel sepoys in Cawnpore took 120 women and children hostage and killed them when they realised that all was lost.

In Lucknow, the besieged British Residency was rescued when a small column of relief soldiers managed to overcome the rebels.

REBELS DEFEATED

The last of the rebels were defeated in Gwalior in June 1858.

The bloodshed had sent shockwaves throughout colonial Britain, which had hitherto taken India for granted. The rebellion led to the dissolution of the East India Company with direct control of the region being assumed by the British Government in the form of the new British Raj. •

DISCOVERY OF A SUBTERRANEAN FOUNTAIN OF OIL

(*New York Tribune*, 8 September 1859)

THE PRESENCE OF OIL around Titusville in Pennsylvania had been known for years. Native Americans had been using it in medicinal remedies and by the mid-19th century it was being refined into kerosene for lamp oil.

Early methods of extracting it included digging trenches along Oil Creek or collecting it from seeps in the ground, but it was slow and laborious and not very efficient.

Knowing that there were big bucks to be made from oil, a group of investors formed the Pennsylvania Rock Oil Company and hired former railroad conductor Edwin Laurentine Drake to help them extract it. He had no engineering background and was principally hired because he was entitled to free rail travel, which would save the company money.

In his mid-30s, he retired due to ill health but, when the company became Seneca Oil with some new backers, he was tempted to return by its president, New Haven banker James M Townsend. His mission was to extract oil on a large scale basis at Titusville.

SINKING A SHAFT

Drake, who was hired at $1,000 dollars a year, had been frustrated by his earlier attempts and this time he decided on a new method based on that used by salt-well drillers. He would bore into the ground and sink a shaft straight to the source.

He was given the title of 'Colonel' to impress Titusville residents but they were less than respectful when he and his team arrived in March 1858.

At that time Titusville was a sleepy town, mostly involved in lumber, and the locals laughed at him for digging for oil – it was something that nobody had ever done. His effort was quickly dubbed 'Drake's folly', as they were convinced it wouldn't work.

After setting up the rig, drilling started in early August 1859, using a steam engine to drive a heavy iron bit into the ground to break the rock. The work was slow, averaging just a couple of feet a day, and the Seneca Oil directors were losing faith and interest, but Drake persevered.

PENNSYLVANIA OIL RUSH

On 27 August the drill bit had reached a depth of 69.5ft (21m) when the workers stopped for the day. But they hadn't realised that they had finally made it. The next morning when Drake's driller, Billy Smith, looked into the hole he saw crude oil rising up.

He excitedly rushed to tell Drake that they had struck oil and 'Drake's folly' became the prototype for future oil well construction. It was the first commercially viable oil well in the United States, producing 25 barrels a day and was the beginning of the Pennsylvania oil rush.

The town's population of 250 swelled to 10,000 as eight refineries were built between 1862 and 1868, spawning an ever-growing oil support industry.

BOOM TOWNS

New towns grew out of what were previously small settlements, oil wells springing up around the unimaginatively named Petroleum Center, while nearby, Pithole grew from nothing to have more than fifty hotels, three churches and a population of at least 20,000.

Prior to the oil boom, Titusville, which was originally called Edinburgh when Jonathan Titus founded the settlement in 1796, had around 250 residents, most of whom were involved in the lumber business. The town very quickly expanded to have a population of more than 10,000 and, unlike Petroleum Center and Pithole which became almost ghost towns when their oil ran dry, Titusville is still thriving today, albeit with a greatly reduced population.

OIL MILLIONAIRES

The first oil millionaire was Jonathan Watson, who owned the land where Drake's well was drilled. He was soon joined by many other millionaires but Drake was not one of them. He was to die an invalid, confined to a wheelchair and virtually penniless.

The Seneca Oil Company, which was now earning a fortune, paid him off with $2,167 in June 1860. Drake's subsequent business ventures were not a success. He lost what money he had made in bad investments and by May 1866 he was so down on his heels that he wrote to a friend asking for money. His wife supported their family by sewing dresses and taking in boarders.

In 1873, the state of Pennsylvania, by way of thanks for founding the oil industry, granted him an annuity of $1,500. He died on 9 November 1880. ●

THE WAR BEGUN

(*New York Herald*, 13 April 1861)

THIS SUCCINCT HEADLINE marked the start of the bloodiest war in American history, which was to last four years and result in the deaths of around 600,000 people.

The article was a despatch from Charleston, on the previous day which read, 'Civil war has at last begun. A terrible fight is at this moment going on between Fort Sumter and the fortification by which it is surrounded.'

Hostility between those in the North and South had been going on for years. The agricultural South favoured strong state government and relied on slaves to work on their land, while the more industrial North wanted a unifying federal government and sought to curtail the use of slaves.

The election of Abraham Lincoln as President in November 1860 was the final trigger for war between the two sides. Lincoln wanted to limit the expansion of slavery, but not abolish it. He was sworn in on 4 March 1861, and in his inaugural address he stated he had no intention to invade Southern states, nor did he intend to end slavery where it existed, but that he would use force to maintain possession of Federal property in the South.

SOUTHERN STATES SECEDE

The South did not want a Republican to be its President and abhorred Lincoln's views. As a result many Southern states left the Union. South Carolina had been the first to secede on 20 December 1860, now several others followed. Civil war was brewing as the two sides began to build up their armies.

THE BLUE AND THE GREY

The Union's soldiers in the North were called either 'Federals', 'Northerners' or 'Yankees' and wore blue uniforms. And the Confederacy in the South dressed in grey uniforms and were often referred to as 'Rebels' or 'Johnny Rebs'.

One of the Federal government's key forts in the South was Fort Sumter, because controlling it was integral to controlling Charleston harbour, one of the busiest ports in the South.

In charge of the fort was Major Robert Anderson, who sent a message to Lincoln that their supplies were running low in the fort and would only last six more weeks. Lincoln ordered new supplies to be delivered but the Confederates were determined to drive the Union out of their states and increased the pressure on the weakened Fort Sumter.

DEAL REJECTED

On 11 April 1861, Confederate General Pierre Beauregard demanded that Major Anderson evacuate the fort. Anderson played for time, saying he would leave the fort at noon on 15 April. But as Beauregard was aware that supplies would be delivered by then, he rejected the deal and at 4.30am the following day, he gave the order to open fire on the fort.

Short of ammunition, as well as food, the Federals did not return fire until about 7am. The firing stopped at night before re-starting the following day. When a cannonball set the barracks alight, Anderson agreed to a truce at about 2pm.

STRAY SPARK TRAGEDY

Incredibly, no one on either side had been killed. But when Anderson was allowed to stage a 100-gun salute to the U.S. flag, a pile of cartridges blew up from a spark, killing two of his men.

In the aftermath, Lincoln called for 75,000 men to enlist in the army to protect Federal property in the South and the Confederates were also swelled by eager young men willing to fight for their rights.

BLOODIEST BATTLE

A number of inconclusive engagements were fought during 1861-62 as the Confederates repulsed Union attempts to capture their capital at Richmond, Virginia, although the Confederates were defeated in Maryland at the Battle of Antietam in September 1862.

In 1863, General Robert E. Lee struck north and was eventually halted by Union forces at Gettysburg in Pennsylvania, where more lives were lost than in any other battle of the war. Union forces fared far better in the west and, when western commander Lieutenant General Ulysses S. Grant took charge of Union forces in the east, it spelled the end for the Confederacy.

After four years of warfare, including ferocious battles for Atlanta and Richmond, Robert E. Lee ultimately surrendered to Grant on 9 April 1865 at Appomattox Court House in Virginia.

As a result, slavery was outlawed throughout the nation and the role and influence of the Federal Government was enormously enhanced. •

IMPORTANT ASSASSINATION OF PRESIDENT LINCOLN

THE PRESIDENT SHOT AT THE THEATRE LAST EVENING

(*New York Herald*, April 15 1865)

IT WAS THE NEWS that shocked the nation. Many could scarcely believe it and crowds took to the streets in alarm and bewilderment.

The long-running American Civil War was just coming to a close as the victorious President Abraham Lincoln took time out with his wife, Mary, to enjoy a night at the theatre. But it would prove to be his final act as the curtain came down abruptly on his extraordinary life.

The Lincolns and their guests, Major Henry Rathbone and his fiancée Clara Harris, arrived at Ford's Theatre in Washington, D.C., at 8.40pm on Good Friday, 14 April 1865, to watch the British play *Our American Cousin*.

THE PRESIDENT BOWS

As they walked across the balcony to the Presidential Box, the wealthy theatregoers broke out into a round of applause, because of the satisfactory end of the Civil War. A delighted Lincoln paused to bow to the audience before continuing on his way.

The curtain went up and the play got under way and the audience enjoyed much of the humour. Then, during the third and final act a man made his way through a corridor to Lincoln's box, armed with a derringer and a hunting knife, and shot him in the back of the head at the moment when a particular line was said in the play which routinely elicited the biggest laugh.

The sound of the laughter partially muffled the gunshot and for a while the audience didn't quite know what had happened until they saw the President slump forward in his seat. Mary screamed and Major Rathbone grappled with the gunman but was stabbed in the arm. The attacker then leapt from the box to the stage, eleven feet below. He landed awkwardly, snapping the fibula bone in his left leg just above the ankle. Stumbling across the stage, he brandished his knife at the startled audience, and shouted, 'Sic Semper Tyrannis!' (Latin for 'Thus always to tyrants', and the state motto of Virginia).

THE GUNMAN ESCAPES

He made his escape backstage and out onto the street where he had left his horse with a theatre employee, and rode off.

A couple of doctors in the audience rushed to the President's aide but on seeing the bullet hole in the back of his head, they knew the wound was fatal. However, he was still breathing and so needed to be moved. They thought better of a bumpy carriage ride back across town to the White House and instead he was carried across the street to William Petersen's boarding house, where he was laid on a bed in a first-floor room.

Here a vigil took place for the dying President. The New York Herald reported how he was surrounded by his Cabinet, many in tears. As the news spread, people thronged the streets outside, anxious for more information.

Meanwhile, some members of the theatre's orchestra had identified the gunman as the actor John Wilkes Booth. He had performed throughout the country and was the lead in several of Shakespeare's plays. He had also played at Ford's Theatre on 12 occasions and so knew the layout well.

Booth was a Southern sympathiser who was incensed by Lincoln and his Emancipation Proclamation, which freed all slaves within the Confederacy.

By January 1865, he had organised a group of co-conspirators to capture Lincoln when he attended a play at a hospital just outside Washington and hold him in return for the release of Confederate prisoners of war. But the plot was foiled when the President changed his mind about attending.

CONFEDERATE SURRENDER

With numbers of the Army of Northern Virginia – the main army of the Confederacy – having dwindled to 35,000, General Robert E. Lee accepted the inevitable against General Ulysses S. Grant's Union soldiers of 120,000. He surrendered on 9 April , thereby ending the war.

But Booth refused to give up the fight and decided on drastic action. When he heard that Lincoln would be going to Ford's Theatre with General Grant, he saw it as a perfect opportunity to kill them both. At around the same time his gang of co-conspirators would kill Vice President Andrew Johnson and Secretary of State William Seward.

In the end, Grant didn't attend and Rathbone took his place. Lincoln died on the morning of 15 April, aged 56. No attempt to kill Johnson was made and Seward was stabbed at his home but it failed to kill him.

Booth was discovered 11 days later with a co-conspirator in a barn at a farm in rural Virginia by Union soldiers. After Booth had shouted that he would not be taken alive, one of the soldiers crept up behind the barn and shot him dead.

Abraham Lincoln was the first American president to be assassinated. He left a lasting impression on the United States, preserving the Union, cementing democracy and laying the foundation for the abolition of slavery. He is widely regarded as being the greatest President in American history. •

AUDIBLE SPEECH BY TELEGRAPH

PROF. A. GRAHAM BELL'S DISCOVERY

SUCCESSFUL AND INTERESTING EXPERIMENTS BETWEEN BOSTON AND CAMBRIDGEPORT

(*New York Times*, 21 October 1876)

A REPORTER FROM the *New York Times* was impressed by a demonstration given by Alexander Graham Bell and his assistant, Thomas Watson, on the evening of 9 October, 1876.

Telephones were placed at either end of a telegraph line from an office in Boston to a factory in Cambridgeport – two miles away. It was the first, long-distance, two-way telephone call.

'Articulate conversation then took place through the wires,' said the report. 'The sounds, at first faint and indistinct, became suddenly quite loud and intelligible. Mr Bell in Boston and Mr. Watson in Cambridge then took notes of what was said and heard, and the comparison of the two records is most interesting, as showing the accuracy of the electrical transmission.'

As with most inventions, there were several others working on similar ideas at the same time but Bell is credited with inventing the first practical telephone, having submitted an application for his model on 14 February 1876, just two hours before his rival, Elisha Gray.

WRITTEN SYMBOLS

Born in Edinburgh, he developed an interest with forms of communication from his father and grandfather, who both taught elocution. His mother was deaf and his father pioneered a method of communication called 'Visible Speech' – a set of written symbols designed to aid the deaf in speaking.

By the time the family emigrated to Canada in 1870, Bell junior was also teaching the deaf to communicate and later travelled to Boston in the U.S. to give lectures on Visible Speech.

He became professor of vocal physiology at Boston University in 1873. A year later he met an experienced electrical designer and mechanic named Thomas Watson and he hired him as his assistant in experimenting with the idea of transmitting speech over telegraph wires.

Their work eventually led to their succeeding in making their first telephone message on 10 March 1876, when Bell, in his Boston laboratory, summoned his colleague via the device from the next room with the now famous words, 'Watson, come here. I want to see you.'

In his journal, Bell later wrote, 'To my delight he came and declared that he had heard and understood what I said.'

The following year, Bell and Watson went on a tour of the Northeast, demonstrating their invention with great success to enraptured audiences.

The Bell Telephone Company was founded in 1877 and by 1886 over 150,000 people in the U.S. owned telephones.

CLARITY IMPROVED

In the succeeding years, there were numerous developments to improve clarity of telephone conversations and the distance over which they could be made. But the Bell Company, which used a liquid microphone transmitter, was nearly eclipsed by Thomas Edison's rival telephone company, which had patented a superior carbon version that enabled the telephone to be used over longer distances without needing to shout into the mouthpiece. Bell were saved when it developed a carbon device of its own.

Bell's invention had made him very wealthy and, inspired by Edison's huge scientific laboratory at Menlo Park in New Jersey, he set up Volta Laboratories, which later became Bell Labs. In 1885 a team working under him here developed an improved version of Edison's phonograph, called the graphophone, playing recorded sounds with the use of wax cylinders. He also experimented with kites and hydrofoils. But it would be the telephone that would mark his name in history. •

THE INDIAN WAR

GENERAL TERRY'S OFFICIAL REPORT OF THE CUSTER MASSACRE

(*Helena Daily Herald*, 14 July 1876)

THE MASSACRE OF General George Armstrong Custer's battalion in the Battle of the Little Bighorn was the worst U.S. Army defeat of the day.

Yet it was to portray the man responsible for the disaster as a hero and the popular description of the battle, Custer's Last Stand, captured the imagination of generations for ever more.

This newspaper article, three weeks after the defeat, reported General Terry's official account of the massacre and the general tone is one of gallantry against overwhelming numbers.

CUSTER THE SHOWMAN

Custer had built a reputation fighting for the Union Army in the Civil War and became one of the youngest generals at the age of 23. He had also found a flair for publicity and showmanship. Keen to show his bravery he put himself forward for battles, petitioned for promotion and sought to capture attention with swagger and bravado. He also caught the eye with his 'dandy' style of dressing which included the likes of shiny cavalry boots, tight olive-coloured trousers, a wide-brimmed hat and a red neckerchief. At the end of the war he fought the Indians and took to wearing buckskin outfits. But despite his vanity, Custer had the respect of his men by fearlessly leading from the front, unlike some other officers.

GOLD IS DISCOVERED

The white settlers' expansion had continually pushed out the Plains Indians from their lands. The U.S Government 'allowed' the Plains Indians to live in certain areas, or 'reserves' but not in others, regularly reneging on treaties and agreements. And when gold was discovered in the Black Hills in Dakota, the U.S. decided to drive away all remaining free Plains Indians. The government set a deadline of 31 January 1876 for them to report to their designated reserves or be considered 'hostile'.

Tension was high and Sitting Bull called a gathering of Sioux and Cheyenne Indians at Ash Creek in Montana in late 1875 with the intention of fighting for their rights. Two victories in clashes with the U.S. Army the following spring spurred their confidence.

LITTLE BIGHORN RIVER

The 7th Cavalry, a unit of around 500–600 men, led by Custer, departed from Fort Lincoln on 17 May 1876 as part of a larger army force determined to round up remaining free Indians.

On 25 June, Custer's scouts sighted the large Indian encampment along the Little Bighorn River – where Sitting Bull and various Indian tribes had gathered.

Custer divided his men into three battalions. One, led by Major Marcus Reno, was to cross the river at the south end, attacking the encampment from the east, while Custer and his men would head west to attack from the other end. Captain Benteen's men would advance south and west to cut off any retreat through the upper valley.

But Custer had underestimated the size of the Indian contingent – an estimated 1,800 warriors – as well as the difficulty of the terrain, which was full of hills and ravines.

When Reno's men made their charge on the encampment, they were met by a massive counter-attack and after a brief ten-minute skirmish, they made a hasty retreat, taking cover in the trees along the river.

To the north and west, Custer and his 208 men – many of whom had crossed the river – were met head on by Cheyenne and Sioux Indians, who forced them back. Meanwhile, another force, largely Oglala Sioux under Crazy Horse's command, swiftly moved downstream in a sweeping arc, enveloping the Army in a pincer movement.

Custer ordered his men to shoot their horses and stack the carcasses to form a wall. But they were far outnumbered and in less than an hour they had all been killed.

Meanwhile, Reno and Benteen's now combined force continued fighting for another day until the Indians learned that a further two columns of soldiers were on their way, and fled.

CORPSES MUTILATED

When the main column under General Terry arrived two days later, the army found most of the soldiers' corpses stripped, scalped and mutilated. Custer's body had two bullet holes, one in the left temple and one just above the heart. Inexplicably, he had not been scalped. Some believe that because he was dressed in buckskin instead of blue uniform, the Indians may have not thought he was a soldier. Another explanation is that his hair had been cut short for battle, which may have made scalping difficult. A more romantic view was that his bravery had been respected.

The Indians had achieved their greatest victory at Little Bighorn, but retribution was swift. Within a year, the Sioux nation was defeated and broken. •

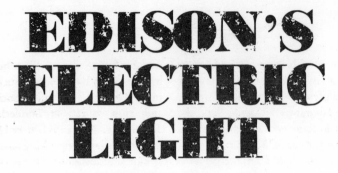

EDISON'S ELECTRIC LIGHT

(*New York Times* 28 December 1879)

ON 21 OCTOBER 1879, prolific inventor Thomas Edison – who had invented the phonograph in 1877 – developed a practical electric light at his laboratory in Menlo Park, New Jersey.

Shortly after, he invited a *New York Times* reporter into his laboratory to witness the spectacle which was to make gas lamps redundant.

The reporter described how he was shown a glass globe containing a thread of carbonised paper held by two platinum clamps from which two wires ran outwardly through a small glass tube contained within a larger one leading out of the glass globe. Inside the tube the platinum wires were met by two copper ones connecting with the conductors of the electricity. Edison explained to him how the carbonised paper became incandescent by a current of electricity. He then proceeded to give a demonstration.

Edison was standing under a chandelier in which two of the bulbs were already burning. He removed one of them and the light went out. When he replaced it, the light shone brightly once more.

BRILLIANT INCANDESCENCE

The reporter was enraptured by what he saw. 'Mr. Edison then, by turning a screw in the lamp, brought the light down to a spark, turned it off completely, as gas can be turned off, and turned it on again to a brilliant incandescence by a twist of his fingers. He certainly demonstrated that in his own laboratory at Menlo Park, the electric light is as obedient to his will as the gas light is to the general public. The light from each lamp is of about the power of an ordinary gas-jet, but Mr. Edison claims that by increasing the electricity, he can raise the power to 15 gas-jets.'

Edison had a total of eighty-four lights burning in his laboratory, all supplied with electricity by an 80 horsepower engine in the basement.

He told the reporter, 'The electric light is perfected and all the problems which have been puzzling me for the last 18 months have been solved. I expect to have every house here lighted and a number of street-lamps going within 10 days.'

LIGHT BULB NOT EDISON'S

Never one to hide his light under a bushel, Edison had not, in fact, invented the light bulb but, by improving on the work of others before him, had come up with a practical version.

It was English inventor Joseph Swan who received the first patent for the incandescent light bulb in 1879 and his home in Gateshead was the first in the world to be lit by one. Swan had reported success to the Newcastle Chemical Society and at a lecture at Sunderland Technical College in February 1879 he demonstrated a working lamp.

But Edison and his team at Menlo Park focused on producing a light bulb that was more robust and that would burn for longer.

The former salesman had his mind on commercial success: mass producing the bulbs and designing a system for the generation and distribution of electricity to illuminate streets, businesses and homes.

Edison continued to improve his design and by 4 November 1879, filed for a U.S. patent for an electric lamp using 'a carbon filament or strip coiled and connected to platina contact wires'. It was granted on 27 January 1880.

COURT BATTLE AVOIDED

Edison made the first public demonstration of his 'own' incandescent light bulb on 31 December 1879.

To avoid a possible court battle with Joseph Swan, he teamed up with him to form a company called Ediswan, which allowed Edison to sell the lights in America while Swan retained the rights in Britain.

WIZARD OF MENLO PARK

On New Year's Eve 1879, Christie Street, just outside Edison's Menlo Park laboratory, became the first street in the world to be lit by incandescent lamps, using a power system devised by Edison.

By the summer of 1880, the man sometimes known as 'The Wizard of Menlo Park' was mass producing light bulbs and had wired up two houses. The first was the nearby home of mathematician Francis Upton, who worked for Edison, and the second was the boarding house run by Sarah Jordan who was the widow of one of Edison's former business partners. Some of Edison's single employees lodged at the house and it was where Edison's entire team came together for social occasions.

Edison's business went from strength to strength as he demonstrated how electricity could be delivered to homes, to deliver power for domestic lighting, from a central generating station. He applied for around 400 patents for inventions devised at Menlo park over the years. Within ten years the wizard had outgrown Menlo Park and moved into a purpose-built facility in West Orange, New Jersey, which would be the inventor's headquarters until his death in 1931 at the age of 84. •

JESSE JAMES, THE BANDIT, KILLED

(New York Tribune, 4 April 1882)

A PAGE FIVE ARTICLE datelined 'St Joseph's Mo [Missouri] April 3', begins... 'A great sensation was created in this city this morning by the announcement that Jesse James, the notorious bandit and train robber, had been shot and killed here.'

It goes on to say how crowds rushed to the quarter of the city where the shooting occurred, anxious to see the body.

That his killing made national news showed how this most notorious of outlaws had become famous in his own lifetime. And he was to become a legendary figure after his death.

He was born in Clay County, Missouri, on 5 September 1847, and his father, Robert, was a prosperous commercial hemp farmer and Baptist minister who owned more than 100 acres of farmland and six slaves.

He travelled to California during the gold rush to minister the mining community and died there when Jesse was three years old. Jesse, his older brother, Frank, and younger sister, Susan, were then brought up by their mother, Zeralda.

GUERILLA FIGHTERS

After the outbreak of the Civil War he and Frank joined a band of Confederate guerrilla fighters whose other members included brothers Cole and James Younger. As well as attacking

Union troops the band also robbed mail coaches and shot supporters of Abraham Lincoln.

After the war Jesse and Frank became outlaws, forming the James-Younger gang, which included their former guerrilla Confederates, Cole and James, along with Bob Younger. Other members were Bill Chadwell, Clell Miller and Charlie Pitts.

On 13 February 1866, the gang robbed a bank at Liberty, Missouri, and over the next few years they took part in twelve bank robberies, seven train robberies, four stagecoach robberies and various raids on stores.

As well as their home state of Missouri, they were also active in West Virginia, Alabama, Arkansas, Iowa, Kansas and Minnesota. During these robberies at least eleven citizens were killed by the gang.

ROBBERY GOES WRONG

But the gang was virtually wiped out on 7 September 1876 during a robbery attempt on the First National Bank at Northfield, Minnesota. Residents who realised what was happening opened fire. Chadwell, Miller and Pitts were killed and the three Younger

brothers wounded and captured. Only Jesse and Frank escaped.

They went into hiding in Nashville and Frank appeared to settle down but a restless Jesse began to recruit a new gang in 1879 which included brothers Robert and Charlie Ford and Dick Liddel.

But Jesse was nervous and didn't trust his new gang like he did his former Confederate guerrilla colleagues.

During a robbery of train passengers as it slowed down to pass through an area of Missouri known as Blue in September 1881, the gang killed the conductor and a pensioner. The enraged governor of Missouri, Thomas Crittenden, offered a reward of $10,000 for the capture of Jessie James dead or alive. Robert Ford contacted Crittenden and offered his services.

LIVING IN DISGUISE

Jesse was living with his wife and children in a house at St Joseph, Missouri, under the pseudonym of J. D. Howards, and had asked the Ford brothers – whom he trusted more than others in his gang – to live at his house for extra protection.

Dick Liddel feared that Jessie wanted to kill him after he and

Robert Ford shot dead his cousin, Wood Hite. He turned himself in at Kansas City and told them what he knew about the James gang.

Ford knew he had surrendered but kept it secret from Jesse. When, three weeks later, he found Jesse reading a newspaper report about it while at home on the morning of 3 April 1882, Jesse accused him of knowing about it because he was in the neighbourhood at the time.

SHOT DEAD

Jesse glared at him but then seemingly changed his mood, saying it didn't matter. Ford, however, was certain that he was a marked man. Jesse was pretending not to mind because he didn't want to shoot him while his wife and family were at home. Jesse took off his gun belt and threw it on the bed. Then he stood on a chair to dust a picture on the wall and Ford took his chance to shoot him behind the ear while his back was turned.

Ford was arrested for murder but two hours later he was reprieved after Crittenden stepped in to give him his reward.

The legend of Jesse James grew and grew after his death with 'dime novels' of the 'James Gang' adventures in which he took on the mantle of a latter-day Robin Hood who stole from the rich to give to the poor. He was eulogised in songs and there have been numerous films about him over the years, all of which have kept him alive as an enduring icon of popular culture. •

THE WHITECHAPEL HORRORS

(*London Evening News*, 1 October 1888)

A DOUBLE MURDER in the early hours of 30 September 1888 sent terror through Whitechapel in the East End of London as the legend of Jack the Ripper gained pace and spread around the world.

The body of Elizabeth Stride was found by the steward of a working men's club in Dutfield's Yard near Berner's Street. Her throat had been cut. Just three-quarters of an hour later, a second body, Catherine Eddowes, was discovered with her throat cut in Mitre Square, Aldgate, along with an abdominal mutilation.

'LEATHER APRON'

Fear throughout the area had already been heightened by two similar murders – those of Mary Ann Nichols and Annie Chapman on 31 August and 8 September. Lurid newspaper accounts had nicknamed the attacker 'Leather Apron' – the description given to police by local prostitutes of a violent man who would demand a share of their earnings. But that was to change when a letter, dated 25 September 1888, was posted to the Central News Agency. The frenzied writing included the line, 'I am down on whores and I shant quit ripping them till I do get buckled.'

It was signed, 'Jack the Ripper'.

After the letter was forwarded to the police, the name was made public and excited people's imagination – not least that of headline writers. The double murder that occurred just days later intensified the general frenzy. The name Jack the Ripper stuck as news spread through the country and abroad.

And there was more to come, as on 1 October a postcard was sent to the agency, written in spidery red ink, which spoke of the 'double event' and again signed off as Jack the Ripper.

FIEND IN HUMAN SHAPE

The sales of newspapers soared as people were eager to hear the latest about 'this fiend in human shape'. His nerve and outrageous audacity in making such brutal attacks in the centre of London shocked the public.

The *London Evening News* reported, 'The public cannot fail to be impressed with one fact – the apparent bravado of the assassin. He seems to revel in brutality and the more energetic the police become in tracking him, the more contemptuously does he defy their efforts.'

From the similarity of the murders – cut throats and disembowelment – Jack seemed to be accountable for the murders of Nichols, Chapman, Stride and Eddowes. Police believed that he had been interrupted in his attack on Elizabeth Stride by the arrival of the local club steward in his trap and had to flee before completing the usual mutilation.

Some believed that The Ripper may also have murdered two other Whitechapel women, Emma Elizabeth Smith and Martha Tabram, who were both savagely attacked with a knife earlier in the year.

SCOTLAND YARD CALLED IN

The killing spree was considered too much for the Whitechapel police, headed by Detective Inspector Edmund Reid, and so Scotland Yard was called in, along with City police. But although many suspects were questioned and trails followed, they all ultimately led to nothing.

On 9 November, Mary Jane Kelly was found lying on her bed in the single room where she lived in Miller's Court, Spitalfields. Her throat had been cut, her abdomen virtually emptied of its organs and her heart was missing.

Throughout the period from 1888 to 1892, there were 11 women murdered in Whitechapel. No one can say for sure how many were the work of Jack the Ripper, but it is generally considered that five can be reasonably attributable to him – Mary Nichols, Annie Chapman, Elizabeth Stride, Catherine Eddowes and Mary Jane Kelly. All were killed between 31 August and 9 November 1888.

RIPPER REMAINS A MYSTERY

No one was ever convicted of the murders and the identity of Jack the Ripper has remained a mystery, although there has been a deluge of books and documentaries from those claiming to have identified the killer.

The murders drew attention to the poor living conditions of humble women in unsanitary and unsafe areas of the East End of London who had few options when it came to earning money, resulting in many turning to prostitution.

In the aftermath, some of the worst slums were demolished, there was improved lighting and charities were set up to help people through their hardship. •

THE WOMAN'S SUFFRAGE BILL ASSENTED TO

(*Auckland Star*, 19 September 1893)

NEW ZEALAND became the first self-governing country in the world to grant all women the right to vote in parliamentary elections.

The Governor, Lord Glasgow, signed the new Electoral Act into law in September 1893, following increasing pressure from suffragettes and their supporters.

The movement was spearheaded by Kate Sheppard. Born in Liverpool in 1847, she emigrated to settle in Christchurch in her early twenties. In 1885 she helped form New Zealand's Women's Christian Temperance Union, which advocated women's suffrage as a means to fight for liquor prohibition. But it was suffrage that was to become an end in itself for Sheppard.

She led an intensive seven-year campaign for the right for women to vote, speaking eloquently at public meetings, lobbying politicians with telegrams and letters and writing many pamphlets to keep the debate alive. Opposition was fierce but the suffragists gained increasing support when women outside the temperance movement joined them.

Sheppard argued, 'We are tired of having a "sphere" doled out to us, and of being told that anything outside that sphere is "unwomanly".'

BILLS FAIL IN PARLIAMENT

Such was the growing support that it could not be ignored and in 1878, 1879 and 1887 bills or amendments extending the vote to women only narrowly failed to pass in Parliament.

The WCTU compiled a series of petitions from the public in support of their aims which they presented to Parliament. In 1891 over 9,000 signatures were gathered, in 1892 almost 20,000 and in 1893 nearly 32,000.

A number of New Zealand's leading politicians, including John Hall, Robert Stout, Julius Vogel, William Fox and John Ballance, supported women's suffrage. But there was considerable opposition both in and out of Parliament.

Scaremongers warned that meddling with the 'natural' gender roles of men and women could have terrible consequences. And the powerful liquor industry, fearing the WCTU's aim to prohibit alcohol, lobbied sympathetic Members of Parliament and organised counter-petitions.

WHEELBARROW PETITION

The massive third petition was transported theatrically to Parliament in a wheelbarrow and the 766-foot-long scroll was unrolled across the chamber of the House of Representatives with dramatic effect. It was the largest petition ever presented to Parliament. The bill was passed on 8 September 1893 by 20 votes to 18.

But the long battle was still not over as new anti-suffrage petitions were circulated and some members of the Legislative Council petitioned the Governor to withhold his consent. It was not until 11 days later that Lord Glasgow signed the bill into law. Suffragists celebrated throughout the country, and congratulations poured in from campaigners in Britain, Australia, the United States and elsewhere.

Suffrage opponents had warned that delicate 'lady voters' would be jostled and harassed in polling booths by 'boorish and half-drunken men'. But the election on 28 November of that year, when 65 per cent of women took the chance to vote for the very first time, was described as the 'best-conducted and most orderly' ever held.

Even so, New Zealand women still had a long way to go to achieve political equality. They would not gain the right to stand for Parliament until 1919, and the first female Member of Parliament, Elizabeth McCombs, was not elected until 1933.

THE WHITE CAMELLIA

During the campaign for women's suffrage, those who supported the

1893 Electoral Bill were presented with a white camellia to wear in their buttonhole. The white camellia has since become a symbol of women's suffrage in New Zealand.

Sheppard continued to work at home and abroad for women's rights – from contraception to freedom from the corset. She became president of the National Council of Women of New Zealand and editor of the *White Ribbon*, the first newspaper in New Zealand to be owned, managed and published solely by women. In 1909 she was elected honorary vice president of the International Council of Women.

She died on 13 July 1934, a year after she saw Elizabeth McCombs, enter Parliament. •

LUMIERE'S CINEMATOGRAPHE

(*Sydney Morning Herald*, 22 September 1896)

THE LUMIERE BROTHERS, who can justifiably claim to have 'invented' the cinema, were wowing audiences the world over with their moving pictures in the late 19th century.

Their exuberant father, Antoine, worked as a sign painter before becoming interested in an article about a new technique for manufacturing photographic dry plates, pioneered by the Belgian chemist Van Monkhoven.

He set about making his own plates in his small studio in Lyon, but with little success. Frustrated, he turned to his bright teenage son, Louis, who excelled at science at the technical school he attended with his brother, Auguste.

At the age of 17, Louis was able to improve on Van Monkhoven's design, creating a new form of dry plate which was far more sensitive.

The brothers started to work for their father – Louis as a physicist and Auguste as a manager – and as photographic portraits became a fashionable trend, the Lumières became very wealthy. To meet the demand for their product, they opened a big new factory in the Lyon suburb of Monplaisir.

CREATIVE VISIONARY

The brothers took control of the company around 1882 but Antoine continued to be a creative visionary source and in the autumn of 1894 he was inspired when a friend showed him one of Thomas Edison's new Kinetoscopes. These were popular novelty arcade devices. By dropping a coin through the slot of the heavy wooden cabinet, the spectator activated a small motor inside that moved spools of celluloid. An electric light flashed onto the film and, by peering down through a lens, the spectator was able to watch crude moving pictures — usually performing animals, boxing matches and circus performers.

An excited Antoine hurried to Louis and told him they should be making film like this. Determined to eclipse Edison by taking a share of this new market, he decided that they would need to develop a camera and projector of their own. The problem lay in moving the strip of film smoothly through a camera. But it was Louis who, once again, found the solution. He adapted the sprocket mechanism of the newly popular sewing machine to move a strip of film along. It was housed in a wooden box which acted as both camera and projector.

THE CINEMATOGRAPHE

Significantly, by projecting pictures onto an exterior screen, they were able to be watched by groups of people instead of just one. They named the device the cinematographe, derived from the Greek word for movement. It was the birth of cinema.

Although Auguste gave credit to Louis, the successful machine was patented in France on 13 February 1895 in both of their names.

In March they used it to shoot a short film of their employees called, *La Sortie des Usines Lumière* (*Workers Leaving the Lumière Factory*).

Later that month, the Lumières arranged intimate screenings of the film for French scientific institutions and then arranged for a larger public viewing in the basement of the Salon Indien du Grand Café in Paris on 28 December.

Just hours before this first show, Antoine was still desperately drumming up support for the event which was payable on admission. Only 33 people turned up. At first they saw a series of still pictures projected onto a screen and there were some disgruntled noises about this lack of innovation. But then one of the pictures, a horse and cart, started to move towards them. It was followed by other moving vehicles and people walking down a street. It was an incredible sight.

EVERYDAY SCENES

The series of ten short films screened were of such simple everyday scenes as Auguste Lumière and his wife feeding their baby, a gardener using a hose and the workers leaving the

Lumière factory. Each lasted around 50 seconds.

News of the films swept across France and overseas. Before long, 2,500 people a day were queuing to watch them.

The Lumières made over 200 cinematographes and employed agents to demonstrate them around the world, shooting scenes and screening them.

OVERWHELMING RESPONSE

One of the first overseas shows was organised in London by the illusionist Felicien Trewey, a friend of Antoine, at the Marlborough Hall on Regent Street on 20 February 1896. Such was the overwhelming response that the show soon transferred to the far bigger Empire Theatre in Leicester Square, where it would play for almost eighteen months.

The *Sydney Morning Herald* contained a small report about the cinematographe's arrival in Australia, having been 'drawing the crowds at the Empire Theatre, London'. Following its success at a private viewing at the Lyceum Theatre in Sydney, it would shortly have a public exhibition. •

OSCAR WILDE IN JAIL

(*Daily Inter Ocean*, 6 April 1895)

THE TRIAL OF OSCAR WILDE was eagerly followed around the world, the sensational revelations making the story compulsive reading as Wilde went from complainant to defendant in the blink of an eye.

The famous playwright and poet had delighted audiences with his comedy plays *The Importance of Being Earnest, Lady Windermere's Fan* and *A Woman of No Importance.*

And he had charmed high society with his flamboyant dress and sparkling wit. But at the height of his fame things took a downward turn when he decided to prosecute the Marquis of Queensberry for libel after he accused him of 'posing as a sodomite'.

The Chicago newspaper, *The Daily Inter Ocean*, reported the sensational moment at London's Old Bailey Court when, on 5 April 1895, Wilde withdrew his libel action, thereby practically admitting the truth of Queensberry's accusation.

WILDE ARRESTED

He was arrested at the Cadogan Hotel shortly after the court closed and spent the night in a cell at Bow Street Police Station. His name was promptly withdrawn from play bills and advertising from two theatres, the St James and the Haymarket, where his plays were running.

While at university at Oxford, Wilde, a brilliant scholar, took a keen interest in the philosophy of aestheticism, which he later portrayed in his stories and poems that were published in magazines.

On 29 May 1884 he married Constance Lloyd, and they settled in a house in Chelsea, West London, and had two sons, Cyril and Vyvyan. Wilde began an affair with a young man named Robert Ross in 1886 and afterwards with 22-year-old Oxford undergraduate Lord Alfred Douglas, the son of the Marquis of Queensberry. Wilde was then 38.

MALE PROSTITUTES

Acts of homosexuality were at that time illegal and it was the rather self-centred Douglas who introduced Wilde to London's 'underground' world of young male prostitutes.

The Marquis of Queensbury, a Scottish nobleman born John Sholto Douglas, was a founder of the Amateur Athletics Association and a very keen boxer, having given his name to boxing's 'Queensbury Rules'. He was absolutely furious about his son's 'friendship' with Wilde and demanded that it end, but Alfred stubbornly refused to stop seeing Wilde.

Queensbury was determined that Wilde should not be allowed to lead his son astray. His eldest son, Francis, was widely rumoured to be having a homosexual affair with the Prime Minister, Lord Roseberry, and, in October 1894, Francis was to die in a mysterious hunting accident. Queensbury had no qualms about confronting Oscar Wilde.

In June 1894, Queensberry visited Wilde at his home and told him, 'I do not say that you are it, but you look it, and pose at it, which is just as bad. And if I catch you and my son again in any public restaurant I will thrash you.'

At the premiere of *The Importance of Being Earnest*, at St James's on 14 February 1895, Queensberry arrived determined to publicly insult Wilde by throwing a bouquet of rotting vegetables onto the stage. But Wilde had been tipped off and had him barred from entering the theatre.

Four days later, Queensberry left his calling card at Wilde's club, the

Albemarle, inscribed, 'For Oscar Wilde, posing somdomite [sic]'.

Wilde, encouraged by Alfred and against the advice of his friends, initiated a private prosecution against Queensberry, who was arrested on a charge of criminal libel.

THE TRIAL BEGINS

The trial opened on 3 April 1895 amidst great publicity and excitement in the packed public and press galleries. Queen's Counsel for the defence, Edward Carson, questioned Wilde about his acquaintances with younger, lower-class men. Wilde insisted they were just friends but admitted lavishing gifts on them.

He responded to many of Carson's questions with his usual mix of wit and aesthetic intellect, which, although entertaining, did not help his plight.

The following day at court, Carson announced that he had located several male prostitutes who were to testify that they had had sex with Wilde. Sir Edward George Clarke, Wilde's counsel, left the courtroom to consult with Wilde who was in another room. On his return he dramatically announced

the withdrawal of the case on behalf of his client.

QUEENSBURY NOT GUILTY

The jury, as directed by Justice Collins, found Queensberry not guilty of libel and he left court triumphant, smiling and surrounded by friends. A warrant for the arrest of Wilde was quickly applied for. He was arrested at the Cadogan Hotel and spent the night at Bow Street police station.

Wilde wrote a letter to newspapers in which he said, 'It was not possible to prove my case without putting Lord Alfred Douglas in the witness-box against his father. Lord Alfred was extremely anxious to go into the box but I would not allow it. Rather than put him in such a painful position I determined to retire from the case, bear upon my own shoulders whatever shame and ignominy might result from not prosecuting the Marquis of Queensberry.' He was placed on remand at Holloway Prison until his trial opened at the Old Bailey on 26 April. Wilde pleaded not guilty and the trial ended with the jury unable to reach a verdict.

WILDE JAILED

The final trial on 25 May was presided over by Mr Justice Wills and here Wilde was convicted of gross indecency and sentenced to two years' imprisonment. He was first incarcerated in Pentonville, then Wandsworth and later Reading.

Wilde's health suffered badly in prison and after his release on 19 May 1897 he moved to France and was reunited with Alfred at Rouen three months later. They lived together in Naples for a few months towards the end of the year but Wilde was a broken man who had lost everything and after Queensberry threatened to cut off Alfred's funds, he returned home.

By 25 November Wilde had developed cerebral meningitis. He was now living in a dingy hotel in Paris, alone and with very little money. He died on 30 November 1990. •

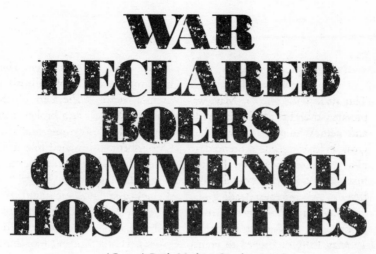

WAR DECLARED BOERS COMMENCE HOSTILITIES

(*Grocott's Daily Mail*, 12 October 1899)

THIS SOUTH AFRICAN newspaper reported the start of a gruelling three-year war which would result in great suffering and many deaths and change the face of the country.

Hostilities between Britain and the descendants of Danish settlers, the Boers (farmers), had broken out in 1880 in the first Boer War. This was in the wake of around 15,000 Boers making the 'Great Trek' out of the British-owned Cape Colony across the Orange River into the interior of South Africa between 1835 and 1847.

They established two independent republics – the Transvaal and the Orange Free State – which were recognised by Britain in 1852 and 1854.

In 1867 diamonds were discovered near the confluence of the Orange and Vaal Rivers, prompting a diamond rush.

BOER ARMED RESISTANCE

British Colonial Secretary, Lord Carnarvon proposed a confederation of South African states in 1875. The Boers began armed resistance against annexation of the Transvaal in 1880 and the republic was reinstated.

In 1886 gold was discovered in the Transvaal but the republic did not have the manpower or industrial base to be able to properly mine it and so the Boers reluctantly agreed to the immigration of fresh waves of uitlanders (foreigners), mainly from Britain, who came to work there. This resulted in the number of uitlanders in the Transvaal eventually exceeding that of Boers, which caused resentment and conflict.

In September 1899 Britain sent an ultimatum to the Boers, demanding full equality for those uitlanders resident in the Transvaal.

BOERS THREATEN WAR

Paul Kruger, the President of the Transvaal, issued his own ultimatum, giving the British 48 hours to withdraw all their troops from the border. If they did not then the Transvaal, allied with the Orange Free State, would declare war against the British.

On 11 October 1899, the second Boer War broke out after Britain rejected the ultimatum.

The Boers attacked British-held territory in Natal and the Cape Colony, besieging their garrisons at Ladysmith, Mafeking and Kimberley.

In the New Year reinforcements of British troops arrived under the command of Lord Roberts in an attempt to relieve the sieges.

The siege of Mafeking was to last 217 days before it was finally relieved on 17 May 1990. Colonel Robert Baden-Powell, in command of the defence of the town, was hailed as a hero back home in Britain, where people were overjoyed with the news.

Once Natal and the Cape Colony were secure the British were able to invade the Transvaal and the republic's capital, Pretoria, was captured on 5 June 1900.

SCORCHED EARTH POLICY

In November Lord Herbert Kitchener, who succeeded Roberts as commander in South Africa, implemented a 'scorched earth' policy in which towns and farms in the republics were burnt or ravaged, destroying crops and livestock. Citizens – especially women and children who had been made homeless – were confined in appalling conditions in camps.

Kitchener's reasoning behind this policy which caused great suffering was that the commandos would no longer be able to obtain food from women on the farms, and would surrender in order to reunite their families.

The war struggled on for another two years before the Boer forces finally surrendered on 31 May 1902. The peace settlement, the Treaty of Vereeniging, brought to an end the Transvaal and the Orange Free State as Boer republics. But the British granted the Boers £3 million for restocking and repairing farm lands and promised eventual self-government. In 1910 the four provinces – Cape, Natal, Transvaal and Orange Free State – were incorporated into the Union of South Africa, a dominion of the British Empire. On 31 May 1961 the nation became a republic, under the name of the Republic of South Africa. •

WIRELESS SIGNALS ACROSS THE OCEAN

(*New York Times*, 15 December 1901)

A FAINT SOUND OF three taps heard over a radio receiver in Newfoundland, Canada, marked a new era of global communications.

Guglielmo Marconi had managed to transmit a radio signal across the Atlantic and defied fellow scientists who thought it could not be done.

Born in Bologna, the son of a wealthy Italian father and Irish mother, he became interested in science at school and carried out many experiments in the attic at home. It was here that his fascination with wireless telegraphy began. Having read about German scientist Heinrich Hertz's work with electromagnetic waves, Marconi hit on the idea of sending messages as signals through the air instead of along wires in the telegraph and telephone.

One night in 1895 he called his mother into the attic to show her how he was able to press a switch on a transmitter to send out radio waves to a receiver about nine metres away and ring a bell. He was later able to send messages in Morse code between a transmitter and receiver in the garden, two kilometres apart.

Marconi quickly realised the commercial possibilities that lay ahead but he could find little interest in his home country, which seemed content with the current system of transmission by telegraph lines and underwater cables.

SIGNALS OVER LONDON

His mother felt that his best opportunities lay in England and they came to London in 1896. That July he sent signals a mile over central London and by September, two miles across Salisbury Plain. Marconi's main aim was to use his system as a means for helping ships in distress. In May 1897 he transmitted across the Bristol Channel and in December from the Isle of Wight to a ship in the English Channel.

He formed the Wireless Telegraph and Signal Company Limited with his cousin Henry Jameson Davis.

In 1898 Marconi installed radio equipment on the Royal Yacht so that Queen Victoria, who was staying at Osborne House on the Isle of Wight, could communicate with the Prince of Wales (later Edward VII), lying off Cowes, who was convalescing on board.

Marconi's system was first used as a practical aid to the ship in distress on 11 March 1899 when a ship went aground on the Goodwin Sands, in the English Channel off the east coast of Kent, amidst a thick fog. The South Goodwin Lightship fired gun signals but this system often failed because when wind was blowing off-shore the guns could not be heard on land. However, on this occasion they were heard by the East Goodwin Lightship, which communicated by wireless telegraphy to the South Foreland Lighthouse, and from there telegraphic messages were sent to the authorities.

INTERNATIONAL MESSAGES

Marconi pushed the boundaries further when, on 27 March 1899, he transmitted the first international wireless message across the Channel from Wimereux near Bologne, France, to the South Foreland Lighthouse.

Marconi had become something of a celebrity by now and, with a flair for showmanship, he set out to perform his biggest experiment yet – transmitting signals across the Atlantic.

It was an enormous financial gamble costing around £50,000 and there were many who said it could not be done because of the curvature of the earth.

At Poldhu in Cornwall, he set up a powerful radio transmitter and an aerial system at Cape Cod in Massachusetts. But after bad weather damaged the aerial Marconi and his assistant, George Kemp, at short notice, switched the location to the appropriately named Signal Hill in St John's, Newfoundland, Canada.

Here Marconi and his assistants set up a radio receiver connected to a makeshift aerial consisting of 500 feet of wire supported by flying kites. It was nowhere near as powerful or sophisticated as the set up at Poldhu but Marconi felt it sufficient for his needs.

Marconi and Kemp sat in a hut at Signal Hill on 12 December waiting for a pre-arranged signal from the station at Poldhu – three dots, the Morse code for the letter 's', chosen for its simplicity. At 12.30pm (GMT), Marconi heard three faint clicks in his telephone connected to the radio receiver. The clicks had come all the way from Cornwall.

MURDERER CAPTURED

In 1909 1,700 lives were saved through wireless distress calls when two liners collided and one of them sank off the coast of the USA. The following year saw more success when Marconi's wireless system made headline news after it was used to apprehend Dr Hawley Crippen, who was fleeing England with his lover, Ethel Le Neve, after murdering his wife and burying the body in his cellar. The captain of the SS *Montrose* asked his Marconi operator to send a brief message to England: 'Have strong suspicions that Crippen London cellar murderer and accomplice are among saloon passengers. Accomplice dressed as a boy. Voice manner and build undoubtedly a girl.'

A detective from Scotland Yard boarded a faster ship and arrested him before SS *Montrose* docked in Montreal. •

DAYTON BOYS EMULATE GREAT SANTOS-DUMONT

(*Dayton Daily News*, 18 December 1903)

THIS RATHER UNDERWHELMING headline 'celebrated' one of the greatest human achievements in history – the power of flight.

It was on page eight of the *Dayton Daily News*, newspaper of the home town of brothers Orville and Wilbur Wright.

Brazilian aviator Alberto Santos-Dumont had become a celebrity from pioneering and flying steerable air balloons and although the newspaper spoke of the Wrights emulating him, they had actually ushered in the modern age of aviation.

The brothers had become interested in flying at an early age. In 1878 their father had given them a toy helicopter powered by rubber bands. They played and experimented with it and built their own versions of the toy. They also learned the fundamentals of flight by playing with kites. After opening a bicycle sales and repair shop in Dayton in 1892, they began making their own bikes and this mechanical knowledge of movement and steering led them to building gliders.

GLIDER PILOT KILLED

But it was the widely publicised fatal crash of famed German glider pioneer Otto Lilienthal in 1896 that really focused their attention on flight. They built and experimented with gliders at Kitty Hawk, North Carolina. They chose this location because of the steady winds there which would lift their gliders whilst the sand dunes offered a soft landing ground.

FIRST FLYING MACHINE

The Wrights' third glider, built in 1902, was a dramatic success and they were able to make numerous controlled flights in it – the best lasting for twenty-six seconds. They were convinced that they were close to powered flight and the following year they began experimenting with a piloted 'flying machine' at Kitty Hawk.

The *Wright Flyer* was a biplane which had light timber wings spanning 40ft 4in (12.3m) covered with canvas. It was 21ft 1in (6.4m) long, 9ft 4in (2.8m) high and weighed 605lbs (274kg).

It was fitted with two propellers mounted behind the wings and connected to a small gasoline engine. Underneath this sat the navigator, who controlled a rudder of canvas which could be moved from side to side and up and down.

On 14 December 1903 they were ready to make the first attempt at powered flight at Kitty Hawk. A flip of the coin had decided that Wilbur would pilot the *Wright Flyer* but it stalled during take-off and they had to repair it before trying again three days later.

This time it was Orville's turn in the pilot seat. It was launched from a trolley on a track on an incline. As it gathered speed, Orville started up the engine, which worked the propellers, and it was lifted into the air, obtaining an altitude of 60ft and flying for 120ft in 12 seconds.

AIRCRAFT DESTROYED

The brothers took turns each in the pilot seat for the next three flights that day. The longest was the final flight with Wilbur at the controls managing 852ft in 59 seconds. But it landed badly, damaging the front rudder. After removing the rudder and carrying the machine back to camp, the brothers stood discussing the flights with their team when a gust of wind turned the machine tumbling over and over, smashing it beyond repair.

But it mattered little. The Wright brothers had discovered the secret of flight. During the design and construction of their experimental aircraft they also pioneered many aspects of future aeronautical engineering such as the use of a wind tunnel.

Not everyone, however, was convinced of the Wright brothers' claims to have achieved powered flight, despite the fact that they had witnesses. In France, where there was great enthusiasm for aeronautics, many simply refused to believe that the Americans had been the first to fly, and maintained that the French would win the race to conquer the sky.

Wilbur and Orville were reluctant to travel to Europe as they thought that others would simply steal their ideas. Alberto Santos-Dumont made the first European heavier-than-air flight in France in 1906, piloting an aeroplane he had designed, rather than the balloons that had made him famous. The Wright brothers shied away from competitions and the prizes that were being offered to pioneer aviators, instead concentrating on improving their aircraft and patenting it.

It was not until Wilbur visited France in 1908 and demonstrated how the Wright brothers' latest machine could stay aloft, by now for many minutes, under complete control, that all of Europe, including even the French, acknowledged the superior engineering of the Dayton boys' flying machine. •

THE CONQUEST OF THE SOUTH POLE

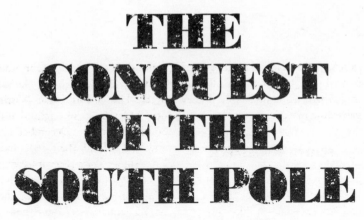

(*Manchester Guardian*, 9 March 1912)

AFTER A BRUTAL and heroic trek across the frozen wastelands of Antarctica, British explorer Captain Robert Scott and his team, who were striving to be the first to reach the South Pole, finally reached their destination... only to find Norwegian rival Roald Amundsen had beaten them to it.

News of the Norwegian expedition's achievement took several months to reach Europe. This report in the *Manchester Guardian* rather grudgingly congratulates Amundsen on his success but sows a hint of doubt into his story.

'Whether Amundsen was the first to reach the South Pole remains, of course, to be seen; no word has yet come of Captain Scott, and until we know whether he reached the Pole, and, if so, when, the question who is the victor in the race remains uncertain.'

The two expeditions had employed very different strategies. Amundsen relied on dogs and sledges to transport supplies over the ice while Scott preferred ponies and mechanical sledges. But the ponies suffered in the cold and the mechanical sledges failed and so the men ended up pulling them. The Norwegians eschewed the usual thick woollen clothing for wolfskin fur suits that had been adapted from Inuit garments, in addition to Burberry suits made of a lighter gabardine material.

SCIENTIFIC RESEARCH

Scott's agenda was to continue his scientific research, which he had undertaken on his *Discovery* expedition of 1901–4 which reached further south than anyone before them and had turned him into a national hero. But Amundsen focused on being the first to reach the South Pole. These are just some of the factors that led to success for the Norwegians and failure and tragedy for the British who were to die on their way home.

Amundsen and his team left Oslo on 3 June 1910 aboard the ship *Fram*, heading south. At that time Norway was a relatively new nation having only achieved its independence from Sweden in 1905. They needed diplomatic support from Britain and so the expedition was kept secret for fear of upsetting the British.

They arrived at the eastern edge of the Great Ice Barrier on 14 January 1911 and set up base camp named Framhein. After a first attempt at reaching the Pole failed,

Amundsen set off with four others, Olav Bjaaland, Helmer Hanssen, Sverre Hassel and Oscar Wisting, on 19 October. They arrived at the South Pole on 14 December 1911 and left behind their tent and a letter stating their accomplishment, in case they did not return home safely. The team reached Framhein on 25 January 1912 and news of their success became public after they sailed to Hobart, Australia, on 7 March.

TERRA NOVA SETS SAIL

The British expedition left West Indian Dock, London, aboard the ship *Terra Nova* on 1 June 1910, on the start of her voyage to Antarctica. On arrival in January 1911 they set up base camp in Ross Island. Scott made his selection of the men who were to accompany him on the final stage – Petty Officer Evans, Lieutenant Bowers, Dr Wilson and Captain Oates – and they set off on 1 November.

Ten miles from their destination, Bowers saw a black speck on the horizon. Later they came across sledge and ski tracks and the imprints of dog paws. When they arrived on 17 January 1912, they entered the tent and read

Amundsen's note, which confirmed that he had arrived a month earlier and had now departed.

A crushed Scott wrote in his journal that evening, 'Great God! This is an awful place and terrible enough for us to have laboured to it without the reward or priority.'

From the start of the return journey, Evans was weak and continued to deteriorate in the arduous conditions.

LOST SUPPLY DROPS

Amundsen had placed well-marked depots of food and supplies en route, while Scott had fewer and badly marked depots that often could not be found in the blizzards. Evans had cut his hand some weeks before on one of the sledge runners and it had swollen and turned gangrenous. He died on the Beardmore Glacier on 17 February.

By March Oates was suffering from severe frostbite. Scott described in his journal how Oates had said he couldn't go on but they refused his suggestion of leaving him behind in his sleeping bag and encouraged him to trek on with

them. But on the morning of 17 March he awoke and commented, 'I am just going outside and may be some time.' He then walked out into the howling blizzard and they never saw him again.

Scott, Wilson and Bowers all died from exposure and hunger while sheltering from a blizzard in their tent on 29 March 1912.

The last entry to Scott's journal on that day read, 'We had fuel to make two cups of tea apiece and bare food for two days on the 20th. Every day we have been ready to start for our depot 11 miles away, but outside the doors of the tent it remains a scene of whirling drift. I do not think we can hope for any better things now. We shall stick it out to the end, but we are getting weaker, of course, and the end cannot be far. It seems a pity, but I do not think I can write more. R Scott. For God's sake look after our people.'

Eight months later, on 12 November 1912, a search party found the tent, the bodies and Scott's diary. The bodies were buried under the tent, with a cairn of ice and snow to mark the spot. •

TITANIC SUNK

TERRIBLE LOSS OF LIFE FEARED
COLLISION WITH AN ICEBERG

(*The Times*, 16 April 1912)

CRACKS WERE appearing in the once mighty British Empire and the 'old world' of privilege, power and prosperity enjoyed by the upper-classes was about to be rocked by the outbreak of World War I.

But glamour and overt affluence was still to be had and none more so than a first-class transatlantic ticket aboard the White Star Line's new pride and joy, the RMS *Titanic*.

It was billed as the largest passenger steamship in the world and offered luxurious First Class accommodation, with large state-rooms, a Parisian café, a swimming pool and restaurant. What's more, special watertight compartments made her 'practically unsinkable'.

The *Titanic*'s maiden voyage from Southampton to New York City on Wednesday, 10 April 1912, attracted some of the most eminent people of the day as millionaires, businessmen, industrialists, aristocrats, politicians and bankers waved family and friends a final farewell from the upper decks before departing on the trip of a lifetime.

But as well as the wealthy, the *Titanic* offered many working-class people the chance to try a new life in America with reasonably priced accommodation in Third Class, tucked away in the lower decks.

ICEBERG COLLISION

Four days into the journey, the unthinkable happened. The ship struck an iceberg at night, piercing the starboard side and popping out rivets. At first, everyone remained calm. This, after all, we the unsinkable *Titanic*. But one of the passengers aboard was Thomas

Andrews, a naval architect who worked for Harland & Wolff, the Belfast shipyard that had built *Titanic*. He was part of the company's 'Guarantee Group', a team of experienced engineers and tradesmen who sailed on every Harland & Wolff ship's maiden voyage to troubleshoot problems, iron out teething difficulties and suggest practical improvements to the design.

Andrews very quickly realised that the extent and position of the damage spelt disaster. He knew that if the watertight compartments in the ship's bow flooded, the water would rise up above the level of the compartments and flood the whole ship. That the ship would sink was, as he put it, 'a mathematical certainty.' It was just a matter of time.

Titanic struck the iceberg at 11.40pm on 14 April. By 2.20am the following morning, just two hours and forty minutes later, she would be gone. The ship's captain, Edward Smith, ordered 'mayday' signals to be broadcast.

The nearest ship to pick up the distress signal was the *Carpathia* but she was 58 miles (93 km) away and, despite travelling at full steam, she would not reach the area until three and a half hours later.

PASSENGERS PANIC

As the *Titanic* began to sink there was increasing panic aboard and lifeboats left the ship only partially full. The first to pull away, with a capacity of 65, contained 27 people. Another, with a capacity of 40, left with just 12. Third class passengers couldn't find their way to the upper decks where the lifeboats were stored and many were still below deck when the ship sank.

In less than three hours, *Titanic* had sunk and the lucky ones who had managed to get in lifeboats, spent three hours on the freezing cold water before *Carpathia* was spotted on the horizon with the coming of dawn and took them aboard.

The official British inquiry concluded that Titanic had sunk after colliding with an iceberg due to excessive speed of 22 knots.

The incident was to bring about many changes in maritime regulations. It was found that the provision of lifeboats was woefully inadequate. Just 20 boats could hold a maximum of 1,178 people. But on board the *Titanic* was a total of 2,201 passengers and crew. In the end, just 711 people were rescued.

THE AFTERMATH

No proper lifeboat drill had taken place and that would become a legal requirement, as would easier access throughout all future ships for passengers following the revelation that just 25 per cent of those in Third Class, below decks, were saved, compared with 62 per cent and 41 per cent in First and Second, respectively.

Other changes would be in hull and bulkhead design, improved life-vests and improved radio communications.

The sinking of the *Titanic* shook the world's confidence in the infallibility of modern technology and underlined the importance of safety and common sense. •

SENSATIONAL DERBY SUFFRAGIST'S MAD ACT

KING'S HORSE BROUGHT DOWN WOMAN AND JOCKEY INJURED

(*Morning Post*, 5 June 1913)

SUFFRAGETTE Emily Wilding Davison hit the headlines when she caused a sensation at the Derby by throwing herself in front of the King's horse.

The *Morning Post* described it as a 'mad act'. Jockey, Herbert Jones, survived the tumble but Davison died from her injuries four days later.

On the day of 4 June 1913, cheering crowds lined the packed course for the prestigious event. As the horses galloped towards the famous Tattenham Corner,

Davison ducked beneath a barrier and rushed across the course, where she attempted to grab the bridle of the King's horse, Anmer, as it rounded the corner.

The horse knocked her down and the impact fractured the base of her skull. The horse did a somersault on the ground and dragged Jones for a short way before he managed to free himself. He suffered concussion and minor injuries and refused hospital treatment.

Davison was taken by ambulance to Epsom Cottage Hospital, where she later died without regaining consciousness. She was wearing a suffragist flag of purple, white and green wrapped round her waist at the time of the incident and was a well-known activist in the movement for female emancipation.

FORMER SCHOOLTEACHER

Born in Blackheath, southeast London on 11 October 1872, she studied at Royal Holloway College and at Oxford University. In November 1906 she joined the Women's Social and Political Union (WSPU), founded by Emmeline Pankhurst. Three years later she gave up her job as a schoolteacher and went to work full-time for the suffragette movement.

She became increasingly militant and some members of the WSPU did not look favourably on her somewhat maverick behaviour.

She was arrested and imprisoned on numerous occasions. Her long list of convictions included those of causing a disturbance, burning post boxes, throwing stones and hiding in the House of Commons in the crypt and air shaft on three occasions.

In 1909, she was sentenced to a month's hard labour in Strangeways Prison in Manchester after throwing rocks at the carriage of Chancellor of the Exchequer David Lloyd George. Her customary way of protest for imprisonment was to go on hunger strike but this time the prison officers tried to force-feed her.

Davison pushed her cell furniture against the door to prevent them from entering. An irate warden climbed a ladder outside, pushed a hosepipe through the window and turned on the water. She remained defiant until the door was eventually forced open.

LEGAL ACTION

On her release, James Keir Hardie, the leader of the Labour Party, complained in the House of Commons about the hosepipe treatment. Davison was encouraged to take legal action and on 19 January 1910, Judge Parry pronounced in her favour, awarding damages of forty shillings.

There was mixed feeling about her intention at the Derby. Some witnesses felt that it was an accident and that she had just been making her way across the course to the centre in order to see a friend and had mistakenly thought that all the horses had passed. But others were convinced that it was a deliberate act. Even Emmeline Pankhurst and her daughter, Sylvia, were not united in their beliefs.

Sylvia argued, 'Emily Davison and a fellow-militant in whose flat she lived, had concerted a Derby protest without tragedy – a mere waving of the purple-white-and-green at Tattenham Corner – which, by its suddenness, it was hoped would stop the race. Whether from the first her purpose was more serious, or whether a final impulse altered her resolve, I know not. Her friend declares she would not thus have died without writing a farewell message to her mother.'

But Emmeline was in no doubt. In her autobiography, *My Own Story*, she wrote, 'Emily Davison clung to her conviction that one great tragedy, the deliberate throwing into the breach of a human life, would put an end to the intolerable torture of women. And so she threw herself at the King's horse, in full view of the King and Queen and a great multitude of their Majesties' subjects.'

WOMEN WIN THE VOTE

A combination of the events surrounding World War I, continuing protest by the suffragettes and the growth of the Labour Party eventually led to women being granted the vote. As the law stood at the end of the war, only men who had been resident in the country for twelve months prior to a general election were entitled to vote. This effectively disenfranchised a large number of troops who had been serving overseas in the war.

With a general election imminent, politicians were persuaded to extend the vote to women. The 1918 Representation of the People Act was passed, which allowed women to vote with the caveat that they were over the age of 30 and owned property. Although 8.5 million women met these criteria, it only represented 40 per cent of the total population of women in the U.K.

It was not until the Equal Franchise Act of 1928 that women over 21 were finally able to vote on the same terms as men. •

HEIR TO AUSTRIA'S THRONE IS SLAIN

WITH HIS WIFE BY A BOSNIAN YOUTH TO AVENGE SEIZURE OF HIS COUNTRY

(*New York Times*, 29 June 1914)

THE ASSASSINATION OF the Archduke Franz Ferdinand and his wife whilst visiting the Bosnian capital of Sarajevo set in motion a chain of events that led to the start of the Great War.

The Archduke and his wife, Duchess of Hohenberg, were shot dead in their car in an incident that would have far-reaching consequences around the world.

Bosnia and Herzegovina had been under Austro-Hungarian occupation since 1878 and was annexed by the mighty empire in 1908. The majority of the population were Serbs, furious with Austrian rulers who wanted unification with neighbouring Serbia.

Franz Ferdinand, nephew of the aged Emperor Franz Josef, who had been made head of the army, knew of the hostility and potential danger prior to his visit to Bosnia, where he had been invited to inspect the manoeuvres of the Austrian Army Corps stationed in the province.

On the morning of 28 June 1914 he and the Duchess were in

a car as it processed through the capital. There were many Serbian flags raised as a sign of protest.

FAILED BOMB ATTACK

He caught sight of a bomb being thrown at the car and managed to swipe it away with his hand. As his car moved on and the bomb fell to the ground, it exploded by the following car in the procession, injuring the occupants, Count von Boos-Waldeck and Colonel Morizzi, along with six spectators.

The Archduke's car increased speed and took him to a reception at the Town Hall where he was officially received by the Major.

Afterwards he asked to be driven to hospital to visit Col. Morizzi, who had been taken there after the bomb incident.

The driver took a wrong turning and as he slowed to turn around a second assassin took his chance and fired shots from a pistol. One struck the Duchess in the abdomen, while another hit the Archduke in the neck and pierced the jugular vein. Both died shortly after.

The men behind the assassination were part of the Black Hand, a Serbian nationalist secret society who had sent seven of their members to mingle with spectators during the Archduke's procession in Sarajevo to kill him.

The bomb had been thrown by a Serbian compositor named Gabrinovics. He was arrested within 20 minutes of the incident. The gunman was 19-year-old Gavrio Princip.

Austro-Hungary strongly suspected that the killing of the Archduke was part of a wider political plot involving the Serbian government and so it took the opportunity to try to crush the nationalist movement with military force.

It issued a list of demands designed to undermine Serbia's sovereignty, accusing the government of complicity in the assassination and insisting on delegates of the Austro-Hungarian government taking part in the investigation against those involved in the assassination plot.

WAR IS DECLARED

Although Serbia agreed to implement most but not all of the demands, Austro-Hungary declared war three days later on 28 July 1914.

But a set of historic alliances between countries throughout

Europe caused a domino effect. Serbia had ties with Russia and whilst not really expecting that Russia would be drawn into the dispute other than by words of protest, the Austro-Hungarian government sought assurances from her ally, Germany, that she would come to her aid should Russia join the war.

Germany, under Kaiser Wilhelm II, was becoming increasingly aggressive in its plans to extend its empire and had been building up its navy, which alarmed other powerful maritime nations such as Britain and France.

Germany readily agreed to help Austro-Hungary but when Russia unexpectedly committed military to aid Serbia, other countries were drawn into the conflict, one by one. France, which was bound by treaty to Russia, found itself at war with Germany and Austro-Hungary.

After Germany invaded Belgium on 4 August, Britain, which had an alliance with both Belgium and France, declared war against Germany on the same day. The move also brought in countries within her empire such as Australia, Canada, India and New Zealand.

Japan, honouring a military agreement with Britain, declared war on Germany on 23 August 1914.

The stage was thus set for a war that would cause great bloodshed and would last for four years. •

LAST BARRIER IN CANAL IS REMOVED

(*Oakland Tribune*, 10 October 1913)

THE HEADLINE IN THIS Californian newspaper referred to the longest and greatest technological achievements of the age.

In Washington, U.S. President Woodrow Wilson pressed a button in the Oval Office at 2pm on 10 October 1913, sending a signal to Panama to blow the Gamboa dyke, thus removing the last practical obstruction in the creation of the huge waterway known as the Panama Canal.

In a project that was first begun more than 40 years before and had cost the lives of over 27,000 workers, the Atlantic and Pacific Oceans were at last joined by a Trans-Isthmian waterway.

But the dream of such a thoroughfare had gone back much further into history. In the early 1500s explorer Christopher Columbus had searched in vain for a route in Panama that would take him from one ocean to another.

In 1534, Charles I of Spain ordered the first survey of a proposed canal route through the Isthmus of Panama to facilitate their ships in plundering the riches of Peru, Ecuador and Asia.

INHOSPITABLE TERRAIN

Others pondered the idea of a link over the centuries and in 1835 U.S. Army Colonel Charles Biddle was sent on an exploratory mission to evaluate its feasibility. But after four days in the sweltering, mosquito-infested jungle, he returned saying that the inhospitable terrain made it impractical.

It was to be another 40 years before construction finally began in 1879, led by the French entrepreneur Ferdinand de Lesseps, who had managed the successful Suez Canal project.

Following the Suez model, de Lesseps' plans were for a canal to be built at sea level across the Central American isthmus. But the mountainous Panamanian jungle was very different from the flat desert at Suez. Labourers had to cope with snakes, mosquitoes carrying yellow fever and malaria, collapsing hillsides, quagmires and insanitary conditions. More than 22,000 workers died.

The slow process and increasing cost resulted in his company being declared bankrupt in 1889.

NEW CANAL PLAN

Ten years later, the U.S. began, once more, to see the advantage of controlling a waterway linking the two oceans. After becoming President in 1901, Theodore Roosevelt put the plan into operation.

A payment of $40 million bought the rights to what was left of the French canal but the constantly changing Colombian government, which was then the colonial power in Panama, refused to sell the land to the U.S.

Roosevelt abandoned attempts at negotiation and, instead, aided Panamanian revolutionaries in their fight for independence by providing a fleet of warships to both coasts of Panama, preventing Colombia from landing troop reinforcements.

He was then able to cut a deal with the new independent nation, paying $10 million in 1903 for the land needed for the canal.

Work began and, after initial deaths amongst the workforce, improved conditions were put in place in which swamps were drained, running water and sewage pipes laid and adequate accommodation built.

The French plan to build a canal at sea level was dumped for a lock-and-lake canal that would utilise the power of the rainy climate and the mighty Chagres River.

But the work was still tough and during American construction more than 5,000 died.

LANDSLIDE PERIL

One of the toughest challenges was the Culebra Cut that was to form a valley through the highest point on the route – the continental divide. More than 300,000 tonnes of rock had to be dug out and disposed of. It was prone to frequent landslides, setting the work back by months.

The Panama Canal officially opened to the world's shipping on 15 August 1915, each ship taking an average of nine hours to pass through the 50-mile (80km) long crossing from ocean to ocean.

Under American control the canal allowed their battleships easy transit between the two seas and confirmed the U.S. as a twentieth century superpower. •

FIVE DAYS INSIDE THE CORDON

THE INSURRECTION AS SEEN FROM WITHIN THE CITY

(*Guardian*, 2 May 1916)

AN UPRISING AGAINST British rule in Ireland lasted seven days before it was crushed by troops. Yet it became the impetus for change and an enduring symbol of nationalism.

With the outbreak of World War I, Irish militants saw the opportunity to take advantage of Britain's preoccupation with fighting the Germans to mount their own battle – for independence.

In May 1915 a military committee (later the military council) was formed, consisting of Patrick Pearse, Joseph Plunkett and Éamonn Ceannt, who were all members of the Irish Republican Brotherhood and of the Irish Volunteers. Later, Seán MacDiarmada, Tom Clarke, James Connolly and Thomas MacDonagh also joined.

In January 1916 the seven men planned to mount a joint insurrection by members of the Irish Volunteers, the Irish Citizen Army and Cumann nam Ban, and to seize key locations in Dublin and proclaim an Irish Republic with themselves as its provisional government.

On Easter Monday the military committee led around 1,600 poorly armed men to take over the General Post Office in Sackville Street, which was to be used as their headquarters, and also to Liberty Hall, St Stephen's Green, the Four Courts, Boland's Mill and Jacob's biscuit factory.

IRISH REPUBLIC PROCLAIMED

Outside the GPO, Pearse proclaimed the establishment of the Irish Republic and hoisted two Republican flags, to the bewilderment of locals going about their normal day.

When two troops of British cavalry arrived to investigate the commotion, they were fired upon. There were a few other skirmishes that day but the following day extra British troops arrived and the shelling of the rebels' defences began in earnest. As the week progressed, more and more troops arrived and it became obvious what the outcome would be.

The British crushed the rebellion with superior numbers and firepower, forcing them to surrender in order to save further

lives. By the end of the fighting, 64 insurgents had died as well as 132 soldiers and police and around 230 civilians. Some 2,000 were wounded.

The high rate of civilian casualties was due to a combination of indirect fire from artillery and because they were directly attacked by both sides. The British troops tended to treat all of the Irish as enemies but, in truth, many resented the actions of the rebels in taking over the city where they lived and worked. And when they resisted orders, they were set upon.

SENTENCED TO DEATH

The seven signatories of the Proclamation and eight others were court-martialled and executed by firing squad. A sixteenth man, Roger Casement, was tried in open court in London and hanged in Pentonville Prison for his part in negotiating a shipment of arms from Germany. In the event, the ship carrying the weapons, disguised as a Norwegian fishing trawler, was intercepted by the Royal Navy.

Ninety-seven others were also sentenced to death, but had their sentences commuted to various terms of imprisonment. All of them were released within a relatively short period, the last in June 1917.

Although most Irish nationalists had considered the insurrection to be a foolhardy undertaking, doomed to failure, the Easter Uprising was to change people's views. The bravery and patriotism shown was seen as commendable and certain atrocities committed by the British troops, such as the execution of six civilians at Portobello Barracks, caused widespread and continuing anger which served to unite people against Britain. And the calls for independence became louder.

The Irish Volunteers became the Irish Republican Army and together with the political party, Sinn Féin, they pushed for independence, resulting in the Act of Partition, which came into effect in 1922. The mainly Protestant counties of Ulster would remain part of the United Kingdom, as Northern Ireland, while the predominantly Catholic counties in the south were given a measure of independence as the Irish Free State, before gaining full independence as the Republic of Ireland in 1948. •

ABDICATION OF CZAR

IS FOLLOWED BY THAT OF GRAND DUKE MICHAEL, WHICH ENDS ROMANOFF DYNASTY IN RUSSIA

(*Asheville Citizen*, 17 March 1917)

ON 3 APRIL 1917, exiled Russian political activist Vladimir Lenin returned to St Petersburg on a train from Finland and precipitated a second revolution in Russia, which ushered in the Communist era and brought about the shocking execution of the Royal Family.

In February of that year, resentment of Tsar Nicholas II's autocratic rule, the unfair balance of wealth between landowners and ordinary working people, along with Russia's involvement in an unpopular war, were causing much anger and ill-feeling.

Poor living conditions amongst the working class were exacerbated by the men being sent off to fight in the Great War. In the first few days of the war at the Battle of Tannenberg, the Russian army was comprehensively beaten, suffering 120,000 casualties to Germany's 20,000. Further losses continued and by 1916 morale amongst the soldiers, as well as on the home front, was at an all-time low. The Tsar was being blamed for the situation.

FOOD SHORTAGES

On 23 February there was a protest in St Petersburg against food shortages, which led to workers going on strike. The Tsar ordered the military to intervene but he could no longer count on their loyalty and many refused. With protests and looting breaking out, the Tsar felt his position untenable and abdicated his throne in March, handing power to his brother, Michael. But he deferred the throne until properly elected, leaving the country without a head of state and bringing an end to the Romanov dynasty.

A Provisional Government was quickly formed by leading members of the Russian parliament, the Duma, led by Alexander Kerensky, until elections could be held. But Kerensky, to the dismay of the public and soldiers, did not want to end the war.

LENIN RETURNS

Into this heated arena entered Lenin, who had been aided in his secret return by the Germans in the hope that he would unite the people to overthrow the Provisional Government and take Russia out of the war.

Throughout the spring and summer, Lenin made rousing public speeches, calling for Russia's withdrawal from the war, better working conditions, more food and the redistribution of wealth.

Some soldiers on the Eastern Front deserted and returned home, using their weapons to seize land from the nobility.

On 19 July, Kerensky gave orders for the arrest of leading members of the Bolshevik party campaigning against the war, which included Lenin and fellow activist Leon Trotsky.

The following month, the Royal Family were placed in the former Governor's mansion where they lived in considerable comfort.

Kerensky was forced to ask the Bolsheviks for military aid when he feared his Minister of War, Kornilov, was aiming for a military dictatorship. By the autumn, the Bolsheviks were growing in stature and Lenin knew the time was right to seize power from the Government.

BOLSHEVIK TAKEOVER

On 24 October 1917, a coup d'état took place as the Bolsheviks stormed the city, taking up strategic posts and meeting with little resistance. By the following day every key building in St Petersburg was under their control, except the Winter Palace where Kerensky and other ministers were holed up with a small guard. But after Kerensky fled, the Palace was taken on 26 October. Lenin's revolution had been achieved with the minimum of bloodshed. But the country was plunged into a civil war between the Red Guard (Communists) and the White Army (a loose alliance of Nationalists, Imperialists and other anti-Bolsheviks) which was to last four years at the cost of millions of lives before the Reds triumphed, establishing the Soviet Union in 1922.

ROYAL FAMILY IMPRISONED

In the meantime, the Russian Royal Family had been moved to the town of Yekaterinburg in the spring of 1918, where they were confined to the house of a successful local merchant which had been commandeered by the Bolsheviks. Here their guards treated them badly, with little or no respect.

The intention was to put the Tsar on trial but the civil war was raging and by mid-July a contingent of the White Army was approaching Yekaterinburg. Fearing that the Royal Family would be rescued, their guards were ordered to execute them.

In the early hours of 17 July 1918, the Tsar, his wife, five children and servants were herded into the cellar of their prison house and shot. Those who did not die straight away were viciously bayoneted. •

HOW LONDON HAILED THE END OF WAR

(*Daily Mirror*, 12 November 1918)

THERE WERE THOSE on both sides who thought that the Great War would last for a few months and it would all be over by Christmas. Few imagined that it would drag on through four long and bloody years.

When the Allied victory finally came over the Central Powers there was a huge sigh of relief and a great outpouring of celebration and euphoria.

The front page of the *Daily Mirror* was taken up with a montage of images from central London depicting the King and Queen on the balcony of Buckingham Palace, a soldier kissing his loved one, and a little girl waving a flag.

It had been a war fought mainly in the trenches, which had seen some epic battles at the Somme, Passchendaele and Gallipoli amongst others, and an estimated 10 million military deaths.

The end unravelled quickly as the final Allied push towards the German border began on 17 October 1918 and resistance collapsed. Turkey signed an armistice at the end of October and Austro-Hungary followed on 3 November.

ARMISTICE SIGNED

On 9 November the Kaiser abdicated and, two days later, Germany signed an armistice in a railroad car outside Compiégne, France, agreeing to a cessation of fighting along the entire Western Front to begin at precisely 11am that morning. The Great War was at an end.

In London, huge crowds took to the streets in celebration. Outside Buckingham Palace they chanted, 'We want the King' until he appeared with the Queen on the balcony.

The Royal couple waved to the crowd to joyous cheers. Later in the day they re-appeared and King George V gave a short speech saying, 'With you I rejoice and thank God for the victories which the Allied arms have won, bringing hostilities to an end and peace within sight.' A band played 'God Save the King', 'Tipperary' and 'Auld Lang Syne'.

CHURCH BELLS RING

Church bells, silent throughout the war, sounded their joyous peal. Crowds formed at Trafalgar Square, Downing Street, Admiralty Arch and Mansion House. And The Strand was packed with people walking up and down. Revellers sang and waved flags and clambered aboard double-decker buses.

In the afternoon, the King and Queen drove through the City and again received a tremendous ovation. The following day they attended a service of thanksgiving at St Paul's Cathedral and celebrations continued throughout the week.

For the next few months the Allies, led by the 'Big Three' of David Lloyd George, Georges Clemençeau and Woodrow Wilson, the leaders of Britain, France and America, negotiated a peace treaty at the Palace of Versailles in Paris.

Negotiations were difficult with each of the Big Three wanting different things. Finally the Germans were shown the Treaty and they were appalled by the unfairness of it. But there was to be no negotiation.

AIR FORCE BANNED

The main points of the Treaty were an establishment of the League of Nations which excluded Germany; German troops banished from the Rhineland; The Saar, with its rich coalfields, given to France for 15 years; Alsace-Lorraine returned to France; fertile farm lands in eastern Germany given to Poland; all colonies placed under League of Nations mandates; Germany not allowed to unite with Austria; the army restricted to 100,000 men, navy to six battleships and no submarines and the banning of an air force; Germany to pay reparations which was eventually settled at 132 billion reichsmarks (around 22 billion pounds).

German hatred and resentment of the punitive terms agreed at Versailles was later to give rise to the Nazis and World War II twenty years later. •

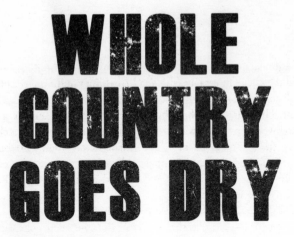

WHOLE COUNTRY GOES DRY

(*Washington Times*, 16 January 1919)

THE NEWS ARTICLE which accompanied this headline announced that the nation would be 'bone dry within a year from today' following the ratification of the prohibition amendment making it illegal to consume, sell and transport alcohol in the U.S.

The ban came into effect on 17 January 1920 and was to last for 13 years, causing an upsurge in violence and criminal behaviour as those still wanting a drink turned to the black market and racketeers.

The ban evolved as a consequence of the activities of a combination of pressure groups, and as a result of America's involvement in World War I. The Anti-Saloon League in particular had campaigned hard that alcohol was damaging American society. And many vocal religious groups announced it was against God's will. Other active organisations included the Women's Church Federation, the Women's Temperance Crusade and the Department of Scientific Temperance Instruction

WARTIME PROHIBITION

After the U.S. joined the Great War in April 1917, a wartime prohibition act was passed which banned the sale of beverages with an alcohol content greater than 2.75 per cent. This was said to have been done to save grain for the war effort. It led to the Volstead Act of 1919, which established the enforcement of prohibition. Finally, the 18th Amendment to the Constitution of the United States made prohibition throughout the country the law after it was certified on 16 January 1919.

But there were many people who objected to prohibition and sought to carry on drinking alcohol. In this climate, illegal drinking dens flourished, becoming known as 'speakeasies'. These were usually bars that claimed to sell soft drinks but served alcohol behind the scenes.

THE BLACK MARKET

Chicago, in particular, became notorious for gangsters making millions of dollars from selling illicit liquor and doing battle with others who wanted a part of the lucrative black market trade. Al Capone and his rival Bugs Moran indulged in frequent gang warfare. The most infamous incident was the St Valentine's Day massacre in 1929 when Capone's men,

disguised as police, 'raided' a trucking warehouse which served as Moran's headquarters. They lined seven men up against a wall and shot them dead with machine guns, firing more than 150 bullets into the victims. The photographs of the dead and bloodied bodies that appeared in newspapers shocked the public.

By the end of the decade, Capone controlled around 10,000 speakeasies in Chicago and ruled the bootlegging business. In addition he owned bookmakers, gambling houses, brothels, horse and race tracks and nightclubs.

Gangland violence, intimidation, theft, protection rackets and murder proliferated and the 1,500 prohibition agents commissioned to enforce the law were overwhelmed. Many also turned a 'blind eye' in exchange for a pay-off.

'BATHTUB GIN'

Making alcohol at home was very common with home-distilled spirit known as 'bathtub gin' in the northern cities and 'moonshine' in the south.

Stores sold grape concentrate with warning labels that listed the steps that should be avoided to *prevent* the juice from fermenting into wine.

With violence on the increase, the black market booming and the law being increasingly difficult to administer, public feeling against prohibition began to change.

In 1929 the Wickersham Commission reported that Prohibition was not working. On 23 March 1933 President Franklin D. Roosevelt signed the Cullen – Harrison Act, which allowed the manufacture and sale of alcohol of 4 per cent proof. And on 5 December of that year, prohibition was repealed with the 21st Amendment. •

MR MACDONALD'S CROWDED DAY

(*Guardian*, 23 January 1924)

A RATHER LOW-KEY headline in the *Guardian* detailed James Ramsay Macdonald's busy schedule on the previous day, which included two visits to Buckingham Palace where he was sworn in as Britain's first Labour Prime Minister.

Born on 12 October 1866 in Lossiemouth, Morayshire, Scotland, the illegitimate son of a crofter, MacDonald worked as a teacher locally and then moved to London where he became a clerk at the House of Commons.

He became increasingly interested in politics and joined the Fabian Society where he met many high-profile socialists of the day such as George Bernard Shaw, Emmeline Pankhurst and H. G. Wells. In 1893, a group of independent socialists, including James Keir Hardie, formed a new national working-class movement called the Independent Labour Party.

MacDonald joined in 1894 and the following year was selected as the ILP candidate for Southampton.

ANTI-WAR CAMPAIGNER

MacDonald was bold in speaking out against the Boer War, which he viewed as a consequence of imperialism. He wrote that, 'Further extensions of Empire are only the grabbings of millionaires on the hunt.' But his resolution to condemn the war at a meeting of the Fabian Society was defeated. Following this failure he, along with thirteen others, resigned from the Fabian Society.

Hardie, the leader of the Independent Labour Party, and George Bernard Shaw of the Fabian Society, realised that the way for socialists to win seats in parliamentary elections would be to form a new party made up of various left-wing groups.

On 27 February 1900, representatives of all the socialist groups in Britain met with trade-union leaders at the Congregational Memorial Hall in Farringdon Street, and the Labour Representation Committee (LRC) was formed with MacDonald as the secretary.

The LRC put up fifteen candidates in the 1900 general election and between them they won 62,698 votes. Two of the candidates, Keir Hardie and Richard Bell, won seats in the House of Commons.

1906 ELECTION VICTORIES

The LRC did much better in the 1906 general election with 29 successful candidates winning their seats, including MacDonald as MP for Leicester. On 12 February, the group of MPs decided to change the name from the LRC to the Labour Party. Hardie was elected chairman and MacDonald was the party's secretary.

After the 1910 election, when 40 Labour MPs were elected to the House of Commons, MacDonald became party chairman. His opposition to the Great War caused him much criticism, particularly in the right-wing press, which labelled him a traitor.

But by the early 1920s, MacDonald was the dominant figure in the Labour Party, impressing people with his mix of intelligence, moderate and practical policies, oratory skills and imposing presence. At the 1922 general election he was elected to represent Aberavon, and the Labour Party won 142 seats, eclipsing the Liberals as the main opposition to the governing Conservative Party.

No party won an overall majority in the general election of December 1923, with the Conservatives taking 258 seats, Labour 191 and the Liberals 159. The Conservatives kept power, but lost a vote of confidence in the House of Commons in January 1924.

PRIME MINISTER RESIGNS

The Prime Minister, Stanley Baldwin, went to Buckingham Palace to tender his resignation to King George V. Shortly after, MacDonald was summoned to the Palace and the King asked him to form a government.

MacDonald was cheered by a group of supports as he left. Later that evening he returned to the Palace as Prime Minister to present to the King his list of government appointments.

McDonald later recalled that the King had complained about the singing of the historic socialist songs, *Red Flag* and the *La Marseilles*, at the Labour Party meeting in the Albert Hall a few days earlier. MacDonald apologised but claimed that there would have been a riot if he had tried to stop it. •

THE "TELEVISOR"

SUCCESSFUL TEST OF NEW APPARATUS

(*The Times*, 28 January 1926)

This rather low-key headline on page nine of the London *Times* was the first report of one of the biggest life-changing inventions of the 20th century.

The reporter told how he, along with members of the Royal Institution and other visitors, were invited to a laboratory in an upper room in Frith Street, Soho, London, on Tuesday, 26 January, where they saw 'a demonstration of apparatus invented by Mr J. L. Baird, who claims to have solved the problem of television'.

Here they were shown a 'transmitting machine', consisting of a large wooden revolving disc containing lenses. The holes were arranged in a spiral, and as the disc turned it scanned the scene in front of it. Behind the disc was a revolving shutter and a light-sensitive cell.

Baird first demonstrated with the head of a ventriloquist's dummy placed in front of the transmitter, which reappeared on a receiver in the same room and then on a receiver in another room. When he moved the head, they could see the movements on the receiver screen. Baird then did the same with a human face.

FAINT, BLURRED IMAGE

The *Times* reporter stated, 'The image as transmitted was faint and often blurred, but substantiated a claim that through the "Televisor" as Mr Baird has named his apparatus, it is possible to transmit and reproduce instantly the details of movement, and such things as the play of expression on the face.'

Born in Helensburgh, Scotland on 14 August 1888, Baird suffered from poor health most of his life, something that spurred him on to experiment with electrical gadgets and communications. He once created a mini telephone exchange in his bedroom that allowed him to talk directly to friends living nearby.

Baird studied at the West of Scotland Technical College and the University of Glasgow, although he never completed his degree course as it was interrupted by the outbreak of World War I. His poor health made him unfit for military service, and he worked as an engineer with the Clyde Valley Electrical Power Company during the war.

Following a short spell in business, Baird moved to the south of England in the hope of improving his health, settling on the coast in Hastings where he concentrated on developing a system for transmitting moving images.

On 2 October 1925, using a ventriloquist's dummy he nick-named Stookie Bill, he transmitted a 30-line vertically scanned greyscale image at five pictures per second. Excited, he went downstairs and fetched 20-year-old office worker, William Edward Taynton, to see what a human face would look like. Taynton became the first person to be televised in a full tonal range.

DAILY EXPRESS LUNATIC

Baird later took his machine to the *Daily Express* in order to get publicity but the editor was alarmed when he heard he was in the building and shouted to his newsroom, 'For God's sake, go down to reception and get rid of a lunatic who's down there. He says he's got a machine for seeing by wireless! Watch him – he may have a razor on him!'

Following the successful public demonstration in Frith Street, the Baird Television Development Company Ltd was formed.

In 1927, he sent a live 30-line television signal 438 miles (730km) from London to Glasgow along telephone cables. A year later, his company transmitted pictures of a man and a woman to an astonished gathering watching in New York.

COLOUR TELEVISION

Baird also invented an early colour TV system and made the first television programmes for the British Broadcasting Corporation (BBC) in 1929. His broadcast system for the BBC included sound, but never had more than 240 lines – almost the limit of his mechanical system.

Baird's electromechanical system was eventually superseded by purely electronic systems.

Although the development of television was the result of work by many inventors, each with an integral part to play, Baird was the first person in the world to demonstrate a practical working television system and to bring it to the attention of the world. •

SEEK CONGRESSIONAL MEDAL OF HONOR FOR LINDBERGH

(*Stamford Advocate*, 23 May 1927)

THE FIRST SOLO FLIGHT across the Atlantic turned 25-year-old American aviator Charles Lindbergh into an instant hero and celebrity of the day.

Born in Detroit, Michigan, on 4 February 1902, Lindbergh spent much of his first 18 years on his family's farm in Minnesota and was fascinated by the occasional aeroplane that flew over the fields. It was to become a lifelong passion and, when he was 20, he joined a flying school, learning first about the mechanics before making his first flight as a pilot.

Four years later he enrolled at a U.S. Army flying school at San Antonio, Texas, and graduated first in his class.

In 1926, he became the first airmail pilot between Chicago, Illinois, and St Louis, Missouri. And it was during this time that he determined to take part in an exciting challenge that had been laid down by New York hotel businessman Raymond Orteig in 1919, offering $25,000 for the first non-stop flight between New York and Paris.

SPIRIT OF ST LOUIS

Lindbergh persuaded a group of St Louis businessmen to back his venture and then helped design and supervise the building of a plane that would soar him into the history books. The result was a single-engine monoplane called the *Spirit of St Louis*.

He was thought by many to have little chance of success as other contenders opted for multi-engine planes and at least one other crew member aboard.

On 20 May 1927, he took four sandwiches, two containers of water, a compass and map aboard the *Spirit of St Louis* and then gunned her down a dirt-track runway in Roosevelt Field, Long Island, and, at 7.52am, took to the air.

Along the way he encountered some sleet, which made him consider turning back but he soon put such notions out of his mind and continued on his epic flight.

Lindbergh later described how he flew low over the coast of Europe to call out to a fisherman on his boat, 'Which way is Ireland?' but that the man did not understand him.

LE BOURGET FIELD

On the evening of 21 May he crossed the coast of France, followed the Seine River to Paris and touched down at Le Bourget Field at 10:22pm (local time). The 3,600-mile journey had taken thirty-three and a half hours.

A jubilant crowd rushed forward to welcome him and were delighted when he thrust his face out of the window and asked, 'Where am I?'

As he opened the door, he was lifted onto the shoulders of officials who carried him away from the enthusiastic crowd who all wanted to shake his hand, pat his back or simply touch him.

Despite his long journey, Lindbergh insisted he did not feel tired and happily conducted a press conference standing up.

His achievement excited the world. It was the heroic, daredevil, adventurous stuff that boy's dreams are made of. The following morning he waved to crowds gathered below him as he stood on the balcony of the American Embassy.

In the days that followed, his fame grew and grew. The President of France, Gaston Doumergue, pinned the Legion of Honor upon his lapel. When he returned home to America aboard the USS *Memphis*, a convoy of warships and aircraft escorted him up the river to Washington where President Coolidge bestowed him with the Distinguished Flying Cross.

MEDAL OF VALOR

New York City gave him the largest tickertape parade ever, with about four million people lining the parade route. The Mayor pinned New York's Medal of Valor upon him.

Lindbergh's achievement inspired others to take an interest in aviation not only in his homeland but around the world.

He embarked on a sponsored, three-month nationwide tour in the *Spirit of St Louis*, touching down in 49 states, visiting 92 cities and giving 147 speeches.

On 21 March 1929, President Coolidge presented him with the nation's highest military decoration, the Congressional Medal of Honor.

Throughout the rest of his life, Lindbergh acted as an adviser to America on aviation. He taught American fighter pilots how to get increased range from their planes, was appointed a Brigadier General in the Air Force Reserves and made many goodwill visits around the world. •

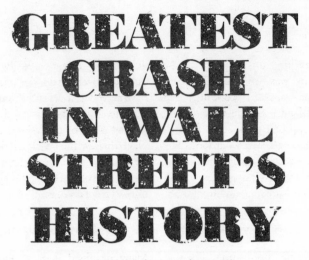

GREATEST CRASH IN WALL STREET'S HISTORY

(*Daily Mail*, 25 October 1929)

THE FEEL GOOD factor of the 'Roaring Twenties' was to end abruptly at the end of the decade with a shocking collapse of share prices on New York's Wall Street stock market. As investors lost huge sums of money, confidence in the economy was shattered and it was to usher in the 'Great Depression' of the thirties.

In the 1920s the United States was enjoying a boom time of prosperity and easy money was to be made on the stock market. Potential investors didn't even need to have much money up front. Such was the confidence in the economy that banks were willing to lend more than two-thirds of the face value of the stocks, which the investor could later sell at a profit before paying the loan.

All was well so long as the price continued to rise and few saw any reason to doubt that it would. But if the unthinkable were to happen, and the bubble burst, then huge losses would be incurred.

There seemed no reason, however, for investors to suspect

that any kind of downturn in the economy was anywhere in sight. A much-respected economist and financial guru of the time, Irving Fisher, proclaimed that 'Stock prices have reached what looks like a permanently high plateau.' Many believed that share prices would simply continue to rise indefinitely.

FLORIDA DISASTER IGNORED

Yet there had been some signs that the economy was not as rock steady as was believed when land prices in Florida collapsed in 1926. Florida had been enjoying a property boom, with building projects forging ahead in a state that was being promoted as a tropical paradise. Speculators snapped up tracts of land and investors funded new developments, fuelling a rapid rise in property prices.

The rapid rise, unfortunately, proved to be a huge discouragement to potential buyers and the devastating 1926 Miami hurricane, which left almost 400 dead and caused damage estimated at $100 million ($1.3 billion in today's terms), left many investors' projects quite literally in ruins.

The Florida experience, and the fact that farm produce prices were being driven steadily lower due to over-production, should have served as a warning that there was no firm foundation for the soaring price of stocks and shares. Nevertheless, the stock market hit an all-time high on 3 September 1929, before it dropped sharply, only to rise and drop again.

INVESTORS IN PANIC

Many dismissed it as a blip. The market had dropped before and recovered in rude health. But when it declined sharply again on 4 October, some began to get jittery. And as it continued to decline, panic started rising. There was an avalanche of selling on 21 October as frightened investors who had pumped so much of their money into the stock market began to sell their shares at any price. On 24 October – a day that was to become known as 'Black Thursday' – 12,894,650 shares were sold, overwhelming the Exchange as it struggled to keep up with transactions.

There was panic on the Exchange floor, too, as traders screamed and shouted and watched in despair at collapsing prices.

That evening, five of the country's bankers issued a statement saying that due to the heavy selling of shares, many were now under-priced. But still, people were desperate to sell.

WORLD FINANCIAL CRISIS

Over the weekend the events were covered by newspapers across the United States, fuelling further fear and panic. And on 28 October, 'Black Monday', more investors decided to get out of the market. The following day, 'Black Tuesday', around 16 million shares were traded. The market had lost over $30 billion in the space of two days.

America had loaned huge sums of money to European countries and, following the Wall Street Crash, they suddenly recalled the loans, which had a big impact on the European economy, causing a general world financial crisis.

Lack of money led to mass unemployment in America and Europe as businessmen could no longer borrow sufficient amounts to run their companies. The Roaring Twenties had skidded to an abrupt halt as the world economy entered the 'Great Depression' of the thirties. •

GHANDI SEIZED BY BRITISH

FOR INDEFINITE DETENTION; TROOPS POSTED FOR CRISIS

(*New York Times*, 5 May 1930)

MOHANDAS 'MAHATMA' GANDHI was arrested and imprisoned by the British authorities in India for his campaign of civil disobedience, which he called satyagraha (insistence on truth).

His incarceration caused widespread international publicity as did the violent beatings that British-led Indian police and troops perpetrated on peaceful protesters.

Known as 'Mahatma' (great soul), Gandhi was the leader of the Indian nationalist movement against British rule, and his policy of non-violence frustrated and ultimately embarrassed the colonial power.

Born on 2 October 1869 in Porbandar, Gujarat, he attended university and went to London to train as a barrister.

In 1893, he accepted a job at a law firm in Durban, South Africa. Appalled by the treatment of Indian immigrants in the country, he campaigned for their rights and was sent to prison many times during his 20-year stay.

RETURN TO INDIA

In 1915, he returned to India and four years later he led a protest against the Rowlatt Act, which allowed the British to imprison for a maximum of two years, without trial, any person suspected of terrorism living in the Raj.

Gandhi's continuing campaign of peaceful non-cooperation with the British included the boycotting of British goods, which led to arrests of thousands. In 1922, Gandhi was sentenced to six years' imprisonment but was released after two years.

After a quiet period he began his biggest and most audacious satyagraha campaign in 1930 with a protest against the tax on salt.

Britain's Salt Acts prohibited Indians from collecting or selling salt and they were compelled to buy it from the British who levied a heavy tax on the commodity.

On 12 March 1930, Gandhi set off from Sabarmati near Ahmedabad with 78 followers on a 241-mile march to the coastal town of Dandi.

ILLEGAL SALT

As they passed through one village after another he stopped to talk to local people and many joined the march so that by the time they arrived on 5 April their ranks had grown to many thousands. The following day, Gandhi walked down to the sea, raised a lump of muddy salt and declared, 'With this, I am shaking the foundations of the British Empire.'

He then boiled it in seawater, producing illegal salt, and encouraged the others to copy his example. In the days that followed, thousands more did likewise in coastal cities such as Bombay and Karachi.

Civil disobedience broke out all across India, soon involving millions of Indians, and British authorities arrested more than 60,000 people.

Gandhi himself was arrested and imprisoned on 5 May en route with his followers to protest at the Dharasana Salt Works in Gujarat, 25 miles south of Dandi.

Shortly after midnight, while Gandhi was fast asleep, two Indian officers and thirty heavily-armed policemen arrested him. But the march continued under the leadership of a female poet and activist named Sarojini Naidu. It was to result in the 2,500 marchers being ruthlessly beaten by policemen at the Salt Works on 21 May.

The protesters refused to retaliate and the incident gained widespread international coverage in newspapers.

BRITISH FORCED TO NEGOTIATE

In January 1931, Gandhi was released from prison. Faced with mass disobedience across India, along with international criticism and condemnation for their unfairness and brutality in dealing with dissenters, the British government was compelled to negotiate with Gandhi.

At a meeting with Lord Irwin, the Viceroy of India, Gandhi agreed to call off the satyagraha in exchange for an equal negotiating role at a London conference on India's future. In August, Gandhi travelled to the conference as the sole representative of the nationalist Indian National Congress.

India's independence was finally granted on 14 August 1947, under the guidance of the last Viceroy, Lord Louis Mountbatten, when the country was split and the new dominion of Pakistan came into being.

Gandhi was one of many opposed to the partition of India and it caused great bloodshed amongst those who were cut off by the newly imposed boundaries. Nearly one million people died in the violence that ensued between Hindus and Muslims.

Gandhi went on a hunger strike, saying he would not eat until the violence stopped but his efforts to achieve reconciliation between Hindus and Muslims were to lead to his death.

On the way to a prayer meeting on 30 January 1948, he was shot dead by a fellow Hindu named Nathuram Godse, who felt that he had betrayed the Hindu cause. •

HITLER MADE CHANCELLOR OF GERMANY

(New York Times, 31 January 1933)

THE NAZIS' RISE to power caused concern throughout Europe after their nationalistic leader, Adolf Hitler, was elected Chancellor of Germany.

German resentment and anger over the Treaty of Versailles, which they had been forced to sign in 1919, continued to run deep. The loss of land, heavy financial compensation, the stripping of her army and her exclusion from the League of Nations was humiliating.

The governing democratic Weimar Republic was seen as weak and the bleak economic climate added to the misery and feeling of hopelessness at the country ever recovering.

Hitler had made an earlier attempt to sieze power. The Nazi Party had started out as a small party in Bavaria called the German Worker's Party, which was opposed to the Treaty of Versailles and communism. Hitler's enthusiasm and flare for rhetoric saw him quickly rise to leadership.

THE NAZIS EMERGE

The party was renamed the National and Socialist German Workers Party and, with inflation running high, the Nazis, as they were known, attempted a political *coup d'etat* in November 1923. They had plotted to seize control of Munich and then stage a march on Berlin, but it was a disastrous undertaking. The police opened fire on the marchers, they dispersed and Hitler was arrested. Two days later he was given a five-year prison sentence.

In the event, he only served two years. He took the time whilst inside to write *Mein Kampf*. On his release, the economy was picking up and most Germans felt he had little to offer them. But then came the Wall Street Crash of 1929, followed by the Great Depression.

The rise in unemployment, fears of a communist uprising and the continuing heavy load of wartime reparation put the German economy in crisis. Disillusioned by the Weimar, Hitler's extremist but patriotic ideas found an audience.

PERSECUTION OF JEWS

In such a climate, he became ever more popular. A charismatic and inspiring public speaker, people responded to his talk of tearing up the Treaty of Versailles, rearmament and territorial expansion. It was intoxicating stuff after years of brooding resentment and misery. And he even managed to pass on his anti-Semitism by attributing some of the blame for Germany's economic plight to the greed of Jews, talking of his nation's Aryan 'master race'.

He said what many wanted to hear – higher prices for farmers' produce, construction jobs for the unemployed, help for small businesses – and he encouraged people to boycott Jewish-owned shops. The Nazis became ever more menacing and the feared stormtroopers would stand outside these shops, painting slogans on the windows and scaring off potential customers. Jewish professionals such as doctors, lawyers and local government officials were forced to give up their jobs.

Once he became Chancellor, his stormtroopers crushed any opposition or dissent as he sought to control the influential institutions – economy, education, business – and his propaganda machine went into overdrive under Dr Joseph Goebbels.

MILITARY EXPANSION

Young people were encouraged to join Nazi Party organisations such as the Hitler Youth, for boys, and the League of German Maidens, for girls. Trade unions were banned and replaced by the German Labour Front. Education was controlled by the state, and newspapers, radio, cinema and the theatre placed under Nazi control. Books were heavily censored or burnt if they did not fit Nazi ideology.

Hitler increased the size of the German army to 550,000 by 1936, and to 850,000 by 1938. A further 900,000 men were trained as reserves and he embarked on the making of a modern air force and navy.

Unemployment figures fell rapidly, mainly due to the increase in the number of men in the armed forces and public-works schemes constructing municipal buildings, motorways and bridges.

Under Hitler, Germany was fast becoming a mighty nation once more and he was eager to claim new territory. •

EDWARD VIII ABDICATES
KING RENOUNCES CROWN FOR LOVE

(*London Herald*, 13 December 1936)

A CONSTITUTIONAL CRISIS in 1936 shocked the British public when the King walked away from the throne to marry the woman he loved. Edward's decision to abdicate rather than live without his beloved Wallis was to change the course of British history.

As a divorcee and a Catholic, Wallis Simpson was not constitutionally suitable for King Edward VIII on both counts: the monarch is nominal head of the Church of England which did not allow divorcees to re-marry.

Edward first met Baltimore-born Wallis at a house party on 10 January 1931. He was then Prince of Wales and she was married to businessman Ernest Simpson, following her divorce from navy pilot Earl Winfield Spencer.

She made little impression on the Prince then but they bumped into each other again in May and in January 1932 he dined at the Simpsons' London flat, staying until 4.00am. At the end of the month, the Simpsons were invited to spend a weekend at Edward's country retreat, Fort Belvedere in Berkshire.

SUNSHINE HOLIDAYS

Things took a more serious turn when, in August 1934, Edward took a party, including Wallis Simpson, on holiday to Biarritz, followed by a cruise along the Spanish and

Portuguese coasts. Notably, Ernest Simpson was not among them. That November, Wallis attended a party at Buckingham Palace in honour of the Duke of Kent.

Edward succeeded his father, George V, on 20 January 1936, becoming King Edward VIII. In July, Ernest Simpson moved out of the couple's home and the following month Wallis joined the King and other guests for a cruise along the Yugoslav, Greek and Turkish coasts. Photographs of the pair together appeared in the American and continental press but British newspaper editors turned a blind eye to the gossip and speculation, as did the British establishment. And nothing appeared in the press.

But the situation could not be ignored much longer. In October, after the King had begun renting a house for Wallis in Regent's Park, Prime Minister Stanley Baldwin confronted him over the relationship, asking him if he could be more discrete and to try to persuade Wallis to put off her plans to divorce her husband. But he failed in his endeavour and on 16 November the King sent for Baldwin and told him he wanted to marry Mrs Simpson.

KING THREATENS ABDICATION

Baldwin insisted that the British public would not accept her as Queen and he was shocked when the King replied that he was prepared to abdicate if the government opposed his marriage.

The King later suggested that Parliament bring in new legislation that would enable him to have a 'morganatic marriage' in which he would still be King but she, as a 'commoner', would not be Queen. But when this was rejected, Baldwin told him he had three choices: to finish his relationship with Mrs Simpson, to marry against the advice of his ministers who would then resign, or to abdicate.

On 3 December, the story broke in the British press and the tone was widely disapproving. The general feeling in the country was that she was more in love with status than with Edward. Wallis went to France to escape the furore. Then, on 9 December, the King informed the government of his decision to abdicate.

'After long and anxious consideration I have determined to renounce the throne, to which I succeeded on the death of my father, and I am now communicating this, my final and irrevocable decision.'

HISTORIC BROADCAST

He was to be succeeded by his younger brother, Albert George 'Bertie', the Duke of York. The following day, Edward signed the Instrument of Abdication and on 11 December he made an historic broadcast to the nation.

'At long last I am able to say a few words of my own. I have never wanted to withhold anything, but until now it has not been constitutionally possible for me to speak. A few hours ago I discharged my last duty as King and Emperor, and now that I have been succeeded by my brother, the Duke of York, my first words must be to declare my allegiance to him. This I do with all my heart.

'You all know the reasons which have impelled me to renounce the throne. But I want you to understand that in making up my mind I did not forget the country or the Empire, which, as Prince of Wales, and lately as King, I have for 25 years tried to serve. But you must believe me when I tell you that I have found it impossible to carry the heavy burden of responsibility and to discharge my duties as King as I would wish to do without the help and support of the woman I love.'

Bertie was crowned King George VI on 12 May 1937 and his wife, Elizabeth Bowes-Lyon (later, the Queen Mother), Queen Elizabeth.

Their two young daughters, Princesses Elizabeth and Margaret became first and second in line to the throne. And on 3 June 1937, Edward, now the Duke of Windsor, married Wallis Simpson in France. •

OWENS COMPLETES TRIPLE AS 5 OLYMPIC MARKS FALL

(*New York Times*, 6 August 1936)

ADOLF HITLER'S NOTION of a superior Aryan race took a battering at the 1936 Olympics in Berlin when black American athlete Jesse Owens was the star of the show, winning four gold medals.

Berlin had been chosen to host the event by the International Olympic Committee before the Nazis had risen to power. Some countries talked of boycotting the event but none did. In fact, more countries entered than ever before.

It was Nazi Propaganda Minister Joseph Goebbels who had pushed for the games, persuading Hitler that it would be a great showcase for a resurgent Germany with her athletes showing their superiority.

An impressive Olympic sports complex stretching 325 acres was built about five miles from West Berlin with the centrepiece being a huge stadium that could seat 110,000 spectators.

FINEST OLYMPIC FACILITIES

The Olympic Village of 140 buildings contained a post office and a bank. There were stewards on hand who could speak various languages and the training facilities included a 400-metre track and a full-sized indoor swimming pool. These were the best facilities that

Olympic athletes had ever seen.

But there was an international outcry over the exclusion of Jewish athletes from Germany's team. Some of those excluded were top tennis player Daniel Prenn, boxing champion Erich Seelig and four-time Word Record holder in track and field events Lilli Henoch. The Nazis also disqualified athletes of Romani origin, including another boxing champion, Johann Trollmann.

In a move to appease critics, the Nazis put Jewish fencing star, Helene Mayer, who had won gold at the 1928 Olympics, into their team.

BERLIN SANITISED BY NAZIS

In the weeks leading to the start of the Games, the streets were 'swept' of 'undesirables' and the many 'Jews Not Welcome' signs taken down from restaurants, hotels and other public places.

When visitors from around the world descended on Berlin for the opening ceremony on 1 August, they walked through streets that were gleaming clean and marvelled at the size and spectacle of the imposing sports complexes where Olympic flags flew alongside the swastika.

The main stadium was packed to capacity and the impressive airship Hindenburg flew low over the stadium trailing the Olympic flag. When Hitler and his entourage walked in, the *Deutschland Über Alles* national anthem was sung. As the teams paraded, there was speculation about who would and wouldn't give the Nazi salute to Hitler as they passed by his seat. Some athletes did and others did not, but there was some confusion because the Olympic salute with right arm held out sideways was not dissimilar.

The climax of the opening ceremony was the arrival of the Olympic torch, which had been carried, by relay, from Olympia, Greece – the first time this had been done, something that was to become a regular feature at future Games.

CONTEST BEGINS

The following day, the competition began with the track and field events. Jesse Owens, 23, had broken three world records and tied a fourth the previous year at an athletics meeting in Michigan.

During the course of that opening Olympic week he outsprinted and out-jumped everyone to win four gold medals in the 100m, 200m, long jump and as a member of the 4x100m relay team.

There was much mention in the foreign press of Hitler being furious at Owens's success. But Owens himself never felt any resentment. He later recalled Hitler standing up and waving to him when he glanced up at him in his box seat.

In the end, the Olympics were a triumph for Germany both on and off the track. They came first with 33 gold medals, followed by the U.S. with 24 and Hungary with 10.

The Games had been the most impressive to date with superb facilities and organisation. It was the first time that the Olympics had been televised and they were preserved on film by Hitler's favourite director, Leni Riefenstahl. Her four-hour film, *Olympia*, was released in two parts, beginning in April 1938.

The next Olympics, in 1940, were scheduled for Tokyo, but Hitler's plans for far greater victories meant that there would be no more Olympic Games until after World War II, in 1948. •

HINDENBURG BURNS IN LAKEHURST CRASH;

21 KNOWN DEAD, 12 MISSING; 64 ESCAPE

(*New York Times*, 7 May 1937)

THE MAJESTIC Hindenburg airship – the biggest in the world – offered a speedy alternative to transatlantic crossing by liner. But when disaster struck, the horrifying pictures and news footage shocked the world, shattering confidence in airships and ending their golden era.

The mighty LZ 29 Hindenburg was the pride of the German Zeppelin passenger-carrying airship fleet. At 245m (804 feet) in length the Hindenburg was more than three times as long as a modern Boeing 747 Jumbo Jet and over twice the 747's overall height.

The airship could not, however, compete with the 747's passenger capacity, accommodating just 72 guests as opposed to more than 400 in a Jumbo. Hindenburg passengers, however, travelled in great style.

Passenger cabins were cramped, with an upper and lower bunk, a folding wash basin and a collapsible writing table but for most of the voyage passengers would be expected to use the lounge, restaurant, reading room or promenade areas (where there were large, sloping windows looking down at an angle), all in the belly of the great silver-skinned beast. While the public areas were not as luxurious as the finest ocean liners of the time, the lounge did have its own, custom-built baby grand piano, made mainly from aluminium and covered with pigskin. Unlike a modern airliner, therefore, there was plenty of space for passengers to move around aboard the Hindenburg.

INAUGURAL FLIGHTS

It began its first transatlantic services in 1936 and the airship's inaugural flight for the 1937 season had attracted much attention from the media, who had gathered at Lakehurst Naval Air Station, New Jersey, to watch the Hindenburg arrive from Frankfurt.

The previous year, the Hindenburg had completed ten successful trips with a full capacity of 72 passengers but for this first flight of 1937 it was only half full with 36 passengers and 61 crew.

Around 7:00pm local time, on 6 May, at an altitude of 650 feet (200m), the Hindenburg approached Lakehurst and, 18 minutes later, it began to drop water ballast from the stern to level out. After this was accomplished, two mooring lines were dropped from the bow, which were to be secured to the mooring winch. The port line was connected but before the other could be secured, witnesses on the ground saw flames from the top and side of the airship. On board, some people had heard a muffled explosion just moments earlier.

The flames rapidly spread and within 34 seconds the Hindenburg was engulfed.

MIRACULOUS SURVIVORS

With little time to react, some passengers leapt to their deaths from the blazing airship when it was still some 300 feet in the air. Others managed to jump to safety when it was lower or were rescued from the burning wreck after it had hit the ground. Of the 97 people on board, 35 died along with a member of the ground crew.

Because there were so many news teams at Lakehurst, the full horror of the incident was captured on both moving and still images. Some commentators described the Hindenburg crash as being 'the *Titanic* of the sky'.

Nobody is sure where the fire started or what caused it. Initially, there were those, including the Captain, Max Pruss, who thought it was sabotage and various passengers and crew members came under suspicion. But subsequent enquiries by both German and American investigators showed no evidence of any sabotage.

Another suggestion was that engine failure had caused sparks to ignite either the airship's outer skin or leaking hydrogen, the highly flammable gas used as a lifting agent.

One of the more popular theories is that the fire was caused by static electricity, which built up in the airship after it had passed through a storm. But there is much debate about whether it caused hydrogen or the outer skin to ignite.

The tragedy killed off the air-ship era and two years later Pan American Airlines provided a much faster means of travel as they inaugurated the world's first transatlantic aeroplane passenger service. •

BRITAIN'S FIRST DAY OF WAR
CHURCHILL IS NEW NAVY CHIEF

(*Daily Mirror*, 4 September 1939)

AFTER EFFORTS to appease German Chancellor Adolf Hitler failed to quell his ambition, British Prime Minister Neville Chamberlain finally gave in to the inevitable and declared war on Germany.

This historic newspaper had the dramatic opening sentence, 'Britain and Germany have been at war since 11 o'clock yesterday morning.' It went on to say that a war cabinet of nine had been set up and that Winston Churchill, who had been First Lord of the Admiralty during WWI, was returning to that post.

The paper also contained what were to become famous speeches by Chamberlain and King George VI.

In his broadcast at 11.15am on 3 September, the PM, in a clipped English accent, announced, 'I am speaking to you from the Cabinet Room at 10 Downing Street. This morning the British Ambassador in Berlin handed the German Government a final note stating that unless we heard from them by eleven o'clock that they were prepared at once to withdraw their troops from Poland a state of war would exist between us.

'I have to tell you that no such undertaking has been received and that consequently this country is at war with Germany.'

THE KING'S SPEECH

That evening the King had his own personal battle to overcome – a crippling stutter – to make his broadcast to the nation. 'In this grave hour, perhaps the most fateful in our history, I send to every household of my people, both at home and overseas, this message, spoken with the same depth of feeling for each one of you as if I were able to cross your threshold and speak to you myself.

'For the second time in the lives of most of us we are at war. Over and over again we have tried to find a peaceful way out of the differences between ourselves and those who are now our enemies. But it has been in vain. We have been forced into a conflict...'

It was a stirring yet measured speech urging the nation to stand 'calm and firm and united' and he did not underestimate the difficulty of the undertaking.

'The task will be hard. There may be dark days ahead and war can no longer be confined to the battlefield. But we can only do the right as we see the right, and reverently commit our cause to God.'

With the harrowing World War I having ended only 21 years earlier,

the British had no appetite for another war, but Hitler's aggressive expansion in Europe could not be ignored.

After being defeated in WWI, Germany was forced to accept a humiliating agreement under the Treaty of Versailles that reduced her territory, imposed huge reparations and put limits on the size of her army.

EXPANSION CAMPAIGN

A growing feeling of resentment in the country inspired the charismatic Nazi Party leader Adolf Hitler and, in 1933, he had been appointed Chancellor of Germany. He set about re-armament and embarked on a campaign of expansion in Europe, annexing Austria and part of Czechoslovakia.

The British and French objected but conceded the territories to Hitler so long as he promised no further expansion. But Hitler was encouraged by their weak response and went on to take over the remainder of Czechoslovakia. With his eyes next on Poland, Britain and France guaranteed their support to the Poles. So when Germany invaded Poland on 1 September, Britain committed herself and her colonial countries to war. A few hours later, France did likewise. It was to become a global conflict.

Churchill had been among the first to recognise the growing threat of Hitler and many were pleased to see him at the heart of the war cabinet – although others criticised him as a 'warmonger'.

In the spring of 1940, Chamberlain came under mounting pressure to resign. He finally gave way and Churchill became Prime Minister on 10 May. •

175 NAZI PLANES DOWN

RAF TRIUMPHS IN BIGGEST AIR BATTLES OF WAR

(*Daily Herald*, 16 September 1940)

ON 18 JUNE 1940, British Prime Minister Winston Churchill gave a speech in the House of Commons saying, 'The Battle of France is over. The Battle of Britain is about to begin.'

Four days later, France surrendered to Germany and Hitler turned his attention towards Britain.

A fleet of invasion barges was assembled in French, Belgian and Dutch ports, with German troops practising embarkation and landing drills on adjacent beaches. Hitler and his military chiefs identified landing sites along the south coast of England and laid detailed plans about how each objective would be captured, how paratroops would be deployed inland to encircle the coastal defences, exactly which German units would be allocated to each stretch of coastline and precisely how far inland they expected to push in the hours and days following the landings.

The Germans also drew up lists of influential people in major towns across Britain who would immediately be arrested. Some were earmarked for execution. Hitler even went as far as to choose Senate House in Bloomsbury, the administrative centre of the University of London but then being used as Britain's Ministry of Information, as his London headquarters.

RAF TO BE DESTROYED

Before any invasion could be launched, however, Hitler knew that he had to gain air superiority. The invasion, codenamed 'Operation Sea Lion' called for vast minefields to be laid at sea, sealing off the English Channel to stop Royal Navy ships from decimating the invasion fleet. Some Royal Navy vessels were bound to get through, but the Luftwaffe would hold them at bay.

In order that the German aircraft could operate freely, and to ensure that the invasion fleet was not bombed out of existence by the British, Hitler required that the RAF be destroyed. He instructed Herman Goering, the head of the Luftwaffe, that the RAF must be 'beaten down to such an extent that it can no longer muster any power of attack worth mentioning against the German crossing.'

'Operation Sea Lion' was planned to take place in mid-September 1940.

The Luftwaffe's principal weapons were its Messerschmitt 109 fighters along with a variety of bombers and hybrid fighter-bombers.

The RAF's 700 or so Spitfire and Hurricane fighters were hugely outnumbered, but the Germans' numerical superiority was countered by the fact that they had the disadvantage of having to fly further, operating at the limit of their fighter aircraft's range. Britain also had the advantage of an excellent radar early-warning system, an effective fighter plane in the Spitfire and the remarkable ability to be able to manufacture more planes at an astonishing rate.

The battle began in mid-July, with the Luftwaffe attacking shipping in the English Channel as well as coastal towns and defences. From 12 August attacks were made directly on RAF airfields and radar bases and there were intense battles. By the end of the month the Germans had lost more than 600 aircraft and the RAF about half that number.

RAF BOMBS BERLIN

At the beginning of September, Britain took the offensive and infuriated Hitler by launching air attacks on some of Germany's industrial areas – and Berlin itself. In retaliation, Hitler ordered the bombing of London and other major British cities from 7 September. It was the beginning of 'the Blitz'.

On 15 September more than 1,000 enemy aircraft flew in and

carried out a day-and-night attack on London. It became known as 'Battle of Britain Day'. The RAF battled them in the skies above the capital and as they flew over the south coast.

At the end of the day, the RAF announced that they had shot down 175 enemy aircraft and the newspapers duly trumpeted the triumph. It did wonders for the morale of civilians who had to shelter on a daily basis during the Blitz. But it was far from the truth. In reality the Germans had lost 56 planes to the RAF's 27. But it was a decisive moment in the conflict between the two countries. Hitler had failed to gain air superiority and postponed his plans to invade Britain. On 17 September, he focused on the invasion of Russia, although the Luftwaffe continued to bomb Britain until the end of the war.

INVASION CANCELLED

In mid-October, Hitler ordered his invasion fleet to be dispersed. Britain had successfully defended herself in battle and had gained the upper hand. It was a huge boost to the nation and was considered to be Hitler's first major defeat – a crucial turning point in the war.

It is estimated that between 10 July and the end of October, the Luftwaffe lost 1,887 planes to the RAF's 1,023. Nearly 500 British pilots and aircrew had been killed and thousands of civilians died during the bombings.

In one of his most memorable speeches, Churchill saluted the achievement of the RAF with the words, 'Never in the field of human conflict was so much owed by so many to so few.' •

JAPAN, U.S. AT WAR

104 DIE IN HAWAII RAID; 2 U.S. TRANSPORTS SUNK

(*Seattle Post-Intelligencer*, 8 December 1941)

A SURPRISE ATTACK by Japan on the U.S. Pacific Fleet at Pearl Harbor, on Oahu, the third largest and chief island of Hawaii, on 7 December 1941, shocked America to the core.

At 7.55am the first of two waves of Japanese aircraft – fighters and bombers – were launched from six aircraft carriers and opened fire on the base. A second wave followed at 9.00am, pounding the fleet for an hour. Within two hours, five battleships had been sunk, another 16 damaged and 188 aircraft destroyed. Over 2,400 Americans were killed, another 1,178 injured, but under 100 Japanese had died.

The U.S., which had followed a policy of isolationism during the war, was stunned and incensed by the action. It came during a time when Japanese officials in Washington were negotiating with U.S. Secretary of State Cordell Hull on lifting U.S. sanctions imposed after continuing Japanese aggression against China.

U.S. DECLARES WAR

The following day, the United States declared war on Japan. In a speech to Congress, President Roosevelt called the attack on Pearl Harbor, 'a day that will live in infamy'. Within an hour of the speech, Congress passed a formal declaration of war against Japan and officially brought the U.S. into World War II.

On 11 December, Germany and Italy declared war on the U.S. and America immediately reciprocated.

Adolf Hitler made his announcement at the Reichstag in Berlin, saying he had tried to avoid direct conflict with the U.S. but under the Tripartite Agreement, Germany was obliged to join with Italy to defend her ally.

Following the Pearl Harbor attack, there were queues of volunteers at U.S. armed forces recruiting stations, all eager to fight for their country.

The background to the attack could be traced back to a decade earlier when, in 1931, Japan embarked on a policy of expansion, moving in to Manchuria in northern China and exploiting the resources there.

JAPANESE AGGRESSION

Having gained confidence from the occupation, Japan became more aggressive and expanded further into Indochina. The U.S., which had territories in the area, imposed trade sanctions on Japan in 1939. Then, on 27 September 1940, Japan signed the Tripartite Agreement with Germany and Italy, becoming a formal member of the Axis alliance fighting the European war.

Early in 1941, a concerned Roosevelt moved the Pacific Fleet from San Diego to Hawaii in a show of power to try to discourage further Japanese expansion in the Far East. In July, he stopped oil exports to Japan, but this only had the effect of encouraging Japan to invade the oil-rich Dutch East Indies in January 1942.

Hostility between Japan and the U.S. was growing. Japan had ambitions to invade more territories in Southeast Asia belonging to the U.S., Britain and the Netherlands. Fearful that the U.S. might step in to try to prevent them, Japan had begun planning a strike on the Pacific Fleet in early 1941.

OFFICIAL INVESTIGATIONS

There was much bewilderment as to why the U.S. had been so taken by surprise by the attack. Six wartime and one post-war investigation revealed a lack of coordination and communication between Washington and Oahu and an underestimation of Japan's aerial strength.

As a result, Lieutenant General Short, Commander for the defence of military installations in Hawaii, was relieved of his post on 17 December 1941. So too was Navy Commander Admiral Kimmel.

A commission headed by U.S. Supreme Court Associate Justice Owen J. Roberts, known as the Roberts Commission, was held soon after the attack on Pearl Harbor. It accused the two men of being unprepared and said that they did not take seriously enough an earlier warning from Washington that there might be an air attack at Pearl Harbor.

A later report in 1945 was more fairly balanced. It stated, 'The underlying cause of this error of judgement was General Short's confidence that Japan would not then attack Pearl Harbor. In fairness to him it must be borne in mind that this belief was shared in by almost everyone concerned including his superior officers in the War Department in Washington. He was undoubtedly influenced in such a belief by the then prevailing psychology which completely underestimated the Japanese military capabilities and particularly the advance which they had made in the use of aircraft.' •

VE-DAY – IT'S ALL OVER

ALL QUIET TILL 9PM – THEN THE LONDON CROWDS WENT MAD IN THE WEST END

(*Daily Mail*, 8 May 1945)

IT WAS THE NEWS that the world had been waiting for. After six long years of fighting, suffering and hardship, Germany had finally surrendered and the war in Europe had ended.

It had happened on 7 May 1945 but was not to be officially announced until a day later. However, as news spread, Londoners could not contain their joy any longer. And that evening, around 9pm, celebrations broke out in the capital.

The *Daily Mail* reported how, 'Bonfires blazed from Piccadilly to Wapping. The sky once lit by the glare of the blitz shone red with the Victory glow.'

It described people linking arms singing, dancing and waving flags. Favourite cockney wartime songs were sung at the tops of their voices – 'Roll out the Barrel', 'Tipperary', 'Bless 'em All' and 'Pack Up Your Troubles'.

They needed to let their hair down after being blitzed and then facing the fear of the dreaded German V1 'Doodlebug' missiles which flew over from 1944. They also had to endure food rationing. If ever there was a time to party, this was it.

Since the beginning of the year, the end had been in sight following a series of capitulations. The German forces in Italy surrendered on 2 May and then in Northern Germany, Denmark and the Netherlands.

SURRENDER DOCUMENT SIGNED

The final document of unconditional surrender was signed at General Dwight Eisenhower's headquarters in Rheims at 2.41pm on 7 May 1945. But it was the following day that would be declared 'Victory in Europe' (VE) Day and back in Britain people sat by their radios at 3.00pm to hear Churchill announce that the war with Germany over.

In Trafalgar Square a large crowd gathered to hear Churchill's voice relayed over loudspeakers. Despite the jubilation there was an extraordinary hush when he began talking.

In a broadcast from the Cabinet Room at Number 10 Downing Street, Churchill paid tribute to Russia and the allies.

'Today, perhaps, we shall think mostly of ourselves. Tomorrow we shall pay a particular tribute to our Russian comrades, whose prowess in the field has been one of the grand contributions to the general victory.'

He went on to say, 'After gallant France had been struck down we, from this Island and from our united Empire, maintained the struggle single-handed for a whole year until we were joined by the military might of Soviet Russia, and later by the overwhelming power and resources of the United States of America.

'Finally almost the whole world was combined against the evil-doers, who are now prostrate before us. Our gratitude to our splendid Allies goes forth from all our hearts in this Island and throughout the British Empire.

JAPAN'S TREACHERY AND GREED

'We may allow ourselves a brief period of rejoicing; but let us not forget for a moment the toil and efforts that lie ahead. Japan, with all her treachery and greed, remains unsubdued. The injury she has inflicted on Great Britain, the United States, and other countries, and her detestable cruelties, call for justice and retribution. We must now devote all our strength and resources to the completion of our task, both at home and abroad.'

Shortly after Churchill's speech, King George VI, Queen Elizabeth and Princesses Elizabeth and Margaret came out onto the balcony at Buckingham Palace to acknowledge the cheering throng. When the Royal Family made a further appearance at 5.30pm they were accompanied by Churchill and a huge cheer went up.

That evening, at 9.00pm, King George VI made a speech to the nation and empire. 'Today we give thanks to Almighty God for a great deliverance. Speaking from our Empire's oldest capital city, war-battered but never for one moment daunted or dismayed – speaking from London, I ask you to join with me in that act of thanksgiving.

'Germany, the enemy who drove all Europe into war, has been finally overcome.' •

FIRST ATOMIC BOMB BROPPED ON JAPAN;

MISSILE IS EQUAL TO 20,000 TONS OF TNT; TRUMAN WARNS FOE OF A 'RAIN OF RUIN'

(*New York Times*, 6 August 1945)

IT WAS A TERRIFYING new bomb of massive destruction, killing thousands of Japanese civilians, that was the final act in ending World War II.

Germany had surrendered to the Allies on 7 May 1945 but the war was dragging on in the Far East with Japan determined to continue fighting.

The U.S., Britain and China had called for Japan to surrender in the Potsdam Declaration of 26 July 1945. It carried the threat that if they did not do so it would result in 'the inevitable and complete destruction of the Japanese armed forces and just as inevitably the utter devastation of the Japanese homeland'. But this was rejected.

Angered that, despite intense bombing of Japanese cities, America was sustaining heavy casualties in fighting at Iwo Jima and Okinawa, U.S. President Harry S. Truman gave the order to drop the ultimate weapon – the atom bomb.

Since 1939, American, British and Canadian scientists had been working in the U.S. on harnessing the power of the atom for military purposes. This top-secret work was known as the Manhattan Project and was later put under control of General Leslie Groves of the U.S. Army Corps of Engineers. The race was on because it was known that Germany was also working on an atomic bomb.

A special laboratory was also set up near Santa Fe under the direction of physicist Dr J. Robert Oppenheimer. The first test of the atomic bomb took place on 16 July 1945, in a remote desert section of New Mexico. Oppenheimer and other eminent scientists, who had gathered to witness it, were said to have been nervous about just what they were unleashing on the world.

ENOLA GAY TAKES OFF

Following the successful testing, a B-29 aircraft, nicknamed Enola Gay after the mother of the pilot of the plane, Colonel Paul Tibbets, took to the air on the morning of 6 August 1945. It was carrying the atom bomb and was accompanied by two other B-29s as it made its way on a six-hour flight to Japan.

The city of Hiroshima had been targeted because it contained a military-supplies depot and was an assembly area for troops. But it was also a heavily populated civilian area. When the bomb was dropped, it devastated an area of five square miles (13 square kilometres). Around 40,000–70,000 people were killed outright and a further 100,000 would die of radiation poisoning over the next five years.

President Harry S. Truman announced the news from the cruiser, USS *Augusta*, in the mid-Atlantic, saying that the device was more than 2,000 times more powerful than the largest bomb used to date.

A RAIN OF RUIN

His statement carried the warning of more to come. 'It was to spare the Japanese people from utter destruction that the ultimatum of 26 July, was issued at Potsdam. Their leaders promptly rejected that ultimatum. If they do not now accept our terms, they may expect a rain of ruin from the air the like of which has never been seen on this earth.'

Truman added, 'What has been done is the greatest achievement of organised science in history. We are now prepared to obliterate more rapidly and completely every productive enterprise the Japanese have above ground in any city. We shall destroy Japan's power to make war.'

U.S. Secretary of War, Henry L. Stimson said that this new weapon 'should prove a tremendous aid in the shortening of the war against Japan'. And in a prophetic note, he remarked, 'The scientists are confident that over a period of many years atomic bombs may well be developed which will be very much more powerful than the atomic bombs now at hand.'

But despite the devastation, Japan refused to give up the fight. And so on the morning of 9 August, a second atomic bomb headed for the city of Nagasaki, one of the largest sea ports in southern Japan, which produced ships and military equipment.

The bomb killed another estimated 40–70,000 instantly and the following day the Japanese government presented a letter of protest to the government of the U.S. via the government of Switzerland. Then, on 12 August, Emperor Hirohito finally gave the order to surrender. In his declaration to his people he said, 'The enemy now possesses a new and terrible weapon with the power to destroy many innocent lives and do incalculable damage. Should we continue to fight, not only would it result in an ultimate collapse and obliteration of the Japanese nation, but also it would lead to the total extinction of human civilization.' •

STATE OF ISRAEL IS BORN

(*Palestine Post*, 14 May 1948)

THE STATE OF ISRAEL was proclaimed on 14 May 1948 in Tel Aviv – the first Jewish state in 2,000 years.

In a ceremony at the Tel Aviv Art Museum, Jewish Agency Chairman David Ben-Gurion, who was to become Israel's first premier, pronounced the words 'We hereby proclaim the establishment of the Jewish state in Palestine, to be called Israel' to applause from the crowd that had gathered.

There had been much fighting over the years leading to this moment and it resumed the very next day as Arab armies from the neighbouring countries of Jordan, Egypt, Lebanon, Syria and Iraq invaded Israel but were resisted.

Britain had taken over Palestine after the collapse of the Ottoman Empire during the Great War and, in 1917, the 'Balfour Declaration' stated that Britain intended to establish a Jewish homeland in Palestine.

BRITISH RULE EXTENDED

But because of Arab opposition and continued fighting in the region, British rule continued throughout the 1920s and 1930s.

In 1947, the British government announced it would withdraw from

Palestine, stating it was unable to arrive at a solution acceptable to both Arabs and Jews. The newly created United Nations approved the Partition Plan for Palestine on 29 November, which would divide the country into two states – one Arab and one Jewish. The Jews were to possess more than half of Palestine, although they made up less than half of Palestine's population.

There was fierce objection from Palestinian Arabs and, aided by supportive Arab nations, they fought against the Jews, determined to claim territory, but the Jews managed to protect the land that had been agreed as theirs and Partition went ahead.

The fighting continued for a year until a ceasefire was declared and temporary borders, known as the Green Line, were established. Jordan annexed what became known as the West Bank and East Jerusalem, and Egypt had control of the Gaza Strip.

SUEZ CANAL CLOSED

In 1950, Egypt closed the Suez Canal to Israeli shipping and armed clashes took place along Israel's borders. On 26 July 1956, President Nasser of Egypt nationalised the Anglo-French Suez Canal Company, declaring that the revenue from the canal would finance the building of a dam at Aswan.

Israel joined a secret alliance with Britain and France to free the Canal from Egypt and in November an Anglo-French aerial and ground assault began on Cairo. In April 1957 the canal was fully reopened to shipping

But conflict between the two sides has continued to break out. In May 1967, a number of Arab states began to mobilise their forces, which led Israel to make a pre-emptive strike on 5 June against Egypt, Jordan, Syria and Iraq.

SIX-DAY WAR

The battle that ensued became known as the Six-Day War. It resulted in Israel increasing its borders, capturing the Sinai Peninsula, the Gaza Strip, the West Bank, the Golan Heights and old Jerusalem.

The Six-Day War, named by Chief of the Israeli Defence Force and future Prime Minister Yitzhak Rabin after the biblical days of creation, may not have been a long, drawn-out affair, but it was brutal and bloody. The Israelis lost almost 1,000 personnel, while the Egyptians are estimated to have had over ten times that number killed, wounded or missing in action. Jordan is thought to have suffered as many as 6,000 fatalities while there were 1,000 Syrian deaths, with many more wounded.

In 1979, Israel and Egypt signed an historic peace agreement in which Israel returned the Sinai. And in 1993, Israel and the Palestine Liberation Organization (PLO) signed a major peace accord, in which they agreed the gradual implementation of Palestinian self-government in the West Bank and Gaza Strip.

But fighting between Israelis and Palestinians resumed in Israel and the occupied territories and tension and resentment remain. •

MAO HEADS PEIPING REGIME

(*New York Times*, 1 October 1949)

MODERN DAY CHINA was born on 1 October 1949 when Mao Tse-tung (Zedong) proclaimed the founding of the People's Republic of China.

The day before, he had been elected Party Chairman of the new communist regime after they had finally defeated the Nationalists to seize power.

The *New York Times* reported on the historic moment, referring to the capital of Beijing as Peiping, as it was known by many at the time. The paper also mentioned that Western powers were worried about this new development, which meant that the Soviet Union had a new Eastern ally.

Mao was born on 26 December 1893 into a peasant family in Shaoshan, in Hunan province, central China. After training as a teacher, he travelled to Beijing and worked as a library assistant where he read Marxist literature. Influenced by Lenin and the Russian Revolution, he became a founder member of the Chinese Communist Party (CCP) in 1921 and set up a branch in Hunan.

MAO IN RETREAT

In 1923, the Kuomintang nationalist party allied with the CCP to defeat the warlords who controlled much of northern China. But four years later the Kuomintang leader Chiang Kai-shek launched an attack on the Communists and Mao and his colleagues retreated to southeast China.

In October 1934, with the Kuomintang army circling the Communists' base in Jiangxi province, Mao led his men on a mammoth journey across difficult terrain to the northwest on an escape route said to have been 8,000 miles (12,500km) long and to have taken 370 days.

Named the 'Long March' it gained Mao enormous respect and symbolised the determination and struggle of the Communists to reach their goal.

During eight years of war with Japan, from 1937 to 1945, there was an uneasy alliance between the Communists and Kuomintang, but shortly after the end of World War II, civil war broke out between them.

It ended in victory for the Communists and Mao proudly announcing the founding of the People's Republic of China.

STATE OWNERSHIP

Mao set out to reshape China and was initially aided by the Soviet Union. Industry came under state ownership and farmers were organised into collectives. Those who objected were ruthlessly dealt with.

But as relationships with the Soviet Union began to cool he attempted to introduce a more 'Chinese' form of communism in 1958, with what he called the 'Great Leap Forward'. This involved a drive for increased agricultural and industrial production with huge communes running their own collective farms and factories.

Each family received a share of the profits and also had a small private plot of land. But three years of floods and bad harvests severely damaged levels of production, leading to famine and the deaths of millions. In 1962 it came to an end and the country resorted to a more traditional form of economic production. Mao's position was weakened but he was determined to forge ahead with reform.

THE 'CULTURAL REVOLUTION'

After having publicly criticised the Soviet Leader Nikita Khrushchev for backing down over the Cuban Missile Crisis, Mao launched the 'Cultural Revolution' in 1966, to distance China from the Soviet model of communism and to purge political opponents whose views were too conservative. He warned the Red Guard and students that the revolution was in danger and that they must stop the emergence of a privileged class, which he said had happened in the Soviet Union.

Some of his writings at this time were gathered in a handbook called *Quotations of Chairman Mao* *Tse-tung*, and widely distributed to Chinese citizens.

The purges resulted in violence and death as opposition was crushed. Mao remained in charge of the nation until his death in 1976. •

TRUMAN ORDERS U.S. AIR, NAVY UNITS TO FIGHT IN AID OF KOREA

(*New York Times*, 27 June 1950)

PRESIDENT TRUMAN ordered the Air Force and Navy into the Korean War following a call from the United Nations Security Council for member nations to help South Korea repel an invasion from the North.

In the aftermath of World War II the Allies replaced Japan as the colonial power of Korea. Seven days before the end of the war, the Soviet Union had seized the moment by entering Korea. Now, at the Allied summit meetings, it was agreed to divide Korea at the 38th parallel, with the USSR in charge north of this line, and the U.S. in the south. This was to be a short-term measure until the return of Korean independence.

The Soviets backed a Stalinist regime in the north under Kim Il-sung and created the North Korean Peoples' Army, equipped with Russian tanks and artillery. In the south, elections were held and Syngman Rhee was made President.

Both occupying forces withdrew from Korea by 1949. A well-equipped and trained army of around 135,000 in the north contrasted sharply with little more than a constabulary force in the south of 98,000.

Emboldened by its military superiority, the north crossed over the 38th parallel in the early hours of 25 June 1950.

A unified Korea was the goal of both sides but one wanted a communist country and the other a democracy.

U.S. FORCED TO RETREAT

U.S. troops were hurriedly sent from bases in Japan but, caught off-guard, they were compelled to retreat. President Truman called on the newly formed United Nations Security Council for support and the council passed a resolution which called on all members to help repel the invasion.

Fourteen nations agreed to help, committing a force of some 300,000. The bulk of the troops were American, with Britain, Canada and Australia all making significant contributions.

By 25 September, the U.N. force had recaptured Seoul and reclaimed the rest of the territory but Truman saw the chance to unify Korea under a single, pro-Western government and ordered the American General Douglas MacArthur, Commander of the U.N. forces in Korea, to pursue the northern invaders across the 38th parallel and deep into their own territory.

They pushed on towards China, ignoring warnings that China would enter the war if the troops invaded North Korea.

On 15 October, a confident MacArthur told Truman that it would all be over by Christmas, but ten days later the Chinese army, which had been secretly massing at the border with Korea, attacked the U.N. troops. They beat a hasty retreat and by the New Year were fighting to hold a line to the south of Seoul.

After a few more months of fighting they were able to push the enemy back to the area of the 38th parallel. With the situation at 'stalemate' the U.N. pushed for a ceasefire.

MACARTHUR DISMISSED

MacArthur wanted to extend the fight against the Chinese and 'communism' and openly criticised Truman for his orders to contain the fighting to Korea. Truman then sacked MacArthur as commander of the U.N. forces in Korea and of U.S. forces in the Far East. He was replaced by General Matthew Ridgeway

The two sides held peace talks in April 1951 but they dragged on for two years. One of the main sticking points was the repatriation of prisoners. Tens of thousands of communist prisoners were held in camps on Koje Island off the coast of South Korea. While the north demanded that all prisoners be returned, there were many in the camp who didn't want to go back. Eventually it was agreed to offer asylum to the latter. Prisoners from both sides were returned when an armistice was signed on 27 July 1953. •

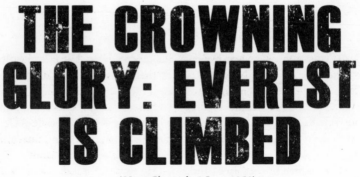

THE CROWNING GLORY: EVEREST IS CLIMBED

(*News Chronicle*, 2 June 1953)

THE NEWS THAT a British expedition was the first to reach the summit of Mount Everest – the highest point in the world – didn't reach newspapers until a few days after the event. But it was perfect timing, coming on the day before the coronation of Queen Elizabeth II.

The expedition, led by Colonel John Hunt, set off for the Himalayas in February. Hunt had named two two-man teams for the final assault on the summit – Tom Bourdillon and Charles Evans; and Edmund Hillary and Tenzing Norgay.

Hillary was a New Zealander who found a love of mountaineering on a school trip to Mount Ruapehu, south of Auckland, when he was 16.

After spending two years as a navigator in the Royal New Zealand Air Force, he joined an alpine club to take on all the national peaks. In search of bigger challenges, he travelled to the Himalayas and then set his sights on becoming the first man to climb Mount Everest.

Tenzing was a Sherpa mountaineer from Nepal, who had been part of several other mountaineering teams that had attempted, but failed, to conquer Everest.

CHANCE OF GLORY

Hunt's team set up its final camp at 25,900 feet (7,890m) and Bourdillon and Evans had their chance of glory when they set off for the summit on 26 May. But they had to turn back 300 feet

(91m) from the top, when Evans's oxygen system failed. Now it was down to Hillary and Tenzing.

After a gruelling climb up the southern face, they reached the top of the world at 11.30am on 29 May.

The two men hugged each other with joy and Hillary took a now-famous photograph of Tenzing holding his pick aloft. But no pictures were taken of himself.

Tenzing buried sweets and a pencil given to him by his daughter as a Buddhist offering to the gods. Hillary left a cross that had been entrusted to him by John Hunt.

OXYGEN RUNNING OUT

They remained on the summit for just 15 minutes because they were low on oxygen, before making their descent. Snow had covered much of their tracks, which made retracing their route more difficult.

The first person they met was teammate, George Low, who had climbed up to meet them with hot soup. Hillary greeted him with the down-to-earth victorious phrase, 'Well, George, we knocked the bastard off.'

Hunt initially mistook Hillary and Tenzing's exhausted appearance

for one of defeat but after hearing of their success, the team hugged each other in celebration.

Hillary later described the peak, which is 29,028 feet (8,847m) above sea level, as 'a symmetrical, beautiful snow cone summit'.

He was knighted, along with Hunt, on return, by the new young Queen, and Tenzing was awarded the George Medal.

AFTER EVEREST

After the ascent, Hillary led a number of expeditions to the South Pole but shunned the celebrity spotlight to devote his life to helping the Sherpas of Nepal's Khumbu region. He set up a trust to help build hospitals, schools and bridges. In 1985, he was made New Zealand's High Commissioner to India and lived in Delhi.

He spoke out about what he considered to be the commercialisation of Everest and climbers who left rubbish behind and ignored others in distress as they passed them en route to the summit. He was made an honorary Nepalese citizen in 2003 and died in 2008.

Tenzing received many honours and continued to work in his beloved mountains as a guide. He went on to become head of field training at the Himalayan Mountaineering Institute in Darjeeling and established Tenzing Norgay Adventures, a trekking and guiding company, in 1978. When he died in 1986 at the age of 71, the company was taken over by his son, Jamling, who climbed Everest ten years after his father's death and, along with Peter Hillary, the son of Edmund Hillary, he was part of an expedition to climb the mountain again in 2002, on the 50th anniversary of their fathers' conquest.

Peter Hillary was part of the team for the assault on the summit and, after their successful attempt, he put in a call to his father using a satellite phone, something that would have been almost beyond imagination in 1952. •

WHY YOU ARE YOU

NEARER SECRET OF LIFE

(*News Chronicle*, 15 May 1953)

THE DISCOVERY OF the secret of life was greeted with a subdued reception. Despite later being described by some as the most significant contribution to science since Darwin's theory of evolution, it took a while for people to become aware of what had happened.

The unravelling of the structure of deoxyribonucleic acid (DNA) – the material that makes up genes which pass hereditary characteristics from one parent to another – was made by biologists Francis Crick and James Watson on 28 February 1953 at their laboratory in Cambridge.

PUB ANNOUNCEMENT

Later that day, a euphoric Crick walked into the local public house, The Eagle, and announced that he and his colleague 'had found the secret of life.'

It may have sounded like an outrageous boast from a pub bore but it was true. The pair had discovered the elusive 'double helix' structure of DNA in which two strands coil around each other, both consisting of complementary elements that fit together and when uncoiled can produce two copies of the original. It confirmed theories that it carried life's hereditary information.

Crick, who was born near Northampton, studied physics at University College, London, and then biology at Cambridge University.

By 1949 he was working at the Medical Research Council unit at the Cavendish Laboratory in Cambridge under the general direction of Lawrence Bragg, who had won the Nobel Prize for Physics in 1915 at the age of 25.

In 1951 an American student from Chicago, James Watson, who at 23 was twelve years Crick's junior, arrived and they enjoyed a shared passion for studying the structure of DNA.

X-RAY STUDIES

The pair worked together using some key information that had been obtained by Maurice Wilkins and Rosalind Franklin, both working at King's College, London, who had been using X-ray diffraction to study DNA.

This helped them to finally crack the 'double helix' structure and Bragg proudly made the announcement at a conference in Belgium on 8 April 1953. It went unreported by the press.

Crick and Watson's findings were published in the scientific journal *Nature* on 25 April 1953. Their comment, 'This structure has novel features which are of considerable biological interest,' has become famous as one of science's most famous understatements.

Bragg then gave a talk at Guy's Hospital Medical School in London on 14 May, which resulted in an article by Ritchie Calder, science editor of the *News Chronicle*, the following day. It was the only British newspaper to carry a report on the ground-breaking discovery.

In 1962, Crick, Watson and Wilkins all won the Nobel Prize. Rosalind Franklin had died of cancer four years earlier, aged just 37, and so missed out on receiving the Prize for her crucial work in the discovery of DNA.

CREDIT TO OTHERS

Like most scientific discoveries, it is the work of many others who have led the way or contributed to the understanding of the subject that makes the achievement possible.

Back in 1868, almost a century before the Nobel Prize was awarded to Watson, Crick and Wilkins, a young Swiss physician named Friedrich Miescher, isolated something no one had ever seen before from the nuclei of cells. He called the compound 'nuclein' which is today called nucleic acid – the 'NA' in DNA.

In the late 1940s, the scientific community were aware that DNA was most likely the molecule of life, but breaking down the structure of it proved to be beyond them. After Crick and Watson found the answer, it provided a launching pad for a rapid advance in molecular biology that led to genetic engineering, stem cell research and DNA fingerprinting. •

RUTH ELLIS TO HANG

THE ONLY VERDICT, SAYS JUDGE – 'JEALOUSY NO DEFENCE'

(*Evening News*, 21 June 1955)

THE TRIAL OF Ruth Ellis, who shot dead her lover, was a controversial and landmark case as she became the last woman in England to be hanged.

The story had all the ingredients of a movie. Platinum-blonde Ellis, 28, was a former model from Wales who became a nightclub hostess after moving to London. At the age of 17 she had become pregnant by a Canadian soldier and gave birth to a son. She brought him up as a single parent for a while until he went to live with her mother.

In early 1950, she became pregnant by one of the customers at the nightclub where she worked but had the pregnancy terminated. Later that year she married another customer of the club who proved to be a jealous and violent alcoholic, who was convinced she was having

an affair. After she gave birth to a daughter in 1951, he refused to acknowledge that he was the father and they separated shortly afterwards.

GLAMOUR GIRL

In 1953 she became a manager of another London nightclub and attracted a number of celebrity friends. Her glamorous looks and vivacious personality also caught the eye of promising racing driver, David Blakely, who moved into her flat above the club. She became pregnant for a fourth time but aborted the child.

She then began seeing a former WWII RAF pilot, Desmond Cussens. When she was sacked as manager of the club she moved in with him at his home in Oxford Street. But her tempestuous relationship with Blakely continued, causing increasing jealousy and anger between the two men.

On Easter Sunday, 10 April 1955, she went in search of Blakely and found his car parked outside a pub called The Magadala in Hampstead, north London. At around 9.30pm he emerged with his friend Clive Gunnell. She called to him but he ignored her and carried on walking towards his car. She then took a gun from her handbag and fired at him. It missed and he started to run. She ran after him and hit him with her second shot. He collapsed on the pavement and she fired three more bullets into him.

'I AM GUILTY'

In a state of shock, she asked Gunnell to call the police and was shortly arrested by an off-duty policeman who heard her say, 'I am guilty. I'm a little confused.' She was taken to Hampstead police station where she made a detailed confession to the police and was charged with murder.

Her trial at the Old Bailey opened on 20 June and the jury took just 14 minutes to find her guilty of murder. Mr Justice Havers sentenced her to death.

The case received much publicity in the press and there was a groundswell of sympathy for her from those who felt that she had been ill-treated by the men in her life and that the law should be more lenient towards what many considered to be a 'crime of passion'. Thousands signed petitions asking for the death penalty to be lifted in her case.

SINGING AND CHANTING

At midday on 12 July 1955, the day before her execution, Ellis made a statement to her solicitor in the condemned cell saying that the gun had been provided by Cussen and that he had driven her to the murder scene. But the Home Office refused to act on this and there was to be no reprieve.

The night before she was due to be hanged at Holloway Prison, a crowd of 500 formed outside the gates singing and chanting for her. Some broke through police cordons to bang on the prison doors, calling for Ellis to pray with them.

The following morning, the executioner, Albert Pierrepoint, went about his duties and she was hanged at 9.00am.

The case sparked debate about British criminal justice and the death penalty. Two years later, Parliament changed the law to allow a defence of diminished responsibility. The death penalty in the U.K. was suspended in 1965 and permanently removed in 1970.

Ruth Ellis's family continued to campaign for her murder conviction to be reduced to manslaughter on the grounds of provocation. At the Court of Appeal in September 2003, they argued that she was suffering 'battered woman syndrome' and that she had suffered a miscarriage just 10 days before the killing after David Blakely had punched her in the stomach.

The Court rejected the appeal, saying that it could only rule on the conviction based on the law as it stood in 1955. Diminished responsibility did not then exist and she had been properly convicted of murder. •

FIRST BLOWS BY NAVY AND R.A.F

CRUISER SINKS AN EGYPTIAN FRIGATE

(*Guardian*, 1 November 1956)

THE ATTACK BY BRITAIN and France on Egypt, part of which became known as the 'Suez Crisis', was a worldwide political disaster and the last gasp of the British Empire.

Construction on the canal began on 25 April 1859 after former French diplomat, Ferdinand de Lesseps, persuaded the Viceroy of Egypt, Mohamed Said, to allow a shipping canal through the 100 miles of desert between Africa and Asia. The Universal Company of the Suez Maritime Canal was set up but Britain, suspicious of France, declined the offer of shares in the company. And so Egypt acquired 44% of the shares.

The canal opened in November 1869 and, during the first year of its existence, some three-quarters of the vessels using it were British.

Said had been succeeded after his death in 1867 by his nephew, Ismail. When he fell into debt he offered his country's shares in the canal for sale. The British Prime Minister, Benjamin Disraeli, bought Egypt's shareholding for £4 million.

ACCESS TO OIL

Not only did the waterway provide Britain with a quicker route to her empire but, as oil became an increasingly important commodity at the beginning of the twentieth century, it also meant quicker access to the oilfields of the Persian Gulf.

Britain and France defended the Suez Canal through both World Wars and, despite Egypt being declared an independent state in 1936, there continued to be a heavy British presence in the country. In 1951, when Nahas Pasha became leader of the recently elected nationalist Wafd party, there was a backlash with attacks on the British garrison. Fighting continued on and off between the sides as relationships deteriorated.

In 1954, Colonel Gamel Abdul Nasser came to power, intent on ending British occupation, on building up Egyptian forces for an attack on Israel and on constructing a high dam at Aswan to irrigate the Nile valley.

CANAL NATIONALISED

It was agreed on 19 October 1954 that British troops were to be withdrawn from Egypt by June 1956 but could return if the canal was threatened by anyone. On 26 July 1956, President Nasser nationalised the Anglo-French Suez Canal Company to finance his dam.

Britain and France were alarmed, while America and Israel were concerned that Egypt was looking to the Soviet Union for arms. A secret meeting was held between Britain, France and Israel in which it was agreed that Israel should attack Egypt, thereby providing a pretext for an Anglo-French invasion of Suez.

Israeli troops began an invasion on 29 October 1956. The next day, Britain and France issued ultimatums to both sides to stop the fighting immediately. Two days later the two colonial powers launched an aerial bombardment on military airfields. Troops were parachuted in and overpowered the defence. Arab countries expressed their readiness to come to the aid of Egypt should she ask for it.

CEASEFIRE IMPOSED

The canal was almost back under Anglo-French control when a ceasefire was called on 6 November, after pressure from the United Nations.

The U.S. President, Dwight D. Eisenhower, was furious at being left out of the loop. In a TV broadcast he said that the 'armed attack' by Britain had been launched 'in error'. He added, 'We do not accept the use of force as a wise or proper instrument to settle international disputes.'

In Britain there was considerable outrage too over Britain's military offensive, with petitions to Downing Street and a mass demonstration in London's Trafalgar Square in which protestors carried banners proclaiming 'LAW not WAR!'.

The Labour Party said that Britain's attack was 'in clear violation of the United Nations charter'.

Under world pressure, Britain, France and Israel withdrew their forces and a U.N. peacekeeping force was sent in to supervise the ceasefire and to restore order.

British Prime Minister, Anthony Eden, denied any prior knowledge of the planned attack by Israel. The incident marked the end of historical colonial powers Britain and France acting independently of world opinion. Britain's relationship with the Middle East was severely damaged. Harold Macmillan, who succeeded Eden, repaired relationships with America, becoming friends with President John F. Kennedy and persuaded him to let Britain have the Polaris nuclear missile. The two countries have continued to support each other in general terms ever since. •

SOVIET FIRES EARTH SATELLITE INTO SPACE

IT IS CIRCLING THE GLOBE AT 18,000 M.P.H.; SPHERE TRACED IN FOUR CROSSINGS OVER U.S.

(*New York Times*, October 5 1957)

AT JUST UNDER 23 inches (58cm) in diameter it was the size of a beach ball but it was a scientific marvel, causing fear and wonder in equal measure, which was to make a huge impact around the world.

With the U.S. and Soviet Union in the midst of the Cold War, each was trying to do outdo the other to prove superiority. Although both countries had talked about launching satellites into space, the U.S. was caught napping when the Soviets successfully launched the world's first artificial satellite, Sputnik 1, on 4 October 1957.

Sputnik weighed just under 184 pounds, had four antennae and contained a radio transmitter, batteries and a thermometer. It was a tremendous propaganda coup for the communist system, with Soviet scientists describing it as the first stage in interplanetary travel.

The U.S. only found out about the launch at a reception at the Soviet Embassy that night. The following day's reports in the newspapers caused much unease amongst the American public, who had no real idea what a satellite actually was.

The Russians had been developing rockets with which to launch missiles at the U.S. and, in August 1957, one of their R-7 rockets travelled 6,000 kilometres carrying a simulated H-bomb warhead. Some Americans now feared that Sputnik was either some kind of weapon or was being used to target American cities for atomic-bomb attacks.

SECRET CODE

It was 500 miles up, travelling at 18,000 miles an hour and it circled the globe every 96 minutes, flying over the U.S. seven times a day. The regular 'beeping' sound could be heard by ham-radio enthusiasts and many Americans found it deeply unsettling. In the days after the launch there were several paranoid articles in the newspapers. One asked if the beeping could be some kind of secret code.

At first, President Eisenhower tried to play down Sputnik's launch, claiming that it did not increase his concern about national security and that there would be no change in funding or priority for satellite or missile programs.

But he was criticised for his lack of investment in his country's space programme and for what some considered to be his lack of concern for Americans' safety. General concern increased when the Soviets launched Sputnik 2 on 3 November 1957. At 1100 pounds it was bigger than its predecessor and was carrying a passenger – Laika, the dog.

One near-hysterical U.S. news reporter took a flight of fancy, suggesting the possibility that it had been launched to hit the moon with a hydrogen bomb.

U.S. ROCKET EXPLODES

Meanwhile the U.S. was still to get a satellite off the ground and now it was desperately trying to make up for lost time. Funding was made available for students keen to enrol in aerospace engineering programmes and projects. And the government put pressure on scientists to launch a satellite as soon as possible. A highly publicised launch on 6 December 1957 was a disaster when the rocket carrying the satellite exploded on the launch pad. It was a great embarrassment to the U.S.

Finally they put their first satellite, Explorer, into orbit on 17

March 1958. But they were soon trumped when, fourteen weeks later, the Soviets launched their third and biggest Sputnik yet. It carried more scientific equipment than previous satellites from either country.

On 29 July 1958, Eisenhower signed a bill that created the National Aeronautics and Space Agency (NASA), which ushered in a whole new world of achievement.

Sputnik 1 had shattered American perception that the U.S. was the world's leading scientific and technological superpower. As well as deeply embarrassing them, they were shaken and nervous that their Cold War enemy had shown her superiority.

The race was now on to be the first to get a man into space. •

21 DEAD
7 MANCHESTER UTD
PLAYERS PERISH
IN AIR CRASH

(*Daily Sketch*, 7 February 1958)

THEY WERE THE DREAM TEAM. The 'Busby Babes' – a nickname derived from their manager's name and their youth. With an average age of just 24, they were the most exciting young football players of their generation.

Tragically, these potential world beaters, who were aiming to win the 1st Division Championship for a record-breaking third consecutive time as well as finding glory in Europe, were cut off in their prime when the dream died on 6 February 1958.

There had been speculation that Manchester United might be capable of 'doing the treble' that season – champions of Division 1, the FA Cup and European Cup.

They had beaten Red Star Belgrade 2–1 at their home ground of Old Trafford in January and had flown out to Belgrade for the away leg, which they drew 3–3. It was enough to put United through to the semi-finals.

DIFFICULT LANDING

The following day their British European Airways plane stopped to refuel in Munich on its way home. Snow and ice had made landing tricky but it was even more difficult when they tried to take off again.

Captain Thain aborted take off after noticing an uneven tone in the engines. The passengers, including team, officials and sports journalists, disembarked for refreshments in the terminal building.

The second attempt was also aborted for the same reason, described by Captain Thain to his passengers as a 'slight engine fault', which would need to be checked.

Once more the passengers returned to the departure lounge. Manchester United's star player, left-half Duncan Edwards, sent a telegram to his landlady saying, 'All flights cancelled. Flying home tomorrow. Duncan.' But unexpectedly, they were called back onto the plane, which was ready to leave.

SKID DISASTER

By now, the snow was heavier, causing a layer of slush to build up. The plane gathered speed but was unable to reach the velocity required to get off the ground. It skidded off the end of the runway, ploughed through a fence and struck a nearby house, which tore off the port wing and part of the tail. The starboard side of the fuselage hit a wooden hut.

Inside the aircraft, twenty people were killed outright. Captain Thain got out and shouted to everyone to evacuate before the plane exploded.

Inside, United and Northern Ireland goalkeeper, Harry Gregg, had bumped his head and blood was pouring down his face, but he realised he was alive. He crawled towards a hole in the wreckage and kicked it wider so that he could get out. Gregg saw the Captain shouting and others running away but just then he heard a baby crying.

Heroically he crawled back and found the baby girl under some debris and brought her out where he handed her over to a radio operator. Gregg then went back in and rescued the mother – Vera Lukic, the pregnant wife of a Yugoslavian diplomat.

Outside, he saw his teammates Bobby Charlton and Dennis Viollet hanging half in and half out of the plane, and he dragged them clear by the waistbands of their trousers.

SEVERED ARM

On seeing central defender Jackie Blanchflower with his right arm almost severed, Gregg used his tie to wrap tightly around it.

In the event the plane did not explode and the injured were all rescued and taken to Rechts der Isar Hospital in Munich.

Manager Matt Busby was thought to be the most seriously injured with a punctured lung, fractured ribs and leg injuries. He had blood transfusions and was given the last rites. A hospital spokesman said, 'We do not have much hope of saving him.'

Winger Albert Scanlon was unconscious for three weeks and Duncan Edwards had broken ribs and a fractured right leg. Bobby Charlton suffered minor head injuries.

Seven of Manchester United's talented players had died immediately after the crash – team captain Roger Byrne, Mark Jones, Eddie Colman, Tommy Taylor, Billy Whelan, David Pegg and Geoff Bent.

Also amongst the fatalities were several sports journalists, team officials and plane crew.

The bodies of the deceased were flown home on 7 February and thousands turned out to line the streets for the funerals.

THE LAST RITES

Busby received the last rites for a second time, while Duncan Edwards and the co-pilot Kenneth Rayment were getting worse by the day.

That Saturday, a two-minute silence was observed at football matches around the world. Despite the tragedy, United fielded a team to take on Sheffield Wednesday in a Fifth Round FA Cup tie, which they won 3–0.

Duncan Edwards, United's undoubted star player died from his injuries on 21 February at the age of 21, followed a week later by Kenneth Rayment, which brought the final death toll to 23 of the 44 passengers and crew aboard the flight.

Busby made a miraculous recovery and was sent to Switzerland to recuperate with his wife, Jean.

Meanwhile, under the guidance of assistant manager Jimmy Murphy, United made it to the FA Cup Final on 3 May. Busby, who had returned home, slowly made his way to the bench with the aid of a walking stick to watch them play. They lost 2–0 to Bolton Wanderers.

A few days later, United beat AC Milan 2–1 in the home leg of their European Cup Semi-final. But the following week they were thrashed 4–0 in the away game at the San Siro Stadium, which knocked them out of the Cup.

TITLE CHALLENGE COLLAPSES

United only won one League game after the crash, causing their title challenge to collapse and they fell to ninth place in the League.

The injuries suffered by Jackie Blanchflower and winger Johnny Berry, meant that neither of them would be able to play again.

Matt Busby believed that football should be exciting and his innovative idea to amass a team full of youngsters – many straight from school – that could be honed to play in the attacking, creative style that he wanted, thrilled the public and was the foundation for all that followed.

Manchester United became one of the biggest and best-loved football clubs in the world.

A decade after the Munich Disaster, Busby, the great survivor, led his beloved team to become the first English club to win the European Cup. •

BIRTH CONTROL PILL APPROVED BY COMMISSION

(Reno Evening Gazette, 9 May 1960)

A SMALL NEWS ARTICLE at the bottom of the front page of this Nevada newspaper might easily be missed by a reader but it ushered in one of the biggest scientific, social and cultural events of the century.

It reported how the U.S. Food and Drug Administration (FDA) had approved a pill as safe for contraceptive or birth-control use.

The pill was called Envoid, made by G. D. Searle and Co., Chicago. It was the first commercially available oral contraceptive.

The drug had been on the market for several years but only for treatment of female disorders. One of the most influential pioneers behind the invention of the pill was Margaret Sanger, a Catholic nurse and birth-control campaigner who opened America's first birth-control clinic in 1916.

WOMEN'S RIGHTS

Sanger felt that, in order for women to be able to have an equal place in society, they needed to be able to determine when to have children. She was pro-birth control but anti-abortion. After meeting

American biologist Gregory Pincus in 1951, she persuaded him to research the use of hormones in contraception and managed to raise $150,000 backing through the Planned Parenthood Federation of America, which she had helped to set up. When the money ran out, Pincus was financed by Sanger's associate, women's rights activist and philanthropist Katharine McCormick.

Meanwhile, in Mexico City, Austrian-born chemist Carl Djerassi created a progesterone pill while working at a pharmaceutical research company. Although aware that it could be used for contraception, it was intended for menstrual disorders and infertility. But within a decade it would become known as the contraceptive pill.

It was Pincus and Catholic gynaecologist John Rock who went on to fully test, produce and distribute the pill for contraceptive purposes.

Rock had founded a clinic to teach the rhythm method, the only form of birth control accepted by the Catholic Church. Pincus had successfully tested progesterone on rats and, in 1952, Rock was recruited to lead the clinical trials of the new contraceptive pill.

Meanwhile, Polish-born American Frank Colton, chief chemist at the pharmaceutical company Searle, was also developing a synthetic progesterone.

More successful trials followed and, in 1957, the FDA approved the Pill on prescription for women with severe menstrual disorders. There was an upsurge in women claiming such gynaecological problems until, finally, three years later, it was approved for contraceptive use.

TRIALS IN THE U.K.

There was huge demand for it. Trials were conducted in the U.K. in 1960 and in 1961 it was approved for use in Britain, with the Germans having adopted the pill shortly before the Brits and a string of other western countries following closely behind.

In France, contraception was illegal until December 1967, but thereafter the pill swiftly became the most widely used method of birth control. One of the world's most technologically advanced nations, Japan, was one of the last to adopt the pill as a contraceptive, the Japan Medical Association expressing concerns over the effect its long-term use might have on the women who took it. It was not approved for use in Japan until 1999. There was plenty of controversy and opposition, which included health scares and accusations that it promoted promiscuity and a relaxation of moral standards. But it helped usher in the sexual revolution and gave women control and independence.

The Pill was to become the leading method of birth control used by more than 100 million women around the world. •

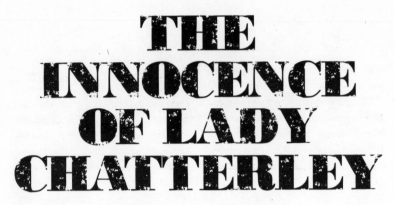

THE INNOCENCE OF LADY CHATTERLEY

(*Evening Standard*, 2 November 1960)

THE TRIAL OF Lady Chatterley sounded like a member of the aristocracy was in the dock for a misdemeanour. It referred, of course, to D. H. Lawrence's novel, but in some ways the court hearing was a class divide. And the daily proceedings provided entertaining reading in the newspapers.

In 1959, a new passage had been added to the Obscene Publications Act, which said that a book considered obscene by some but which could be shown to have 'redeeming social merit' might still be published.

D. H. Lawrence's novel, *Lady Chatterley's Lover*, about a passionate affair between the lady of the house and the family gamekeeper, Mellors, had been banned in Britain for decades because of graphic language and descriptions of sex. Only a heavily censored version was available. The full original version had, however, been published in Italy in 1928 and later in France.

ANNIVERSARY EDITION

Now the book was causing a stir again after the publishers, Penguin, decided to take advantage of the new clause in the Obscene Publications Act and printed 200,000 copies of the unexpurgated novel as part of a complete set of the author's work to commemorate the 30th anniversary of his death in 1960.

Penguin sent 12 copies to the Director of Public Prosecutions, who decided that the text did contravene the Obscene Publications Act and brought about a prosecution – the first novel to be tested under the 1959 clause.

The six-day trial at the Old Bailey began on 27 October. The defence lined up 35 eminent witnesses including bishops and leading literary figures. These included Dame Rebecca West, a novelist, travel writer and journalist who had covered the Nuremberg Trials for *The New Yorker* and been appointed DBE in 1949 for her services to literature.

Also in the defence corner was E. M. Forster, the prolific and much-respected author who wrote *A Room with a View*, *Howards End* and *A Passage to India*. He was joined by Cecil Day-Lewis, the Poet Laureate of the United Kingdom, who also wrote mystery adventure yarns under the pen name Nicholas Blake; and Richard Hoggart, a prominent academic and university professor whose book, *The Uses of Literacy*, was required reading for anyone studying English or the media.

EVERY OBSCENITY NOTED

The prosecution had gone through the book noting every obscenity and given copies of the novel to the jury to read.

In what was to become a famous remark, prosecution counsel Mervyn Griffith-Jones asked the jury, 'Would you approve of your young sons, young daughters – because girls can read as well as boys – reading this book? Is it a book that you would have lying around in your own house? Is it a book that you would even wish your wife or your servants to read?'

There were amused smiles in court as well as disbelief that Griffith-Jones should be so out of touch with the times and assume that the jury of twelve – chosen from ordinary members of the public – would have servants. They were also amazed by his rather sexist notion of females.

Many thought that once these words had come out of his mouth in his opening address, the case was already lost.

The defence team, led by Gerald Gardiner, capitalised on the blunder to show that the prosecution was out of touch and that Penguin represented the common man in the modern world.

PENGUIN'S LONG-TERM BATTLE

In his closing address, Gardiner remarked, 'I do not want to upset the prosecution by suggesting that there are a certain number of people nowadays who as a matter of fact don't have servants. But of course that whole attitude is one which Penguin Books was formed to fight against, which they have always fought against.

'Isn't everybody, whether earning £10 a week or £20 a week, equally interested in the society in which we live, in the problems of human relationships including sexual relationships? In view of the reference made to wives, aren't women equally interested in human relations, including sexual relations?'

After six days, the jury took three hours to acquit Penguin Books of all charges. Most of the newspapers thought the prosecution was silly but avidly reported on it and there were few complaints about the jury's decision. Times were changing and the permissive sixties were on their way.

The court case proved to be wonderful advertising for the novel as all 200,000 copies of it were sold on the first day of publication and two million over the next few months.

It was a watershed moment and other obscenity cases would follow with liberation usually defeating censorship.

PEOPLE APPALLED

But, despite *Lady Chatterley's* victory, there were many people throughout the country – outside of literary or trendy social circles – with strict morals who were appalled by the outcome.

The Home Office received many letters of protest, copies of the book were burned on the streets of Edinburgh and women librarians in South Wales asked permission not to handle it.

In a House of Lords debate, the 6th Earl of Craven made the memorable comment: 'I made a trip on the M1 the other day, on my way to Manchester, and stopped at Forte's restaurant... It was the day that Lady Chatterley's Lover was on sale to the public and there, at every serving counter, sat a snigger of youths. Every one had a copy of the book held up to his face with one hand, while he forked nourishment into his open mouth with the other. They held the seeds of suggestive lust, which was expressed quite blatantly by glance and remark, to the girls serving them. That I saw with my own eyes... Purity is sacrificed on the altar of promiscuity as woolly-headed intellectuals pour their vociferous sewage into the ears of the public.' •

MAN ENTERS SPACE

(*Huntsville Times*, 12 April 1961)

THE RACE TO PUT the first man into space was on. Following Russia's successful launch of the Sputnik satellites in 1957, America was determined to gain the upper hand. They were busy preparing their Mercury capsule but did not realise that the Soviets were secretly forging ahead with their own Vostock space programme.

When they discovered that they had been beaten once again, the country was stunned and embarrassed, while Russia enjoyed her moment of triumph and enjoyed a magnificent propaganda coup.

A big picture of Russian cosmonaut Yuri Gagarin dominated the front page of this Alabama newspaper, as it did many other throughout the world, after he became the first man into space.

The achievement was engineered by the remarkable Sergei Korolev. He had qualified as a pilot and began designing gliders and then rocket engines. In 1933, he successfully launched the first liquid-fuelled rocket in the USSR.

CAPTURED NAZI STORES

After World War II, the Russians captured Nazi stores of V2 rocket components and used them to develop their own missile system. On 21 August 1957, Korolev launched the Soviet R-7 rocket, the world's first intercontinental ballistic missile. This was followed by the world's first satellite,

Sputnik 1, in October, before Korlov then put the first dog, Laika, into space the following month.

Towards the end of 1959, Yuri Gagarin was one of 20 pilots chosen for the Soviet space programme. Slightly built, he was one of the few pilots able to fit into the cramped Vostock 1 capsule and was eventually selected.

On the morning of 12 April 1961, he sat inside the capsule as it was launched from a pad at Baikonur, in Kazakhstan. At 9:07am (local time), the capsule went into orbit around the earth and Yuri Gagarin became the world's first man in space.

One hundred and eight minutes later, after making a single orbit, the 27-year-old cosmonaut parachuted back to Earth.

GAGARIN 'IMMORTAL'

Gagarin became an instant hero. Premier Nikita Khrushchev was elated and telephoned him to say, 'You have brought glory to our homeland. You have shown courage and heroism. You have made yourself immortal.'

Khrushchev compared him to Christopher Columbus, and named him a hero of the Soviet Union.

People gathered in the square and streets of Moscow to celebrate. Streets were named for him in many Soviet cities, monuments were erected, and Government officials pinned medals on his tunic. He was later to travel the world, meeting leaders and royalty as an international celebrity.

Despite America's disappointment, President John F. Kennedy sent congratulations to Moscow with the words, 'The people of the U.S. share with the people of the Soviet Union their satisfaction for the safe flight of the astronaut in man's first venture into space... It is my sincere desire that in the continuing quest for knowledge of outer space our nations can work together to obtain the greatest benefit to mankind.' And he told a press conference that the flight was 'a most impressive scientific accomplishment.'

Responding to American newspaper reporters' criticism of the U.S. space programme, Kennedy admitted, 'We are behind.'

FIRST AMERICAN IN SPACE

Less than a month later, astronaut Alan Shepard became the first American in space. But by now

Kennedy had his mind on what was seen as the ultimate goal – to put a man on the moon. It was a challenge that he could not afford to lose.

On 25 May 1961, just a few weeks after Gagarin's flight, Kennedy made his speech committing the United States to sending a man to the moon and returning him safely before the end of the decade. •

EAST GERMAN TROOPS SEAL BORDER WITH WEST BERLIN TO BLOCK REFUGEE ESCAPE

(*New York Times*, 14 August 1961)

THE RAPID ACTIVITY shortly after midnight on 13 August 1961 caught Berliners napping. The quiet, almost deserted streets of East Berlin was shattered by the sound of screaming sirens as police and troops in cars, trucks and on motorbikes sped through the city.

Working at speed, troops and construction workers set up barbed-wire fences up to six feet (1.83m) high along the border with West Berlin and by daylight the city had been divided.

Nobody was allowed to cross the border and road and train transport between the two sectors of the city was halted.

Thousands of angry demonstrators quickly gathered on the West Berlin side of the divide. At one crossing point, protesters tried to trample down the barbed wire but were driven back by guards with bayonets.

The following day – a Monday – thousands of East Berliners who arrived for their daily commute to work in the West were told it would no longer be possible.

The momentous incident was the dramatic response by East Germany's Head of State, Walter Ulbricht, to the continuing flow of refugees from East to West Berlin.

PERMANENT STRUCTURE

Within days, troops began replacing the barbed wire with concrete blocks and the wall became a permanent structure. It was officially called the 'Antifaschistischer Schutzwall' or 'Anti-Fascist Protection Rampart'.

It eventually stretched some 100 miles around West Berlin. Consisting of a mixture of concrete nearly 12 feet high, wire fencing and various watch towers, it was to become the most potent symbol of the Cold War – a tangible vision of Churchill's 'Iron Curtain' description of Communist Eastern Europe.

The historical background to this divisive edifice can be traced back to the end of World War II when the victorious Allied powers divided Germany into four zones, each occupied by Britain, the United States, France or the Soviet Union. The same was done with Germany's capital city, Berlin, which was located in the Soviet quarter.

But as relations between the Soviet Union quickly began to disintegrate it developed into an East–West, communism–capitalism divide.

In 1949, West Germany became The Federal Republic and East German the Democratic Republic. The two countries developed very differently. The capitalist west experienced a rapid growth in its economy while those in the east experienced hardship, poor living conditions and restriction of movements. This model was encapsulated on a smaller scale within Berlin with the western sector becoming an 'island' of democracy within Communist East Germany.

ARMED GUARDS

There was a regular flow of people leaving East Berlin for the more prosperous west, an exodus which reached around 1,700 daily. After the Wall went up, people attempted to climb across it, despite armed guards keeping an attentive watch. Many paid with their lives.

Towards the end of the 1980s, the 'Iron Curtain' over Eastern Europe began to lift. In 1989 Hungary opened its border with Austria and thousands of East Germans found a route into West Germany.

With the Communist regime crumbling, a huge crowd attended a pro-democracy demonstration in East Berlin's main square on 4 November of that year and the government of East Germany resigned three days later. Two days after that, thousands gathered at the Berlin Wall protesting to be let through. Some started to hack at the wall and to everyone's amazement, the guards stood back. The euphoric crowd then started to knock it down in earnest. Once it had been breached, they streamed across the border that had cut them off for 28 years and were welcomed with open arms by West Berliners who had clambered onto the concrete wall in front of the Brandenburg Gate to look across.

The barrier had come down at last and East and West greeted each other like long lost friends. On 3 October 1990, the two Germanys merged to form a new united country. •

WE BLOCKADE CUBA ARMS

(*Daily News*, 23 October 1962)

FOR 14 TENSE DAYS in 1962, the United States and the Soviet Union appeared to be on the brink of a nuclear war.

The front page of this New York newspaper refers to a U.S. naval blockade of Cuba in response to an aggressive move by the Soviets which was the start of what became known as the 'Cuban Missile Crisis.'

In August and September of 1962, U.S. intelligence services gathered evidence of Russian-built MiG-21 fighters and surface-to-air missiles on the Caribbean island of Cuba.

Then, on 14 October 1962, an American U-2 reconnaissance plane photographed long-range Soviet nuclear missiles on Cuba, capable of being launched at the American mainland. There was also an increase in the number of Soviet ships arriving in Cuba.

President John F. Kennedy was prompted into action. He was in a difficult situation at home with elections due to take place for Congress in two months' time. Public-opinion polls showed that his ratings had fallen to their lowest point since he became president.

INVASION OF CUBA PLANNED

An executive committee of the National Security Council was set up and the fourteen members discussed what to do. Several tense meetings followed in which they debated what their response would be. They ranged from taking no action at all to an invasion of Cuba and the overthrow of Fidel Castro.

Eventually, it was decided to put a naval blockade in place around Cuba to prevent the Soviets from bringing in more military supplies. The U.S. also demanded the removal of missiles already there.

Kennedy announced the discovery of the missiles and his response in a televised address to the nation on 22 October. And he warned that any nuclear attack from Cuba would result in 'a full retaliatory response upon the Soviet Union'.

ACT OF AGGRESSION

The U.S. Air Force was put on stand-by for attacks on Cuba and the Soviet Union. Nikita Khrushchev telegrammed Kennedy warning that the United States' 'pirate action' would lead to war. In a second telegram he said that the blockade was 'an act of aggression' and that his country's ships would be instructed to ignore it. The scene was set and now the world waited to see what happened as Soviet ships continued to make their way to Cuba. If they did not turn back or refused to be searched, a war was likely to begin.

On 24 October, Kennedy was informed that the ships had stopped just before they reached the blockade. An angry Khrushchev sent another telegram to Kennedy accusing him of creating a crisis to gain support for himself and his party. Two days later and the breakthrough came when Khrushchev proposed that the Soviet Union would be willing to remove the missiles in Cuba in exchange for a promise by the United States that they would not invade Cuba. The following day he also demanded that America remove its nuclear bases in Turkey.

SPY PLANE SHOT DOWN

While diplomatic exchanges and demands continued, the U.S. still had to keep track of what was happening at the missile bases being built on Cuba. Their latest information, based partly on photographs taken by the U-2 spy planes, showed that the bases were now operational. Further U-2 flights were scheduled to monitor the situation.

On 28 October, America sustained the only fatality resulting from enemy action during the confrontation when U-2 pilot

Major Rudolf Anderson was shot down over Cuba. The Americans knew that the Cubans did not have the capability to shoot down the high-flying U-2s. Only a Soviet anti-aircraft missile would be able to hit a U-2. They had already decided that, if a U-2 was shot down, they would consider it as an act of aggression on the part of the Russians. They would then have no choice but to strike back at the Soviets.

Fortunately, the Americans decided to change their minds and put the incident down to a regrettable error of judgement. It was later disclosed that the Russians had ordered that their missiles should not be used against the U-2s because they knew that the Americans would be likely to retaliate. The missile that downed the spy plane had been launched on

the orders of an over-zealous local commander in Cuba. The incident had brought the world one step closer to all-out nuclear war.

Kennedy publicly agreed not to invade Cuba and privately promised the removal of the nuclear bases in Turkey.

The Cuban Missile Crisis was finally over on 28 October. The 'unthinkable' had been averted and the world began to breathe again.

The event appeared to frighten both sides, who found it difficult to 'lose face' in public by backing down. A result of this was that America and the Soviet Union set up a direct private communications link that became known as the Hot Line.

A Test Ban Treaty was signed between the two countries in August 1963, prohibiting the testing of nuclear weapons in the atmosphere. •

PROFUMO QUITS

(*Daily Mail*, 6 June 1963)

BRITISH SECRETARY OF STATE for War, John Profumo, resigned from government over a notorious 'sex scandal' after admitting he lied to Parliament about his relationship with good-time girl, Christine Keeler.

The Conservative MP confessed that he had misled the House of Commons in an earlier statement about his relationship with Keeler. Prime Minister Harold Macmillan said that he had no option but to accept his resignation, adding, 'This is a great tragedy for you, your family and your friends.'

Profumo, who was married to the actress Valerie Hobson, had first met Keeler at a pool party in July 1961 at Cliveden, the beautiful Buckinghamshire home owned by Lord Astor. The host was party-loving London osteopath Stephen Ward, whose list of high-profile clients included Lord Astor, Winston Churchill, Ava Gardener and Frank Sinatra. Lord Astor allowed him the use of a cottage on the Cliveden estate, and at the party he introduced 46-year-old Profumo to 19-year-old Christine Keeler

TOPLESS SHOWGIRL

Ward had a penchant for pretty young women from lower-income backgrounds, whom he introduced to high society. Keeler worked as a topless showgirl at a cabaret club in London's Soho, where she met fellow dancer, Mandy Rice-Davies. It was here that they met Stephen Ward who introduced them to his world of racy parties and celebrity friends.

Both girls got a lot of attention at the Cliveden party, where other guests included Yevgeni Ivanov, the senior naval attaché at the Soviet Embassy. Profumo's first sight of Keeler was as she stepped naked from the pool. Before leaving he asked for her telephone number, which she gave him, and they embarked on an affair. But what he didn't know was that she was also in a relationship with Ivanov.

Rumours about the affair began to circulate because it compromised national security. It was the height of the Cold War and the country was still reeling from the revelations that intelligence officers Guy Burgess and Donald Maclean were Soviet spies. As War Secretary, Profumo would be privy to the most sensitive and secret information regarding the security of the country. What if Keeler was passing on secrets told to her by Profumo to Ivanov?

After MI5 learned of the liaison, Profumo ended the affair but by the time he had, Westminster was buzzing with gossip and word had reached the newspapers.

HOUSE OF COMMONS SHOCK

Profumo sought to distance himself from the Cliveden set but on the evening of 20 March 1963,

the whispers turned into direct confrontations when the Labour MP Barbara Castle stood up in the House of Commons and asked whether the Secretary of State for War had been involved with Christine Keeler.

In the House the following day, Profumo declared that there had been 'no impropriety whatsoever' in his relationship with Keeler. He continued to deny anything improper but events were already spiralling out of control. The previous December a petty criminal and jealous lover of Keeler's went after her and fired shots outside Ward's flat in London, where she had been visiting with Mandy Rice-Davies.

Stephen Ward faced a trial for living off immoral earnings, and newspapers ran lurid stories about a world of decadence and orgies.

FAMOUS RIPOSTE

While giving evidence at Ward's trial, Rice-Davies made what was to become a famous riposte to the prosecuting counsel's statement that Lord Astor denied an affair with her or had even met her. She replied, 'Well, he would, wouldn't he?'

On 5 June 1963, Profumo decided to confess. In his letter

of resignation from Parliament he expressed 'deep remorse' at the embarrassment he had caused his colleagues and his constituents.

Stephen Ward was prosecuted for living off immoral earnings. On the last day of his trial, he killed himself with an overdose of sleeping tablets.

The scandal rocked the Conservative government and was instrumental in the party's defeat by Labour in the 1964 election.

A few days after his resignation, Profumo had arrived at the door of a charitable settlement for the deprived in the East End of London called Toynbee Hall, and asked whether there was anything he could do to help.

He began by cleaning and washing dishes, eventually becoming its chairman and then president. In the last 40 years of his life he was a tireless worker for charity at Toynbee and in 1975 his selfless work was officially recognised when he was appointed CBE on the advice of the Labour Prime Minister Harold Wilson. •

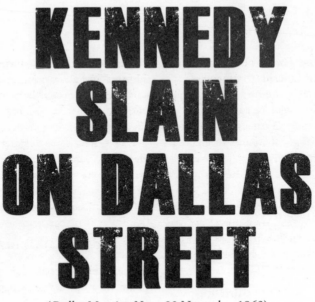

KENNEDY
SLAIN
ON DALLAS
STREET

(*Dallas Morning News*, 23 November 1963)

SHORTLY AFTER NOON on 22 November 1963, President John F. Kennedy was assassinated as he rode in a motorcade through Dealey Plaza in downtown Dallas, Texas.

The incident was captured on news footage and shown around the world with many barely able to believe their eyes.

The charismatic Kennedy had been preparing his campaign for the next presidential election and was touring Texas to meet and greet the people.

On the morning of 22 November, the presidential party flew from Carswell Air Force Base to Dallas and were greeted on their arrival by a crowd of well-wishers.

The First Lady, Jacqueline Kennedy, dressed in pink, was handed a bouquet of red roses, which she took with her to the waiting limousine – an open-topped Lincoln Continental.

Texas Governor John Connally and his wife, Nellie, were already seated in the car as the Kennedys entered and sat behind them. Vice President Lyndon Johnson and his wife occupied another car in the motorcade.

The procession left the airport and travelled along a ten-mile route to the Trade Mart where the President was scheduled to speak at a luncheon.

SUDDEN GUNFIRE

People lined the route, cheering and waving as the motorcade passed by, and the Kennedys happily waved back. But then all hell broke loose as gunfire suddenly reverberated in the plaza and the President slumped to one side, falling into Jacqueline's arms. He had been shot in the neck and in the head.

Governor Connally was hit in the back, probably by one of the bullets that had passed through the President. Witnesses said that three shots were fired from the window of a building called the Texas School Book Depository.

The security forces leapt into action and all the passengers were told to keep their heads down as the cars sped to Parkland Memorial Hospital just a few minutes away.

Police and Secret Service agents rushed into the School Book Depository building and recovered a rifle with a telescopic sight but the assassin had fled. However, a witness gave police a description of a man he had seen leaving a building a few minutes earlier.

POLICEMAN SHOT DEAD

Patrolman J. D. Tippitt, 38, driving alone in a squad car, stopped to question a man who he thought fitted the description but as he got out of his car, the man shot him dead with a revolver.

The gunman fled and entered a cinema a few blocks away but the cashier phoned police saying that there was a man there who looked suspicious and constantly changed seats.

Police entered the cinema, the lights went up and the killer rose from his seat and aimed his revolver at one police man and pulled the trigger – but the weapon failed to fire.

The police arrested him. His name was Lee Harvey Oswald, a 24-year-old recently hired employee at the Texas School Book Depository.

Meanwhile, the President and Governor Connally were operated on at the Parkland Memorial Hospital. Connally was saved but nothing could be done for the President. A Catholic priest was summoned to administer the last rites, and at 1:00pm John F. Kennedy was pronounced dead.

Vice President Lyndon Johnson was sworn in as the new U.S. leader and on Sunday morning, 24 November, households across the country were glued to their TV sets to catch a glimpse of Oswald being transferred from police headquarters to the county jail. Suddenly a man aimed a pistol and fired at point-blank range. The assailant was identified as Jack

Ruby, a local nightclub owner. Oswald died two hours later at Parkland Hospital.

The Warren Report, commissioned to investigate the President's death, concluded he had been killed by shots fired by Lee Harvey Oswald from the Texas School Book Depository building. But conspiracy theories have abounded ever since. Was Oswald a hired hitman and, if so, who hired him? And did Jack Ruby kill Oswald in order to silence him?

Many books and documentaries have been made, aiming to shine more light on the truth behind the assassination. The tragic incident continues to intrigue and fascinate successive generations. •

3,000 FANS GREET BRITISH BEATLES

(*New York Times*, 8 February, 1964)

'**B**EATLEMANIA', which had swept Britain and Europe, surged across the Atlantic after the 'Fab Four' made their first U.S. visit on 7 February 1964.

Their Pan Am plane touched down just after 1.00pm local time at New York's Kennedy Airport to a scene of hysteria as 3,000 fans screamed in excitement, crowding the ground, balconies and roof of the terminal.

When the plane door opened and George Harrison appeared, the exhilaration was a wall of sound. Harrison was followed out by John Lennon, Paul McCartney and Ringo Starr – all looking like they couldn't quite believe what they were seeing and hearing.

Home-made placards were held aloft beseeching them, 'I love you, please stay'. The crowd chanted 'We Want the Beatles' as the mop-haired, be-suited lads from Liverpool made their way down the steps.

POLICE DRAFTED IN

Around 200 photographers and reporters were there to record this momentous event, bigger than any visit by a royal or head of state. And more than 100 policemen were drafted in to keep things under control.

The Beatles' schedule included three appearances on America's biggest variety TV show of the time, *The Ed Sullivan Show*, plus a handful of concert dates. But first they were ushered into the airport for their first U.S. press conference. Such was the noise and commotion that they could barely hear the questions shouted at them.

IRREVERENT HUMOUR

McCartney commented, 'We've never seen a reception like this. It's fantastic.' And Lennon showed some of their typical cheeky, irreverent humour when asked what the appeal of their music was. 'If we knew, we'd form another group and be managers,' he replied.

America had been anticipating their arrival for a few months after reports came through of this musical phenomenon from across the Atlantic.

Time and *Newsweek* were among the first U.S. publications to take notice of the 'Beatlemania' craze and ran articles in mid-November 1963, after the Beatles had the honour of performing before the Queen Mother at the Royal Variety Show in London.

Lennon had got a big laugh from the audience at the prestigious royal event when he had remarked, 'For our last number I'd like to ask for your help. Will the people in the cheaper seats clap your hands, and the rest of you, if you'll just rattle your jewellery.'

In October 1963, Ed Sullivan and his wife were in London, stuck at Heathrow Airport, because of the chaos surrounding a Beatles arrival from Sweden. When he discovered the cause of the delay he took note.

In November and December, 'Beatlemania' began to make short news reports on U.S. TV, and when their single, 'I Want to Hold Your Hand', was first played on radio there by disc jockey Carroll James at Washington's WWDC on 17 December, it shot to the top of the U.S. charts.

On the morning of their impending arrival at Kennedy airport, radio stations were stoking the mounting excitement amongst America's youth by playing Beatles songs.

TV RECORD BREAKERS

Their first performance on the *The Ed Sullivan Show* on 9 February would go down in history as one of the most-watched shows of all time, reaching a record-breaking audience of 73 million.

They performed the songs 'All My Loving', 'Till There Was You', 'She Loves You', 'I Saw Her Standing There' and 'I Want To Hold Your Hand'.

They appeared twice more on the show in subsequent weeks and by the time they left for home, America had been charmed.

The Beatles were the first British band to break into the American market and became an integral part of pop music and popular culture around the world. •

U.S. FORCES OUT OF VIETNAM;
HANOI FREES THE LAST P.O.W.

(*New York Times*, 29 March 1973)

THE LAST OF THE U.S. troops finally left Vietnam on 29 March 1973, after a long, tiring and bloody conflict, which failed in its objective and made America determined never to repeat the same mistakes again.

American involvement in Vietnam began in the 1950s after communist forces in the north of the country, led by nationalist Ho Chi Minh, successfully defeated the colonial power of France in 1954.

During this Cold War period, America's foreign policy in Asia revolved around the 'domino theory' that if one country fell to communism then surrounding countries would also fall. And so they had sent aid to France and the south Vietnamese, but after the defeat the country was split into communist north and pro-American south.

The split was to cause much suffering as plans eventually to unify the country never materialised. The communists killed thousands of landowners in the north and their farming policies lead to extensive famine. And in the south, the corrupt Saigon government of Ngo Dinh Diem ruthlessly crushed any opposition, killing tens of thousands.

Diem's regime sparked a guerrilla resistance movement of communists in the south known as the Vietcong, who were supported and supplied by communists in the north via a route known as the Ho Chi Minh Trail. This led to an increased involvement by the U.S.

Diem was killed in a coup in 1963 by dissident military officers and eventually General Nguyễn Văn Thiệu took control.

OPERATION ROLLING THUNDER

Following an attack by the North Vietnamese Army (NVA) in August 1964, when they torpedoed a U.S. destroyer in the Gulf of Tonkin, the U.S. launched aerial strikes on the enemy's naval bases. And in February 1965, with the South Vietnamese Army struggling against the Vietcong, the U.S. launched Operation Rolling Thunder, a sustained bombing campaign against targets in North Vietnam.

This was followed in July by the deployment of 100,000 U.S. soldiers. Australia, New Zealand, Korea, the Philippines and Thailand also contributed troops.

But the Vietcong guerrillas proved to be very effective in their tactics. They made good use of jungle cover, which led to the U.S. army spraying a toxic solution called Agent Orange over the jungle, as well as napalm to burn through the thick foliage. And Vietcong guerrillas were often difficult to distinguish from civilians. Even women and children were used to set booby traps. Troops became demoralised trying to fight an enemy they could seldom identify.

By the end of 1967, there were 485,000 U.S. soldiers in Vietnam and they were sustaining a high rate of casualties. Back home, a general feeling of pointlessness and horrific pictures of napalm victims in news footage led to a groundswell of protest about U.S. involvement.

In addition, a concentrated movement by the NVA and Vietcong, known as the Tet Offensive, caught the Americans off guard when they attacked 36 provincial capitals and five major cities, including Saigon, where they penetrated the U.S. embassy compound. They were eventually beaten back but the offensive showed that the enemy was still strong and capable, and any thoughts of U.S. nearing victory quickly receded.

NIXON ELECTED PRESIDENT

Political support for President Johnson waned despite his calling for peace talks. Richard Nixon was elected President in November 1968 and sought to extricate U.S. troops without losing face. The following June, U.S. troops began training and equipping the South Vietnamese Army to be able to look after themselves, and over the next three years more than 500,000 U.S. solders returned home.

Ho Chi Minh died in 1969, but his successor Le Duan continued to fight. A peace deal was finally negotiated in January in which U.S. forces would leave and South Vietnam would have the right to determine its own future. But peace was short-lived after the last U.S. troops left with both the south and north accusing each other of breaking the terms of the truce.

In early March 1975, the NVA mounted an invasion of the south. As they approached Saigon, Thiệu fled to Taiwan and, on 30 April, the tanks rolled in. Thousands of south Vietnamese left the country, fearing reprisals.

Saigon was renamed Ho Chi Minh City on 2 July 1976. Vietnam was reunited as a communist country, the Socialist Republic of Vietnam. •

4 CHILDREN DIE, 160 MISSING IN S. WALES HORROR

(*South Wales Echo*, 21 October 1966)

IT WAS ONE OF THE most poignant of British disasters that caused the small Welsh mining village of Aberfan to be evermore associated with the tragic incident that occurred on 21 October 1966.

At 9.15am of that morning a waste tip of coal began to slide down the mountainside to the village of Aberfan, near Merthyr Tydfil, in South Wales. It was sunny on the higher ground but fog had enveloped the valley and so visibility below was poor.

The tipping gang up the mountain had seen the slide start, but could not raise the alarm because their telephone cable had been repeatedly stolen. But it was later accepted that it would have been too late to escape the impending disaster even if a call had been made.

FARM COTTAGE DESTROYED

Down in the village, nobody saw anything, but everybody heard the rumbling noise getting louder and louder. The waste first destroyed a farm cottage in its path, killing all the occupants, and gained momentum as it headed towards Pantglas Junior School, just below. The children had just returned to their classes after singing 'All Things Bright and Beautiful' at their assembly.

There was little time to move and children and teachers were mostly 'frozen' where they were as the waste hit the school with devastating consequences. After demolishing the school and around 20 houses, the slide came to a rest. A total of 144 people were killed in the Aberfan Disaster, 116 of them school children.

When news of the incident spread, people were so horrified that many rushed there to try to help rescue those trapped. But nobody was rescued alive after 11 on that day and it was nearly a week before all the bodies were recovered.

LOCAL WORRIES ABOUT TIP

At a subsequent enquiry into the incident it was revealed that there had long been local worries over the stability of the tip. The Chairman of the National Coal Board (NCB) claimed that the disaster had been unforeseeable and that the tip moved due to springs that no one had known about surfacing beneath the giant mound of waste.

In fact, concerns had been raised up to three years before about the amount of spoil being dumped on the hillside above the school and the springs were marked on various maps dating back to before the NCB began dumping there. Local villagers remembered playing there when they were young, long before the NCB began dumping operations.

The NCB blamed abnormally high levels of rainfall for causing the coal waste to move, but the enquiry established that there had previously been several minor slips and that a range of NCB personnel, from those working in the tipping gangs to senior management, had known that the tip was not stable.

The Inquiry of Tribunal found that the NCB was wholly to blame for the disaster and should pay compensation for loss and personal injuries. They were ordered to pay grieving families just £500 per child. The report stated, 'The Aberfan Disaster is a terrifying tale of bungling ineptitude by many men charged with tasks for which they were totally unfitted, of failure to heed clear warnings, and of total lack of direction from above. Not villains but decent men, led astray by foolishness or by ignorance or by both in combination, are responsible for what happened at Aberfan.'

NEW REGULATIONS IMPOSED

The enquiry found that there was no legislation in place for dealing with the safety of tips. In future all tips should be treated as civil-engineering structures and that managers and surveyors should as soon as possible be made aware of the rudiments of soil mechanics and ground-water conditions. Provision should be made for regular inspection of all tips by qualified persons

In the wake of the tragedy major changes were made in the way mine waste was managed across Wales and the rest of the U.K. And Aberfan was to become enshrined as an enduring memory of the tragic loss of innocent young lives. •

MAN WITH A NEW HEART

(*Cape Argus*, 6 December 1967)

CHRISTIAAN BARNARD performed the first human-to-human heart transplant, on 3 December 1967, in Cape Town, South Africa.

For the first few days the patient was reported to be doing well but, sadly, died 18 days later. However, the operation had been successfully carried out and hundreds more heart transplants were to take place all over the world following this medical achievement.

The idea of replacing a heart with another one had fascinated medics, as well as science-fiction writers, for years.

In Moscow during the 1930s and 1950s, Vladimir Demikhov had transplanted a heart into another animal and had managed, rather bizarrely, to graft a second head onto a dog.

HEART TRANSPLANT DOG

In America, fellow transplant pioneers, Norman Shumway and Dick Lower, succeeded in bringing a dog's heart back to life after it had been stopped and stored in saline for one hour. It led to them performing their first successful canine heart transplant. The dog lived for eight days before tissue rejection set in.

Christiaan Barnard, a director of surgical research at Cape Town

University's medical school in South Africa, had become fascinated by this work. His attention had turned towards heart surgery while studying at Minnesota Medical School. Later, he visited Demikhov in Moscow and, on his return to Cape Town, he too grafted a second head onto a dog.

Shumway had been one of his contemporaries at Minnesota, and Barnard closely followed his progress. Barnard was soon able to replace diseased heart valves with artificial ones.

By September 1967, advances in a new anti-rejection drug in kidney transplants encouraged Shumway to announce his intention, once he had the right donor, to perform a human heart transplant.

'WE ARE READY ...'

Meanwhile, Barnard was eager to beat Shumway in the race. After performing his first kidney transplant, he stated, 'The machinery of the transplant team had functioned perfectly. We are ready to undertake a heart transplant.'

On 14 September 1967, a grocer named Louis Washanksy had been admitted to Groote Schuur

Hospital in Cape Town with diabetes and incurable heart disease. Velva Schrire, Groote Schuur's chief cardiologist, recommended him as a potential heart transplant recipient. Barnard then awaited a suitable donor.

On 2 December, 25-year-old Denise Ann Darvall was involved in a fatal car crash. She was admitted to Groote Schuur Hospital and declared brain dead. After her blood type was found to be compatible with Washkansky's, her father gave his permission for the doctors to use her heart for the transplant.

Mr Washkansky had just an 80 per cent chance of surviving the operation but without it he faced certain death.

WASHKANSKY'S HEART REMOVED

The donor heart was removed and kept working via mechanical means while Washkansky's heart was also removed and the process of suturing and cauterising veins and arteries began.

With the new heart beating strongly inside Washkansky, a wide-eyed Barnard looked at his team and said in Afrikaans 'Dit gaan werk! [It's going to work!]'

Thirty hours after the operation, Washkansky was able to speak, but remained in critical condition.

He lived 18 days after the operation before dying of double pneumonia attributed to his suppressed immune system. Despite the setback, the transplanted heart had functioned normally until his death.

Barnard's success turned him into a celebrity but the operation caused controversy on ethical grounds. Nevertheless, over 100 heart transplants were performed around the world in 1968.

In the 1970s, the development of better anti-rejection drugs made transplantation more viable. Dr Barnard continued to perform heart transplant operations, and by the late 1970s many of his patients were living up to five years with their new hearts. •

MARTIN KING SHOT TO DEATH

(*Daily News*, 5 April 1968)

THE AMERICAN civil rights leader, Dr Martin Luther King, Jr., was shot dead by a single bullet to the neck as he stood on a hotel balcony in Memphis.

An inspiring orator, he had encouraged black people to rebel against injustice by peaceful means but his violent death led to rioting on the streets and accusations of government or FBI involvement in the shooting.

Born in Atlanta, Georgia, on 15 January 1929, King came from a family of ministers. While studying at a theological seminary he learned about Mahatma Gandhi's non-violent civil disobedience campaign that he used successfully against British rule in India. King became convinced that the same methods could be employed by blacks in their civil rights struggle in America.

After his ordination, King took a doctoral degree at Boston University and married Coretta Scott, with whom he was to have four children. In 1955, he became pastor of the Dexter Avenue Baptist Church in Montgomery, Alabama, and it was here that he became actively involved in civil rights.

ROSA PARKS ARRESTED

On 1 December 1955, a 42-year-old black woman named Rosa Parks was arrested after she refused to give up her seat on a bus to a white man, as was expected. This caused anger amongst the black community and King was at the forefront of a campaign to end such inequality. It grew into a mass boycott of buses by black people, which lost the transport companies revenue and received world-wide publicity. During this time, King was amongst many who were arrested and his house was fire-bombed. The boycott lasted for several months until it ended in victory.

His non-violent strategy was the blueprint for similar protests across America's southern states, which included sit-ins that eventually ended segregation in restaurants, public parks, swimming pools, theatres, museums and on beaches.

In 1957, King founded the Southern Christian Leadership Conference to rally his fellow Negro ministers throughout the South and he led several peaceful protest marches.

DREAMS OF FREEDOM

He was a stirring and inspiring speaker with a soulful, lyrical voice, using biblical references and talking of dreams of freedom to great effect in rallying speeches across the country, increasingly becoming the figurehead of the civil rights movement.

He made one of his most famous speeches to a huge crowd that had marched to Washington for 'jobs and freedom' on 28 August 1963. He was the last speaker and captivated his audience with poetic words such as, 'I have a dream that one day on the red hills of Georgia, the sons of former slaves and the sons of former slave owners will be able to sit down together at the table of brotherhood.'

Meanwhile, President John F. Kennedy's Civil Rights bill was still being debated in Congress when he was assassinated in November 1963. The new President, Lyndon Baines Johnson, kept up the pressure and was able to get the legislation passed in 1964, making racial discrimination in public places illegal and requiring employers to provide equal employment opportunities.

In 1964, Martin Luther King was awarded the Nobel Peace Prize. He continued to campaign against the war in Vietnam, which provided him with enemies in high places in America. He also encouraged black people and white people living in poverty to unite and to strive for a fairer society.

SANITATION WORKERS STRIKE

In early 1968, he supported sanitation workers in Memphis –

90 per cent of whom were black – who sere striking against poor working conditions.

Meanwhile, Senator Robert F. Kennedy was running for President, promoting similar policies to King – pro-civil rights and anti-war and -poverty.

On 3 April 1968, King made another famous speech at the Mason Temple, in Memphis, in which he said, 'I would like to live a long life – longevity has its place. But I'm not concerned about that now. I just want to do God's will. And he's allowed me to go up to the mountain. And I've looked over, and I've seen the promised land. I may not get there with you. But I want you to know tonight, that we, as a people, will get to the promised land.'

After the meeting, King and his party went to the Lorraine Motel. The following day he was shot dead on the balcony.

His death was followed by rioting in 125 cities. A convicted armed robber named James Earl Ray, who had escaped from prison, was arrested at London's Heathrow Airport and extradited to America. He pleaded guilty to having shot Martin Luther King and was given a prison sentence of ninety-nine years.

Ray was to later say that he had been framed as part of an FBI plot to kill King, and there are certainly those who believe that he was not acting alone. However, his appeals for a new trial were rejected and he died in prison in 1998. •

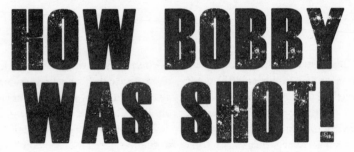

HOW BOBBY WAS SHOT!

(*Chicago Daily News*, 5 June 1968)

FIVE YEARS AFTER his brother, President John F. Kennedy, was assassinated in Dallas, 42-year-old Robert F. Kennedy was shot dead during his campaign to become U.S. President.

Robert Kennedy had put himself forward to be the Democratic Party's nominee for President on 16 March 1968.

After winning the primary in California, he gave a victory speech to his campaign supporters in the Ambassador Hotel's Embassy Room in Los Angeles at around 12.10am on 5 June 1968. In euphoric mood, he was then taken on a shortcut through the hotel kitchen en route to a press conference in the Colonial Room. As he walked along a corridor he took time to shake hands with hotel workers when a gunman rushed towards him repeatedly firing a revolver.

Kennedy was struck three times at point-blank range from behind. One bullet struck behind his right ear from about an inch (2.54 cm) away, the others near his right armpit and in the back of the neck.

SCENE OF CHAOS

Pandemonium broke out. The *Chicago Daily News*'s west coast bureau chief, who was there at the time, described how there was 'screaming and angry confusion' all around him. There was added chaos as reporters and photographers, hearing the shots and screams, rushed in to see what was going on.

As Kennedy slumped to the floor, his security man, Bill Barry, punched the gunman in the face and others forced him against a table and disarmed him before he was led away by police.

After a while, Robert Kennedy's wife, Ethel, who was also at the hotel, was brought in to be with her husband. She knelt beside him and, still conscious, he appeared to recognise her before he was taken away on a stretcher and rushed for emergency treatment at the Central Receiving Hospital. He lost consciousness and medics tried to revive him before he was taken several blocks away to the Hospital of the Good Samaritan for surgery, about 30 minutes later.

GUNMAN IDENTIFIED

As the shocking news of the incident spread, the gunman was identified as 24-year-old Jordanian immigrant Sirhan Bishara Sirhan.

Although Sirhan was born in Jerusalem, he was a Jordanian citizen and emigrated to America with his family when he was 12 years old. They lived for a short time in New York before moving to California.

Sirhan's motive for the murder was patriotic, but his loyalty lay with the Arab nations in the Middle East, not with his adopted country of America. He claimed that he had decided Robert Kennedy must die because the presidential candidate had promised that, as soon as he was elected, he would send fifty fighter aircraft to Israel to help the Israelis defend their borders.

This promise, coupled with the fact that Kennedy had supported Israel during the Six-Day War in which so many Arabs had died, had made Sirhan decide to kill Kennedy on the anniversary of the start of that conflict.

That evening, at 5.30pm, Kennedy's press aide, Frank Mankiewicz, announced that Kennedy's doctors were 'concerned over his continuing failure to show improvement' and that his condition remained 'extremely critical as to life'.

He was pronounced dead at 1.44 am on 6 June, nearly 26 hours after the shooting.

SENTENCED TO DEATH

Sirhan was convicted of murder and sentenced to death but this was commuted to life imprisonment after the California Supreme Court invalidated all pending death sentences imposed in California prior to 1972.

Like his elder brother before him, Robert Kennedy's death has been the focus for 'conspiracy theories' ranging from there having been more than one gunman to CIA involvement.

His body lay in repose at St Patrick's Cathedral in New York for two days before a funeral mass was held on 8 June. He is buried near his brother, John, at Arlington National Cemetery. •

MAN ON THE MOON

AND THE MESSAGE FROM EARTH: WE'RE BREATHING AGAIN!

(*Daily Mirror*, 21 July 1969)

HAVING STATED HIS intention in a 1961 speech to land a man on the moon by the end of the decade, U.S. President John F. Kennedy's goal was achieved when Neil Armstrong became the first man on the lunar surface on 20 July 1969.

Millions around the world watched enthralled as the space craft, *Columbia*, was launched from Cape Kennedy, Florida, four days earlier. On board were Commander Neil Armstrong, lunar module pilot, Edwin 'Buzz' Aldrin, and command module pilot, Michael Collins.

After establishing an orbit around the Moon, Armstrong and Aldrin crawled into the lunar module *Eagle*, which detached from the command module and was rocket boosted towards the

Moon as *Columbia* continued its orbital flight.

TENSION IN HOUSTON

Back on Earth in Mission Control at Houston, Texas, tension was building. And as the *Eagle* neared the Moon's surface, some of the shirt-sleeved flight controllers sat or stood silently at their consoles, barely able to breathe.

There was a moment of panic at 300 feet above the Moon's

surface when Armstrong saw that they were heading towards a large crater and he took over semi-manual control, guiding the *Eagle* to safety.

Armstrong was later to recall, 'The auto-targeting was taking us right into a football-field-sized crater, with a large number of big boulders and rocks.'

Finding a more level place to land, Armstrong lowered the module down onto the rocky surface in the Sea of Tranquility. There was a dramatic pause before he radioed back, 'Houston, Tranquility Base here. The *Eagle* has landed.'

'WE ARE BREATHING AGAIN.'

A relieved Mission Control replied, 'Roger, Tranquility. We copy you on the ground. You got a bunch of guys about to turn blue. We are breathing again. Thanks a lot.'

About six-and-a-half hours later, Armstrong opened the landing craft's hatch, made his way down a ladder and set foot on the Moon, making the comment, 'That's one small step for a man; one giant leap for mankind.'

He described the surface as being like powdered charcoal and he left deep footprints as he walked around. After 19 minutes he was joined by Aldrin. They set up a television camera and jumped across the landscape to test movement, also collecting dust and rock samples. In a patriotic moment, which must have been galling for their Soviet space rivals, they planted the Stars and Stripes flag into the soil and unveiled a plaque bearing President Nixon's signature and an inscription reading, 'Here men from the planet Earth first set foot upon the Moon July 1969 AD. We came in peace for all mankind.'

HISTORIC PHONE CALL

The astronauts then heard from Nixon, who said, 'This certainly has to be the most historic telephone call ever made.' He congratulated them on their achievement, adding with a flourish, 'For one priceless moment in the whole history of man all the people on this Earth are truly one; one in their pride in what you have done and one in our prayers that you will return safely to Earth.'

Armstrong and Aldrin spent 21 hours on the Moon. After rejoining the *Columbia* mothership, all three astronauts returned to Earth on 24 July, splashing down in the Pacific Ocean.

Their leap into the unknown had scientists wondering whether they might have picked up an alien infection and so they were held in quarantine for almost three weeks before being released, waving and cheering to the crowds.

That evening they were guests of honour at a State Dinner in Los Angeles. And they went on to visit 25 countries in a celebratory tour.

The lessons learned paved the way for further space exploration and visits to the moon in years to come, although the dangers inherent in sending men into space would lead to several tragedies and near misses along the way. •

UP, UP AND AWAY!

(*Daily Mirror*, 3 March 1969)

THE SUPERSONIC AIRLINER, Concorde, made a faultless maiden flight on 2 March 1969.

The *Daily Mirror* splashed with a huge front-page picture of the striking-looking, delta-winged and droop-nosed plane taking off from Toulouse.

Strong winds meant the test flight was in doubt for much of the day. But as it sped down the runway, there was a spontaneous burst of applause from watching reporters and cameramen when the wheels lifted off the ground. Just 27 minutes later, it landed.

The French pilot, André Turcat, commented after landing, 'Finally the big bird flies, and I can say now that it flies pretty well.'

The test flight was a gentle one, reaching 10,000 feet (3,000m), with a top speed of 300mph (480kph), although it was capable of 1,300mph (2,080kph).

It was hoped to start flying commercially in 1973 with an eye to transatlantic flights, cutting the flying time between London and New York from 7 hours 40 minutes to 3 hours 25 minutes.

CONCORDE PARTNERSHIP

Concorde was the result of separate British and French projects to create the world's first passenger-carrying commercial supersonic aircraft. To keep the cost of the enterprise down they joined in 1962 to develop the plane together. The partnership led to the British Aircraft Corporation (later British Aerospace) and Aerospatiale of France building 20 Concordes.

They were powered by four Olympus 593 engines, built jointly by Rolls-Royce and the French Snecma company.

Following its successful maiden flight, Concorde embarked on a sales and demonstration tour on 4 September 1971, completing its first supersonic flight on 1 October 1969. But it had a bumpy ride when it came to securing deals.

Heavy fuel consumption – 5,638 imperial gallons every hour – threatened to make it uneconomical for airlines to buy such a plane at a time when fuel prices had shot up.

SUPERSONIC SERVICE

British Airways bought five Concordes on 28 June 1972, but it wouldn't be until four years later, on 21 January 1976, that it commenced commercial supersonic travel from London to Bahrain, and Air France from Paris to Rio.

On 22 November 1977, Concorde made its first London–New York commercial flight.

It began operating daily flights to America out of London Heathrow and Paris's Charles de Gaulle airports, cruising at around 1350 mph at an altitude of up to 60,000 feet (11 miles). The flight took around three-and-a-half hours

– less than half the normal flying time for other jets.

It set a record time in February 1996 between New York and London taking just 2 hours 52 minutes and 59 seconds.

But the hopes and dreams for Concorde never really took off when it came to demand from paying customers. Then, on 25 July 2000, its previously unblemished safety record was scarred by a horrific crash shortly after taking off from Charles de Gaulle Airport, which killed 113 people.

The fleet of just 20 was grounded while a full investigation took place and £17m was spent on safety improvements. Flights resumed in November 2001 but public confidence had been lost. In April 2003, British Airways and Air France announced the plane would be retired due to falling passenger revenue and rising maintenance costs.

FINAL FLIGHT

Concorde's final commercial flight was on 24 October 2003 from New York to London.

The aircraft was such a symbol of national pride that thousands of spectators turned up at Heathrow to witness Concorde's decommissioning.

At a 2003 auction of Concorde memorabilia and artefacts at the Olympia exhibition centre in Kensington, London , pieces being sold ranged from seats and cutlery to cockpit instruments and even a nose cone.

A number of enthusiasts are working to raise the vast amounts of money required to restore the most complete surviving Concordes in order that the aircraft might one day take to the air again, if only for display flights at air shows.

Despite a number of alternative supersonic airliner design studies having been proposed since the demise of Concorde, including one that could carry 300 passengers at more than five times the speed of sound and reach Sydney from Brussels in less than five hours, the age of supersonic travel is currently suspended. •

THREE SPACEMEN ARE HOME SAFE

SPLASHDOWN FOUR MILES FROM SHIP

(*Houston Chronicle*, 18 April 1970)

IT WAS TO BE THE third lunar-landing attempt in the U.S. space programme, as Apollo 13 was launched on 11 April 1970.

On board were astronauts Commander James A. Lovell, command module pilot John L. 'Jack' Swigert and Fred W. Haise as lunar module pilot. And, despite a few glitches, things were going so well that, after two days, Joe Kerwin, the capsule communicator back at Mission Control, remarked, 'The spacecraft is in real good shape as far as we are concerned. We're bored to tears down here.'

But he wasn't going to be bored for long, as the mission became the most fraught to date after an explosion on board left the astronauts fighting for survival.

COMFORTABLY WEIGHTLESS

Nine hours later, as the crew finished a 49-minute TV broadcast showing how comfortably they lived and worked in weightlessness, a relaxed Lovell said, 'This is the crew of Apollo 13 wishing everybody there a nice evening, and we're just about ready to close out our inspection of *Aquarius* [the lunar module] and get back for a pleasant evening in *Odyssey* [the command module]. Good night.'

Minutes later, oxygen tank No. 2 blew up in the service module, which damaged No.1 tank, and reserves of oxygen began to leak into space. It left the command module without power or air and short of water. They were about 200,000 miles from Earth.

In words that have since become famous, Swigert calmly reported, 'Houston, we have a problem.'

MISSION ABORTED

The mission was aborted and it was decided that the only chance they had of saving the crew was to shut down the command module entirely to conserve batteries for re-entry into the earth's atmosphere later. In the meantime they would move into the lunar module, which had a separate oxygen supply, and use its engines (that had been intended for the moon landing) to set them on a course that would take them home. But it was fraught with problems. A module equipped for two men for two days would have to sustain three men for four.

It was estimated that the crew would run out of water after about five hours of normal usage, so they rationed themselves to six ounces each per day, which was about one fifth of normal intake, and drank extra fruit juices.

Sleep was almost impossible because of the cold. When the electrical systems were turned off, the spacecraft lost an important source of heat. The temperature dropped to 38 degrees Fahrenheit and condensation formed on all the walls.

SIGHS OF RELIEF

Four hours before landing, the crew jettisoned the damaged service module and, two and a half hours prior to re-entry, it was time to see if the plan of firing the command module back to life would work. When the systems came back on there were sighs of relief on board, in Mission Control and from people following the drama around the world.

An hour later, the lunar module was also jettisoned and Mission Control felt it was losing an 'old friend' as it radioed, 'Farewell, *Aquarius*, and we thank you.'

Re-entry to the earth's atmosphere on an Apollo mission

routinely involved four minutes of radio blackout as a layer of ionized air built up around the command module, blocking communications. Not knowing whether *Odyssey* had sustained any damage, the radio blackout brought heightened tension to Mission Control, especially when the silence continued for 33 seconds longer than expected.

But the radio crackled back into life as the command module parachuted out of the sky to splash down safely in the South Pacific on 17 April at 1.07pm local time (7.07pm BST).

Within minutes, helicopters were on the scene and the astronauts were airlifted onto the recovery ship, *Iwo Jima*, where they spent the night before flying to Samoa to be reunited with their families. •

THE DEATH STEPS

(Daily Record, 4 January 1971)

THE TRADITIONAL New Year derby football match between historic rivals Celtic and Rangers on 2 January 1971 had failed to live up to expectations on the pitch.

On a drizzly, overcast day, the mist hanging over the Rangers ground, Ibrox Stadium in Glasgow, summed up the mood of the spectators who were feeling downcast at having had little to cheer about during a rather dull game.

But just a minute from the end, it suddenly flared into life when Jimmy Johnstone scored for Celtic. A huge roar went up and that seemed to be that... until Rangers equalised during injury time with a goal by Colin Stein. This time it was the Rangers fans who roared their approval and, as the final whistle blew, they turned to make their way out of the stadium with spirits considerably lifted.

Those heading towards the Stairway 13 exit felt the usual squeeze of a crowd leaving the stadium. They had become used to it at big games. But as they made their way down the steep steps, people felt themselves being pushed forward and many were lifted off their feet. The momentum of the crowd made it impossible to stop or push back and the crush squeezed the life out of those trapped.

CLAMBERING TO SAFETY

Some managed to clamber over the fences at the sides of the stairs. Others helped push people over to safety.

Meanwhile, the players had left the pitch, unaware of what was happening. The Celtic team were on their coach within 15 minutes of the end when their manager, Jock Stein, heard that there had been an accident. He told the driver to take the players back to their home ground while he and his backroom staff returned to help out.

Ambulances were called and bodies were lined along the side of the pitch. Others were taken to the changing rooms.

Sixty-six people died, a third of whom were aged 16 or under, and 145 were injured. It was the worst tragedy in the history of Scottish football and united both rival teams and their supporters in their grief.

PUBLIC ENQUIRY

Initial reports suggested the tragedy had been caused by supporters rushing back up the stairs after the late Rangers' goal and colliding with those leaving the stadium. But a public inquiry discounted this theory, concluding that the deaths were the result of the crush of fans pouring down Stairway 13.

A police officer told the inquiry that bodies were 'like a pack of cards that had been thrown forward, the lower ones were horizontal, others were semi-upright and the last were upright'. Many had died standing up.

THE DEATH STEPS

The Glasgow-based *Daily Record* carried a huge picture of the stairway, alongside which they ran the grim, stark headline, 'The Death Steps'.

Rangers' manager Willie Waddell vowed to make Ibrox a stadium that was both safe and comfortable. He championed a major redevelopment of the ground, visiting Dortmund where the brand new, state-of-the-art Westfalenstadion (now called Signal Iduna Park) was opened in time for the 1974 World Cup matches.

Once plans for redesigning, refurbishing and rebuilding Ibrox were approved, the work took three years and led to most of the stadium being replaced by all-seater grandstands. The capacity of the ground was reduced to 44,000 (80,000 had attended the match on the day of the disaster) and the new Ibrox was opened with a special 'Old Firm' derby match on 19 September 1981.

Sadly, there were several more disasters to come at football stadia across Britain before all of the major grounds were given a proper safety overhaul. •

13 KILLED AS PARATROOPS BREAK RIOT

(*Guardian*, 31 January 1972)

THE SHOOTING OF 13 civilians by British troops in the Bogside area of Northern Ireland on 30 January 1972 became known as 'Bloody Sunday' and was greatly to increase hostilities for decades to come.

In the late 1960s, the Catholic minority in Northern Ireland began organising protest marches against what they saw as unfair treatment by the Protestant-dominated authorities over issues such as housing allocation and voting rights.

Increasingly violent clashes between the two sides and the Royal Ulster Constabulary led to the British Army moving in to try to restore order. But the fighting escalated, and the troops came under repeated attack from bottle- and brick-throwing Catholics. Clashes between the Army and the

Provisional IRA led to deaths and injuries on both sides.

In the face of this, internment without trial was introduced and all marches and parades banned. However, the Northern Ireland Civil Rights Association organised a protest march in Derry to protest against internment and the authorities decided to allow the march to proceed in the nationalist areas of the city, but to stop it from reaching Guildhall Square, as intended, in order to prevent a clash.

The 1st Battalion, the Parachute Regiment was drafted in to Derry to arrest any unruly rioters on the day of the march. Barricades were set up, and the march, consisting of around 10,000 people, was redirected to Free Derry Corner. But a splinter group broke off from the main procession and tried to push back the barricade to get to the Guildhall. They threw heavy stones at the Army, who responded with a water cannon, tear gas and rubber bullets.

VIOLENCE ESCALATES

As the violence escalated, a civil rights organiser began to walk through the crowd, telling them through a megaphone that a meeting was starting at Free Derry Corner.

Shortly after, armoured cars appeared in William Street and roared into Rossville Street, causing several thousand people to run away.

Paratroopers from the 1st Battalion piled out of their vehicles and rushed towards the crowd. Then they opened fire with their rifles. Thirteen civil rights marchers were shot dead and others were wounded. A further person later died from his injuries sustained on the day.

The Army's official explanation for the killings, backed by the Home Secretary the following day in the House of Commons, was that their troops had fired in response to a number of snipers who had opened up on them from nearby buildings.

But there were many witnesses, including journalists, who maintained that the soldiers fired indiscriminately into an unarmed crowd.

PARATROOPERS 'RECKLESS'

In April, an inquiry by Lord Widgery reported that the paratroopers' firing had 'bordered on the reckless'. But it concluded that the soldiers had been fired upon first and some of the victims had handled weapons. The Catholic community rejected these findings, calling it a 'whitewash' and began the long campaign for another inquiry.

It finally came in 1998, under Lord Sackville, and after another long wait of twelve years, the Sackville Report, on 15 June 2010, found that none of those killed or injured were 'posing a threat or causing death or serious injury', despite soldiers' claims; they did not fire in response to attacks or threats; members of the official IRA did fire some shots but paratroopers shot first.

Prime Minister David Cameron made a formal apology on behalf of the United Kingdom, calling the shootings 'unjustified', saying that he found the report 'shocking' and that he was 'deeply sorry.'

In the aftermath of 'Bloody Sunday' there was a resurgence of violent opposition to the British presence in Northern Ireland. Many Catholics, angry and resentful, joined the IRA and other militant groups. And Protestant unionists recruited members into rival organisations such as the Ulster Defence Association and Ulster Volunteer Force.

'The Troubles', as these years of hatred and fighting were labelled, were to result in many more deaths. •

NIXON RESIGNS

(*Washington Post*, 9 August 1974)

IN THE EARLY HOURS of 17 June 1972, five men were arrested for burgling the headquarters of the Democratic Party in the Watergate complex in Washington, after a security guard had contacted the police when he noticed tape covering the latches on several doors in the complex, allowing them to close but remain unlocked.

The incident was to lead to the revelation of corruption and lies at the highest political level and to prosecutions and the eventual resignation of the President of the United States.

The five intruders had with them photographic equipment and bugging devices. Intrigued by the story, two young reporters on the *Washington Post*, Carl Bernstein and Bob Woodward, investigated further.

The following day saw the first of a series of their sensational reports, which revealed that one of the burglars was on the payroll of President Nixon's re-election committee.

SECRET IDENTITY

The two journalists' findings were corroborated by a top ranking official source – a contact of Woodward's that they nicknamed 'Deep Throat'. They agreed to keep his identity a secret, and it wasn't until 2005, 33 years later, that he was revealed to be FBI Director, Mark Felt.

Meanwhile, the FBI stepped up its investigation, and many of their findings found their way into the pages of the *Washington Post*. But despite it becoming clear that the burglars were working for Nixon's re-election team by spying on their rival Democrats in an attempt to sabotage their campaign for the Presidency, Nixon was re-elected by a landslide on 7 November 1972.

He continued to deny any prior knowledge of the burglary or of organising a 'cover-up' operation but, by the summer of 1973, the Watergate Affair – as it had become known – had blown up into a national scandal and was the subject of two official investigations.

NIXON INVOLVED

A White House aide revealed that Nixon was instrumental in being part of the cover-up operation. Then, in July 1973, another aide disclosed that the President recorded all of his phone calls in the Oval Office.

Nixon was ordered to hand over the tapes, but a lengthy legal battle ensued after the White House cited 'executive privilege' that the President is entitled to candid and confidential advice from aides.

But the pressure on him mounted when, in March 1974, the special prosecutor indicted former Attorney General John Mitchell, former aides Haldeman and Ehrlichman, and four other staffers for conspiracy, obstruction of justice and perjury in connection with the Watergate burglary.

The Supreme Court eventually ordered the White House to hand over the tapes to the special prosecutor on 24 July 1974. Three days later, the House Judiciary Committee sensationally recommended the President of the United States be impeached and removed from office.

One of the tapes – dubbed by the press as 'the smoking gun' – showed that, despite his denials, he had played a leading role in the cover-up from the start. Nixon lost what remaining support he had and his closest aides told him he had to resign or face the almost certain prospect of impeachment.

PRESIDENT RESIGNS

On 8 August 1974, Nixon announced his resignation as President in a televised address from the Oval Office in which he still failed to admit his guilt.

'By taking this action,' he said, 'I hope that I will have hastened the start of the process of healing which is so desperately needed in America.'

Following his short speech, he shook hands with his successor, Vice President Gerald Ford, on the White House lawn, clambered into a waiting helicopter with his wife, Pat, and daughters, Julie and Tricia, and flew off.

Gerald Ford was sworn into office on 9 August 1974, declaring, 'Our long national nightmare is over.' One month later, he granted Nixon a full pardon for any offences he might have committed as Present, saving him from possible prosecution. •

KING ELVIS DEAD

(*Sun*, 16 August 1977)

'THE KING OF ROCK 'N' ROLL' was found dead on his bathroom floor at his Graceland home in Memphis, Tennessee, following a heart attack.

For years his health had been deteriorating due to a reliance on prescription drugs and a fondness for junk food. But his sudden death at 42 came as a shock to his millions of fans around the world.

Elvis had changed the face of popular music with his high-energy performances of such songs as 'Hound Dog' and 'Blue Suede Shoes'. The wide range of genres he performed encapsulated, rock 'n' roll, blues, gospel, country and western, pop and ballad.

Born into a poor family, on 8 January 1935, in Tupelo, Mississippi, he was heavily influenced by local gospel choirs. After entering various talent contests, his special quality was

noticed and, under the guidance of his manager, Colonel Tom Parker, he was to become a worldwide icon.

He took the music industry by storm during the fifties with hits like 'Heartbreak Hotel', and 'All Shook Up'. His unique body movements, good looks and gleaming smile had teenage girls going wild. But many of the older generation were appalled by his grinding hip movements which earned him the nickname of 'Elvis the Pelvis'.

A series of network-TV appearances raised his profile, although on some he was only shown from the waist up. But despite the controversy, every TV show he appeared on was a ratings winner. Elvis had brought rock 'n' roll to the masses and the masses loved him.

FILM DEBUT

In November 1956, he made his film debut in *Love Me Tender*, and many similar light-hearted musicals followed throughout the sixties. All were panned by critics but that didn't stop his fans from watching them and they made a healthy box office profit.

While Elvis's movies played all over the world, the King himself never did. Apart from a few appearances in Canada in the 1950s, Elvis never took to the stage outside the United States.

Some say that he was keen to tour abroad. He spent two years in Germany when he was in the army doing national service and enjoyed visiting Paris while he was on leave. He would like to have seen more of Europe, but it was not to be.

There were rumours that Colonel Parker quashed any proposed foreign tour plans because, despite having served in the U.S. Army, Parker was an illegal immigrant (he was born Andreas van Kuijk in Holland) and if he left America, he might not be allowed back. Others believed that there were serious security issues at venues big enough to take the

millions of fans who would want to see their idol.

The films, however, were to be the closest any foreign audience ever got to the King, who kept his feet firmly on U.S. soil.

On 1 May 1967, he married Priscilla Beaulieu with whom he had his only child, Lisa Marie, born a year later. He divorced Priscilla in 1973.

LAS VEGAS ACT

During the 1970s he became a resident act in Las Vegas and then made a series of concert tours. But he was looking far from the sexy, lean and energetic Elvis that had rocked the world. Now he was something of a showbiz caricature with a puffy face, an expanding waistline and wearing white, rhinestone-studded jump suits. In more than one concert he appeared remote, and mumbled and slurred his way through his hits.

On the evening of 16 August 1977, he was scheduled to fly out of Memphis to begin another tour. That afternoon his new girlfriend, Ginger Alden, found him lying out on his bathroom floor.

Attempts to revive him failed, and death was officially pronounced at 3:30pm at Baptist Memorial

Hospital. The official report stated that he died of heart failure.

OPEN CASKET

Thousands gathered to file past Elvis Presley's body, which lay, state-funeral-like in an open casket at Graceland the day after his death. And a huge turn-out of around 80,000 people lined the processional route for his funeral from his home to Forest Hill Cemetery where he was buried next to his mother on Thursday, 18 August.

Following an attempt to steal his body later that month, Elvis and his mother were reburied in Graceland's Meditation Garden.

Graceland was opened to the public in 1982 and it regularly continues to attract over half a million visitors each year.

Within a few days of his death, his last single, 'Way Down', topped the U.S. and U.K. pop charts.

U.S. President Jimmy Carter said of Elvis, 'His music and his personality, fusing the styles of white country and black rhythm and blues, permanently changed the face of American popular culture.' •

TEST TUBE MOTHER HAS GIRL

(*Guardian*, 26 July 1978)

A PICTURE OF A new-born baby, eyes screwed up against the light and yawning, dominated the world's front pages. Not a remarkable picture in itself but the birth of Louise Brown introduced a new era of human reproduction.

She was the world's first 'test tube baby' conceived by in vitro fertilization (IVF).

Her parents, Lesley and John Brown, had been trying to conceive for nine years but without success because of blocked fallopian tubes.

In 1976, Lesley was referred to Oxford-born gynaecologist Dr Patrick Steptoe, who worked at Oldham General Hospital. He recommended that she try a new experimental procedure that would bypass the fallopian tubes.

Steptoe had been experimenting with laparoscopic (or keyhole) surgery in retrieving an egg from an ovary. Meanwhile, Manchester-born biologist Dr Robert Edwards had realised the potential of IVF as a treatment for infertility since the late 1950s and knew from the work of others that it was possible to take an egg from an animal, like a mouse or a rabbit, and fertilise it with sperm in a test tube. He became focused on trying to do the same thing with a human egg.

After reading about Steptoe's work, he contacted him and the two began working together in 1968 to try to accomplish human in vitro fertilization.

After their pioneering work was rejected for funding by the Medical Research Council, they had to find a private benefactor in order to set up their clinic just outside Cambridge.

ETHICAL DEBATE

Their research became the subject of an ethical debate, with several religious leaders and even some scientists calling for it to be stopped. The pair responded by setting up an ethics committee where they worked at their Bourn Hall Clinic.

After more than 100 attempts, which all led to short-lived pregnancies, they eventually found a successful technique. And when the Browns contacted them, they were ready.

Lesley, 32, had a mature egg removed by Steptoe via laparoscopy, and Edwards cultured it in the laboratory where it was fertilized by John's sperm. A few days later a developing embryo was placed by Steptoe into Lesley's uterus.

It was a success. Louise Joy Brown was delivered by planned Caesarean section at Oldham General Hospital at 11.47pm on 25 July 1978. She weighed 5 pounds 12 ounces.

IVF treatment quickly spread around the world, giving hope to infertile couples. Louise Brown's younger sister, Natalie, was also conceived through IVF, four years later, and became the world's fortieth IVF baby.

Louise married nightclub doorman Wesley Mullinder in 2004, with Dr Edwards attending their wedding. Their son, Cameron, conceived naturally, was born on 20 December 2006.

Edwards and Steptoe continued working together at their clinic – the world's first IVF centre – teaching other doctors haw to carry out the procedure. Steptoe died in 1988. Edwards was awarded the Nobel Prize for medicine in 2010.

Millions of babies around the world have since been born by IVF. Edwards and Steptoe's achievements attracted many other researchers to the field of fertility treatment and advances continue to be made on the foundation of their success. •

MRS THATCHER TAKES OVER

(*Daily Telegraph*, 5 May 1979)

MARGARET THATCHER became the first female Prime Minister of Britain and the first woman to be voted into such high office in the western world on 3 May 1979. Her forceful leadership won her as many critics as supporters but she was to remain in place for 11 years, winning three successive general elections.

In January 1975, when the Labour Party was in power, Thatcher challenged Edward Heath for the leadership of the Conservative Party and, on, 4 February she defeated him by 130 votes to 119, to become the first woman leader of a major political party in Britain.

The Labour government at that time faced difficult economic circumstances, with inflation and unemployment soaring. Harold Wilson was succeeded as PM by Jim Callaghan but, despite Callaghan denying there was any crisis, things failed to improve. Public spending cuts caused unease amongst the workforce, which led to strikes during a period known as the 'Winter of Discontent'.

Callaghan lost a vote of confidence and announced that there would be a general election on 3 May 1979.

Margaret Thatcher firmly blamed the government for the

Winter of Discontent during her campaigning and said that the Conservatives would cut income tax, reduce public expenditure, make it easier for people to buy their own homes and curb the power of the unions.

CONSERVATIVE VICTORY

The Conservatives soared ahead in the public opinion polls and won the election with 43.9 per cent of the vote.

On the steps of Number 10 Downing Street, she quoted St Francis of Assisi: 'Where there is discord, may we bring harmony. Where there is error, may we bring truth. Where there is doubt, may we bring faith. And where there is despair, may we bring hope.'

Britain's new Prime Minister was born in Grantham, Lincolnshire, in 1925. The daughter of local grocer and Mayor of Grantham, Alfred Roberts, Margaret Hilda Roberts and her older sister, Muriel, were brought up in a flat above one of their father's two shops.

Having won a grammar school scholarship to Kesteven and Grantham Girls' School, Margaret went on to study chemistry at Oxford in 1943, graduating with a Second Class Honours degree in 1947.

Like her father, she became heavily involved in politics and was President of the Oxford University Conservative Association. She worked as a research chemist for a time before marrying businessman Denis Thatcher and balancing a budding political career with studying law. She qualified as a barrister in 1953.

Also in 1953, Thatcher gave birth to twins, Carol and Mark, politics taking a back seat for a short while before she returned to the fray as the Conservative candidate for Finchley. Having previously stood in Dartford and Orpington, she was at last successful in the 1959 election. Her career progressed through various ministerial positions until she became leader of the Conservative party in 1975.

In the years following the Conservative election victory in 1977, Thatcher changed the face of the country by curbing union powers, privatising nationalised industries and allowing people to buy their council houses. She became an influential world figure who developed good relationships with U.S. President Ronald Reagan and President of the Soviet Union, Mikhail Gorbachev. The Soviet media nicknamed her the 'Iron Lady'.

In Europe, she fought strongly to renegotiate Britain's contribution to the European Economic budget. But as unemployment rose above 3 million in the early 1980s, she lost a great deal of support. However, that was to change with the Falkland Islands conflict in 1982, which united Britain as the country fought and succeeded in removing Argentine troops from the British overseas territory.

POLL TAX RIOTS

In 1984, she faced down the miners in their bitter strike and she attracted widespread anger and resentment for the introduction of the Community Charge – commonly known as the Poll Tax – which caused public demonstrations and several riots throughout the country in the late eighties and early nineties.

But it was her strident Euro-sceptic stance that was to lead to her downfall as she fell out with several of her party colleagues.

Thatcher was challenged for the leadership of the Conservative Party by backbench MP Sir Anthony Meyer in the 1989 leadership election. She overwhelmingly defeated him but, with public opinion polls now showing that Labour had established a considerable lead over the Conservatives, the rumblings of discontent amongst the party grew ever louder.

On 1 November 1990, Geoffrey Howe, the last remaining member of Thatcher's original 1979 Cabinet, resigned from his position as Deputy Prime Minister over her refusal to agree to a timetable for Britain to join the European single currency. It was a fatal blow for Thatcher.

The following day, Michael Heseltine mounted a challenge for the leadership of the Conservative Party. Opinion polls had indicated that he would give the Conservatives a national lead over Labour and many within Thatcher's Cabinet thought he would win but, true to her 'Iron Lady' persona, she was not going without a fight.

She won the first round of the contest but the majority was not enough to prevent a second round. After consultation with her Cabinet colleagues she announced her resignation on 22 November and was replaced by her Chancellor, John Major.

To the surprise of many, the Iron Lady shed a tear as she left Downing Street. Soon afterwards, she entered the House of Lords as Baroness Thatcher of Kesteven.

Major oversaw an upturn in Conservative support in the 17 months leading up to the 1992 general election, which they won before being toppled by Labour in 1997 when Tony Blair became Prime Minister. •

BOMB ON BOAT KILLS LORD MOUNTBATTEN

(*Irish Times*, 28 August 1979)

LORD LOUIS MOUNTBATTEN, second cousin to Queen Elizabeth II and beloved great uncle of Prince Charles, was murdered, along with three others, by a bomb planted by the Provisional Irish Republican Army while he was on a boating holiday in Sligo, Republic of Ireland.

One of the earl's grandsons, Nicholas, 14, and Paul Maxwell, 15, a local lad employed as crew member, also died in the explosion. Nicholas's grandmother, the Dowager Lady Brabourne, 82, was fatally injured and died the following day.

Nicolas's twin, Timothy, his mother Lady Brabourne (the earl's daughter, Patricia) and her husband, Lord Brabourne, were injured.

Just hours later, 18 British Army soldiers were killed in an ambush in Warrenpoint, Northern Ireland.

Mountbatten, 79, was enjoying his annual summer family holiday in his castle at Mullaghmore, County Sligo, and on the morning of 27 August 1979, they boarded a boat, *Shadow V*, in the harbour, intent on spending the day fishing.

BOMB ON BOARD

But overnight, IRA member Thomas McMahon had planted a 50lb (23kg) bomb aboard and when the boat was 100 yards out, en route for Donegal Bay, it was detonated.

The boat was blown to pieces, and all seven occupants were hurled into the water. Nearby fishermen rushed to the rescue.

McMahon, 31, had been detained in the area by police on suspicion of driving a stolen car two hours before the bomb went off.

Five hours later, 18 British soldiers were killed in two bomb attacks near their base in Warrenpoint, County Down. The first bomb, weighing half a ton, was planted under some hay on a flatbed lorry beside a dual carriageway on the Irish border 44 miles (71km) from Belfast.

It exploded, killing six soldiers of the 2nd Battalion, Parachute Regiment as they travelled past in a lorry at the end of a three-vehicle army convoy.

SECOND BOMB DETONATED

Members of the Queen's Own Highlanders flew in by helicopter from their base at Bessbrook, County Armagh, to take the injured away to hospital. But just after the helicopter took off, a second bomb weighing 800lbs (363kg), concealed in milk pails near the gate house, was detonated, thirty minutes after the first, killing twelve more soldiers – ten from the Parachute Regiment and two Highlanders.

The following day, the IRA admitted carrying out the attacks on both the Mountbatten family and the soldiers. McMahon was convicted of the three boat murders.

Lord Mountbatten was given a state funeral. A navy man, through and through, in World War II he had commanded the destroyer, HMS *Kelly*, which was sunk by German dive bombers off Crete with the loss of 130 men.

In 1942, Winston Churchill appointed him Chief of Combined Operations, and then Supreme Allied Commander for Southeast Asia the following year, conducting the campaign against Japan that led to the recapture of Burma.

VICEROY OF INDIA

In March 1947, he became last viceroy of India with a mandate to oversee the British withdrawal, leading to partition and the independence of two nations, India and Pakistan.

He was created Viscount in 1946 and Earl Mountbatten of Burma the following year. He was later made First Sea Lord and Chief of Defence Staff.

Mountbatten had enjoyed a close relationship with Prince Charles and had been responsible for bringing together the Prince's parents. He had arranged the visit of King George VI and Queen Elizabeth to Dartmouth Royal Naval College on 22 July 1939, making sure to include the young Princesses, Elizabeth and Margaret, in the invitation. They were looked after by his naval cadet nephew, Prince Philip of Greece.

His close association with the Royal Family made him a much-loved and admired figure amongst its members. ●

POLAND YIELDS ON INDEPENDENT TRADE UNIONS

(*Washington Post*, 31 August 1980)

THE UNLIKELY FIGURE of a stocky, working-class shipyard electrician was the impetus behind the collapse of the communist regime in Poland. He was later to find himself as President of a new government.

The summer of 1980 saw a series of strikes in Poland in protest at soaring prices and the slow growth of wages. There was anger and resentment towards the government and, in the Lenin shipyard in Gdansk, activist Lech Walesa encouraged workers to strike to underline their demand for higher pay and for the establishment of independent trade unions.

The workers were reluctant to do so at first, fearing reprisals, until popular crane operator Anna Walentynowicz was sacked for her militant behaviour.

This was the nudge they needed to declare a strike on 14 August 1980. A committee was set up and, with a new-found sense of unity and power, they set out 21 demands, including the right to have an independent trade union and the right to strike. They also secured Walentinowicz's swift reinstatement and she joined the committee.

The strike damaged both the economy and the government's image. It became international news and it was finally agreed to recognise the right of independent trades unions – the first in any Eastern Bloc country – with a deal signed on 31 August.

The following month, Solidarity was formed, the workers' first independent trade union, led by Walesa, who was hailed as a working-class hero. It was seen as the start of a movement for political freedom and improved economic conditions in Poland but things soon took a grim turn once more.

MARTIAL LAW

On 11 February 1981, General Wojciech Jaruzelski was appointed Prime Minister, replacing Stanislaw Kania. And on 12 December he imposed martial law.

Solidarity was banned, its leaders were arrested overnight and more than 2,000 workers were dismissed. Full censorship and a six-day working week were re-imposed and the coal mines were placed under military control.

The dream seemed to have ended abruptly. By late 1982, the government was confident that control had been restored and Walesa was released from prison but prevented from returning to work as he was investigated for alleged tax irregularities. He was also barred from speaking at rallies. But he remained an influential figure and in 1983 was awarded the Nobel Peace Prize.

Meanwhile, the economy was in a bigger mess than ever. The government increased food prices by 40 per cent in February 1988 and, in May, Walesa organised a series of strikes in protest. As support for Solidarity swelled once more, a second wave of widespread strikes took place in August. The government then decided that it was time to negotiate properly with Solidarity.

SOLIDARITY LEGALISED

The trade union was formally legalised again in 1989 and allowed to campaign as a political party in the upcoming elections on 4 June. Meanwhile, the government announced a new economic plan and promised more freedom.

Solidarity had little financial support with which to campaign and polls predicted the party would be defeated in Poland's first free elections. But in the event they won a landslide victory.

The party changed its name to the Citizens' Parliamentary Club, with Walesa as President and, on 25 August, Tadeusz Mazowiecki, a Catholic newspaper editor and Solidarity adviser, became the first non-communist Prime Minister in Eastern Europe for nearly 40 years.

Walesa credited Pope John Paul II for giving him, and others, the confidence to rise up against communism. As Polish Archbishop Karol Wojtyla, he was elected Pope in 1978, and the following year returned to his homeland where millions turned out to greet him.

Walesa met the Pope on several occasions and was amongst many Poles inspired by him. 'Before his pontificate, the world was divided into blocs. Nobody knew how to get rid of communism,' said Walesa. 'In Warsaw in 1979, he simply said, "Do not be afraid."'

After five years as President, Walesa was defeated in an election by the ex-communist minister Aleksander Kwasniewski, in 1995. •

JOHN LENNON SHOT DEAD

(*Liverpool Echo*, 9 December 1980)

'**J**OHN LENNON, leader of the legendary Liverpool pop group, The Beatles, was shot dead in New York today by a crazed gunman,' reported the *Liverpool Echo* – the newspaper that had tracked the rise of their local lads throughout the 'Beatlemania' years of the 1960s.

The shocking event was mirrored in newspaper headlines around the world. The killing had occurred at 11.00pm local time in New York, outside Lennon's apartment in the Dakota Building in Manhattan. The news reached the U.K. in the early hours of the following day.

Lennon, 40, was shot four times in the back by Mark Chapman. He was rushed to St Luke's Roosevelt Hospital Center in a police car but was pronounced dead on arrival.

After years out of the limelight, Lennon had returned to recording again and had recently released an album called *Double Fantasy* and a single, 'Starting Over'.

Earlier in the fateful day of his murder, he and his wife, Yoko, walked out of their apartment to a waiting car, which was to take them to a recording studio. He was used to being stopped by fans asking for his autograph and so happily obliged 25-year-old Mark

Chapman in signing his copy of *Double Fantasy*.

Chapman, a security guard from Honolulu, Hawaii, had a history of depression and mental illness. He was obsessed with Lennon but had come to hate him for what he saw as his hypocrisy in preaching about peace and the simple things in life whilst enjoying a wealthy and privileged lifestyle.

DEMONS TOLD HIM TO KILL

Chapman was also obsessed with J. D. Salinger's classic novel, *The Catcher in the Rye*, and strongly identified with the protagonist, disillusioned teenager Holden Caulfield. Chapman later claimed to hear 'demons' in his head telling him to kill John Lennon.

In late October 1980, he bought a gun and flew to New York with the intention of doing so but changed his mind after watching the film *Ordinary People*, in which Timothy Hutton plays a suicidal teenager caught up in the midst of a dysfunctional family.

Coming to his senses, he went home but, on 6 December, he returned to New York, with murder once more on his mind.

He began staking out the Dakota Building but, after Lennon graciously gave him his autograph, Chapman was taken aback by his kindness and then tried to battle against the demons in his head.

When the Lennons returned from the recording studio at 10.50pm, Chapman shot him in the back four times. Bleeding profusely, Lennon staggered up five steps to the Dakota reception area and fell to the floor. The concierge rushed to his aid and called the police. Outside, the doorman shook the gun from Chapman's hand and kicked it across the pavement but Chapman was not struggling. He calmly sat down and started reading his favourite book, *The Catcher in the Rye*.

FIRST NEWS REPORTS

The first report of Lennon's death was during the middle of a televised football game on ABC's *Monday Night Football*, which was announced by sports broadcaster Howard Cosell.

Chapman pleaded guilty to murdering John Lennon and received a life prison sentence. He later explained that, as well as hearing demons in his head, he also thought that killing Lennon would make him as famous as his hero.

The death of John Lennon brought worldwide mourning. On 14 December, millions responded to Yoko's request for a ten-minute silence in memory of her husband. Over 200,000 people gathered in Central Park, across the road from the Dakota Building, where John and Yoko liked to walk.

And in Lennon's home town of Liverpool, around 30,000 sang his songs, such as 'Give Peace a Chance' and 'Imagine' in front of St George's Hall.

Sales of his records, both as a solo artist and as a Beatle, soared.

A 2.5-acre memorial was set up in Central Park called 'Strawberry Fields', after the title of the classic Beatles song. Annually, on Lennon's birthday, 9 October, and on the anniversary of his death, visitors and fans from all over the globe flock to Strawberry Fields to pay homage to him. •

POPE SHOT

(*New York Post*, 14 May 1981)

ST PETER'S SQUARE in Vatican City was full of cheering and waving people with smiles on their faces as Pope John Paul II slowly made his way through the crowd, standing in a specially designed open jeep so that he could see and be seen.

He was reaching out to touch some people – especially the children – when shots rang out and he slumped into his seat, blood staining his white cassock.

Two bullets had struck him in the stomach, another in his right arm and a fourth hit his little finger.

There was a moment's shocked silence before people started screaming and crying and the Pope was driven at speed to the confines of the Vatican, with police and bodyguards running along, keeping the crowd back.

The Pope was taken by ambulance to nearby Gemelli Hospital, with Vatican Radio appealing to the world to pray for his survival.

Police instantly arrested the gunman who had fired a 9mm pistol some 15 feet away at around 5.15pm local time on 13 May 1981. He turned out to be a Turkish citizen named Mehmet Ali Agca, a former member of a far-right terrorist group known as the Grey Wolves, who had been jailed for the killing of a Turkish human rights journalist named Abdi Ipecki in February 1979 but had escaped and was on the run.

As he was led away from St Peter's Square he kept repeating, 'I couldn't care less about life.' In his pocket was found a note on which he had written, 'I, Agca, have killed the Pope so that the world may know of the thousands of victims of imperialism.'

EMERGENCY OPERATION

Meanwhile, surgeons performed a five-hour operation on the Pope. None of the shots had damaged vital organs and his life was not in danger.

The hospital director, Professor Luigi Candia, said one bullet passed through the Pope's body and a section of his intestine was removed.

In St Peter's Square, hundreds had remained behind, praying and singing hymns for the Pope's survival. When loudspeakers from Vatican Radio announced that he was out of danger, a cheer went up and they started to drift home.

The Pope came out of hospital two weeks later. He was re-admitted on 21 June with a lung infection but eventually made a full recovery.

Mehmet Ali Agca was sentenced to life imprisonment in July 1981 for the shooting. There were all sorts of conspiracy theories with a central core that Agca was not working alone. One of the most prominent suggestions was that

he was working for the Soviet and Bulgarian intelligence services who were angered by the Pope's support of the Solidarity movement in his home country of Poland and its commitment to shaking off the Communist regime imposed by Moscow.

POPE FORGIVES GUNMAN

Two days after Christmas, in 1983, John Paul II visited Agca in prison and forgave him. They spoke privately for 20 minutes and the Pope later said, 'What we talked about will have to remain a secret between him and me. I spoke to him as a brother whom I have pardoned and who has my complete trust.'

In June 2000, with the agreement of the Pope, Agca was released after serving 19 years.

On his return to Turkey he was re-arrested and compelled to serve the rest of his sentence for the killing of Abdi Ipekç in 1979. He was released in January 2006.

The Pope, who had always in his life felt a strong attachment to Mary, Mother of Christ, later credited her for saving his life.

'Could I forget that the event in St Peter's Square took place on the day and at the hour when the first appearance of the Mother of Christ to the poor little peasants has been remembered for over sixty years at Fátima, Portugal? For in everything that happened to me on that very day, I felt that extraordinary motherly protection and care, which turned out to be stronger than the deadly bullet.' •

RARE CANCER SEEN IN 41 HOMOSEXUALS

(*New York Times*, 3 July 1981)

THE *NEW YORK TIMES* was the first newspaper to carry a report on a disease that alerted the world to the biggest health concern in generations.

The article told how doctors in New York and California had diagnosed amongst homosexual men 41 cases of 'a rare and often rapidly fatal form of cancer'. The disease usually first appeared in violet-coloured spots on the body and eight of the victims died less than 24 months after the diagnosis was made. 'The cause of the outbreak is unknown.'

Doctors had been perplexed by the increase in the incidence of Pneumocystis carinii pneumonia (PCP) and of the cancer, Kaposi's sarcoma (KS). Neither were new diseases but the outbreak amongst young male homosexuals prompted an investigation.

When the Centers for Disease Control and Prevention in America reported the new outbreak they called it GRID (Gay-Related Immune Deficiency). But as it spread into the heterosexual community and particularly amongst drug addicts and people who received blood transfusions, it became known as AIDS (Acquired Immune Deficiency Syndrome).

RESEARCH CONTROVERSY

Throughout 1982 there was a marked rise of cases in Europe and Africa. Medical scientists around the world investigated what was causing the disease and there was to be some controversy over who identified the virus first.

In France, Dr Montagnier and Professor Barre-Sinoussi of the Institut Pasteur in Paris, isolated a retrovirus that they felt was related to AIDS, in 1983. But a year later, scientist, Dr Robert Gallo of the National Cancer Institute, National Institutes of Health, in Bethesda, USA, also isolated a retrovirus that he too claimed was responsible for AIDS.

It was later discovered that both had discovered the same thing, which an international committee of scientists later named Human Immunodeficiency Virus (HIV).

IMMUNE SYSTEM DESTROYED

The virus infects and gradually destroys the cells in the body that combat infections, leaving the body susceptible to diseases. Without treatment, the immune system will become too weak and a person with HIV may develop diseases that their body will be unable to fight. They are then said to have AIDS.

The most common ways in which HIV is spreading throughout the world is through sexual contact. Other ways include the sharing of needles and by transmission from infected mothers to their babies during pregnancy, birth or breastfeeding.

Tens of millions of people have died of AIDS around the world since 1981 and many more are infected with HIV – the majority living in Africa.

The death of movie star Rock Hudson from AIDS, in 1985, brought the disease even more into the public conscience.

Scientists continue to look for a cure but advancement in new drug therapies means that they are now able to stop HIV from reproducing and allow immune systems to recover. •

GOTCHA

(*The Sun*, 4 May 1982)

THIS MEMORABLE and controversial headline in the *Sun* newspaper during the Falklands conflict inspired nationalist pride in some and appalled others for being jingoistic and insensitive.

It referred to the sinking of the Argentine cruiser *Belgrano*, on 2 May 1982, by torpedoes fired from the Royal Navy submarine, HMS *Conqueror*, resulting in the loss of 323 crew. Controversially, the *Belgrano* was outside of the 200-mile exclusion zone that Britain had imposed around the Falkland Islands and reportedly heading away.

But in a television interview with David Frost, British Prime Minister Margaret Thatcher claimed that the ship was sunk because 'it was a danger to our boys'.

The conflict between the two countries began with an incident on 19 March of that year which took Britain and the Falkland Islanders by surprise. A group of scrap-metal workmen, accompanied by a military presence, landed on South Georgia Island and hoisted an Argentine flag. Within a week the Argentine leadership decided to invade and reclaim the islands.

There had been long historical friction and resentment over possession of the islands, which lie some 290 miles to the east of Argentina. The Argentines had settled there in 1826 but a British expedition took control of the territory in 1832 and declared sovereignty the following year.

ARGENTINE ECONOMIC CRISIS

But Argentina, which has always referred to the Falklands as the Malvinas, has never accepted British sovereignty and has yearned for their 'return'. During the 1970s and 1980s, Argentina was facing an economic crisis and there was widespread dissatisfaction with the military junta that had been governing the country since 1976.

In a move to restore popularity, President General Leopoldo Galtieri, hatched an ambitious plan to reclaim the Malvinas. After the raising of the flag on one of the smaller islands, South Georgia, Argentina sent a fleet of ships and troops to the Falklands. When they were spotted near South Georgia, British Foreign Secretary Lord Carrington said that a diplomatic solution was being pursued.

ENEMY INVASION

On 2 April, the Argentine troops landed on the Falklands and easily brushed aside the resistance from a small base of Royal Marines before Governor Rex Hunt ordered them to surrender. There were enthusiastic public celebrations in Buenos Aires.

Many people in Britain had either never heard of the Falklands or had no idea where they were or that they were a U.K. colony, 8,000 miles away in the South Atlantic. The Argentine junta believed that Britain would not physically defend

the islands but, to their surprise, on 5 April, Britain sent a task force of 28,000 troops and over 100 ships to fight for them.

On 22 April, the task force arrived in the area and a 200-mile exclusion zone was set around the islands. Three days later, a small commando force re-took South Georgia, and Margaret Thatcher called on the nation to 'Rejoice at that news.'

On 1 May, British planes attacked enemy planes at Port Stanley airport. And in the days that followed, several ships were sunk and planes shot down on both sides. These included the sinking of the British destroyer HMS *Sheffield*, on 4 May, with the loss of 20 men, two days after the hit on the *Belgrano*.

The first major British troop landing was at San Carlos on 21 May and, from here, attacks were made on Goose Green and the capital of Port Stanley.

FALKLANDS D-DAY

On 28 May, British troops defeated the Argentines at Darwin and Goose Green and 1,400 prisoners were taken. Now the British were free to march towards Port Stanley, which was liberated on 14 June when

Commander Mario Menendez signed a surrender document – 9,800 Argentine troops laid down their arms. Britain formally declared an end to hostilities on 20 June.

Although sometimes referred to as the 'Falklands War', neither side officially declared war and so it is regarded as a 'conflict' in which 649 Argentines died and 255 British, plus three Falkland Islanders.

The praise and respect that Argentina's military junta had sought and briefly gained quickly evaporated. By contrast, Margaret Thatcher received a tremendous boost in popularity as the British celebrated their victory in regaining a remote colonial island of which many in Britain had previously been completely unaware. •

MURDER

(*Daily Mirror*, 13 October 1984)

A single emotive word, unusually placed vertically down the right-hand side of the front page of the *Daily Mirror*, alongside the subdued face of Margaret Thatcher and the wrecked façade of a hotel.

But Mrs Thatcher, then British Prime Minister, was one of the lucky ones who escaped with her life when an IRA bomb exploded in the Brighton Grand Hotel on 12 October 1984. Inside were members of the Conservative Party, the British government of the time, who had gathered to attend their annual party conference in the seaside town.

The bomb had been planted three weeks earlier by IRA 'operative' Patrick Magee, who checked into Room 629 under the alias of 'Roy Walsh' and concealed the device beneath the bath. He used the timer from a TV video recorder to prime it.

It detonated at 2.54am, crumbling the front of the hotel on the top floors and sending masonry crashing down below. Most were sleeping but Mrs Thatcher was still working in her first-floor suite, finishing off her speech for the next day's conference. At 2.50am, her private secretary entered to hand her an official paper to read and five minutes later there was an explosion.

'I KNEW IT WAS A BOMB'

She was later to recall, 'A loud thud shook the room. There were a few seconds' silence and then there was a second, slightly different noise, in fact created by falling masonry. I knew immediately that it was a bomb.

'Denis [her husband] put his head around the bedroom door, saw that I was alright and went back inside to dress.'

Mrs Thatcher and her husband were entirely unscathed but there were obvious fears that there would be further attempts on the Prime Minister's life. Once Mrs Thatcher had changed her clothes, her security team whisked them both out of the hotel's rear exit, taking them directly to the safety of Brighton police station. They were then transferred to Sussex Police Headquarters at Lewes, spending the rest of the night there.

Back in Brighton, guests who were evacuated or had fled from the hotel mingled in confusion on the sea front, most wearing only their dressing gowns and pyjamas, some shocked, dazed and coated in plaster dust. Five people died in the blast and 34 were injured. The fatal casualties were Anthony Berry, MP, Roberta Wakeham (wife of Chief Whip John Wakeham) north-west area chairman Eric Taylor, Muriel Maclean (wife of Scottish chairman Donald Maclean) and Jeanne Shattock (wife of the president of the south-west Conservative association).

NORMAN TEBBIT RESCUED

Memorable TV news pictures showed Norman Tebbit, President of the Board of Trade, being dug out of the rubble and, in considerable pain, being carried away on a stretcher. His wife, Margaret, who had been trapped alongside him, was paralysed by her injuries.

Within a few hours of the blast, the IRA issued a statement claiming responsibility, adding, 'Mrs Thatcher will now realise that Britain cannot occupy our country and torture our prisoners and shoot our people in their own streets and get away with it. Today we were unlucky, but remember we only have to be lucky once. You will have to be lucky always.'

At Mrs Thatcher's insistence, the conference opened on schedule, less than seven hours after the blast, at 9.30am. She walked onto the conference platform to a thunderous ovation.

'THIS ATTACK HAS FAILED'

In her redrafted speech she briefly alluded to the incident before carrying on as normal. 'The bomb attack was an attempt not only to disrupt and terminate our conference, it was an attempt to cripple Her Majesty's democratically elected government,' she said. 'That is the scale of the outage in which we have all shared. And the fact that we are gathered here now, shocked but composed and determined, is a sign not only that this attack has failed, but that all attempts to destroy democracy by terrorism will fail.'

Magee was caught after finger prints on a hotel registration card assigned to 'Roy Walsh' were a match for those of Magee's in police records, dating back to a time when he was arrested as a juvenile. He was sentenced to 35 years but released in 1999, under the Good Friday Agreement. •

WORLDBEATER!

(*Sunday Mirror*, 14 July 1985)

The world's biggest rock festival, organised by Bob Geldof to raise money for famine relief in Africa, kicked off at Wembley Stadium with a rousing rendition of 'Rocking All Over the World' by Status Quo.

Described as the 'Woodstock of the eighties', Live Aid was a truly global event and a remarkable achievement of organisation from arranging and sound checking the acts to satellite link ups and screening the event around the world.

At the same time as the Wembley concert was taking place, another was happening in the U.S., at the JFK stadium in Philadelphia. There were also small ones in African countries and the likes of Austria, Norway and Yugoslavia.

An estimated final figure for the money raised from the concerts was £150 million. Astonishingly, for such a mammoth undertaking, Live Aid was arranged in just ten weeks.

The background to the event can be traced back to some harrowing BBC TV news footage of the African famine. Geldof, lead singer of the Boomtown Rats, was so moved by what he saw that he got together with singer Midge Ure from Ultravox to help raise money for the crisis. They co-wrote a song called 'Do They Know It's Christmas' and persuaded some top British singers of the day to record it, under the name of Band Aid. They included Boy George, Sting, George Michael and Paul Young.

CHART TOPPER

The song was rush-released, on 7 December 1984, in time for the Christmas market and became the fastest-selling single ever, hitting the top of the charts both in the U.K. and U.S. and raising £8m. It inspired American pop artists to do something similar. with a song written by

Michael Jackson and Lionel Ritchie called 'We Are The World' featuring both singers on vocals, along with the likes of Bob Dylan, Cyndi Lauper, Harry Belafonte, Paul Simon and Bruce Springsteen.

Surprised by how much money was raised, Geldof set his sights on a huge, famine-busting concert. And in his typical forthright, determined style, played a hands-on part in gathering together the cream of the British music industry to perform and in persuading TV networks around the world to screen the event.

On 13 July 1985, a packed crowd of 72,000 at Wembley Stadium heard a voice over the sound system announce, 'It's twelve noon in London, seven AM in Philadelphia, and around the world it's time for Live Aid.'

ROYAL PATRONS

With Prince Charles and Princess Diana in attendance, music 'royalty' included Queen, David Bowie, Elton John, Dire Straits, George Michael and Paul McCartney. U2 cemented their reputation as stadium rockers and Freddie Mercury had the audience in the palm of his hand. David Bowie

and Mick Jagger sang together in an amusing video performance of 'Dancing in the Street'.

In Philadelphia the 100,000-strong stadium crowd watched top acts including Madonna, The Who, Crosby, Stills and Nash, Hall and Oates, and Led Zeppelin. Mick Jagger and Tina Turner duetted on 'It's Only Rock and Roll' and Phil Collins managed to play at both concerts by crossing the Atlantic on Concorde.

GELDOF SWEARS ON AIR

Throughout the day there was footage of the African famine and televised appeals for people to donate money. At one point, Bob Geldof was so passionate that he swore on live television. News footage of starving African children accompanied by the haunting song 'Drive' by Cars, contained the emotive line, 'You can't go on, thinking there's nothing wrong.'

Prior to the concert, there had been strong rumours that it would feature a reunion of surviving Beatles, Paul, John and Ringo. But this proved to be no more than a rumour. Headline act Paul McCartney sang on his own at the piano but, unfortunately the first two minutes of 'Let It Be' were beset by microphone problems.

After a long day in which 52 acts had been on and off stage at Wembley, David Bowie led the ensemble in the final song, 'Do They Know It's Christmas'. Six hours later, the U.S. concert ended with 'We Are the World'.

The mammoth event was televised to over 1.5 billion people in 160 countries and really made individuals feel that they could help change the world. Bob Geldof was given an honorary knighthood in 1986. ●

EXPLOSION STUNS NATION

(*Florida Today*, 29 January 1986)

THE WORST ACCIDENT in the history of the American space programme was watched live on TV by millions around the world in shock and disbelief.

The graceful shuttle, *Challenger*, launched at 11.38am local time on 28 January 1986, on its tenth mission into space.

The crew of seven was led by Commander Dick Scobee, 46, and one of the astronauts had received worldwide publicity as she was chosen to be the first school teacher in space.

Christa McAuliffe, 37, was picked from among 10,000 entries for a competition to find a teacher to be sent into space so as to encourage children across the country to take a keen interest in space and science education and learn from the shuttle. She was due to give two lectures from space, which would be broadcast on TV to schools.

EXPLOSION HORROR

On the day of the launch, children in classrooms across the country were avidly watching with mounting excitement as, after a delay, *Challenger* took to the skies. But just a minute later, the thrilling spectacle turned to horror as the shuttle exploded above Cape Canaveral, Florida.

There was a moment's stunned silence at the airbase where a crowd, including the astronaut's families, had gathered to watch the take-off. Amongst them was Christa McAuliffe's husband, Steve, and her nine- and six-year-old children. The eerie silence was shared by around 1,200 adults and children watching on a giant television screen erected at the New Hampshire school where Christa McAullife taught. People at home around the world watching on TV shared the shock. Nobody was quite sure – or could quite believe – what had happened.

MISSION CONTROL STUNNED

Even Stephen A. Nesbitt of Mission Control took a moment to react. His voice was heard to report that there had been 'a major malfunction'. Shortly after, he added, 'We have no downlink,' referring to the loss of communication with *Challenger*. This was followed by, 'We have a report from the flight dynamics officer that the vehicle has exploded. The flight director confirms that.'

All seven of the crew aboard were killed. That evening, President Ronald Reagan made a televised address to a stunned nation in which he talked of the bravery and inspirational qualities of the astronauts and vowed that the space programme would continue.

'There will be more shuttle flights, more shuttle crews, more volunteers, more teachers… nothing ends here. Our hopes and journeys continue,' he said. He ended, 'We will never forget them, nor the last time we saw them this morning as they prepared for their journey and waved goodbye and slipped the surly bonds of earth to touch the face of God.'

OPERATIONS SUSPENDED

NASA immediately suspended operations of the shuttle indefinitely until the findings of a board of inquiry. The report, when it arrived in May, stated that the accident had been caused by a leak through a faulty seal or 'O-ring' in one of the solid rocket boosters, which had caused the hydrogen fuel to explode.

The flight was the twenty-fifth by the fleet of shuttles since 1981, and NASA had gained confidence at being able to send reusable manned craft into orbit and bring them back again.

The schedule for 1986 was the most ambitious in the history of the shuttle programme with 15 flights planned. But in the wake of the disaster there were no further manned flights until September 1988 when NASA resumed shuttle missions with the launch of *Discovery*.

But tragedy struck once again, on 1 February 2003, when the *Columbia* shuttle disintegrated over Texas as it was attempting re-entry, leaving another seven crew members dead. The heat shield that protects the shuttle from the searing temperatures of re-entry was fatally damaged on lift-off by a piece of insulating foam that broke away from an external fuel tank.

Two years later, President George Bush announced that he would be cancelling the space shuttle programme. •

NUCLEAR NIGHTMARE IS HERE

(Daily Express, 30 April 1986)

THE WORST NUCLEAR power plant explosion that had ever occurred shot radioactive debris up to 1km (3,300ft) into the air and was blown by the wind for hundreds of miles. Yet the Soviet authorities tried to keep it a secret.

In the early hours of 26 April 1986, engineers at the Chernobyl nuclear power station in the Soviet republic of Ukraine were carrying out an electrical power test at reactor number four. They were taking advantage of a planned shutdown of the reactor for routine maintenance but, at 1.24am local time, an uncontrollable power surge occurred, sparking two explosions which destroyed the reactor and sent a plume of more than 50 tons of deadly radioactive material into the air.

It was carried by air currents for miles around with some of it blown as far as Western Europe.

One worker was killed instantly by the explosions and another died a few hours later in hospital as a result of his injuries. A team of 14 firemen arrived minutes later to battle the fires and were later joined by dozens more. All received high doses of radiation.

RADIATION DEATHS

Twenty-eight rescue workers and plant staff would die of acute radiation syndrome in the coming weeks and dozens more suffered radiation burns.

Soviet leader Mikhail Gorbachev who had won praise for his glasnost policy of greater Soviet openness, tried to cover the incident up and it took two days before the authorities confirmed the incident – and that was only after monitoring stations in Sweden, Finland and Norway began reporting sudden high discharges of radioactivity in the atmosphere.

The first sign was when workers arriving at the Forsmark nuclear power station, 60 miles north of Stockholm, set off warnings during a routine radioactivity check. Believing there to be a leak at their own power station, 600 workers were sent home. After similar high radioactive readings at other power plants in Scandinavia, attention focused on the Soviet Union. But when they were contacted, the authorities denied any knowledge of an accident.

ACCIDENT CONFIRMED

The admission, when it came, was low-key. Tucked away on the Soviet news television bulletin on the evening of 28 April, after the farm reports, a statement said, 'An accident has occurred at the Chernobyl nuclear power plant and one of the reactors was damaged. Measures are being taken to eliminate the consequences of the accident. Aid is being given

to those affected. A government commission has been set up.'

To try to contain the fire, Chernobyl's managers pumped water into the reactor core but when this proved unsuccessful they turned to dumping boron carbide and a total of 4,000 tons of lead, sand and clay on the facility via helicopters. By May, an input of nitrogen into the reactor cooled it down.

Subsequent international reports blamed the poor design, a lack of safety culture at the plant and errors by operators.

RADIOACTIVE DEBRIS

Because the reactor was not housed in a reinforced concrete shell, as is standard practice in most countries, it allowed large amounts of radioactive debris to escape.

The building of such a shelter then took place and was completed by October, preventing further leakage from reactor number four and allowing the other reactors to continue producing power.

Estimates of those who died or have been subjected to radiation poisoning from the explosions vary wildly but it has been reported that there were fewer than 50 deaths, mostly workers at the plant, but up to 9,000 could eventually die due to radiation exposure.

Radioactive fallout from the disaster caused a pine forest downwind of Chernobyl to die. Wildlife and livestock across Europe were also badly affected, with unusually high instances of birth defects amongst animals even as far away as Britain, where slaughter restrictions remained in place for years for sheep that may have fed on hillsides contaminated by the fallout.

The city of Pripyat, established mainly to house workers at Chernobyl, had a population of around 50,000 by the time of the disaster. It was completely evacuated and remains a ghost town within the exclusion zone around the nuclear plant.

Further afield, in areas where the fallout cloud is known to have caused some contamination, there were increased numbers of human birth defects and unusually high figures for certain cancers which have been associated with the catastrophe.

Chernobyl continued to produce electricity for another 14 years, until international pressure forced its closure in December 2000. •

HUNDREDS DIE AS JUMBO JET PLUNGES INTO VILLAGE

(*Independent*, 22 December 1988)

A JUMBO JET EXPLODED over Lockerbie, Scotland, killing all 259 passengers and crew aboard and 11 people on the ground.

It turned into a murder investigation when evidence was found of a bomb having been concealed inside a cassette player packed in a suitcase. The incident caused a huge international furore, which rumbled on for 11 years before anyone was brought to trial.

The Pan Am flight 103 from Frankfurt to New York, via London, on 21 December 1988, was carrying a large proportion of Americans – 189 in total – many of whom were students or military personnel looking forward to returning home for Christmas.

EXPLOSION OVER LOCKERBIE

As it cruised at 31,000 above the town of Lockerbie in the Dumfries and Galloway region of south-west Scotland, the quiet normality of life below was to be shattered just after 7.00pm local time when the plane exploded.

A Semtex bomb aboard was activated with a timer, which blew

the plane to pieces. Plane debris and dead bodies fell to the ground, scattering over an area of 845 square miles. The fuel it was carrying caused fireballs that set houses, trees and cars alight. Twenty-one of Lockerbie's houses were completely destroyed and 11 residents died.

An eyewitness remarked, 'There was a terrible explosion and the whole sky lit up. It was virtually raining fire – it was just liquid fire.'

BOMB TIMER TRACED

During the investigation, pieces of a circuit board belonging to the bomb's timer device was traced to its Swiss manufacturer and fragments of clothing that were said to have been inside the suitcase led to a tailor in Malta. Both ultimately led to the identity of a Libyan intelligence officer and head of security for Libyan Arab Airlines (LAA), Abdelbaset Ali Mohmed al-Megrahi. His co-conspirator was named as al-Amin Khalifa Fhimah, the LAA station manager at Luqu airport, Malta.

Investigators claimed that the booby-trapped suitcase had been loaded onto the plane at Frankfurt from an earlier flight from Malta.

Both men were formally charged with murder in November 1991

and a warrant for their arrest was issued. But Libya's leader, Colonel Gaddafi, refused to hand the men over, saying that they would be tried in their own country.

Britain and the U.S. obtained a U.N. Security Council Resolution in January 1992 ordering Libya to surrender the Lockerbie suspects. When the demand was refused a threatened worldwide ban on air travel and arms sales came into effect.

LIBYAN ASSETS FROZEN

A year later, tightened sanctions were imposed, including the freezing of Libyan assets in foreign banks and an embargo on oil industry-related equipment.

It wasn't until 5 April 1999 that Libya finally handed over the accused for trial at a military base called Camp Zeist, in the Netherlands, where Scottish judges presided over the court proceedings. U.N. sanctions against Libya were suspended as agreed.

The trial finally got underway on 3 May 2000. Eight months later, on 31 January 2001, Megrahi was convicted of mass murder and sentenced to life imprisonment. His co-accused, Al-Amin Khalifa

Fahimah, was found not guilty and freed.

But Megrahi spent just eight-and-a-half years in Scotland's Greenock Prison. On 20 August 2009, the Scottish authorities released him on compassionate grounds after he was diagnosed as suffering from terminal prostate cancer. He was allowed to fly back to Libya to be with his family. •

OUR DAY OF TEARS

(*Sunday Echo*, 16 April 1989)

AN FA CUP SEMI-FINAL clash between Nottingham Forest and Liverpool ended in tragedy just minutes after the kick-off – the worst disaster, to date, in British football history.

The match was at Sheffield Wednesday's ground, Hillsborough, on Saturday, 15 April 1989. For some years, football in Britain had been blighted by hooliganism amongst the fans. Fighting, pitch invasions and the throwing of objects at players had led to segregation and fences erected between spectators and the pitch.

The policy of keeping opposing supporters apart meant that Nottingham Forest fans were placed in the 'stands' at the Spion Kop End of the ground and the Liverpool contingent in the Leppings Lane End of the stadium. These terraces were divided into a series of 'pens' by iron railings.

TRAFFIC DELAYS

With the kick-off at 3.00pm, many Liverpool fans arrived with little time to spare – heavy road traffic had been reported – and a large crowd formed at the turnstiles. They became anxious at the slow process of entering the ground and, concerned that they would miss the start of the match, began pressing forward.

With many fans still desperate to enter, worried police asked for the exit Gate C to be opened and around 2,000 people passed through, the majority making their way in to the already overcrowded central 'pens' of the Leppings Lane end.

Gate A was opened a few minutes later, followed by Gate B. It resulted in a rush as those at the front were pushed forward, pressing into the fence to accommodate those who had just arrived.

CROWD SURGES FORWARD

Four minutes into the game, Liverpool player Peter Beardsley took a shot that hit the crossbar at the Leppings Lane end of the ground. It caused the standing crowd to surge forward in excitement, crushing people into the fence.

A few managed to clamber over and onto the pitch and, for a moment, it looked like another pitch invasion. A police officer saw what was happening and ran onto the pitch to tell the referee to stop the game.

For those packed ever more tightly against the fences, however, there was little that could be done. Many of the fatalities were due to compressive asphyxia. They were crushed so tightly that they simply could not expand their chests enough to breathe.

Police and match officials attempted to help those trapped clamber over the fence and others were pulled to safety by fellow supporters in the seating areas above.

But the police, the stadium stewards and the ambulance crews in attendance for the match were overwhelmed by the number of injured.

Fans attempted CPR on friends whom they had managed to drag to safety on a pitch that began to look like a battlefield. For many, the lifesaving attempts simply came too late.

BODIES ON PITCH

Bodies were laid out on the pitch – many of them teenagers and children. Fans assisted the injured by tearing down advertising boards and using them as stretchers.

A total of 96 people were crushed to death and around 766 others injured. Liverpool's *Sunday Echo* newspaper carried the following day's headline, 'Our Day of Tears'.

Lord Justice Taylor was appointed to conduct an inquiry into the disaster. The report found that the main cause was the failure of police crowd control. One of the key elements was the failure to close off the tunnel leading to overcrowded 'pens' once Gate C had been opened.

Following the inquiry, new safety measures were introduced at major football grounds around Britain. Fencing was torn down and standing terraces made way for all-seater venues. •

CRACKDOWN IN BEIJING

TROOPS ATTACK AND CRUSH BEIJING PROTEST

(*New York Times*, 4 June 1989)

AN ATTACK ON protestors by Chinese troops in the centre of the capital of Beijing shocked the world with its brutality and resulted in many deaths and injuries.

The protests began after the death of former General Secretary of the Chinese Communist Party (CCP), Hu Yaobang, who had gained many enemies amongst the party for his liberal policies including the introduction of a free market and more transparency of government.

Following a series of student protests across China in 1987, Hu was blamed for the incidents and was forced to resign as party General Secretary, although he was allowed to retain a seat in the Politburo.

On the eve of Hu's funeral on 15 April 1989, a crowd of students converged on Tiananmen Square to commemorate him and demand that his contribution to the country be reappraised. It grew into a crowd of around 100,000, who called for Hu's reforming liberalisation to continue.

THOUSANDS GATHER IN SQUARE

Over the following days more and more people joined the students to campaign for political reform and calling for the resignations of repressive party leaders. On 22 April, tens of thousands gathered outside the Great Hall of the People in Tiananmen Square as Hu's memorial service was held. They delivered a petition of demands and insisted on a meeting with Premier Li Peng but it was rejected.

Worried authorities placed armed troops on the outskirts of the crowd. Protests also broke out in cities throughout China, including Shanghai and Wuhan. They were mostly peaceful, although some things were hurled at buildings and there were some clashes with troops.

On 15 May, Soviet leader Mikhail Gorbachev arrived in Beijing for the first Sino-Soviet summit in 30 years. His visit was seen as a formal end to years of hostility between the two communist nations. But large protests forced the cancellation of plans to welcome him in Tiananmen Square, which was a huge embarrassment for the government.

MARTIAL LAW DECLARED

Five days later, martial law was declared in several districts in Beijing as troops moved ominously towards the city centre.

What had begun as a relatively small protest had grown to around one million in numbers by its seventh week with people from all walks of life arriving to support the movement.

Many were chanting 'General strike!' and TV footage was shown all around the world from Western news teams who had been invited in to cover Gorbachev's visit. They were now ideally placed to film what was happening. With the crowd refusing to disperse, the government sent in troops and tanks, which fired indiscriminately, mowing down anyone in their way.

UNARMED CIVILIANS SHOT

The noise of gunfire filled the air. Ordinary, unarmed civilians were stunned that their own army was shooting at them. As people fell dead or injured, they were either carried to hospital or taken there on bicycle rickshaws. Ambulances arrived but were turned away by the troops and two drivers were shot and injured.

A defiant crowd shouted 'Fascists!', 'Stop killing!' and 'Down with the government!'

Precise figures of casualties may never be known but it has been estimated that hundreds were killed and thousands injured.

It was dubbed the 'Tiananmen Square massacre', although most of the bloodshed happened in the surrounding streets.

The savagery of the attack on 4 June caused an international outcry. Meanwhile, the CCP conducted widespread arrests of protestors, banned the foreign press from the country and sacked those in the government thought to be too sympathetic to democratic reform. •

MANDELA GOES FREE TODAY

(*City Press*, 11 February 1990)

AFTER 27 YEARS in prison, Nelson Mandela was released on 11 February 1990 and the televised moment was televised live around the world.

Four years later, the man who had long campaigned against apartheid and the white government of the National Party in his homeland was elected as the country's first black president.

The South African newspaper, *City Press*, splashed 'Mandela Goes Free Today' on the morning of his release and it was held aloft by many ecstatic supporters who celebrated in the streets.

Mandela had joined the African National Congress (ANC) in 1943 and when the Afrikaner-dominated National Party came to power in 1948, he actively campaigned against the party for its support of the apartheid policy of racial segregation

He qualified as a lawyer in 1952 and opened a law practice in Johannesburg with his partner, Oliver Tambo. In 1958, he married Winnie Madikizela, who was later to take an active role in the campaign to free her husband from prison.

ANC OUTLAWED

Mandela became vice-president of the ANC and, after it was outlawed in 1960, he went underground but was eventually arrested and charged with sabotage and attempting to violently overthrow the government.

In the winter of 1964, he was sentenced to life in prison and spent

18 years on Robben Island before being transferred to Pollsmoor Prison on the mainland in 1982.

In 1980, Oliver Tambo, who was in exile, and Winnie Mandela, launched an international campaign to release Nelson Mandela. Many countries tightened sanctions on South Africa and there was growing pressure for Mandela to be released.

MANDELA REFUSES RELEASE

In February 1985, he refused President P. W. Botha's offer for early release because of the condition that he should reject violence as a political weapon.

At a rally at the Jabulani Stadium, Nelson's 25-year-old daughter, Zindzi, read out his response. Zindzi's mother, Winnie, was restricted under a government banning order but attended the rally in disguise. Zindzi's address became known as the 'My Father Says . . .' speech.

The words that inspired a renewed vigour in the campaign against apartheid were, 'What freedom am I being offered while the organisation of the people remains banned? Only free men can negotiate. A prisoner cannot enter into contracts.'

On 2 February 1990, President F. W. de Klerk, who had succeeded Botha as leader of the National Party the previous year, lifted the ban on the ANC, and Mandela, at the age of 71, was released from prison nine days later.

Celebrations erupted throughout the country. Mandela had been moved to Victor Verster Prison in 1988 and, as he walked through the gates to embrace Winnie, he greeted a waiting crowd with a huge smile and raised fist salute. He then got into a car, which took him to Cape Town where he addressed a huge, joyous gathering.

His opening words were of peace, 'I greet you all in the name of peace, democracy and freedom for all,' he said. 'I stand here before you not as a prophet, but as a humble servant of you, the people.'

ARMED STRUGGLE CONTINUES

But he went on to warn that the armed fight against apartheid must continue.

'Now is the time to intensify the struggle on all fronts. To relax our efforts now would be a mistake, which generations to come will not be able to forgive.'

In 1991, Mandela became president of the ANC and talks took place about forming a new multi-racial democracy for South Africa.

Nelson Mandela and F. W. de Klerk shared the Nobel Peace Prize in 1993 for their efforts to transform South African society.

Mandela's charisma, warmth, beaming smile, humility and seeming lack of bitterness about his long incarceration endeared him to millions around the world.

On 10 May 1994, the ANC won 252 of the 400 seats in the national assembly in the first democratic elections of South Africa's history and Nelson Mandela became the country's first black president. •

CAPITAL SARAJEVO RACKED BY SERB-MUSLIM CIVIL STRIFE

(*Independent*, 7 April 1992)

ON THE DAY THAT the European Community recognised Bosnia as an independent state, Serbian snipers opened fire on a Muslim peace demonstration in the capital city of Sarajevo.

Although there had been much conflict over the years between rival factions, this was regarded as the opening salvo of the Bosnian War.

The multicultural country of Yugoslavia had been created after the Great War by the victorious Western Allies. It comprised several ethnic and religious groups that had been historical rivals, in particular the Serbs (Orthodox Christians), Croats (Catholics) and ethnic Albanians (Muslims).

During World War II, Yugoslavia was invaded by Nazi Germany and was partitioned. A resistance movement sprang up led by Josip Tito. After Germany's defeat, Tito reunified Yugoslavia, merging together Slovenia, Croatia, Bosnia,

Serbia, Montenegro and Macedonia, along with two self-governing provinces, Kosovo and Vojvodina.

But after Tito's death in 1980, Yugoslavia fell into political and economic chaos as it struggled without his strong leadership.

INDEPENDENCE DECLARED

A new leader arose by the late 1980s, a Serbian named Slobodan Milosevic, who took control of Kosovo. But in June 1991, Slovenia and Croatia both declared their independence from Yugoslavia.

The national army of Yugoslavia, now made up of Serbs controlled by Milosevic, entered Slovenia to subdue the separatists. But with almost no Serbs living there, he withdrew the troops after only ten days of fighting. He then focused on Croatia where a minority of Serbs resided amongst the Catholic population.

During World War II, Croatia had been a pro-Nazi state and Serbs, as well as Jews living there, had been put in concentration camps and killed. In 1991, Serbs living here still felt they were being discriminated against.

Milosevic's forces invaded in July and killed hundreds of Croat men, burying them in mass graves. By the end of the year a U.S.-brokered ceasefire was agreed between the Serbs and Croats fighting in Croatia.

On 6 April 1992, the U.N. officially recognised the independence of Bosnia, which was a predominantly Muslim country, with Serbs making up 32 per cent of the population.

Milosevic wasted no time in responding. Serbian snipers opened fire from the upper floors of a hotel on a peace gathering below. Bosnian police and Muslim fighters stormed the hotel, firing machine-guns. On the outskirts of the city Muslims exchanged artillery and mortar fire with Serbs in the surrounding hills.

MASS SHOOTINGS

In the weeks, months and years that followed, Bosnian Muslims suffered terribly against the better-armed Serbs led by Radovan Karadzic. There were mass shootings of Muslims and internment in concentration camps reminiscent of the Nazi ones during World War II. There was also reported rape of women as the Serbs sought to eradicate the Muslims in what became known as 'ethnic cleansing'.

With Bosnia in terrible turmoil, the U.N. response was a limited one, with troops deployed to protect the distribution of food and medicine to dispossessed Muslims, but taking no military action.

One of the worst atrocities occurred in Srebrenica when nearly 8,000 men and boys between the ages of twelve and sixty were shot dead. It shocked the world and resulted in a NATO bombing campaign targeting Serbian military positions.

Eventually, Milosevic was ready to talk peace and, in November 1995, he joined Bosnian Muslim President Alija Izetbegovic and Croatian President Franjo Tudjman for peace talks in Dayton, Ohio, U.S.

It was agreed to create two separate entities – a Bosnian-Croat federation and a Bosnian-Serb Republic – each with its own president, government, parliament and police. And an international peacekeeping force was sent in to keep the peace. The agreement also called for democratic elections and stipulated that war criminals would be handed over for prosecution.

Karadzic went into hiding and, on 12 February 2002, Milosevic went on trial charged with 66 counts of genocide and war crimes in Bosnia, Croatia and Kosovo. On 11 March 2006, Milosevic died of a heart attack in his cell in The Hague. There was jubilation in the streets with the news that Karadzic had been arrested in Belgrade on 21 July 2008 after 13 years on the run. •

SCIENTISTS CLONE ADULT SHEEP

TRIUMPH FOR UK RAISES ALARM OVER HUMAN USE

(*Observer*, 23 February 1997)

CLONING – A STAPLE ingredient of science-fiction films and novels – became science fact with the birth of Dolly the Sheep.

Mammals reproduce sexually in a process that involves both a male and female. Cloning is the production of a new, genetically identical individual from a single parent animal.

Scientist Dr Ian Wilmut at the Roslin Institute, near Edinburgh, took a single cell from the udder of an adult sheep, turned it into a viable embryo and implanted it into a surrogate mother. The sheep gave birth to a lamb named Dolly who was genetically identical to the sheep from which the cell was taken.

Although biologists around the world had successfully cloned plants and frogs, this was the first mammal to have been successfully cloned from an adult cell.

MORAL ISSUES

The announcement aroused huge interest as the world's press descended on Roslin to take pictures of Dolly. But there was immediate controversy with ethical and moral issues over whether the procedure would lead to the cloning of humans.

Dolly was born on 5 July 1996 but the announcement was not made until 22 February 1997 when the publication of the result could be fully prepared.

Dolly started her life in a test tube. Once normal development was confirmed at six days, the embryo was transferred into a surrogate mother. An ultrasound after about 45 days confirmed the pregnancy, which proceeded without any problem until the lamb was born.

DNA tests showed that Dolly was identical to the ewe who donated the udder cell but unrelated to the surrogate mother.

NEW HEALTH PRODUCTS

Explaining the reason behind the birth of Dolly, Dr Wilmut stated, 'Apart from showing the biological principle that it is possible to get a cell to begin development again in this way – which has fascinating implications for studies of cancer and suchlike – the initial importance is that we will be able to use this for research in biology and also to make new health care products'.

As the debate about the potential for human cloning rumbled on,

Wilmut opposed the notion and called it 'repugnant.'

Despite the spectacular outcome achieved with Dolly, in 2008 Wilmut decided to abandon the technique used to create her. Instead of using embryonic stem cells, Wilmut began working with a procedure developed by Japanese researcher Professor Shinya Yamanaka to generate stem cells from adult skin cells in mice. He hopes this will lead to effective treatments for diseases such as Parkinson's.

DOLLY'S NORMAL LIFE

Dolly was encouraged to lead a normal sheep's life. She was mated with a small Welsh mountain ram and produced six lambs. Later she had arthritisbut then there were fears for something more serious when some of the sheep at Roslin contracted pulmonary adenomatosis. This disease is caused by a virus that induces tumours to grow in the lungs of affected animals. It is incurable and infectious.

A CT scan (computerised tomography) carried out on Friday, 14 February 2003, confirmed the Roslin team's worst fears. Tumours were growing in Dolly's chest. Since a general anaesthetic had been necessary to perform the scan it was decided that it would be best if Dolly did not regain consciousness and an overdose of an anaesthetic agent was administered to end her life.

Her early death raised debate that it may have been due to the cloning process but Roslin scientists stated that they did not think there was a connection with Dolly being a clone and that other sheep on the farm had similar ailments.

Dolly's remains were conserved by taxidermists and she was put on display at the National Museum of Scotland in Edinburgh. •

DIANA DEAD
6AM SHOCK ISSUE

(*News of the World*, 31 Aug 1997)

THE NEWS WAS so sudden and shocking that people could scarcely believe it. Diana, Princess of Wales, had died in a car crash in Paris in the early hours of Sunday, 31 August 1997. So too had her companion, Dodi Al Fayed, and the driver of the car, Henri Paul.

For the past week there had been pictures in the newspapers of Diana in a swimsuit enjoying the sunshine with Al Fayed aboard a yacht belonging to his father, Mohamed Al Fayed, on the French and Italian Rivieras. The couple had stopped in Paris en route for London and, at around 12:20am on 31 August, they left the Ritz Hotel to return to an apartment owned by Mohamed Al Fayed in rue Arsène Houssaye.

The hotel's acting Head of Security, Henri Paul, drove them in a black Mercedes-Benz S280 through Paris where they were pursued by paparazzi. Entering the tunnel under the Place de l'Alma in the centre of the city, he lost control of the car, which smashed into a pillar at an estimated speed of 105kph (65mph). It then spun and hit a stone wall before coming to a halt.

DEAD AT SCENE

Al Fayed and Henri Paul died at the scene but Diana and her bodyguard, Trevor Rees-Jones, were cut from the wreckage and rushed to hospital. They were unable to save her and she died in the early hours of the morning. Of the four people in the car, only Rees-Jones survived. None of them had been wearing seat belts.

The news of the Princess's death – officially declared at 3.00am

(BST) – stunned the world. Newsreaders were visibly choked, stumbling over their words. And the story made the later editions of that day's Sunday newspapers.

Prince Charles broke the news of their mother's death to Princes William and Harry at Balmoral Castle in Scotland where the royal family had been spending the summer.

In a statement, Buckingham Palace said the Queen and the Prince of Wales were 'deeply shocked and distressed'.

STUNNED DISBELIEF

Her death caused overwhelming public grief in Britain, the like of which had never been seen before. The traditional British 'stiff upper lip' was replaced by tears and a general stunned sense of disbelief.

Diana's home at Kensington Palace became a focal point for mourners, many of whom were surprised by the overriding emotion that compelled them to pay their respects. They shared their grief with each other as one bouquet after another was laid on the ground. People also brought flowers to Diana's ancestral home, Althorp Park, in Northampton.

Around one million people lined the streets to see the Princess's funeral cortège as it made its way from Kensington Palace to Westminster Abbey for the service on 6 September.

Inside, Diana's brother, Earl Spencer, criticised the media and took a sideswipe at the royal family's behaviour towards Diana. He pledged to play a greater role in the upbringing of the two princes.

'It is a point to remember that of all the ironies about Diana, perhaps the greatest was this – a girl given the name of the ancient goddess of hunting was, in the end, the most hunted person of the modern age,' he said, in a voice trembling with emotion.

The Earl promised that he and what he called her 'blood family' would look after the welfare of her sons.

'GOODBYE ENGLAND'S ROSE'

Diana's friend, Elton John, memorably sang a re-written version of his hit song, 'Candle in the Wind', replacing lines such as 'Goodbye Norma Jean' with 'Goodbye England's rose.'

The service was watched by an estimated worldwide audience

of 2.5 billion people – one of the biggest televised events in history.

Outside the Abbey and in Hyde Park crowds watched and listened to proceedings on giant outdoor screens and huge speakers.

Afterwards, the hearse made its way to Althorp as people lined the roads, and so many flowers were thrown that the driver had to use the windscreen wipers to clear his view. And at one point the cortège stopped to remove some of the flowers that were piling up on the car.

Inside the estate, the Princess was buried in the idyllic and peaceful setting of an island in a lake where she had played as a child. •

CLINTON ADMITS TO LEWINSKY RELATIONSHIP

(*Washington Post*, 18 August 18 1998)

BILL CLINTON BECAME the second U.S. President to be impeached since Andrew Johnson in 1868 after lying about an affair with 22-year-old White House intern Monica Lewinsky in 1998.

In an affair that gripped a worldwide audience, Clinton finally admitted that he had misled the public in an earlier statement in which he had denied any involvement with Lewinsky. His position as President hung in the balance as the Senate tried him for perjury and obstruction of justice.

Clinton had first got to know 22-year-old Lewinsky in 1995 when she was an unpaid intern at the White House. According to her, they became sexually involved that November. In December she landed a paid position in the Office of Legislative Affairs. But by the following spring, those close to the 49-year-old President were concerned about her hanging around the West Wing so much and what they perceived as her obvious infatuation with him.

LEWINSKY'S NEW FRIEND

Evelyn S. Lieberman, then deputy White House chief of staff, had her transferred to the Pentagon in April 1996, where she struck up a friendship with another employee named Linda Tripp.

That summer Lewinsky confided in Tripp about her intimate relationship with Clinton and, in the autumn of 1997, Tripp began secretly taping their conversations. On 17 December, Lewinsky was subpoenaed by lawyers for Paula Jones who was suing Clinton on sexual harassment charges dating back to when he was Governor of Arkansas. Kathleen Willey, another former White House staffer had recently testified about alleged unsolicited sexual advances made by Clinton in 1993.

LEWINSKY ON TAPE

On 12 January, Tripp made contact with independent counsel Kenneth Star who had been investigating Clinton and his wife Hillary over possible fraudulent land deals when Clinton was Governor of Arkansas. Tripp handed him her tape recordings, which allegedly had Lewinsky talking about her affair and indicating that Clinton asked her to lie about it.

Now working with Starr, Tripp again secretly recorded conversations with Lewinsky. On 17 January 1998, Clinton gave his deposition in the Jones lawsuit, in which he denied having a sexual relationship with Lewinsky and repeated his denial a week later in a live TV address, watched the world over, in which he stressed, 'I did not have sexual relations with that woman, Miss Lewinsky.'

In April, the Paula Jones case was dismissed by Judge Susan Webber Wright but Clinton continued to feel the heat.

On 6 August 1998, Lewinsky told a grand jury investigating Clinton's conduct that she had an 18-month sexual relationship with him and that the pair had discussed ways of concealing the relationship. She also presented one of her dresses as evidence, stating it had been stained with Mr Clinton's semen during one of their sexual encounters.

CLINTON ADMITS DECEPTION

On 17 August, Clinton himself testified before the jury. After the questioning at the White House was finished, he again went on national TV but this time to admit he had an inappropriate relationship with Lewinsky and deceived the American people about it. But he defiantly challenged Kenneth Starr to stop 'prying into private lives'.

He explained that he had not been candid because he wanted to protect himself and his family from embarrassment.

'I did have a relationship with Miss Lewinsky that was not appropriate,' he confessed. 'In fact, it was wrong. It constituted a critical lapse in judgement and a personal failure on my part for which I am solely and completely responsible.' He added, 'I misled people, including even my wife. I deeply regret that.'

Clinton's defence of his statements in the Jones sexual harassment lawsuit appeared to rely on the interpretation of 'sexual relations'. He maintained that it did not include oral sex.

After Starr submitted his report and supportive documents to the House of Representatives, the Judiciary Committee announced that it would begin an impeachment inquiry against President Clinton. It began on 7 January 1999 and ended on 12 February when senators voted to acquit him of the impeachment charges of perjury and obstruction of justice. •

U.S. ATTACKED

HIJACKED JETS DESTROY TWIN TOWERS AND HIT PENTAGON IN DAY OF TERROR

(*New York Times*, 12 September, 2001)

THIS DRAMATIC HEADLINE screamed across the *New York Times* above a big picture of the Twin Towers of the World Trade Center ablaze and billowing thick, black smoke.

When a plane hit the first tower it was initially thought by many to be a tragic accident. But a similar incident on the second tower just 17 minutes later left no one in any doubt that it was a terrorist attack.

On the morning of 11 September 2001, 19 Islamic terrorists, linked to al-Qaeda, hijacked four American passenger planes. At 8.38am local time (12.38pm GMT), the Federal Aviation Administration alerted NORAD (North American Aerospace Defense Command) that American Airlines Flight 11 had been hijacked. Eight minutes later, at the height of New York's morning rush hour, the plane crashed into the north tower of the World Trade Center, where thousands were already working at their desks.

News teams rushed to the site where the scenes of shock and despair were beamed around the world. The news media assumed it was an accident but as they kept cameras on the plane sticking out of the building, millions of viewers around the globe watched in horror as a second plane crashed into the south tower.

Some of those in the south tower had left the building after the first plane crash but many more were still inside. Meanwhile, hundreds of fire-fighters and police were doing their best to rescue those in both buildings.

PENTAGON HIT

More reports of hijackings began to filter through and at 9.37am a plane carrying 64 people crashed into the Pentagon in Washington, causing one section of the building to collapse. All airports across the U.S. were ordered to be shut down and commercial flights grounded. And the White House and the Capitol were evacuated, amid further threats.

Passengers aboard a fourth plane struggled with the hijackers above Pennsylvania, causing it to crash 80 miles (128km) southeast of Pittsburgh, killing everyone on board. The target was believed to have been either the Capitol or the White House.

As the public was struggling to take in all this incredible news, TV pictures relayed the sickening sight of the south tower of the Trade Center suddenly collapsing, sending a wall of smoke into the air and hundreds of people on the streets running for their lives. Twenty-nine minutes later, the north tower also fell.

The intense heat caused by the explosions had melted the steel structural cores in the towers, causing them to collapse. Hundreds of fire-fighters, police officers and people who were trying to escape the towers were crushed.

PRESIDENT VOWS REVENGE

President George W. Bush made an emergency statement on TV in which he pledged to 'hunt down and find those folks who committed this act'.

On the evening of that fatal day, which was to become known as 9/11, after the month and day, President Bush addressed the nation on TV again, in which he stated that 'our military is powerful and it's prepared', adding, 'The search is underway for those who are behind these evil acts. We will make no distinction between the terrorists who committed these acts and those who harbour them.'

The attacks killed 2,974 people. Suspicion quickly fell on al-Qaeda but the group's leader, Osama bin Laden, denied involvement until three years later when he claimed responsibility, citing U.S. support of Israel, the presence of U.S. troops in Saudi Arabia and sanctions against Iraq as motives for the attacks.

The U.S. responded to the attacks by launching the War on Terror.

On 7 October 2001, American and British forces initiated aerial bombing of Afghanistan, targeting the Taliban who had harboured al-Qaeda members. This was followed by an invasion of ground troops.

President Bush's popularity at home soared as Americans united in backing his fight against terrorism. •

BLOODBATH ON HOLIDAY ISLAND

(*New Zealand Herald*, 14 October 2002)

A TERRORIST BOMB caused carnage on the idyllic holiday island of Bali in Indonesia after it exploded in a busy tourist area.

It killed 202 people, mostly tourists, 88 of them holidaymakers from Australia. The death toll included 38 Indonesian citizens and 24 British visitors. A further 240 people were injured.

The bomb was placed in a van outside the Sari Club in downtown Kuta and was detonated just after 11.00pm local time on Saturday, 12 October 2002, when all the bars along the street were packed with customers enjoying themselves.

The blast destroyed the Sari Club and the resulting fire then engulfed a neighbouring bar, Paddy's Pub. Other buildings and several cars were also damaged in the blast and ensuing fire. Barely a shop front was left intact along a 500m stretch.

Rescuers worked through the night and into the following day, pulling the injured from the wreckage, along with dead bodies.

An Indonesian police chief said it was the worst act of terror in his country's history.

TOO FEW AMBULANCES

Bali's emergency services struggled to cope with the scale of the disaster. With so many injured, ambulances were in short supply to transport them to Sanglah Hospital, 10 miles away in the capital, Denpasar.

The hospital was ill-equipped to deal with the situation as more and more injured arrived needing treatment. Dozens of tourists volunteered to give blood or help in any way they could.

Many of the injured were burns victims who had to be flown to hospitals in Australia to receive specialist treatment.

Just prior to the main bomb a much smaller explosive had been set off in Paddy's Bar, which caused many to rush out into the street. Twenty seconds later, the huge van bomb was detonated across the road.

SLEEPING ON THE BEACH

Dozens of tourists, fearing more bombs, left their hotels to sleep on the beach that night, where they felt safer in the open space.

Another, smaller, explosion occurred in Denpasar, close to the United States Honorary Consulate, but there were no injuries.

The violent Islamic group Jemaah Islamiah, considered to be al-Qaeda's Southeast Asian arm, was suspected of being behind the bomb attack.

Although most of their victims in the Bali atrocity were unlikely even to have heard of Jemaah Islamiah, the group had been active for many years, with its roots stretching back to the 1940s. The group's modern incarnation dates back to 1993 and its stated aim is to establish an Islamic superstate incorporating Indonesia, Malaysia, the Philippines, Brunei and Singapore.

In 2001, the security services foiled a Jemaah Islamiah plot to bomb American, Australian, British, Israeli and Singapore diplomatic personnel at embassies, missions and schools in Singapore. At that time, 15 Jemaah Islamiah activists were arrested in Singapore, leading to a further 26 arrests elsewhere over next 36 months.

Bali – a predominantly Hindu island popular with Western tourists – was thought to represent a soft and tempting target for Islamist extremists linked to al-Qaeda

TERRORISTS JAILED

Three men were eventually sentenced to death for the bombings – Amrozi bin Nurhasyim, his brother Mukhlas and Imam Samudra. A fourth, Ali Imron, was sentenced to life imprisonment.

Muslim cleric Abu Bakar Bashir, widely thought to have been one of the masterminds behind the attack, was found guilty of conspiracy and sentenced to two and a half years imprisonment.

On 1 October 2005, Bali was targeted again when three suicide bombers blew themselves up in tourist areas, killing at least 19 people, mostly Indonesians. The incidents happened almost simultaneously just before 8.00pm local time. More than 50 others were injured as blasts ripped through three restaurants – two in the Jimbaran beach resort, the third in Kuta.

Police claimed to have discovered a further three bombs designed to be triggered by signals from cell phones. These failed to detonate as the island's mobile phone network was shut down as a precaution immediately after the initial blasts.

Once more Jemaah Islamiah was suspected of being behind the attack. •

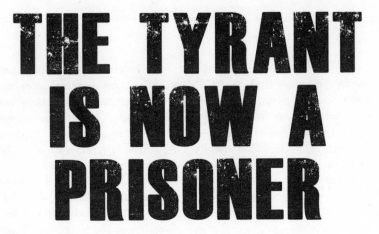

THE TYRANT IS NOW A PRISONER

(*Independent*, 15 December 2003)

HE WAS THE president who brought education, electricity and welfare to his country but also death and destruction to anyone who opposed his regime.

Saddam Hussein had become involved in politics after joining the Arab socialist party, Ba'ath, while at college. After the overthrow of the monarchy in 1958, during a military coup, General Abdul Karim Kassem became the country's new leader but his moderate polices lost him the support of the Ba'ath Party. In 1959, Hussein had to flee to Egypt after being part of a discovered plot to assassinate Kassem. But he returned when Kassem was executed in another military coup in February 1963.

Colonel Abdul-Salam Arif became the new president but he was killed in an air crash in 1966 and was replaced by his brother General Abdul Rahman. Another military coup on 17 July 1968 brought to power Ahmad Hasan al-Bakr and the Ba'ath Party. Over the next ten years, Saddam rose quickly through the ranks of government and became the number two figure behind al-Bakr.

The Ba'ath government ruthlessly suppressed opposition but it did agree to enter negotiations with the Kurdish Democratic Party and, in March 1970, the government promised to grant the Kurds, in the north of the country, a degree of autonomy. But four years later, when nothing had changed, fighting broke out between the Kurds and Iraqi armed forces. Kurdish villages were destroyed and the inhabitants were resettled in specially constructed villages surrounded by barbed wire and fortified posts.

SADDAM BECOMES PRESIDENT

In 1979, Saddam became president after al-Bakr retired, and the ruthlessness continued as he put to death any opposition. He also created the Republican Guard, a presidential security force.

Increasing oil revenues provided him with the money to build schools, hospitals and clinics and start a literacy project, as well as creating an electricity network throughout the country.

Statues and posters of the president appeared all over the country. Some depicted him in military dress, others in traditional garb and others in casual wear with his family or with a young child on his knee, looking like a benevolent father figure.

Seeing himself as the leader and unifying force of Arabs, he poured his army across the border into Iran in September 1980 in an attempt to gain control of the Shatt al Arab Waterway that runs along the border of both countries.

Iraq's war with Iran received support from Britain, the U.S., Soviet Union and France. Iran fought back far more ferociously than anticipated and the war was to last eight years, costing the lives of hundreds of thousands before a ceasefire was agreed.

POISON GAS REVENGE

In an effort to gain their independence from Iraq, the Kurds supported Iran during the war. Saddam's retribution in the spring of 1988 was to send his air force over the Kurdish region releasing poisoned gas, resulting in 5,000 deaths.

But despite this long and bloody war, just two years later, Saddam ordered his army into neighbouring Kuwait – where he had long wanted to extend his territory – after lengthy disputes over oil.

The United Nations immediately imposed economic sanctions on Iraq and demanded a withdrawal from Kuwait. But Saddam refused and in January 1991 a United States-led coalition of 32 countries launched an attack on Iraq. Saddam called it 'the mother of all battles'. It eventually led to a ceasefire on 28 February.

In April he agreed to accept the U.N. resolution calling on him to destroy weapons of mass destruction and begrudgingly allowed U.N. inspectors into his country to monitor the disarmament.

OPERATION DESERT FOX

Convinced that he was hiding biological and chemical weapons, the U.S. and Britain launched Operation Desert Fox in December 1998 – a four-day intensive air strike aimed at destroying Iraqi military bases, weapons factories and airfields. The following month, U.S. and British aircraft began regular bombing attacks on Iraq.

With the arrival of George W. Bush as U.S. President in 2001, and the al-Qaeda attacks on the World Trade Center in September of that year, the War on Terror was stepped up. Bush described Iraq, Iran and North Korea as the 'axis of evil'.

In March 2003, Bush, with the support of British Prime Minister Tony Blair, ordered the invasion of Iraq on the pretext that Saddam was concealing 'weapons of mass destruction', despite having no U.N. resolution authorising the action. In the event, no such weapons were ever found. But it was the beginning of the end for Saddam. His reign was toppled with the fall of Baghdad on 9 April when he went into hiding. News footage of Iraqi civilians hacking away at a towering statue of Saddam in central Baghdad, which was eventually pulled down by U.S. troops, was shown around the world. It was a highly symbolic moment.

SADDAM CAPTURED ALIVE

In December 2003, following a tip-off from an intelligence source, U.S. forces found the wanted dictator hiding in a cramped bunker on a farm near Tikrit, where he was born. The U.S. administrator in Iraq at the time, Paul Bremer, told reporters, 'Ladies and gentlemen, we got him. The tyrant is a prisoner.'

Saddam's two sons, Uday and Qusay, were both killed during the invasion of Iraq when U.S.

special forces, acting on a tip-off, discovered their hiding place in a house in the town of Mosul.

Uday was Saddam's elder son and had been tipped to succeed his father as president, but he was also a notorious torturer, rapist and murderer. He suffered severe injuries in an assassination attempt in 1996 and was eventually deemed too unstable to take over from Saddam, but was in charge of a newspaper and TV station.

Qusay took over from his brother as heir to the presidency. He did not adopt the playboy lifestyle of his brother but tended to keep a low profile, although he was head of the elite Republican Guard and the Special Security Organisation. His 14-year-old son died alongside him in the gunfight that also killed Uday and a bodyguard.

Saddam survived to stand trial in Iraq for crimes against humanity but remained defiant throughout, refusing to accept the legality of the proceedings. He was found guilty, and executed on 30 December 2006. •

'WE SAW THE SEA COMING, WE ALL RAN, BUT GOD SAVES LITTLE'

(*Times of India*, 28 December 2004)

ONE OF THE WORLD'S deadliest natural disasters occurred on the morning of 26 December 2004 when an earthquake under the Indian Ocean caused a huge tsunami, killing more than 200,000 people in 14 countries.

The quake, which occurred off the west coast of Sumatra, Indonesia, at 7.58am local time, measured between 9.1 and 9.3 on the Richter scale, causing the sea floor to jolt vertically by about 10m (33ft). This sent surges of water roaring towards coastlines, travelling at speeds of up to 800kph (497mph). The huge tsunami took everyone by surprise as waves up to 30m (98ft) high smashed down onto beaches, villages and towns on the coasts of countries including Indonesia, Sri Lanka, India and Thailand.

MASSIVE DEATH TOLL

Over 200,000 people were killed – around 170,000 in Indonesia alone – including local people as well as many tourists who had been enjoying holidays in some of the most picturesque locations in the world.

There was little or no warning

that the tsunami was coming. Tragically, there were no tide gauges in the Indian Ocean as there are in the Pacific. If they had been in place, then tens of thousands of lives could have been saved.

The only visible sign was the waterline suddenly retreating on some beaches, causing bewilderment amongst those who saw it. Unfortunately, many were so intrigued by this unusual occurrence that they walked further out to sea to explore when they should have been running away. Other victims drowned after running to retrieve fish stranded on the beach.

SUMATRA HIT FIRST

The tsunami came in several waves with intervals of between 5 and 40 minutes. Sumatra was hit first with Sri Lanka and India roughly 90 minutes to 2 hours later.

In the Sumatran city of Banda Aceh people were going about their business as the sun was rising but within moments they were fighting for their lives when the first gigantic wall of water hit. It surged through the city, sweeping anyone and anything along, causing widespread devastation.

Many witnesses described how the sea appeared suddenly to 'seethe and boil' as it engulfed thousands of miles of coast. Others likened the first sighting of a spec on the horizon which grew and grew into a mountain of water as being 'like something out of a disaster movie'. By the time people realised what was coming it was largely too late. Some managed to flee to higher ground but all too many were washed away.

Many on the beaches, enjoying the sunshine, were engulfed. A woman on honeymoon in Sri Lanka said, 'It was terrifying. The water behind us was ripping through the trees as we ran up a hill to safety.'

BODIES ON THE BEACHES

In the aftermath, the beaches were lined with bodies, and cries and wails filled the air as emergency services did their best to tackle the appalling devastation.

There was a massive international response to the calls for help, with governments pledging aid in rescue operations, supplying food and water and sending in teams to help clear the devastated towns and villages. Ordinary members of the public, all over the world, appalled by the news stories and images, donated large sums of money.

The earthquake was the largest for 40 years and was a shocking reminder of how terrifying the power of nature can be.

The energy released by the initial earthquake has been estimated at the equivalent to 26 megatons of TNT – roughly 1500 times more powerful than the atom bomb that devastated Hiroshima in 1945.

The resulting tsunami was actually a rare occurrence in the Indian Ocean, despite the number of earthquakes in the area. In 2005 a quake of magnitude 8.7 happened in roughly the same area, but produced no major tsunami. In fact, the last tsunami in the region to cause a serious problem was when Krakatoa erupted in 1883.

Nevertheless, in 2005 the United Nations began work to provide the Indian Ocean Tsunami Warning System and by June 2006 the system was active, although the information it provides will only become an effective warning when a tsunami alert can be broadcast by the authorities to everyone in the coastal area danger zones. •

KATRINA STORMS ASHORE

'BIG ONE' LASHES AT NEW ORLEANS

(*Atlanta Journal-Constitution*, 29 August 2005)

THE HURRICANE THAT New Orleans was dreading finally arrived and, as expected, the impact was devastating.

It caused widespread flooding when it ripped through the old city, tearing roofs off buildings, upturning trees and cars and killing over a thousand people. It was the worst natural disaster in the United States for decades.

There had been plenty of warning that it was going to strike. It began as a low pressure weather system which increased to a tropical storm and then a hurricane as it built up over the Bahamas. It then moved towards the Florida coast on the evening of 25 August 2005. By now it was classed as a Category 1 hurricane with 80mph (130 kph)

winds. Passing through Florida, it caused flooding, uprooted trees, caused structural damage and cut off electricity supplies. It resulted in 14 fatalities.

WORSE TO COME

President Bush declared a 'major disaster' in Florida. But there was far worse to come. After leaving Florida, Katrina blew over the warm waters of the Gulf of Mexico, strengthening rapidly overnight.

It had grown to Category 5 by the time it started its approach to the Louisiana coast but had weakened early on Monday, 29 August to Category 4 with sustained winds of 145mph.

New Orleans Mayor Ray Nagin ordered the city of 485,000 to evacuate and warned that the storm could topple its century-old levee system, leaving New Orleans under water.

Homes and buildings were shuttered and boarded up throughout the city and the motorway was jammed with people desperate to get out. But thousands took refuge in the city's Superdome arena. These were people too poor, sick or elderly to be able to leave and others doggedly determined to stay and sit the storm out.

NEW ORLEANS FLOODED

When Katrina finally hit New Orleans it had dropped to Category 3 but the force was still terrifying and immensely damaging, with winds of 125mph (205kph). Boats, bridges, houses and cars were washed inland along the Louisiana coast, New Orleans bearing the brunt of it. Up to 80 per cent of the city was flooded after defensive barriers were overwhelmed.

Howling winds and lashing rain ripped holes in the Superdome but thankfully the roof held and those inside remained frightened but safe.

With the streets flooded, people were trapped in their attics or even on their roofs once the worst of the winds had passed. But rescue took time because emergency workers were hindered by the swift-moving floodwater. Supplies of fresh water and food began to run short in the aftermath of the disaster. Sanitary conditions quickly deteriorated, bringing the risk of diseases such as cholera and typhoid, and military units were despatched to bring emergency aid. The floodwaters lingered for weeks.

DEADLIEST SINCE 1928

At least 1,836 people died, making Katrina the deadliest U.S. hurricane since the 1928 Okeechobee storm that killed nearly 3,000.

The economic effects of the disaster were crippling, oil platforms and refineries having been destroyed as well as roads, homes, businesses and farm land. Thousands of residents were left homeless and unemployed.

The effect on the environment was catastrophic. There was substantial beach erosion, sixteen national wildlife refuges had to close and oil spillage estimated at 7 million gallons (26 million litres) had to be cleaned up.

Over seventy countries pledged money and physical aid as a mammoth undertaking got underway to re-build New Orleans. •

MICROSOFT SAYS GOODBYE TO BILL GATES

(*Seattle Times*, 28 June 2008)

AN OBSESSION WITH computers led Bill Gates to world domination of the software market with his mighty Microsoft company changing the daily business operations and leisure lifestyles of millions around the world.

Along the way, he became the richest man in the world and one of the most influential. He departed from Microsoft after 33 years to devote his life to philanthropy, using his great wealth to help ease global suffering.

Born in Seattle, Washington, on 28 October 1955, he became fascinated by his school's computer as a 13-year-old. Together with three fellow students, including Paul Allen, they explored their interest and Gates wrote a program for a game of noughts and crosses that could be played on it. By the age of 17 he had sold his first program – a timetabling system for the school, earning him $4,200.

THE PAYROLL PROGRAM

The four students were later hired by a company to write a payroll program for them. Gates then enrolled at Harvard College where he continued to spend much of his time understanding the workings of computers. He remained in contact with Paul Allen and took time out to write a program with Allen for computer company MITS, which was a version of the programming language BASIC (Beginner's All Purpose Symbolic Instruction Code). It was used for the Altair microcomputer.

Encouraged by their success, the two friends saw an opportunity to develop software for the next generation of computers and they formed their own company, Microsoft, in 1975. A year later, Gates dropped out of Harvard to concentrate on his work with his new company. Their big break came when computer giant IBM asked them to provide an operating system for a new personal computer they were developing. It was given the code name Project Chess and the team consisted of twelve people directed by Don Estridge with chief designer Lewis Eggebrecht.

GATES' FIRST FORTUNE

Gates adapted a system already in existence called 86-DOS, which became known as MS-DOS. Showing a flair for business he crucially accepted a one-time fee of $50,000 for the system but retained the licensing rights and this was to earn him a fortune.

The IBM PC was launched on 12 August 1981 and revolutionised the home-computer market. The original press release described it as IBM's 'smallest, lowest-priced computer system', which was 'designed for business, school and home'. This 'easy-to-use system sells for as little as $1,565'.

IBM vice president and group executive, C. B. Rogers, said, 'This is the computer for just about everyone who has ever wanted a personal system at the office, on the university campus or at home.'

IBM and Gates fell out after he was asked to develop a separate operating system for them called OS/2. Although he did a first version of it, creative differences led to him focusing on something he had already been working on – a system called Microsoft Windows. Windows arrived on 20 November 1985. This quickly became the standard software for most personal computers around the world and Microsoft became a household name.

SHARP BUSINESS SENSE

Several commentators have said that Gates's real genius is not so much in being original and creative but in his sharp business sense, which has been described as 'aggressive' .

In 1987, Gates was officially declared a billionaire in the pages of *Forbes* '400 Richest People in America' issue, just days before his 32nd birthday, with a fortune worth $1.25 billion. He was the World's Richest Man from 1995 to 2007 and again in 2009. And in 2011 *Forbes* ranked him as the fifth most powerful person in the world.

Gates stepped down as chief executive officer of Microsoft in January 2000 to concentrate on The Bill & Melinda Gates Foundation, which, amongst other things, seeks to reduce global poverty, expand healthcare and encourage education.

On 27 June 2008, he said farewell to Microsoft as he finished his last full-time working day there, although he remained as non-executive chairman. •

OBAMA MAKES HISTORY

U.S. DECISIVELY ELECTS FIRST BLACK PRESIDENT

(*The Washington Post*, 5 November 2008)

DEMOCRATIC SENATOR Barack Hussein Obama defeated Arizona Senator John McCain on 4 November 2008 to become the 44th President of the U.S.

It was a particularly historic occasion for he was the first black President in the country's history.

During an exciting campaign en route to the highest office, he captured the public's imagination with his vitality and freshness. His commitment and determination to change things was stressed by his catchphrase, 'Yes we can', which became a rallying cry amongst his supporters.

After his Republican rival, Senator John McCain, finally and graciously admitted defeat, Obama paid tribute to the former Vietnam prisoner-of-war, calling him a 'Brave and selfless leader' who 'has endured sacrifices for America that most of us cannot begin to imagine'.

Appearing with his family before a crowd of tens of thousands in Chicago's Grant Park on the day of his victory, Obama embodied the

'American Dream' in which anything is possible. 'If there is anyone out there who still doubts that America is a place where all things are possible, who still wonders if the dream of our founders is alive in our time, who still questions the power of our democracy, tonight is your answer,' he said to a cheering crowd.

COMMITMENT FOR CHANGE

He was under no illusions about the difficult times ahead but stressed his commitment for change, with the support of the country.

'The road ahead will be long, our climb will be steep. We may not get there in one year or even one term, but America, I have never been more hopeful than I am tonight that we will get there. I promise you, we as a people will get there.'

Then, turning towards his young daughters, he switched comfortably from the role of being the most powerful figure in the land to that of ordinary father.

'Sasha and Malia, I love you both more than you can imagine, and you have earned the new puppy that's coming with us to the White House.'

Barack Obama was born in 1961 in Hawaii, the only American president to have been born on the island, where his father, Barack Obama Snr., met his mother, Ann Dunham while they were both studying at the University of Hawaii. Barack Snr was Kenyan, and the university's first African student, while Ann came from Kansas.

The couple divorced when Barack Jnr. was only three and his father returned to Kenya. His mother then married Indonesian Lolo Soetoro and Barack moved to live in Jakarta when he was six years old, living there until he was ten.

In 1971, Barack was sent back to Hawaii to live with his grandparents and, having excelled at school, studied at university in California and New York where he studied political science and international relations. He worked in Chicago with a communities organisation before studying law at Harvard where he made national headlines by becoming the first black president of the influential *Harvard Law Review*.

Barack Obama was a civil rights lawyer before pursuing a political career, working his way up the ladder to become Illinois State Senator.

On 10 February 2007, he formally announced his candidacy

for the 2008 Democratic presidential nomination. There followed a gruelling primary campaign, battling against his rival, former First Lady and then Senator from New York, Hillary Clinton, but he clinched victory on 3 June 2008.

As the world headed towards a financial crisis, the economy took centre stage and Obama's campaign agenda was one of reform and change in finance, education and healthcare.

After capturing Republican strongholds Virginia and Indiana and key battleground states Florida and Ohio the result in the race for the White House was a Democratic victory and Obama was inaugurated as President on 20 January 2009.

He cut taxes for working families, small businesses and first-time home buyers and lobbied allies to support a global economic stimulus package. He also managed to persuade Congress – in the face of united Republican opposition – to pass a bill for a complete overhaul in healthcare insurance, making it more easily available for all. •

WORLD TRANSFIXED BY THE GREAT ESCAPE

(*Daily Telegraph*, 14 October 2010)

THE DRAMA UNFOLDED like a Hollywood movie as millions around the world were united in watching live pictures of the Chilean miners great escape from their 'hell hole' underground.

One by one, the 32 miners emerged from the depths and took their first gulp of fresh air in 69 days, their relief and exhilaration shared by a global audience who were fighting with them every inch of the way.

The men had become trapped when part of the San Jose mine in Chile's Atacama Desert collapsed on 5 August 2010. A second collapse two days later blocked rescue access to the lower parts of the mine.

Not knowing whether the men were dead or alive, rescue teams began drilling exploratory bore holes, lowering listening devices. But as the days wore on, and there was no sign of life, hope began to turn towards despair.

RESCUERS FIND NOTE

Then, seventeen days after the accident, rescuers found a note from the miners attached to one of the listening probes saying, 'Estamos bien en el refugio los 33' ['All 33 of us are well inside the shelter.']

It referred to a refuge shelter 700m (2,300ft) down, where the men had been having lunch when the first collapse occurred.

News that the men were alive quickly spread around the world and the miners' families and friends set up camp around the mine, providing emotional support for each other during the ordeal. It was dubbed Campo Esperanza, or Camp Hope.

Communications were set up and emergency supplies and fresh water were sent down the borehole to the miners who had been surviving on rations. The longest and most complex mining rescue in history was about to take place as three different drills were tried out, called Plans A, B and C, to see which would work best. To save time, they bored down into the rock simultaneously.

FREE BY CHRISTMAS?

It was thought that the men would be freed by Christmas but the excellent progress by Plan B drill indicated that breakthrough would happen much quicker than expected. The man at the controls of this rig was an American named Jeff Hart, who had been in Afghanistan drilling water wells for the U.S. military's forward operating bases when he got the call to fly to Chile.

Meanwhile, food, drink, medicine and letters from loved ones were passed on to the miners via two narrow boreholes that became their lifelines.

Plan B drill finally broke through to the miners on 9 October and there was jubilation under and above ground in Campo Esperanza, as well as around the world.

Further good news came after a video inspection of the shaft showed the rock to be quite stable and only the first 96m (315ft) needed to be encased with steel pipes.

A rescue capsule was put in place attached to a winch and pulley and at 11.15pm local time on Tuesday, 12 October (2.15am GMT on Wednesday, 13 October), technical expert Manuel Gonzalez entered the capsule and was lowered down the shaft. He was warmly embraced by the miners as he stepped out the other end, and Florencio Avalos took his place for the return journey.

FITTEST FIRST

The men had been supplied with green boiler suits and sunglasses to wear and an order of rescue had been planned with the fittest and most experienced winched up first in case anything went wrong and a cool head was required. Next would come the weakest, either psychologically or physically, and finally those who were considered to be in good health but not expert mining equipment operators.

Avalos reached the surface at ten minutes past midnight local time on Wednesday, 13 October and was warmly hugged by his sobbing son and wife, along with Mining Minister Laurence Golborne and Chilean President Sebastián Piñera. He was then strapped onto a stretcher and taken away for health checks – a procedure followed for each of the miners.

Next up was the exuberant Mario Sepulveda, who hugged his wife, ran to the rescue workers to exchange 'high fives' and punched the air as he led the crowd in chants of 'Viva Chile!' He also handed Piñera and other dignitaries pieces of rock from his shoulder bag as mementos.

The rescue team was soon able to reduce the time between each ascent from an hour to between 16 to 25 minutes. TV cameras below ground showed remarkable pictures of the trapped men – looking surprisingly fit and healthy – stepping into the capsule and being brought to the surface, one-by-one, with clockwork precision.

The last of the 33 miners to be rescued was shift supervisor Luis Urzua. The very last man left below on his own was rescuer Manuel Gonzalez, who strapped himself into the capsule for its final ride to the surface. •

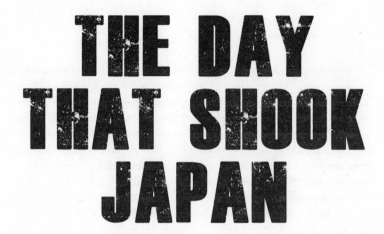

THE DAY THAT SHOOK JAPAN

(*Independent*, 12 March 2011)

JAPAN'S BIGGEST ever earthquake occurred on 11 March 2011 and triggered a huge tsunami that caused widespread devastation. Around 16,000 people died and a further 6,000 were injured.

The quake struck at 2.46pm local time beneath the seabed in the Pacific, 80 miles off Japan's east coast, sending terrifying waves 30ft high rushing towards coastlines at 500mph.

The tremor – the world's fifth biggest since records began in the 1800s – sparked a tsunami alert around the entire Pacific rim. Japan's early-warning system kicked in but things were happening at such a pace that there was little time to evacuate coastal populations.

The city of Sendai on Honshu island, close to the epicentre of the quake, took the worst hit as the tsunami crashed into 1,300 miles of coastline, smashing ships, demolishing houses and washing everything away as the water quickly surged ashore. Three thousand homes were destroyed and a petrochemical complex was set alight, sending huge orange fireballs into the air. Sendai Airport was flooded, causing severe damage.

The capital city of Toyko, some 170 miles away, escaped the worst horrors of the disaster but it was badly rocked. Office workers scrambled to hide under desks, people stumbled in the streets and falling debris caused havoc. At least 20 people were injured when the roof of a hall collapsed onto a graduation ceremony.

THOUSANDS STRANDED

With roads badly damaged, many found themselves unable to flee. All railway services were suspended in Tokyo, with an estimated 20,000 people stranded at major stations across the city.

To the east of the capital in Ichihara, Chiba, a huge fire broke out at an oil refinery. It raged for ten days before being extinguished.

The earthquake was followed by over a hundred 'aftershocks', which caused further damage. A dam burst in north-eastern Fukushima prefecture, sweeping away 1,800 homes.

There were further problems when three nuclear plants were affected by the quake and some were swamped. At the Fukushima Daiichi plant, the tsunami severed its main power supply and also flooded the emergency generator rooms. With no electricity to power electronics systems and the pumps that circulate cooling water around the reactors, they began to overheat.

Over the course of the next few days, three of the reactors went into meltdown and there were several explosions. Military helicopters were used to 'bomb' the reactors with sea water to try to cool them down. Workers battling to restore electrical power were exposed to radiation leaks and were evacuated until radiation levels became more tolerable.

It wasn't until 20 May, more than three months after the earthquake, that the situation was brought fully under control and personnel were able to re-enter the main Reactor Building.

EXTENSIVE DAMAGE

The earthquake and tsunami caused extensive structural damage in Japan, splitting roads, buckling railways and rupturing concrete. Tens of thousands of people were left homeless.

With gas and water pipes and electrical cables destroyed, people were left without power and there was a shortage of water and food.

The force of the quake and tsunami was felt in other countries, too. Russia evacuated 11,000 residents from coastal areas of the Kuril Islands and a tsunami warning was given along some coastal areas of America. In California and Oregon, 8ft-high waves damaged docks and harbours. Thousands of people fled beaches in Hawaii as it was swamped by 7ft waves.

In the aftermath of the disaster, many countries helped with supplies and in sending search-and rescue-teams.

Japanese Prime Minister Naoto Kan said, 'In the 65 years after the end of World War II, this is the toughest and the most difficult crisis for Japan.' •

(*New York Post*, 2 May 2011)

ALMOST A DECADE after the 9/11 terror attack on the World Trade Center and the Pentagon, al-Qaeda leader Osama Bin Laden was killed by U.S. forces in Pakistan. It had taken months of planning but the raid was all over within 40 minutes.

The death of America's 'most wanted' man was announced by President Barack Obama who called it 'the most significant achievement to date in our nation's effort to defeat al-Qaeda'.

It transpired that U.S. intelligence had intercepted a phone call the previous August from a trusted courier of Bin Laden who was identified as Abu Ahmed al-Kuwaiti. The mobile-phone number was traced to a compound in Abbottabad, Pakistan, which was put under surveillance by CIA operatives on the ground and by high-altitude spy planes, which were able to take pictures and video footage of the building undetected.

A man thought to be Bin Laden was often spotted walking up and down within the compound but the CIA were unable to positively identify him even after Obama gave the go-ahead for a raid, which took place in the early hours of 2 May 2011. The operation was top secret. No other country had been informed.

LIVE VIDEO FEED

Two Black Hawk helicopters flew to Abbottabad, carrying 23 Navy Seals who blasted their way through several walls to get into the buildings. Back in Washington, the live events were being watched as they unfolded by Obama and his security team via a video camera with which one of the Seals was equipped.

According to U.S. officials, al-Kuwaiti fired at the troops as they searched the inner confines. They shot him dead along with his wife who made a lunge for them.

They also shot dead al-Kuwaiti's brother and Bin Laden's adult son, Khalid Bin Laden.

COMMANDOS GIVE CHASE

Osama Bin Laden was found on the top floor of the three-storey building, around 20 minutes into the raid, standing at the end of the corridor. He ducked back inside a room and the commandos chased after him. Initial U.S. reports said that Bin Laden shot at them, using his wife as a human shield, but this was later retracted and U.S. officials described how the Seals found two women in front of Bin Laden, screaming and trying to protect him. One of the women was pushed aside and another Seal shot Bin Laden in the head and chest.

His body was taken aboard a helicopter and flown back with the Seals to the U.S. air base in Bagram, Afghanistan.

From there Bin Laden's body was transferred to a U.S. aircraft carrier in the north Arabian Sea where it was prepared for burial. After a Muslim funeral, his body was placed in a weighted bag and dropped into the water.

LOCALS SURPRISED

The large compound in which Bin Laden had been living had towering walls and a high metal security gate which led to inner walls and other security gates. The building was far bigger than any others in the neighbourhood and lay only about a kilometre from the Pakistan Military Academy. Yet the Pakistan security forces said they had no idea that Bin Laden had been living there and residents of the area also expressed their surprise. Some told how the occupants of the compound rarely went out and when they did so – in either a red Suzuki jeep or a van – they passed through security doors that closed immediately afterwards.

After the death of Bin Laden was announced, crowds gathered outside the White House in Washington, D.C., chanting 'USA, USA' and singing 'The Star Spangled Banner'.

Former U.S. President, George W. Bush, who had been in power during 9/11, commented, 'The fight against terror goes on, but tonight America has sent an unmistakable message: No matter how long it takes, justice will be done.' •

STEVE JOBS DEAD

APPLE ICON CHANGED THE WORLD

(*New York Post*, 6 October 2011)

VISIONARY, INVENTOR, maverick, designer, genius, salesman... Steve Jobs had been described as all of these things during a remarkable life in which he stood at the pinnacle of the electronics industry.

Born in San Francisco in February 1955 to unmarried students, he was given up for adoption to a Californian couple and grew up in Cupertino – later to become the headquarters of Apple, the world's most valuable technology company.

After leaving school he helped to design video games for Atari, earning enough money to fund a six-month travelling experience in India. On his return, he went back to work for Atari and joined a local computer club with his schoolfriend, Steve Wozniak, who was designing and building his own computer.

In 1976, he and Wozniak formed the Apple company in his parents' garage and that year they released Apple I – a computer lacking a keyboard and monitor. The following year they made a truly ground-breaking version with the Apple II – the first computer for personal use.

MOUSE AND GRAPHICS

The Macintosh computer in 1984 was a worldwide success with its use of a mouse to bypass the keyboard and its graphical user interface – allowing users to interact with images rather than text commands.

But within the company there were some concerns about Jobs's management style, said by some to be 'autocratic', and he was ousted from the company. However, this just spurred him on to do other things and he founded the NeXT computer development company in 1985, which aimed its products at the business and higher-education markets. A year later, he bought Graphics Group from the *Star Wars* director George Lucas, which had been producing expensive computer-animation hardware used by a number of film makers, including Disney. Jobs shifted away from manufacturing and began producing computer-animated feature films under the new name of Pixar.

HUGE PROFITS FOR PIXAR

The results were stunning. *Toy Story* was a massive hit, generating huge profits. It was followed by the likes of *Finding Nemo*, *Monsters Inc.* and *WALL-E*.

Apple paid more than $400 million for NeXT computers and, in 1996, Jobs was back with the company he founded, becoming CEO in 1997. And he was about to unleash a string of eye-opening technological marvels...

In 1998 he brought design to the forefront of desktop computers, ditching the traditional beige with the colourful iMac. Turning his attention to music, he revolutionised the market with iTunes and iPod, allowing the public to buy their favourite songs easily on the Internet and store and play them on a small portable device.

In 2005, Disney paid $7 billion worth of stock to buy Pixar from Jobs. Apple then entered the mobile-phone business with the sleek iPhone, its touch-screen control icons combining phone, media player, Internet and camera.

This was followed three years later by the iPad – a touch-screen 'tablet' computer providing the services of a laptop with the ease of use of an iPod.

FACE OF APPLE

Each new and exciting product was unveiled by Steve Jobs in theatrical style, wearing his trademark black turtle-neck jumper, faded blue jeans and trainers. He made his inventions look appealing to own and explained their functions in a simple way. He was the face of Apple with a flair for knowing what people wanted before they knew themselves.

His untimely death from pancreatic cancer at the age of 56 on 5 October 2011 robbed the world of one of the most influential men of his generation. He had been fighting cancer for eight years and had a liver transplant in 2009. He took medical leave in January 2011, before resigning as CEO in August, although he remained as Apple's chairman.

On the day of his death, Microsoft founder Bill Gates commented, 'The world rarely sees someone who has had the profound impact Steve has had, the effects of which will be felt for many generations to come.'

And U.S. President Obama said, 'By making computers personal and putting the Internet in our pockets, he made the information revolution not only accessible, but intuitive and fun.

'He transformed our lives, redefined entire industries and achieved one of the rarest feats in human history: he changed the way each of us sees the world.' •

W9-CEW-789

THE

RETURN

OF

IXTAB

A NOVEL

ROBERT ZITELLA

EMERALD
BOOK CO.

This book is a work of fiction. Names, characters, businesses, organizations, places, events, and incidents are either a product of the author's imagination or are used fictitiously. Any resemblance to actual persons, living or dead, events, or locales is entirely coincidental.

Published by Emerald Book Company
Austin, TX
www.emeraldbookcompany.com

Copyright ©2011 Robert Zitella

All rights reserved.

No part of this book may be reproduced, stored in a retrieval system, or transmitted by any means, electronic, mechanical, photocopying, recording, or otherwise, without written permission from the publisher.

Distributed by Emerald Book Company

For ordering information or special discounts for bulk purchases, please contact Emerald Book Company at PO Box 91869, Austin, TX 78709, 512.891.6100.

Design and composition by Greenleaf Book Group LLC and Alex Head
Cover design by Greenleaf Book Group LLC

Cataloging-in-Publication data
Publisher's Cataloging-In-Publication Data
(Prepared by The Donohue Group, Inc.)
Zitella, Robert.
    The return of Ixtab : a novel / Robert Zitella. -- 1st ed.
    p. ; cm.
    ISBN: 978-1-934572-53-5
    1. End of the world--Fiction. 2. Mayas--Prophecies--Fiction. 3. Luck--Fiction. 4. Assassins--Fiction. 5. Adventure fiction. 6. Science fiction, American. I. Title.
    PS3626.I84 R48 2011
    813.6   2010934921

ISBN 13: 978-1-934572-53-5

Part of the Tree Neutral® program, which offsets the number of trees consumed in the production and printing of this book by taking proactive steps, such as planting trees in direct proportion to the number of trees used: www.treeneutral.com

TreeNeutral

Printed in the United States of America on acid-free paper

10 11 12 13 14 15   10 9 8 7 6 5 4 3 2 1

First Edition

For my wife, Lisa, and our six children: Rebecca, Joseph, Jack, Annabella, Luke, and Lucy.

CHAPTER 1

Rocks the size of small moons spiraled toward the silent blue planet. These were no ordinary asteroids. These jagged behemoths were as close to the origins of the universe as anything that still existed. They contained the essence of the universe, the building blocks of all life. They were a part of God. They came from the beginning, the beginning of everything, when the darkness turned to light.

Most of the asteroids' original energy had been spread thinly across an ever-expanding space, but here, in this group of rocks, it was concentrated into a force as powerful as a thousand suns.

The largest asteroid of the group hurtled toward Earth; the others continued their never-ending journey through space. This largest asteroid plummeted through Earth's atmosphere, breaking into thousands of pieces. But its core remained intact, glowing fiery hot.

The rock continued to fall, silently drawing closer to the planet, which was teeming with life. With a shrieking explosion the rock plunged into the ocean, evaporating it in seconds.

A blast of energy spread from the rock in every direction at the speed of light, bringing death in waves.

The energy contracted as quickly as it had spread, returning to its source, back to the remains of the once great asteroid, transforming the rock at an atomic level. The ancient material briefly experienced a mingling of its existence and the destruction it had caused.

The birth of this new entity brought death to an uncountable number of beings instantly; nearly every creature that survived the impact died within weeks due to the massive amounts of debris that shot skyward and blocked the sun that had sustained the flora at the bottom of the food chain.

The core of the killer asteroid remained hidden in a massive crater. Now only a foot or two wide, it glowed a shade of purple that had not previously existed on this planet. The rock lay cooling, its glow dimming but never dying out completely. Time covered and uncovered it. It waited, hidden, incomplete. Calling. Waiting.

CHAPTER 2

Steve Soto stood waiting for the fat guy to get off his favorite chest-exercise machine. Metal clanked and men grunted, and Steve tried to ignore the smell of his gym.

The guy using Steve's machine looked about thirty years old and about nine months pregnant. With a final grunt, he rose to a sitting position. He gave Steve an irritated look as he got up and lumbered to the next machine, leaving a sweat slick on the bench's padding.

Steve had half a mind to remind big boy about common gym courtesy, but considering that the man outweighed him by thirty or forty pounds, and that Steve wasn't eager to cause a scene, he chose instead to wipe the slick with his own towel and begin his set—after dropping the weight down to nearly half of what it had been.

Though he usually ate more than his share, Steve had always been skinny. He was nearly six feet tall, but he weighed less than 170 pounds. Even after a year of working the weights, he remained a beanpole. What little fat he'd had had been replaced with lean muscle, and although he was healthier, it made his already thin frame appear even thinner. Hoping to put on some pounds, he had recently started drinking a powered shake mixture he had stumbled upon, but it didn't seem to be working either.

It was 6:30 a.m., and he would have to shower now to make it to work by seven. When he first joined the gym he made the mistake of coming after work. At night, the place was filled with pumped-up guys yelling at each other for one more set—screaming, spitting, and strutting. Wherever he went on the gym floor in the evenings, there were spandex-wearing meatheads talking too loudly and preening for the women who filled the rows of elliptical machines. Steve more than once imagined they were looking at him and cracking jokes about his physique, and that fear once became a reality when the leader of the meathead pack, after a louder than normal set of squats, looked in Steve's direction and shouted to his friends, "Hey, feed the hungry!" The other meatheads roared with laughter, and a few members of the elliptical peanut gallery cackled.

Humiliated, Steve had marched to the locker room and decided then and there that mornings would be a much better time to work out.

In the locker room now, Steve checked out his reflection as he passed a mirror. He had to stop and do a double take. He looked bigger.

He continued to study himself in the mirror, not caring what the other men in the locker room thought. There definitely was a change: a roundness to his biceps, a little pop to his shoulder muscles. Steve's mood suddenly brightened. After a year of no results, he was finally seeing a payoff for his religiously followed, four-times-a-week workout program.

He jumped into the shower, fantasizing about going back

to his evening workout schedule and outlifting the meatheads. He caught himself in his fantasy and then quickly finished showering.

Steve wore the same clothes combination every day: chino pants, an oxford shirt with the top button unbuttoned, and a dark tie, slack enough to be comfortable but tidy enough to look professional. He worked for the Hubbel Corporation, a midsize third-party administrator of insurance claims. Or, as he told people, a company full of bean counters. He was a senior analyst, which meant he was an analyst who had been at Hubbel for more than a year, and he was one promotion away from having junior analysts report to him. This was supposed to have been a "passing time" job after he graduated from community college, but it had turned into his career. Unable to find work as a computer-game programmer, his dream profession, he had taken a junior analyst position to pay the bills. Five years later he was still at Hubbel, as the analyst with the most seniority in his department.

The job didn't have a high retention rate. It was thoughtless work, basically consisting of matching numbers from one sheet with those on another sheet. He kept his resume at the ready and sent it out occasionally, but it seemed no one was hiring. The economy bottomed out a year after he began working at Hubbel, and it still hadn't recovered. Every department at Steve's location was working with considerably fewer people than when he'd started. He figured he was lucky to have a job.

Steve exited the front door of Joe's Gym and walked into the already hot morning air of Las Vegas. It was October, and the heat had been unbearable for months, even by Vegas standards. He had read something the other day about how 2012 was already one of the top five hottest years in history, and if the temperatures continued at their current levels for much longer, this would be the hottest year ever. Between the extreme weather, the wars, new viruses, a world economy still in the dumps, and the 12/21/12 Mayan calendar prophesy, there was no shortage of end-is-near nonsense. It reminded Steve of the Y2K stuff when he was a kid, but this was far worse. Every television show and bestseller seemed to be about the end of the world.

Steve's back was already damp when he reached his 2009 Toyota Prius. He started the silent engine and made his way into morning traffic.

* * *

By the time Steve reached work, a few miles away, it felt like the temperature had risen another ten degrees, and beads of sweat had collected on his forehead. A blast of frigid air greeted him inside the foyer of Lincoln Plaza, a thirty-story building in which Hubbel occupied multiple floors.

After several security checkpoints, an elevator ride, and two card swipes, Steve was in the nondescript Hubbel lobby. The receptionist sat at her desk surfing the web and, as usual, didn't acknowledge his presence as he walked to his cubicle— the same one he'd worked in for five years. He plopped into his seat, fired up his computer, and went to grab a cup of coffee while his computer booted up on the notoriously slow Hubbel network system.

Steve's cubicle was one of twenty on the floor; a row of private offices lined the exterior walls. His cubicle was in a group of four, one of which no one sat in. Jim Ritter and a woman named Doris occupied the other two.

If Steve had a best friend, it was Jim, but that wasn't saying much. Their relationship was based on office talk, weekly after-work happy hours, and a daily lunch run. Their conversations never did more than scratch the surface of either one's life. Steve knew where Jim lived, that he was single, and that he liked to play online games. He also knew that Jim could turn just about anything Steve said into a sexual innuendo. "I *bet* you want to thank her!" Jim had whispered to Steve the previous morning, after Steve thanked the girl who served him his coffee.

Doris, the occupant of the other cubicle, was a chubby, overly cheery middle-aged woman who was always good for standard office banter. She frequently complained about the boss or how slow Mondays passed. Her cubicle was covered with pictures of her cats, and although Steve didn't really know how many she had, he hoped it was fewer than a hundred.

Pictures of Mr. Doris used to be sprinkled in with the cat photos, but about a year ago, without any explanation or change in Doris's bouncy demeanor, all traces of Mr. Doris had disappeared from the cubicle, along with the ring from Doris's left hand. Steve wanted to ask her what had happened, but he'd decided it would be too awkward and would just lead to her asking questions about his personal life that he didn't want to answer.

The first question Doris would've asked is why he didn't have any pictures in his cubicle. Everybody in the office had something posted on his or her walls—even Jim. He had one picture of his parents and brother and a bunch of pictures of beautiful women, each of them dressed just tastefully enough to not be offensive. Jim claimed the women were his cousins, but most of the photos were cut out of magazines.

The truth was that Steve was alone. His dad had died in a car accident when he was three, and his mom died of cancer when he was twenty. Neither his mom nor his dad had siblings, and his living grandparents—if he had any—were unknown to him.

Steve opened his e-mail and found his list of daily tasks from Hubbel's headquarters. He would print out the files and go through them line by line, looking for mistakes and inconsistencies. This was eighty percent of his job. As Steve began printing out his day's work, Jim and Doris walked past his desk.

"Didn't the weekend just fly by, hon!" said Doris.

Steve answered with insincere enthusiasm. "Sure did."

He quickly turned his attention to Jim to keep himself from thinking of poor Doris sitting alone with her cats for two days.

"Steve-o, that looks like a lot of work, dude. Mondays suck!" Jim said, leaning over the cubicle wall and eyeing the pile of papers in Steve's printer tray.

Steve hated being called Steve-o, but that was Jim's favorite way to refer to him—that and various slang terms for genitalia, when Doris wasn't around to hear. Jim was small, nearly thirty years old, and called himself "Kornese"—half Korean and half Chinese. He had labeled Steve "Mexipean," since his dad was Mexican and his mother's family was a mix of European nationalities.

"I could be done by ten if I wanted to," Steve said slyly, glancing around to make sure his boss, Greg, wasn't around.

He could finish his work by ten most days, but he would stretch it out until quitting time, four o'clock. He used to try to impress his bosses, Greg Hanson being the latest one, but fast work was not rewarded at Hubbel. He had learned from several years of exceeding expectations that working his fastest resulted only in a junior analyst being fired and his or her work being dumped on Steve. Since he learned that corporate lesson, Steve's day consisted of ten-minute bursts of work, walking around the building or outside, a few coffee runs down the street, and the pinnacle of the day, going with Jim to one of three nearby restaurants for lunch hour. On good days, usually Fridays, Greg would leave at two or three in the afternoon, and Steve would put a fast, final push on his work, e-mail it to corporate, sneak out the stairwell exit, and meet Jim for wings and beer.

"Dude, you look like a linebacker today," Jim said, looking Steve up and down.

"You think?" Steve asked, acting uninterested.

"Hell yeah, man! You look like you put on ten pounds of muscle this weekend, steroid boy."

"Ah, thanks, I guess." Steve felt stronger, too. Something had been building in him for a while—a few days or weeks, he wasn't sure. The weight lifting was paying off in more ways than one. He felt as confident and powerful as he ever had.

That confidence quickly drained from his body when Katie Landry, Greg's beautiful assistant, brushed past his cubicle, her sweet fragrance trailing her. Steve snuck a look at her. He had a huge crush on Katie, who was dark-haired and slender, probably a few years younger than Steve.

Jim interrupted his silent adoration. "Hey Kate, wild weekend?" he said with a giggle.

"Morning, Jim," she replied, ignoring his question. She turned her head slightly to catch Steve's eye and gave him the slightest of smiles as she continued through the office.

"Dude, did she just smile at you?" Jim asked as he watched Katie walk away. "And you don't even give her a hello? You're such a puss."

"No, you had that covered, moron. 'Wild weekend'?"

"You better make your move, or I just might. Big Jim is good with the ladies," Jim said, nodding his head.

"Yeah," Steve shot back, "Big Jim is good at getting ladies to take out restraining orders against him. I'm getting to work. Some of us actually *do* work around here."

Jim squeezed his face as though he was sucking on a lemon drop and disappeared behind the divider.

CHAPTER 3

For thousands of Earth years it sat and waited, shining an eerie purple, its once great mass reduced to almost nothing.

The changes around its new form occurred almost immediately after its fiery arrival on Earth. At first, it lay in a lifeless, steam-filled valley, where it was cooled by time and an ever-darkening sky.

Rains came, and soon the sea returned. Cold changed to warm, which changed to hot and then back to cold. Rains turned to snow, and glaciers moved over the rock.

This pattern continued for years, leaving it in a warm gulf teeming with aquatic life. Its brightness compelled the creatures of the sea to come closer, but when they drew near, a screaming sense of danger stopped them and sent them fleeing.

It continued to sit alone, glowing, waiting, unfinished.

CHAPTER 4

Ted Baron stood patiently in the shadows of the Royal Arms apartment building, waiting for Larry Radcliffe to come home.

Ted had never met Larry, but he knew who he was. Ted's employer, Edgar Vega, had given him a file that contained a photo of Larry and his Oklahoma driver's license, which showed a Tulsa address. The file said that Larry was thirty-two and divorced.

He didn't know that Larry had accidentally killed a girl when he crashed his car into another one after a few drinks. The girl had been the daughter of one of Mr. Vega's close associates. Larry served only two months in prison after pleading guilty to manslaughter. Larry probably thought his debt was paid, but Mr. Vega decided it wasn't.

Ted has been working for Mr. Vega for almost ten years. His title at Mr. Vega's multinational conglomerate, Next Industries, was Head of Internal Security. He performed a variety of tasks for Mr. Vega, but this kind was the most profitable.

Ted had done this type of job for Mr. Vega more than a dozen times, and some of the assignments, he knew, were business-related, involving men or women who had ties to Mr. Vega's company. Other times he had no idea what the person had done. But Ted never asked questions, and Mr. Vega appreciated that.

As he waited for Larry, Ted felt the familiar aches in his knees and back. When he was in the Special Forces, he could stay in the same position for hours. But now, at forty, he had a hard time standing in one place for too long.

Ted's many years of training for Uncle Sam prepared him for almost anything, but he never really got to put that training to use for his country. The most action he saw was in the First Gulf War, when he was on the ground in Kuwait for a month. He mainly did prisoner interrogations, pulling information out of terrified Iraqi soldiers who were more than willing to talk; it wasn't a job that required his special skills.

But the army, through extensive testing, could pick out the right types of people for the work it had trained Ted to do. Mr. Vega once told Ted that the thing he liked best about him was his ability to "perform any task without the problems of morals and conscience." The comment didn't offend Ted.

Ted stretched his neck, touching his head to one shoulder and then the other, and felt the satisfying crack of his spine. Inflicting pain or even taking a life didn't bother Ted—as a matter of fact, he almost enjoyed killing. He was a walking God; he could decide life or death. He often smiled to himself as he passed through crowds of people: they didn't know how close they were to death, that he was allowing them to live. He was like a lion moving among a flock of sheep.

A car pulled into the Royal Arms parking lot. He looked at his watch: 11:15 p.m. This should be his latest lamb. For three days he had scouted Larry, and he'd learned that he followed a routine: after working the second shift at a chemical plant, Larry would come straight home, where he would watch television and drink a few beers before falling asleep, usually with the box still on. Larry always used the north stairs to get to his second-floor apartment, and Ted waited on a nearby landing overlooking the parking lot. He didn't like the idea of doing this in the open, but he didn't have a choice; he had been told to make it look like an accident.

Dressed in a tank top and beat-up jeans, with an unshaven face and uncombed hair, Ted blended in nicely with his surroundings. He would have preferred to be in one of his suits, but a large man dressed in Armani was not a common sight at the Royal Arms.

Ted could now see that the car was Larry's. As Larry opened the door to get out, Ted backed halfway up a flight of stairs and waited. He listened to Larry's footsteps approaching quickly, put his head down, and pretended to stumble down the stairs. All of Ted's senses were on high alert for sound and movement, but mostly they were fixed on the footsteps. Larry bounded up to the second floor, almost colliding with Ted.

"Hey, man, watch it!" Larry said as Ted bumped into him. Those were Larry's final words. Ted made eye contact to be sure he had the right man, and Larry must have seen something in Ted's eye, because fear sprung into his face. This was Ted's favorite part. He loved the look people got when they realized they were in mortal danger. He fed on it.

In one swift motion he had learned in the army, Ted knocked into Larry, grabbed him by the head in a sleeper hold, and cracked his neck. The body slumped against Ted, lifeless.

Ted held Larry against him and listened.

Silence.

He quickly dragged Larry down the flight of stairs, smashed his forehead once against the ground, and positioned the body so that it looked as though he had taken a nasty fall. He took a bottle of vodka from his pants pocket, poured a little into Larry's mouth and a little on his shirt, wiped the bottle clean of prints, and placed it on the stairwell floor, near Larry's outstretched hand.

The story lay in front of him: Larry, drunk, was taking a swig as he walked down the stairs when he lost his balance and had a tragic spill.

As Ted left the stairwell he felt the power racing through his veins, the power of life and death. He looked forward to informing his boss of another success. If he hurried, he just might make the red-eye back to San Francisco.

CHAPTER 5

Tec squatted on a tree branch overlooking a river that rushed into the ocean, hidden by the branches around him.

Tec and his twin brother, Que—two sixteen-year-old princes—had snuck out of a temple ceremony celebrating the creation of the world. Usually, he liked to watch the ceremony, mostly because he and his brother were named after the tale's two main characters. As the story went, nothing existed before the goddess Ixtab. But then she bore two sons, Tec and Que, and all three sacrificed themselves: Ixtab became the sun, Tec the Earth, and Que the stars. Through their sacrifices man eventually rose.

This year, Que had been too fidgety to enjoy the show, so he and Tec had snuck out into the jungle. Perched in the tree, Tec listened intently for any sound outside of the existing canopy of noise: the rushing water, birds singing, jungle animals squealing. He waited for Que, determined to catch him by surprise and pin him to the ground. This was a game they had played since they were able to run. The rules were simple: they would begin together in the middle of the jungle and run in opposite directions, but never beyond the valley, and then attempt to take the other by surprise. Since the days they first ventured off as children, they had known the line they could not cross, at the valley's highpoint, where the spear of the gods protruded from the ground.

Que won more often than not, and the few times Tec had won, Que hadn't talked to him for days. Though they were twins, Que was bigger and faster. But Tec was smarter. He was very good at concealing himself, waiting for his brother to walk by, and then springing into attack, but when they played their game, the element of surprise usually wasn't enough to match Que's superior strength and speed.

Even though Tec was older than Que by a few breaths, most of the villagers felt Que would someday be their king. Their father, the great Gukumatz, would soon pick one of his sons to be his successor, and although Tec wanted to be king, he would accept his father's decision. He'd decided that he would help his brother in any way possible if Que became king, though he knew his brother would not return the favor were the roles reversed. It was likely that Que would want to kill Tec to take his place, and that was ultimately why Tec would accept his father's decision. Tec didn't see himself as a coward; he just wanted peace with his brother. He wanted things to remain unchanged.

Tec took a deep breath, inhaling the smell of the jungle, a scent so rich it bordered on unpleasant. As he scanned the trees in front of him, he noticed that the singing birds and squealing animals had become silent.

He thought a jaguar might be close, but that fear lasted only a moment, until he felt a sharp smack to the back of his skull and heard his brother's laughter. Tec fell face-first from the branch to the jungle floor, hitting a rock and opening a gash on his forehead.

"You are bleeding more than I will during the vision ceremony, when I become king!" Que said mockingly from the tree above.

The thought of the vision ceremony made Tec shudder. When a king died, the ascension of the new king began with a ceremony in which he barricades himself in the main temple and ingests the God Medicine, a potion that will let him see as the gods see. The new king then cuts himself on the penis, which bleeds onto a sacred cloth. Once the cloth is soaked in blood, it is set on fire, and the new king sees his own destiny and the future of his people in the smoke.

This ceremony was another reason Tec wasn't interested in becoming king, but the thought of undergoing this ordeal didn't appear to frighten Que. In fact, it seemed to excite him.

"Brother, how did you find me?" asked Tec.

"Ha, if I told you, you would know my secret! Do you think I'm stupid?" Que said.

Tec knew he was on dangerous ground with his brother. He was alone and wounded, and he had no interest in antagonizing his only rival further.

"No, brother, I do not think you're stupid," Tec replied, wiping the blood out of his eye.

Que jumped to the ground from the branch on which Tec had been standing, landing effortlessly on his feet. "Come, brother. Let us return home before the *b'alam* feasts on your skinny body," Que said with a smile.

* * *

They walked back to their village together, Tec occasionally wiping the blood out of his right eye and his brother making good-natured jokes at his expense. This is how Tec liked being with his brother—side by side, not afraid that Que might be plotting against him, like they had been when they were younger and unconcerned with their father's death.

As they approached their village, they could see the main temple, of which their father had overseen construction, rising out of the jungle. The people thought of him as their greatest king: he had led them fearlessly in battle, expanding their domain to many tribes and villages, and had embraced the priests of the village, built temples, and studied the great heavens and the messages from the gods that resided in them. His heroic deeds and his understanding of the gods had led his people through wars, famines, and great storms. Tec knew that the people did not have the highest hopes for the king's sons; he had heard whispers that he and his brother combined might equal a king like their father, but that alone, neither was destined for greatness.

Despite their lack of confidence, the people greeted Tec and Que as they entered the village, and Tec enjoyed the reception, putting his worries about the future out of his head.

CHAPTER 6

Steve entered the Hubbel lobby as if he owned the place. The receptionist wished him a good morning—for the first time ever. Never before had he even warranted a look from the Ice Queen, as Jim referred to her. It was Friday, and Steve was looking forward to some after-work fun with Jim and the rest of the office crew at happy hour. Usually, Jim picked out a place that was running some crazy-sounding deal: dime beer, quarter wings, an all-you-can-eat buffet with no cover charge. Jim actually did research during the week to find these places. Las Vegas had no shortage of dives and near-dives with great deals, and Jim always found a new place to hit that was no more than a fifteen-minute drive from Hubbel.

Steve sat down in his cubicle, started his computer, and kicked back in his chair. Man, he felt great. He'd just had another outstanding workout; in the last week he had gained ten pounds, all of which seemed to be muscle. He was sleeping like a baby at night—and practically jumping out of bed in the morning.

He was going to write a letter to the makers of P80 Muscle Builder, the protein drink he'd been using daily. The P80 had to be what was doing this, but it seemed impossible that anything off the shelf could be that powerful. He started to worry a little: What if there was some steroid hidden in the powder? He considered checking the web to see if there were any complaints about the product. Hadn't there been a story recently about diet supplements from China containing steroids? *Still, it might be worth it,* he thought as he stretched his sculpted arms. His newfound bulk looked great in the mirror, and he was stronger, a lot stronger, on the machines at the gym; he was thinking he would soon move to free weights.

But first things first: he had to investigate the P80 powder. A Google search on his impossibly slow Hubbel computer brought up only advertisements and P80's home page. The website listed the ingredients, none of which jumped out at him. *Maybe hard work does pay off,* he thought. Still, it seemed weird. He'd started on the powder a few weeks ago and seen no results, but now he was seeing rapid changes. *What the hell, I'm due for something good in my life, aren't I?* he asked himself.

As he was pondering the sudden effects of the P80, Katie got off the elevator. His eyes followed her to her cubicle, which was outside Greg's office. He tried to catch her attention as she passed, but didn't have any luck.

Jim and Doris arrived at the same time, smiling as if they had been talking about something amusing. Doris walked around to her desk.

"Dude, I got the place for tonight!" Jim said, waving a flyer in front of Steve's face. Jim often made a Friday flyer for the office that alerted everyone to the location of the latest great deal he had found. Today's happy hour would be held at the

Pour House, which specialized in quarter beer and had a free buffet between 5 and 6 p.m.

"You could be a party planner, Jim," Steve said, impressed.

Steve opened his e-mail and got to work. Before he knew it, he was finished with his day's tasks. He had never finished this fast before; it was barely lunchtime and he had nothing to do. Steve crumpled a piece of paper and threw it into Jim's cubicle.

"You ready for lunch?" Steve asked.

"Ah, yeah," Jim answered, sounding preoccupied.

Steve looked over the cubicle wall and saw Jim surrounded by a mess of paper.

"Oh man, I think I screwed up the consolidation," Jim said, speaking to nobody.

"What does that mean?" Steve had no idea what Jim did; he just knew it involved numbers, lots and lots of numbers. The inbox on Jim's desk was always nearly full; he had a perpetual stack of work waiting to be done.

"Can I help?" Steve asked.

Jim shook out of it. "Yeah, you can buy me lunch, muscle boy. Let's go."

* * *

By midday Steve had cleaned his desk and every drawer in it, replaced his printer's ink cartridge, and filed every paper that could be filed. He occasionally peeked over the cubicle wall and saw Jim, deep in thought and muttering curses under his breath.

Without thinking, Steve walked toward Greg's office. Katie, sitting in the cubicle outside of Greg's door, was busy reading e-mails and looked annoyed. Steve normally would have kept walking past her, but avoiding her just didn't seem like a possibility today.

She was wearing a smart pink business blouse. Steve knew all of her outfits, and this was one of his favorites. *God, she is so hot!*

"Excuse me, Katie?"

She looked up, and her expression quickly softened.

"I was wondering if you were going to the happy hour?" Steve continued.

"I might. Depends, you know," she answered, smiling slightly as her eyes darted back to her computer screen.

"Well, great. Hope to see you there." Steve began to move away, his newfound confidence starting to wane.

"I take it you are going, then?" she asked, half looking at him but still preoccupied with her screen.

"Ah, yeah. Should be fun." Steve immediately regretted the way he said this—he sounded like a teenager going to a high school dance.

"OK, sounds good." She gave her full attention back to her e-mail.

Steve walked away feeling both embarrassed and excited.

CHAPTER 7

Ted entered the Next Industries complex from one of its secure garages. The company, which employed twenty thousand people worldwide, was headquartered here, in a multi-building campus in Silicon Valley. Next Industries, a Fortune 500 operation, developed technology for just about every industry, including aerospace companies and the military. Anything involving electronics, Next was part of it. Its main focus was software, and that's what it had come to be known for. Ted had designed security protocols for Next Industries facilities all over the globe, but the Silicon Valley location had the most interesting setup by far.

He was back in his uniform of choice, a well-tailored Italian suit that fit his muscular figure to a tee. He knew he was an imposing figure, and his manner around other Next employees only added to his intimidating aura. He rarely spoke to anyone but his second in command, and never cracked a joke or even smiled. This demeanor wasn't an affectation; it came naturally to Ted.

He swiped his key card and looked into the camera at the garage entrance. Once the biometrics program had analyzed the bone structure of his face, a green light lit up and he heard the familiar click of the door opening. The first thing he always noticed as he entered the main executive building was the cool air—and its antiseptic fragrance. The building, tightly sealed against the outside world, stood only two floors tall; the remaining fifteen were below ground, the lowest of those being dedicated to the most sensitive research. On the first floor was a row of sixteen elevators; each went to one floor only. Ted stepped onto the second-floor elevator, swiping his key card and pressing his thumb against a scanner to activate the elevator.

On his way into his office he passed Ken Burns, his second in command, who was already hard at work. Ken had a background similar to Ted's: ex-military, willing to do things that crossed certain ethical lines.

"Morning, chief," Ken said as Ted passed by.

"Anything going on?" Ted asked.

"No. Reports are on your desk, and Mr. Vega's office called for you. He would like to see you."

Mr. Vega was already asking for him. It wouldn't surprise Ted if he found out Mr. V worked twenty hours a day. He was first in the office, usually around 4 a.m., and Ted often got e-mails from him long past midnight. Ted entered his office, which had a view of the Next campus through a wall of one-way glass. The other walls were smooth, black, and empty, and the rest of the décor was equally Spartan. The only furniture his office held was a simple chair and a desk that resembled a large, black block. The office contained no photos and no personal items at all, giving it an unoccupied look.

Ted waved his hand over the corner of the desk, where a scanner read his fingerprints and prompted twenty video surveillance screens to appear on the opposite wall and five more screens on the wall behind him. One screen immediately asked for his log-in code, and the other screens lit up a fraction of a second after he keyed it in. There were no server lags at Next Industries, a benefit of working at the world's foremost software and computer systems company.

But the company's status also kept him busy. On a daily basis, hackers, thieves, and corporate spies tried to get pieces of information from Next's systems, its employees, and even its shredded trash. Mr. V's side projects were a welcome respite from these attacks. Ted had seen it all.

He had a floor of programmers whose job it was to fight hackers, analyze data, and do everything they could to thwart future attacks, and Next's group of lawyers and private investigators was always working on one threat or another. He even monitored all the employees at Next, from the night cleaning crew to the corporate vice presidents. He checked their bank accounts for unusual purchases and kept track of their medical records. All the things that a company had no business accessing, he accessed—unknown to everyone, except, of course, Mr. V.

Ted glanced over the records of the previous night's attacks against Next's main servers and looked at a few summary reports of employee activities. One employee in particular stuck out. A Mr. Dale Thorn was exhibiting some curious behavior—most likely it was nothing, but it was interesting nevertheless. Thorn was on loan to Next Industries from neighboring Apollo Industries, which Ted knew was a front for the research being conducted on Vega's underground floors. Thorn had been entering the building at strange times and repeatedly logging in to stations he didn't previously frequent. Ted printed out the record displayed on his screen.

"Ken, let's take a closer look at him," Ted said, pointing to Thorn's name on the printout.

"Sure thing, boss."

"Ken, walk with me," Ted ordered as he left his office.

"Quiet night last night, huh?" Ted asked. He was concerned it was too quiet; there had only been a few minor attempted intrusions into the main servers.

"Seems that way," said Ken.

"I want you to rotate the night security teams, starting immediately," Ted commanded. He had multiple security groups crossed-trained; they never did the same job for more than a few months. The rotation he'd just ordered was early, but maybe an early rotation was what was needed. The summary reports he reviewed showed either a dramatic drop in attempted hacking activity in the last few weeks or a myriad of failures from his group, ranging from illegal activity to laziness. A new set of eyes always seemed to improve operations.

Ted and Ken proceeded to the security elevator that would drop them fifteen floors underground, to Mr. Vega's office. The rest of the building's interior looked much like Ted's office: lots of plain black walls, though here they were broken up by stone columns. The clean, sterile smell in the air that Ted enjoyed so much permeated every area of the complex.

He and Ken passed one of their charges in the hallway. "Stop!" Ted bellowed.

The young man stopped and turned to face them.

"You know our policy on facial hair, don't you?" Ted asked evenly. The obviously scared employee was sporting a goatee.

"Yes, sir. I mean, I guess not. Sir. I thought it referred to full beards."

Ted glared at the boy. His name tag identified him as Larry. *Funny how the universe works*, Ted thought. *Another Larry to slaughter.*

Ted noticed Larry's mannerisms: the tilt of his head, the lack of eye contact, the hand that repeatedly went to his face, the way his body was positioned at an angle to them. Larry was lying. He'd probably thought no one would call him on the goatee. Or worse, perhaps Larry was a nonconformist— not a good type of person to have on the team.

"Fair enough," Ted said, continuing to walk in the direction he had been going. Ken followed silently, and Larry, relieved, continued down the hallway in the opposite direction.

"Fire him," Ted said without sounding angry.

"Yes, sir," Ken replied.

When Ken had first begun working for Ted, he might have questioned such a directive, but he had seen Ted in action and learned to follow his orders without comment.

They stepped into the elevator and glided down to the fifteenth floor, where the doors opened silently.

Ted swallowed to un-pop his ears. He feared very little in life, but this floor always gave him an unsettling feeling. The main hallway branched off in four directions, leading to four separate departments that Mr. Vega directly controlled. One department was called Data Acquisition, where, from what Ted had gathered over the last few years, Mr. Vega had staff working around the clock to find men from around the world who fit a certain profile. No one besides Mr. Vega knew why they did this. Ted figured it had something to do with the out-of-town side jobs he did for Mr. Vega. The department with the most employees was Data Entry, where workers collected and entered information from birth certificates, death notices, newspaper articles, hospital records, police records, and real estate transactions. Ted was sure Data Entry recorded other data, but he didn't know what it was. He also knew that some high-level programmers worked in Data Entry, crunching information in a variety of ways.

The most interesting work was performed by the department Ted and Ken were now passing, Research and Development. Sometimes Ted retrieved certain items for Mr. Vega, in most cases legally but in a few instances through not-so-legal means. These items—ceramic figures, paintings, manuscripts, books, even scraps of paper—ended up here. Ted had personally delivered four meteorites to this lab along with countless papers, most written in a language he was unfamiliar with. Most of the papers were from Mexico or Central America; a few were from Spain. One item, a black rock the size of his hand, had been part of a display in a little museum in Guadalajara, Mexico. Ted had paid a night watchman the equivalent of a hundred dollars for it. When Ted brought the rock to his boss, Mr. Vega acted like it was the finest jewel on earth. Then, after Mr. Vega held it in his hands for a few moments, examining each side closely, Ted could see the excitement slip out of his eyes; the meteorite was not the one Mr. V was looking for. Ted later saw it catalogued and stored with the hundreds, if not thousands, of items Mr. Vega had at one time taken interest in, most of them about as valuable as that rock. Ted figured the true value of the rocks he collected for Mr. V was simply not apparent to him yet, since Mr. V was always one step ahead of everybody else. One thing was for sure: his boss was looking for a particular rock, and he hadn't found it yet.

They entered the lobby of Mr. Vega's offices, which had more of a human touch than the rest of the building. It had the feel of Mr. Vega's home country, Mexico, with its lush tropical plants, large statues, and paintings that had a clear Mexican heritage. The room's focal point was a large, round ceramic wall hanging. It was in the shape of the sun and depicted hundreds of animals, people, and other half-animal–half-human creatures performing acts ranging from peaceful farming to killing one another.

Nellie, Mr. Vega's personal assistant, sat at her desk, smiling coldly at them as they entered.

"Good morning, gentlemen," Nellie said without any emotion. "Mr. Baron, you may go right in."

"Good morning," Ted said as he continued past Nellie, down the long stone hallway decorated with paintings of landscapes. It felt almost like an English castle. Ken had remained in the lobby, where he would wait for Ted to return.

Ted tapped lightly on Mr. Vega's door, which was halfway open.

"Enter," Mr. Vega said coolly and evenly.

Ted entered the office. Mr. Vega sat facing the entrance behind a modern-looking desk, casually moving his mouse around and staring at his computer screen.

"Ah, Ted, welcome back," he said in a tone that was now friendly.

"Good to be back, sir," Ted replied.

Mr. Vega's hair always caught Ted off guard. It was thick, deep black, and had a remarkably healthy sheen. Ted figured Mr. Vega was about forty, but he didn't have a single gray hair on his head or wrinkle on his brow. A graceful six feet tall, he wasn't muscular, but he looked substantial. He was a billionaire from Next Industries alone, but he also came from a family that was one of Mexico's largest landowners. Sometime back, Ted had seen the breadth of Mr. Vega's holdings; in addition to Next they included everything from a huge phone company in Mexico to pig farms in South America.

"I see you were successful," said Mr. Vega.

"If you mean Tulsa, sir, then yes, we were, sir," Ted said, perturbed that he sounded like a nervous little boy. Mr. Vega may not have been a huge or scary-looking man, but there was something about him that let you know he was not to be trifled with.

"Good, good," he said. A few seconds passed. "Ted, I have big plans, and I want you to be part of them."

"Of course," Ted said, but the look in Mr. V's eyes told Ted he had interrupted.

"There are things going on here. Well, things are going on everywhere that you don't know about. Now don't get me wrong—you are one of, if not the most, loyal employees I have, Ted."

Ted noticed that his name was one of the only words that betrayed Mr. Vega's slight Mexican accent. It sounded more like "Teed" than "Ted."

"I want to show you something," Mr. Vega said solemnly. By his tone of voice, Ted could tell this was more than a typical work thing.

"Ted, I have watched you very closely, and you have proven completely trustworthy. I have tested you through the years, in ways you know of and in ways you don't."

"In ways I don't know of?"

"Well, let's just say I like to know who I am dealing with, especially when that person is handling such . . . well, such sensitive projects. My point is, you have never failed me, through word or action."

"Well, I have always tried to do my best, sir . . ."

Mr. Vega interrupted. "I know you have, Ted, and that is why I am going to share with you things that may seem strange to you, or even quite unbelievable. The future holds great things for me, Ted, and I want you to be part of it."

Ted was hearing the words, but he didn't really know what Mr. V was saying. Was he getting a promotion? What could be stranger than bribing people for rocks? "Well, I appreciate that and hope you know I won't let you down," he answered.

Even though Mr. V was offering kind words, Ted still had an uneasy feeling, as if he were playing with a poisonous snake. Mr. Vega was dangerous, even when he was giving compliments.

"Yes, of course, I know, Ted. I know."

With that, Mr. Vega extended his hand toward the door in an after-you motion. Ted exited the office and began walking down the corridor to the lobby.

"Ted," Mr. Vega said from behind him, "this way." Mr. Vega had stopped and was facing one of the hallway's stone walls. He flipped up a small rock that jutted from the wall and pressed his hand against an identification pad that lay beneath it. A green light swept up and down his hand and part of the wall slid silently to the side, revealing an elevator.

Ted looked on in wonder as Mr. Vega invited him into the elevator. Inside were buttons marked "Office," "X," "Y," and "Z." Mr. Vega pressed the X button.

He noticed Ted's confused expression. "Ted, there are three floors below us. X contains Astrophysics and Y contains Medical. Z is a floor I hope we never have to use. It's a sort of bomb shelter, but the largest and most user-friendly bomb shelter in the world. It can function as a self-sustaining colony and can house one hundred people comfortably."

"You did promise that this would be strange, but why do you . . . what is this all for, its purpose?"

"All in good time, Ted, but rest assured that preparations have begun—for anything."

For anything? Ted thought as the elevator door opened. But other matters quickly occupied his mind. The elevator opened to a viewing room above a large, bright chamber in which hundreds of people were bustling around. Rows of computers filled the room, and huge viewing screens covered the walls. Charts, trajectory diagrams, and photographs of outer space filled the screens. It looked like NASA's mission control, but with far better technology.

"Ted, this is Astrophysics. We use telescopes and satellites to look for certain events in the sky."

Mr. Vega held up his hand when he saw that Ted was about to unload a flurry of questions. "Ted, I just want you to see that there is much more than you know going on with the projects you perform for me—much more. And as the time grows near, I will share more with you."

As the time grows near? Ted half expected Mr. Vega to tell him about his plan to take over the world, like some sort of James Bond villain.

"Wait, where do these people come from?" asked Ted. He knew all of the job titles at Next. There were five thousand people who worked on the sprawling Next campus, and he didn't remember any titles in Astrophysics, or Medical.

"They actually work for our neighbor, Apollo. They enter the building next door and leave that way. I like the idea of separation, especially when it keeps their work hidden from certain shareholders."

"Come, Ted." Mr. Vega was walking back to the elevator, and once they were inside, he hit the Z button. The elevator opened to complete darkness. Mr. Vega stepped out and turned on a light, revealing a small room with Sheetrock walls and a dirt and rock floor. It smelled musty.

"This was part of a U.S. military base in the 1950s," Mr. Vega explained. "It was built for California military and government personnel. Of course, I had it updated many years ago. It has its own water supply and enough stored food and diesel fuel to operate for years. And it has other supplies that we'll need to continue our lives, in case certain things happen."

"Certain things happen? You mean terrorist attacks? Wars?" Ted asked.

"I am talking about larger disasters."

"Uh huh . . ." Ted said, having a hard time believing he was having this conversation.

"Ted, we are at a time in which prophecy is beginning to come true. There is something greater than you and I afoot, and it will make me a very powerful man. As a matter of fact, it's already happening, Ted."

"Well, you are one of the world's richest men."

"It goes beyond wealth, beyond any Earth-born power. It is about the universe, forces as wide as creation."

"To be honest, you sound like one of those 2012 end-of-the-world nuts, Mr. V." Ted tried to use humor to lighten his increasing uneasiness.

With an ominous tone that shot fear through Ted, Mr. Vega replied, "They are not nuts, Ted. I know that for sure."

Ted didn't know how to respond. Finally, Mr. Vega spoke again, breaking the uncomfortable silence. "Ted, let's go back up. I have shown you a lot today. I want you to digest it. I brought you down here because I will be asking you to do things that may have not made sense if you hadn't seen this. I'll need your best effort; I don't want you clouded by questions."

They stepped back into the elevator and started moving back toward the surface.

"Ted, you will be doing many more special jobs for me in the near future. Actually, this work will become close to your only job. We also have to involve more people, people I need you to recruit and control. Only you will know about my involvement."

"OK. But I'll need to know what you need," Ted said, trying to regain his bearings.

"Yes, of course, Ted," Mr. Vega said as the elevator opened to his hallway.

Ted felt disoriented as they stepped into the hall and the wall panel slid back into place. He was knocked further off balance by the sight of an old Mexican or Indian man standing in the hallway, dressed in casual clothes. Wrinkles a quarter inch deep ran through his face.

"Ah, Achi, there you are," Mr. Vega called to the old man.

Achi turned slowly toward Mr. Vega, revealing a blank expression.

"Ted, this is Achi, a sort of priest from my hometown. He will be staying with me for a while. He is an expert in Mayan symbols. He has been very valuable to me."

Ted extended his hand to Achi, who stared at it for an uncomfortable three seconds before shaking it, weakly.

"Well, Ted, I am sure you have a busy day. We will speak again soon," Mr. Vega said as he ushered Achi down the hallway, back toward his office.

"OK, Mr. V."

Ted turned and began walking back toward the lobby, where Ken was waiting for him.

"Ted, one more thing," Mr. Vega called out from behind him. "Don't call me Mr. V. My name is *Vega*, and I am very proud of it."

"Of course. I am sorry for the offense."

Mr. Vega walked away and began saying something to Achi, not even acknowledging Ted's apology.

Ted kicked himself for his embarrassing slight.

CHAPTER 8

The bar pressed against Steve's chest, threatening to crush it. He pushed with all his might and raised it enough to place it back on the rack.

He felt the blood rushing through his body, creating a pulsating beat in his temples. He looked up at the trio of forty-five-pound plates on each side of the barbell. He'd just benched over three hundred pounds, more than twice his body weight.

Unbelievable.

In the last month, he had gained twenty pounds, and he was even stronger than he looked. He kept promising himself he would back off on the P80 powder, but the results he was getting made that hard to do. A voice in his head kept repeating, *You know a simple powder couldn't give you results like this.* He chose to ignore that voice.

As Steve left the main floor at Joe's Gym and walked toward the locker room, he could sense people looking at him. He figured they were noticing the changes to his physique. Steve now wore a tank top to the gym to show off his new bulk, and he assumed they were wondering what type of steroid or growth hormone he was on.

In the locker room, Steve stopped in front of his favorite mirror and removed his shirt. *Man, I'm ripped!* he thought.

Then he felt that nagging worry again. How was this possible? No one should grow this fit, this quick. He had spent many nights on the web, looking to see if muscle growth was a symptom of some exotic disease. He hadn't found anything, but muscle wasn't the only symptom he had; he was sleeping only four or five hours a night and waking up refreshed, as though he'd gotten ten hours of sleep. His eyesight, which had been marginal before, was now razor sharp. He could hear his neighbors' conversations through his apartment wall. And when he went online at night and played Jim at Warzone, their favorite shoot-'em-up, he beat him every time. Jim had always kicked his butt before.

Steve felt like a superhero, but a worried superhero. Running through these strange circumstances in his mind, he showered and got dressed.

As he left the gym, his thoughts wandered to Katie. Every Friday he hoped to see her at happy hour, but she never showed. There was no happy hour last week; it was cancelled due to another round of layoffs. No one had been in the mood. Three weeks had passed since he'd last talked to Katie, when he asked if she was going to meet them after work. She hadn't shown up, and he didn't have the nerve to ask again. Since then, she barely made eye contact with him. He often imagined running into her outside of work, but what would he say to her? Maybe they would laugh at what a small world it was. Maybe they'd get a drink.

When he reached his car, Steve stopped daydreaming and began the short drive to work. As he moved into traffic he turned on the radio, which was tuned to a talk station, and once again the debate focused on the supposed end of the world in 2012. It seemed as if at least half of the programming on radio revolved around Earth's impending destruction. From what he had gathered by listening, the end of the Mayan calendar signified everything from the north and south poles reversing to the sun exploding to the universe collapsing to a stray planet hitting Earth to every other God-awful way civilization could be destroyed. Occasionally someone on the radio said 2012 would be the dawn of a great new age for humanity. But those guests didn't get as much airtime.

On this station, someone was arguing that "the Mayan calendar calls for doomsday on December twenty-first, but other religions, including . . ."—Steve changed the station. After surfing through commercials, he returned to the end-of-the-world program. Another person was talking now. He sounded calmer, and Steve figured he was providing the counterpoint to the previous guest's argument. "The Mayan calendar is based on cycles within cycles within cycles. What happens in 2012 is the ending of a major cycle. For the Mayans, 2012 is the end of what is known as the Great Cycle. The Great Cycle is a five thousand, one-hundred-twenty-five-year cycle that began at the date thirteen-zero-zero-zero-zero on the Mayan . . ."

He was interrupted by the shrill voice of the other guest. "So you agree, the Mayan calendar names December twenty-first as the end of the Great Cycle. How could they have known this? This knowledge is too advanced for such a primitive people. The signs are around us. The major religions all point to this doomsday: the Book of Revelation, the Hindu Paranas, the . . ."

The counterpoint man interrupted. "This end-of-the-world stuff and its signs have been misinterpreted by the ignorant for centuries."

A high-pitched "*Ignorant!*" screamed from the radio as Steve pulled his car into the Hubbel lot. He entered the building, pulling at his shirt collar; he missed his old broken-in work shirts, but he'd had to buy new, larger shirts since his old collars wouldn't button around his neck anymore.

He took the stairs for the added exercise and walked into the reception area expecting the Ice Queen to greet him, as she had been doing lately. But her desk was empty. Then Steve remembered last week's layoffs; the Ice Queen had gotten the ax, along with twenty other employees, including Doris. She'd cried as she loaded her belongings into an empty box, a security guard standing behind her. They vowed to keep in touch, but Steve knew chances were good he would never hear from her again, just as he had lost contact with all of the other people who had been let go.

This layoff was more stunning than the others; no one had expected it. Most of the staff thought the company was as close to bare bones as it could get. To make matters worse, Greg, the boss, was not well equipped to lay off people; he lacked empathy. He would have been a better guillotine operator.

Steve felt bad for Katie; she had the job of escorting people to Greg's office, each one knowing why he or she was going there. She'd looked like she was about to cry when she came to get Doris.

Steve, standing in his cubicle, looked across the office. It was mostly empty now. Katie sat at her desk, her eyes fixed on her computer screen. Greg, smiling, breezed past Steve. Steve agreed with Jim's latest assessment of Greg: "That dude is a douche!"

Steve sat in his chair, ready to begin another mindless day, when he noticed movement out of the corner of his eye. Through the opening in his cubicle, he saw that Raymond Tisdale, looking haggard, was moving through the office, scanning the workspaces as though he was trying to find someone. Raymond was an engineer, and a very odd engineer at that, who was often the butt of jokes that Jim whispered to Steve. Most of the jokes had to do with Raymond's lack of personal hygiene; you didn't want to ride in an elevator with Raymond during the summer months. Raymond was one of last week's layoffs, so Steve wondered why he was here. Maybe he was picking up his final paycheck.

Steve almost shouted a hello before he noticed the dangerous look on Raymond's face. His eyes were wild and he seemed to be muttering to himself, and the way he looked made the hairs on Steve's neck stand on end. Raymond had something in his hand, black and shiny. Was that a gun?

Steve's first impulse was to run and get help. Then he thought of Katie. His stomach dropped when he saw Raymond turn up the main aisle and make a beeline toward Katie's desk and Greg's office. Katie, squinting at her computer screen, was oblivious to her surroundings, and Greg had his back to Raymond as he neared Katie's desk.

When Steve looked back at this moment, he would not remember making the decision to charge Raymond. Why didn't he shout a warning? Run to security? He would never have an answer to these questions, nor understand completely what happened next.

Steve moved toward Raymond with no plan for what he'd do when he got there. He could see now that Raymond, walking purposefully, swinging his arms, was indeed carrying a gun, and it looked almost comically long to Steve, as if a flag bearing the word "BANG" would pop out were it fired.

Steve closed up the space between himself and Raymond quickly and silently. It seemed as though he were moving normally and Raymond in slow motion; Steve was a few feet away when Raymond raised the gun. Why was he moving so slowly? Steve saw Katie, looking terrified, turn toward Raymond as he pointed the gun at her. Steve seemed to be in a vacuum devoid of all sound except for the thump of his accelerating heartbeat. Then he heard a scream that sounded warbled, as if he were underwater and hearing the noise from above. It was Katie.

What seemed like a minute to Steve happened in seconds. Greg turned from the entrance to his office when he heard Katie's scream. Steve chopped down on Raymond's arm, and as the gun fired into the floor he heard a loud boom that sounded like a recording played at too slow a speed. Greg moved to close his door, a look of pure panic on his face.

Steve grabbed Raymond's wrist and squeezed as hard as he could until Raymond dropped the gun. Raymond's howl snapped Steve out of what seemed like a trance. Now he could hear the shouts from the other people in the office.

Steve grabbed Raymond by the hair and slammed his head into Greg's door, punching a large, head-shaped dent in it. Raymond's screams stopped immediately, and he slumped to the floor, unconscious, emitting an odor that resembled a mix of bad cheese and ammonia.

"Run!" Steve shouted to Katie.

She stared blankly at Steve for a few seconds and then sprinted down the aisle, stopped, looked back, and then began running again.

She screamed again at the sight of two armed men running down the aisle in her direction, but stopped when she realized who they were.

By the time they reached Steve, the two security guards had their guns drawn.

"Drop it! Drop it!" one of the guards, a chubby guy, yelled at Steve.

"I don't have a gun," Steve said, pointing at Raymond's gun, which lay on the floor.

The other guard, tall and skinny, yelled, "Down on the ground!"

Steve complied, dropping down next to Raymond.

"It was him. I . . . I stopped him," Steve stuttered.

That didn't stop one of the guards from driving a knee into Steve's back, grabbing one of his arms, and twisting it behind his back. "Goddamn it!" Steve shouted.

It felt as if his arm had been torn out of its socket. He pulled it away instinctively, nearly whipping the security guard aside.

The other guard pounced on Steve's back and slapped handcuffs around his wrists. "This guy is out," one of the guards said, looking at Raymond. "Oh shit, his head is bleeding!"

Greg opened his door a crack and then emerged from his office. "Guys," Greg said as he pointed at Steve, "this man on the floor is a hero. He stopped this nutcase."

"Let's just wait until the cops get here," the chubby security guard said.

The tall guard cuffed Raymond, who remained unconscious.

"It's OK," Steve said, his words partially muffled by the carpet under his face. "Just no more pulling my fucking arm out of its socket!"

While one of the guards patted him down, Steve lay on the floor, calmly waiting for the police and tuning out Greg's voice as he excitedly described to the guards what had just happened.

CHAPTER 9

Tec watched as the head priest chanted and stalked around an open fire, tossing different plants and tree extracts into it. In the room with the priest were Tec's father, a few of his father's most trusted warriors, and a handful of lesser holy men.

The priest was viewing the past and the future. He had no name. His predecessors had no names. He was a medium who communicated with the gods, the earth, the sky, nature, and the great king—Tec's father, Gukumatz. Through the priest's visions and counsel, Gukumatz had led his people to prosperity.

For as long as Tec could remember, the tribe had not experienced drought or flood. It had raided its neighbors and enslaved them, forcing them to labor in their corn and bean fields. And his father had found gifts of the gods, the most important of these being the drawings of the houses of the gods on a cave wall. The tribe had constructed tall stone temples and halls based on those images, creating cities that were the envy of all its neighbors. You could run for many days and still be under the protection of King Gukumatz.

The only tragedy that had befallen Tec's people in many years was the death of his mother, who had died giving birth to him and Que. The people of the village believed his father had given his wife to the gods for their prosperity, that their king would do anything for them.

Tec did not sense Que approaching until he was lying next to him on a raised platform that encircled the main floor of the temple. "Brother, I was hoping they were sacrificing one of the captives," Que whispered.

Tec glanced at the crimson-stained stone platform in the center of the room, the place their father sacrificed captives from their raids to the Gods to ensure the tribe's prosperity.

Tec did not share his brother's enthusiasm for the ceremonies, another reason he was more than willing to see his brother become king. He could still see the eyes of a girl near his age, fifteen or sixteen, as his father had plunged the blade into her breastbone and removed her heart as she lay staring up at him in horror. She had seemed no different from the girls in his village.

Tec knew he had to keep these thoughts to himself. If his father learned of his true feelings on this and other matters, he'd get a quick smack to the head—or worse.

Tec was the first-born son, and the first-born son always became king. But none of the tribe's kings had ever had twin sons. His father never spoke of a successor, and Tec assumed that because Que excelled in all the ways a strong king should, he would be the one named king. Tec thought that most of the village shared this view, but his father's silence on the subject both worried and excited him.

Que interrupted his musing. "Tec, let's go find turtle eggs." The priest was now sitting, swaying back and forth in a trance. Tec knew from past ceremonies that this could go on for hours. "Let's go. I will race you," Tec whispered as he got up and walked quickly toward the exit, his brother close behind.

The exit from the upper part of the temple looked like a bright spot on an otherwise dark wall. Tec sprinted for it as the ceremony continued below and burst into the bright light of a humid day. At his feet were a hundred steps, which he quickly descended. Soon his brother came upon him, pushing him lightly as he passed. The ocean was visible for a few seconds, until they descended to a level where the jungle blocked the view.

When Tec reached the ground, his brother was already several steps ahead, looking back and laughing. Tec had never beaten his brother in a race, and today looked like it would be no different. They ran along the trail that lead to the ocean, through the thick brush that bordered the beach. Tec ran as fast as he could, but Que easily outdistanced him.

"To the water!" Que called out triumphantly, again looking back at his brother and laughing. "You look like a—"

Que was cut short by a low-hanging tree branch. It caught him flush across the chest, hanging him momentarily in midair before knocking him onto his backside with a hard thump.

In full stride, Tec jumped over his brother's prone body and sprang onto the beach, rushing into the warm ocean with his arms above his head. Tec was jumping in the air, shouting and celebrating his victory when his brother emerged from the jungle.

Que was rubbing the back of his head and for a second Tec thought he was smiling, but as Que drew within a few feet, he saw it was a scowl on his face, a scowl that was morphing into a scream. Tec stopped jumping, realizing the danger he was in.

Que dropped his hand from the back of his head and Tec

saw that he was bleeding. The blood seemed to make Que even angrier. He lunged at Tec and missed. "Admit you cheated! Admit you didn't win!" Que shouted.

Usually Tec would have given in to his brother, but for some reason—maybe he was enjoying the feeling of being victorious, maybe he was tired of being belittled—instead of agreeing, he answered as loudly as he could, "Admit you lost! I won!"

Que looked surprised and then enraged. He lunged at Tec again, screaming, "I will kill you!"

Tec took a step to his right and then pivoted on his left foot. Que dove at his initial move, landing face-first in the ocean. Tec didn't look back, but he heard the splash and then a roar that caused his testicles to retreat into his body. His brother was coming for him, and he knew he was in mortal danger, maybe the closest to death he had ever been.

Tec ran along the beach, pumping his legs and arms as fast as he could, afraid to look back. The beach was coming to an end. A steep rock wall rose in front of him; the dark jungle was to his right. Tec decided to climb the rocks; Que would surely catch him if he ran into the jungle.

Tec felt a searing pain in his shoulder from where Que had reached out and driven his fingernails into Tec's back when he fell into the sand. Tec ignored the pain, barely losing a step as his brother quickly recovered and continued his pursuit.

Tec reached the rock wall and scurried up. When the rocks became too steep and he could no longer find footholds, Tec grabbed the rocks above him and pulled himself up. He had forty feet or so to climb before he reached the top. He was hoping his brother wouldn't follow. Tec new that at the top of the rock formation was a flat surface about twenty feet wide, and on either side was a forty-foot drop to the beach or ocean below. He hoped Que would realize there was no escape and not climb after him. Then Tec would wait until his brother calmed down or the people from the village came looking for them. The thing that scared him the most was his brother's silence; it showed Tec how much danger he was in.

Tec glanced down and saw that his brother, looking as vicious as a wild animal, had followed him up the rock wall and was only a few feet behind him.

Tec saw an outcropping to his left, too far away to grab safely. Without thinking, he surged toward it anyway, grabbing the outcropping with one hand and swinging dangerously for a few seconds before grabbing the rock with his other hand. He now had a ledge he could slide his feet along to move slowly around the rock. He also now had a head-on view of his brother, who had reached the same point Tec had before swinging to the outcropping. Que measured the distance, unsure whether he could make it.

Instead of jumping, he looked Tec in the eye and said, "Brother, let us go down this rock and talk." Tec knew from his brother's tone that he had no intention of talking.

"No, brother, you get off the rock and I will then follow."

There was no way Tec would leave his perch until Que calmed down or left.

"I will meet you on the beach," Que agreed.

Tec was relieved, but only momentarily: Que suddenly pushed himself off the rock and jumped for the outcropping, barely catching it. After a few unsteady swings, he grabbed the rock, stabilized himself, and followed Tec's path onto the ledge.

They were about thirty feet from the ground. Tec had only one choice. He couldn't continue to climb; his brother would surely grab his leg. He wanted to try reasoning with his brother, but as he turned to face him, Que jumped at him.

Tec pushed off the rock and dove toward the sparkling water. He crashed into it surprisingly fast, in an upside-down dive, the back of his shoulders hitting the ocean first.

Que had lost his balance when he lunged for his brother and missed. His head smacked flush against the rock wall, and he tumbled into the ocean seconds after Tec.

While swimming toward the surface after his dive, Tec saw his brother fall into the water a few feet from him. He expected Que to be a flurry of motion as he tried to grab him, but instead Que continued to fall to the ocean's floor with a blurry red trail behind him. Tec had no choice but to continue swimming to the surface; his lungs were empty.

Soon his head burst from the water, and he took in a deep breath of air before dropping back into the sea. He could see his brother's faint shadow falling along the submerged portion of the rock structure they had just climbed. Tec swam down toward Que, but not without entertaining the thought of letting his brother die. Wouldn't Que have done the same?

But Tec kept swimming; he wasn't his brother.

Tec found Que at the jagged base of the cliff. He was face down against the rock. Still leery of a trick, he kicked Que, but his brother didn't move. A few air bubbles left Que's mouth and blood continued to flow from the back of his head.

Tec grabbed him by the armpits and was dragging him toward the surface when his head exploded with pain. He had smacked into a part of the cliff that jutted out into the ocean. The force of the impact disoriented him, and the flow of blood from his own head blurred his vision. Tec began to panic. Which way was up?

A purple light caught his eye; he swam toward it, dragging his brother. The light grew and was within his reach when Tec realized that it couldn't be the surface; it was too small and dim. Suddenly his head was out of the water, and he was hungrily breathing in large gulps of air while trying to get his brother above the water. Que was not breathing, and the wound on his head was severe; Tec could see his skull.

Tec took in his surroundings. He was in a large cavern within the rock formation he and his brother had just climbed. He realized he must have swum under a lip of rock and into this cavern. In front of him, the rock rose out of the water. He lifted his brother onto the rock, lightly slapped his face, and called his name. "Que! Que!" His voice grew louder, his slapping harder.

When the reality that his brother was dead hit him, he grew angry. "Why did you have to chase me, why?"

Tec sobbed and hit Que in the chest. After a few strikes, Que coughed and choked and emptied the water from his lungs.

Tec rolled him on his side as he continued to cough up water. He cried over and over, "Brother! Brother! You are alive!"

Que struggled to turn his head toward Tec. "What happened?" he asked, coughing hard.

"You hit your head and fell into the ocean," Tec said.

A change occurred in Que's eyes as he remembered the events leading up to his fall. But if he still felt any anger, it quickly waned. "Where are we?" Que asked.

"In a cave, I think," answered Tec.

Tec looked around the cave, hoping to find a spot where the sun was coming in, but he couldn't find any such opening. He then realized the light in the cave was purple; it couldn't be the sun. Looking around the cave, he noticed a half-submerged rock in the corner. It was the size of two men's heads and glowed a fluorescent purple that filled the room.

"What is that?" Tec asked, pointing toward the rock. He wiped blood from his eyes to get a better look and realized how badly his head hurt. He was sure his brother's head felt no better—probably worse, from the look of it.

Que raised himself to a sitting position, grunting in pain. His hand went immediately to the back of his head to touch the wound. "How bad is it?" he asked.

"Not that bad," Tec lied.

Tec got up and moved closer to the glowing rock. He felt a warm sensation, and the rock seemed to glow brighter. It was such a warm glow; he just wanted to get closer. He heard a light humming, a song.

Que was next to him, looking woozy. "Let's take it to the village," he said in a hushed tone.

Together they waded waist-deep into the water.

"I hope it isn't too heavy," Tec said.

It was as though the rock was speaking to him, pulling him in. It was like the calling of the mother he never had. He and Que stood on either side of the rock, but when Que reached down to grab it, he drew back and howled with pain. Tec froze, not sure what to do. He grabbed Que's arm and instinctively pushed against the rock, staring into his brother's face with a look of agony. The room seemed to explode in a glow of purple. A rush of sensations coursed through Tec's body. He wanted to scream, cry, and laugh all at the same time. Pain, love, death, pleasure—he felt everything at once.

He thought the glow would melt his eyes and melt his skin. The pain was raging, and then a second later he was pulsating with power, the pain gone.

He was the world. He felt himself merge with the world, with his brother, with everything.

Tec became aware of the room again, now pitch black. He was back in his body, feeling a sense of power and peace that he had never before experienced. But his hands burned.

"Brother?" he said to the darkness. He was shocked at the sound of his voice. It was deeper, more powerful than it had been.

"I am here," said Que. His brother's voice also sounded different.

Tec lifted the rock, which was still in his hands, with ease; he felt his brother's hands on the other side of the rock.

He didn't feel like himself; he felt like a hundred Tecs. The pain in his head was gone. His eyes had now adjusted to the dark, and he saw his brother across from him.

Tec now noticed all the sounds of the room: the dripping water, the waves hitting the rocks outside—he could actually hear the sound of fish swimming near him. He punched his hand into the ocean, and when he pulled it out he was holding a five-inch fish.

Que saw what his brother had done and, after focusing on the water for a few seconds, plunged his hand in, pulling out a slightly larger prize.

"Que, your wound is healed!" Tec exclaimed. The gaping hole was gone completely; only smudged blood remained.

Tec felt his own head and discovered that his wound was also healed.

"We must tell Father!" Tec said. "Quick, help me with the rock."

Que quickly hoisted the rock out of the water with ease and held it in one palm.

"How do we get out of here?" Que asked.

"There," said Tec, pointing into the water. "I think we swim under and up."

Tec thought about the changes in him. He felt different: his hearing was sharper, he could move more quickly. What had happened? Why had the rock stopped glowing?

Tec felt a connection to everything around him. He felt he could melt into his surroundings, as if he were a natural, swirling energy. Gone was the sense of dread that had always been part of him. He felt strong, invincible. Even his brother didn't scare him.

They waded into the water. Que dove first and Tec followed.

They swam down a few feet and then under a rock lip and into the open ocean. Tec could see every detail under the water; the light was almost blinding. The sounds and sights of the ocean and all its activity were mesmerizing, beautiful. Tec and Que shot to the water's surface. Que hoisted the rock above his head and treaded water with his other arm. The brightness of the day nearly overwhelmed Tec; the sounds around him battered his hearing.

When they reached the shore, Tec looked up at the rock formation. A moment ago it had seemed so imposing, but now he knew he could climb it with ease. Tec could tell by Que's expression that he was thinking the same thing. Then Que's eyes widened. "Brother you look . . . different . . ." Que's voiced trailed off.

Tec moved closer to Que and noticed that his body, too, had changed. His skin was darker and it appeared to glow in the sunshine. His eyes, which had been brown, were now a striking blue, and he looked more like a man—stronger and fiercer.

Que rubbed his head, and a handful of hair came away in his hand. Seeing this, Tec rubbed his own hair, but none of it came loose. Que looked shaken.

Tec looked at his own arms and saw that they were as dark, shiny, and muscular as his brother's. He felt power flowing through his body. He feared nothing; he understood everything. The dark jungle no longer held mystery or fear. He knew he was its most fearsome predator.

"Brother, you have changed also—your skin, eyes . . ." Tec said.

Que nodded, confirming that he felt the same changes.

They walked into the jungle and toward the village. A deep silence greeted them as they entered the dark brush; the jungle also felt their power.

CHAPTER 10

Steve looked away from the bright lights shining on him. He wanted to wipe his hand across his forehead, but the show's producer had already scolded him about doing that. His last wipe led to the makeup person angrily applying an orange paste to his smeared forehead. The set had been made to look like a living room, and he sat next to an empty chair in front of the camera. People scurried about silently, most of them wearing headsets and rushing to or from some emergency. To his far right, a man and woman—the news anchors—were giving a recap of yesterday's newsworthy events. This was the second television interview Steve had given since he became Las Vegas's favorite hero. A reporter had assured him that by this time next week no one would care about him anymore, but for this week he would be king.

And it had been a whirlwind week. First, Katie visited him at the police station, where they both had to give their statements after the attempted shooting. She thanked him through tears of shock and gratitude.

Many different people asked Steve many questions at the police station. The police then put him in front of a group of reporters at a news conference; he was told not to answer any questions about the details of "the event," as the police kept referring to it. To make sure he followed instructions, Steve had a detective standing next to him. He didn't remember many of the questions, or his answers, but the detective never interrupted him, so he guessed he did OK. He did remember one question the reporters kept asking: they wanted to know about Raymond's wrist, and how it got shattered—not broken, but shattered—as though it had been caught in a piece of machinery. Steve told them that he had simply squeezed it, and the police had decided that Raymond must have injured his wrist earlier, before he entered the Hubbel office.

Apparently Raymond had begun that day by shooting his landlord. Raymond, Steve learned, was not well mentally; he'd had serious psychological problems pretty much his whole life. According to various reports, he was one of those people who falls through the cracks in society, with no friends, no family.

Steve noticed a flurry of activity on the studio set to his right. Grace, the female news anchor, was moving to the living room set now. She was going to interview him after the commercial break.

"OK, we ready?" Grace asked, settling into her chair.

"Yes, ma'am!" Steve replied.

Steve wasn't sure how he ended up doing these interviews. It started with a call from the president of Hubbel, Frank Hubbel, thanking him for his bravery, telling him he would be rewarded. Then there were phone calls from newspapers, radio shows, and television stations. Most, if not all of it, was initiated by Hubbel. "Everyone loves a hero, Steve," Frank Hubbel had told him, "and I love having a hero work for me!"

Steve figured this would be the last interview; the public had to be sick of this story by now.

"Your gonna do real well with those baby blues," Grace told him as they waited for the commercial break to end.

He looked at Grace, in her ridiculous orange makeup that matched his shirt. "They're not that blue," Steve said with a little laugh.

"They do the job," Grace replied, looking down.

Was she embarrassed? Was she flirting with him? He wasn't used to women flirting with him. Was this what it was like? She was kind of cute, probably even cuter without the hideous makeup.

A balding man with his headset half on yelled in their direction, interrupting Steve's thoughts. "We're back in thirty!"

"OK," said Grace, "here we go. You'll do fine. Try to keep the answers focused on the question, and look at me, not the camera."

She reached over and gave his hand a squeeze. Good thing Steve had the heavy makeup on, because he felt his face burn up in a blush. The bald man, now with his headset completely on, was giving hand signals to Grace. "And we're back," she said. "I am here with Las Vegas's latest hero, Steve Soto." Smiling, she looked directly at Steve. "Hello, Steve."

"Hello, Grace," Steve replied with a smile.

"So tell me, do you come from a long line of heroes? I mean, taking on an armed man without a weapon?"

"Well, I reacted on instinct and got lucky, I think. I'm just glad no one was hurt—I mean, no one at Hubbel." Steve had remembered the landlord, and that Frank Hubbel had told him to say the word Hubbel as often as possible during interviews. "Any publicity is good publicity, Steve," he'd said.

"From what I understand, there was a woman who was in mortal danger when you stopped the gunman," Grace continued.

"Well, I can't really comment on the specifics. I'm just glad everything worked out for the best at Hubbel that morning, and my sympathies to the family of the man shot at the apartment building preceding what happened at Hubbel."

Grace looked a little perturbed. Steve figured she wanted some more detail, which he wasn't going to give. He wouldn't have even if the police hadn't told him not to. It just didn't seem right.

Grace proceeded to ask more questions, ones he had already answered four or five times for newspapers and the other television program.

"Well, thank you, Mr. Soto, for your time, and good luck to you," Grace said eventually, ending the interview. She offered a few pleasantries while a crew member removed Steve's microphone. He was now free to go.

Steve returned to the makeup room, where he wiped the orange paste from his face. Having mixed with his sweat, it now had the consistency of moist spackle. Steve looked in the mirror and wondered if his fifteen minutes of fame were over. Was this the highpoint of his life, a few newspaper articles and two television interviews? A few months ago he would have been happy for that to have been his destiny, but now he felt he was meant for something greater. It wasn't just the new physique or the added confidence he was feeling. It was more than that. He wasn't just hoping for great things in his future; he knew they were going to happen. He just didn't know what they would be.

He would return to Hubbel next week, to his boring job, and within a few months his heroic actions would likely be forgotten. Where would he be then? He had to make changes to his life; he needed to move forward.

Steve finished cleaning his face, removed his tie, and picked up his jacket to leave. No escort or good-bye from anyone. Steve walked out of the studio alone and unnoticed, already forgotten. He imagined hearing his fame-clock tick to zero.

Steve's cell phone vibrated in his pocket. When he saw that the caller ID showed "Landry, Kathleen," his heart skipped a beat. "Hello?" he said in the manliest voice he could muster.

"Hi, Steve. It's Katie."

"Hi. Good to hear from you." Steve winced when he heard the words come out of his mouth. He sounded like a complete dork.

"I was wondering if I could take you out to dinner . . . you know, to thank you," she said.

"Oh, that's not necessary," Steve answered. *Not necessary? She's asking me out! Play it cool*, he told himself.

"I really would like to, though. I mean, you saved my life," she said forcibly.

"Well, since you put it that way, sure. When were you thinking?"

"When are you coming back to work?" she asked.

"I guess tomorrow. I was told to do the interviews, and my last one was today. So I guess if I want to keep getting paid, I'll be back tomorrow."

"Why don't we go out Saturday night, then?"

Steve's pulse quickened. There was a sweetness to her voice he had never heard in their brief hellos and good-byes. "Sounds good. Can I pick you up?" Steve asked.

"Sure. How is six or seven?"

"Seven sounds good. Where are we going?"

"I was thinking Nick's, on the strip," she said. Nick's was one of those overpriced and overhyped casino steak restaurants frequented mainly by tourists.

"You don't have to spend that much. You'll need a second mortgage."

"It's the least I can do. Let a girl do something nice," Katie said.

"OK, it's a date!" The words escaped Steve's mouth before he could think. A few seconds of silence followed.

"OK, I'll see you at work tomorrow," Katie said, either not noticing that he'd used the word *date* or choosing to ignore it.

"Yeah, OK," Steve said as they both hung up.

His face was burning. He heard his own voice on a loop in his head as he walked to the car: *It's a date! It's a date! It's a date!*

CHAPTER 11

S teve returned to Hubbel the next morning, just as he'd told Katie he would. Nothing happened when he swiped his key card at the entrance by the stairs, so he went to the main entrance, where two security guards were sitting at attention, watching a line of people swipe their cards and pass through a turnstile. This was all new.

Steve felt a pang in his stomach when he recognized the security guards. They were the two from "the incident." The short guard hit the tall guard on the arm when he recognized Steve. "There he is, the hero," the tall guard said, waving Steve over.

"Hi," Steve answered. People were now stopping to look at him.

"Sorry we roughed you up a bit," the short guard said with a smile.

Steve noticed their badges and name tags. The short guy was Ben, and the tall guy was also Steve.

"No problem. I could have been the guy shooting as far as you knew. Better safe than sorry."

"We have your new key card and have been told to send you straight to the sixth floor," Ben said, holding out Steve's new badge.

Steve knew the sixth floor held Hubbel's West Coast management offices. He had been up there only once—to deliver a package sent to him by mistake—and only as far as the lobby.

"Thanks, guys."

Steve took his badge from the guard and slid it through the slot at the turnstile. He went immediately to the sixth floor, though he really wanted to go to his own floor and say hello to Katie, and make sure she hadn't changed her mind about their date. As Steve exited the elevator he was struck by the difference between the sixth floor and his floor; everything here was top-shelf, while his floor was bargain basement. The sixth-floor walls and all its furniture were made of dark wood, and a stunning redhead sat at the reception desk. Apparently the budget cuts were not as deep on the sixth floor.

"Good morning, Mr. Soto. I'll let Mr. Hubbel know you are here," the beautiful woman said to him with a smile.

"Mr. Hubbel?" Steve asked, surprised that he was supposed to meet with Frank Hubbel himself.

"Yes, I believe he flew in last night from New York just to meet you in person," she answered. The look on her face suggested that he should be impressed.

Steve waited less than a minute before Greg and a man he presumed to be Mr. Hubbel greeted him.

"There he is!" Mr. Hubbel said, holding out his hand. He was a balding man in his forties or fifties, wearing a polo shirt and dress pants. *I guess the Hubbel dress code only applies to employees*, thought Steve.

"Frank Hubbel. And it is a pleasure to meet you, young man."

Greg just smiled and nodded his head.

"Hello, Mr. Hubbel," Steve said, meeting his handshake.

"No, no, son. Call me Frank." He'd also asked Steve to call him Frank when they had spoken on the phone.

Mr. Hubbel and Greg led him to a finely appointed conference room. For the next hour, Mr. Hubbel offered compliment after compliment on Steve's bravery. Greg didn't say anything; he just smiled dumbly and nodded his head like a bobble-head doll. Did Mr. Hubbel know how much of a coward Greg was? Through their small talk, Steve discovered that Mr. Hubbel was the grandson of the company's founder. Besides that piece of information, Mr. Hubbel's compliments, and Steve's thank-yous for the compliments, their conversation focused on the security upgrades that Mr. Hubbel had put in place immediately, so that another "Raymond situation" could never happen again.

Mr. Hubbel then took him and Greg to an early lunch via the company limo. They ate lunch at the opulent and exclusive Madras Club, a lush green oasis set against the desert background. "It's invite-only to join," Mr. Hubbel noted as they sat down, before he launched into a description of all the great things the company had done, was doing, and was going to do in the future.

Mr. Hubbel started talking about Steve's future when their meals—elaborate turkey sandwiches—arrived without their having placed an order. "I had the lunch preordered," Mr. Hubbel explained as he flipped open his napkin. "I have limited time." Mr. Hubbel took a bite of his sandwich, swallowed, and continued. "Steve, you are the type of person I can build a team around."

Steve didn't think Mr. Hubbel expected him to answer, so he also began eating instead of responding.

Mr. Hubbel continued to offer broad praise for Steve throughout lunch, while Greg grunted his agreements through his sandwich-stuffed mouth. Mr. Hubbel recounted details from Steve's personnel file—how he never missed a day of work, how he had a 99 percent job-completion rate and positive supervisor reviews. Steve got the impression he was supposed to be wowed by the president's knowledge of such things about a lowly employee. Mr. Hubbel continued, saying that what impressed him most was the way Steve handled himself during the Raymond situation. "That is the type of man I want in my foxhole," he told him.

Lunch ended as soon as they finished their sandwiches. They were back in the company parking lot an hour after they had left. "Steve, I have a gift for you, a token of my appreciation," Mr. Hubbel said as they sat in the idling limo. He handed Steve an envelope. "It contains a year's salary, son." Mr. Hubbel looked eager for Steve's happy reaction.

Steve, a little shocked, thanked Mr. Hubbel, but the expression on the president's face suggested that Steve should have acted more excited.

"OK, Steve, we've taken enough of your time," Mr. Hubbel said. "Take the rest of the day off. Come in bright and early Monday. Greg will show you your new office and talk to you about some new responsibilities."

Now Steve was really shocked. He'd thought all the foxhole talk at lunch was about long-term plans, but apparently things were happening now.

"Again, thank you, Mr. Hubbel. You are more than generous." Steve tried to up his enthusiasm for Mr. Hubbel's benefit.

"Greg, I need you to ride to the airport with me." Mr. Hubbel stated this as a fact, not as a request. He gave Steve a pat on the knee and a quick good-bye and left him standing alone in the parking lot, holding a check worth a year's salary.

Steve wasn't sure how he felt about what just happened. He'd never looked at his job as something he wanted to grow in. He really wanted to go inside and see Katie but figured he had better leave; when the president says go home early, Steve was pretty sure it meant go home early.

* * *

The sun was setting on another oppressively hot fall day in Las Vegas. Steve walked around his apartment in his new shoes and new clothes. When he'd left work after lunch with Mr. Hubbel the day before, he immediately deposited his bonus check into his savings account. He had decided that with some extra disposable income, he might as well upgrade his wardrobe. The clothes he was wearing had looked cool in the store, but now he wasn't so sure.

He got ready way too early for his date with Katie, and now he was now trying to keep from sweating in his new outfit. His apartment building was fairly new, but he had a hard time getting the temperature under seventy-five degrees in his unit when the outside temperature was above ninety-five.

To add to his misery, whatever was happening to his body and senses had raised his resting body temperature. He was always hot; he sweated profusely while he slept.

He didn't want to sit down, afraid that the sweat would bead up on his back and form a wet blotch on his new black shirt. He once again went to his freezer and opened the door. The cold blast felt delightful. After a few seconds he closed the freezer, moved his untucked shirt around so no sweat could blotch it, and resumed his slow walk around the apartment. He had ten minutes to kill before he left to pick up Katie for their date. He could still hear himself saying, "It's a date!" He hoped he hadn't blown it with her.

But he was getting ahead of himself: this was most likely just a thank-you dinner, like she'd said, nothing more.

Steve had called Katie earlier in the day to confirm their date and get her address. To his surprise, she'd said she was looking forward to tonight. "You don't get to take the man who saved your life to dinner often," she had said.

Steve continued pacing around his apartment, going over her words, searching for hints to give him hope that this might be more than a thank-you dinner. His apartment wasn't that big—it consisted mainly of a kitchen that opened into a family room with a thirty-inch flat-screen television as its focal point—so he did a lot of looping around.

A sliding door led from the family room to a small balcony large enough for two little chairs and nothing else. A door in the main room connected to his bedroom and to the one bathroom. Despite its modest size, Steve took pride in his apartment. He had stylish, matching furniture, and he had painted each room a color that complemented the furniture. This was the apartment of a responsible man.

He pictured Jim's apartment. The only thing his place had in common with Jim's was the flat-screen television, which in Jim's case was almost obscured by piles of takeout containers and dirty clothes.

Steve stopped to look at his reflection in the mirror near the apartment's entrance. He was still amazed at his transformation. He had not been to the gym in nearly two weeks because of his suddenly busy schedule, yet he still looked like he was getting bigger. After some more research, he'd found that various medical websites listed night sweats and muscle growth as symptoms of lymphoma and thyroid disorders, but he didn't have the majority of the symptoms for either, and some of his other symptoms contradicted those possibilities. Still, he made a mental note to make a doctor's appointment. He was excited that almost all of the changes to his physique and his senses were positive, but he was also concerned that he couldn't explain why they were happening. There had to be something wrong with him. *Maybe it's a brain tumor*, he thought. He definitely needed to make a doctor's appointment.

Figuring that sitting in the air conditioning of his car would keep him cooler than stalking around his apartment, Steve left and walked down the dark, drab interior hallway to the elevator. He hated waiting for the elevator, especially when there were people waiting with him. Steve usually recognized their faces but never knew their names, and he might grunt a greeting to receive another grunt in return.

In the hallway, he passed a frumpy lady whom he had passed many times before. She usually held her purse close to her chest as they passed each other, but not today. She glanced at him and started to clutch her purse, but then left it dangling and gave him the brightest of smiles. "Hello, Sean," she said with a little uncertainty in her voice.

"Hi. It's Steve."

They passed each other awkwardly; the hallway was not wide enough for them to walk shoulder to shoulder.

"Oh, I am sorry, Steve, hon. OK, bye," she said, continuing to smile.

She wasn't the only neighbor to offer Steve a first-time happy hello; he had received a few in the hallways over the last couple of weeks. It was like everyone in his apartment building was part of a big practical joke being played on him, and he kept waiting for the punch line.

Steve got in his car, started it, and put the air conditioning on full blast. He drove around the city for a half hour to kill time—he didn't want to arrive at Katie's too early. By the time he got there, he had cooled off completely, to the point where he was bone dry and starting to develop a chill.

He found a parking space right in front of Katie's home, a small stucco house in a new subdivision where all the houses looked the same—row after row of them extending into the desert, each with landscaping that consisted of cactus, decorative rock, and an occasional flower pot to add color to a mostly beige scene. He arrived on time, and thankfully clouds were now covering the setting sun, dropping the temperature to a more comfortable level.

Play it cool, Steve thought as he walked to Katie's front door.

* * *

Steve couldn't believe how well his date with Katie was going. They were sitting in a corner booth at Nick's, the dark wood and leather of the restaurant's interior lit mostly by candles. Katie looked even more stunning than usual, and by the looks of passersby, he could tell he wasn't the only one who thought so. She laughed at his jokes and seemed interested in his stories, and as the wine took effect, he started having grander visions for this night. After the waiter took their plates, Steve coolly asked Katie, "Do you think we have any more dates in our future?"

She didn't seem uncomfortable with the question. In fact,

she seemed to embrace it. "I hope so," she answered with a twinkle in her eye.

"So this wasn't a thank-you dinner only?" Steve couldn't believe the words coming out of his mouth. He waited for an answer that would smash his dreams.

"Well it was, at the beginning, but I think I would be disappointed if you didn't ask me out again."

Steve tried to keep calm as his heart leapt in his chest. It actually felt like his heart was pushing through his breastbone. He needed to keep it together. He couldn't blow this.

"I would be disappointed too," he said, in a tone that sounded way too self-possessed to be coming from his mouth.

After deciding against coffee, they went for a walk through the upscale mall attached to the casino. They small-talked as they strolled past stores that he would probably never enter: Gucci and Armani and others with French-sounding names. He had no idea what the names meant or what the stores sold.

He didn't know if it was because of the wine or the atmosphere, but he reached out to grab Katie's hand as they walked. Without skipping a beat, she accepted it as though they were an old married couple. Not even acknowledging her hand in his, she continued talking about her family, how happy they were. She explained that she had a sister and a brother and happily married parents who lived in Los Angeles. "What about you?" she asked, referring to his family.

"Get your violin ready. I'm an orphan," Steve said, trying to add a soft touch to his voice.

"Oh, geez, I'm sorry. How long? Were you young, or was it recent?"

"Both. My dad when I was little, and my mom recently— cancer."

"I'm so sorry. Any other family?"

"No, not really. No aunts or uncles really. I have some

cousins in Mexico. My grandfather—my dad's father—and my dad lost touch when he was a teenager. He ran away from home, in Texas or Mexico. I'm not sure. My mom didn't really know the story completely."

"That had to be hard," Katie said, giving his hand a squeeze.

"Let's talk about your family instead. Mine is a downer for the most part. What does your dad do?" Steve asked, hoping to change the focus of the conversation.

"Well, he's the president of Global National Bank," she said, sounding a little embarrassed.

"The president of one of the biggest banks in the world? Not too shabby!"

"Yeah, he's very successful. But he's also the best dad in the world. He's always there for me." She stopped for a moment. "Actually, he got me the job at Hubbel, or at least the interview. He wanted me to work in the real world at first. Maybe someday I'll go work with him."

"Yeah, GNB is one of Hubbel's biggest customers, if I am not mistaken."

"The biggest," she corrected.

"Something makes me think you would have got the job regardless," Steve said with a smile. He and Jim often joked about Hubbel's hiring practices—in this economy, Hubbel had the pick of the litter when it came to applicants, even for the lowest of positions. But when guys like Greg were in charge of the hiring, the candidates who got the jobs were always pleasing to the eye.

Katie seemed to know what Steve was implying. "Yeah, I know the joke. Greg asks for headshots with the resumes."

They both laughed.

"I think you may be qualified, though. UCLA, right?"

She nodded and smiled.

"NWLVCC," Steve said proudly.

"Huh?"

"Northwest Las Vegas Community College."

Steve hadn't been paying much attention to the crowds of people walking by them in the mall, but now he noticed a well-dressed guy across the walkway. The man was keeping pace with Katie and him, and seemed to be watching them. When Steve looked directly at him, the guy quickly looked into a store window, avoiding his gaze.

"I think that guy likes you, or me. I think he's following us," Steve said jokingly to Katie, tilting his head in the man's direction.

Katie peered at the man, her eyes squinted, and a look of anger crossed her face.

"Oh my God, it's Gabriel."

The blank look on Steve's face prompted her to add more: "My *ex*-boyfriend." Katie marched in Gabriel's direction and Steve followed.

"Are you following me?" Katie asked loudly as she approached Gabriel, who had his back turned toward them.

"Katie? No! What? Following you? Come on," Gabriel replied indignantly.

Steve now noticed that Gabriel was as close to male-model perfection as you can get: the tall, dark, and handsome type. He probably adorned an underwear ad somewhere. Steve suddenly became self-conscious. Why did he ever think he could get a girl like this? She was out of his league.

"I can't go to a mall?" Gabriel was asking Katie when Steve refocused on the argument.

"Well it wouldn't be the first time we've run into each other in the last few weeks: the bank, the grocery store, in front of my building. Now this. You need to leave me alone!"

"Listen, I'm just watching out for you. There are a lot of dangerous people out there." He looked at Steve directly for the first time. "I can't stand to think about you in danger. Look, you almost got shot."

"Like that's my fault? That doesn't give you a reason to follow me. We're done! Get it? You had your chance and you showed who you were."

People walking by had started to pay attention.

"Let's calm down and get a coffee, talk about it."

"Go take out your other girlfriend for coffee, you pig," Katie shot back.

"You're embarrassing me," Gabriel said, as he moved closer to Katie. He had a serious look on his face as he towered over her.

Steve stepped in, grabbing Gabriel's arm. "OK, buddy, let's move on. The lady . . ." Before Steve finished his sentence, Gabriel raised his other arm and punched Steve squarely in the nose. Steve stood dumbfounded: he wasn't fazed at all by the punch. It was as if a two-year-old had hit him. That blow should have laid him out.

"Gabriel! You asshole!" Katie screamed.

"Are you OK?" she asked Steve.

"Yeah. Fine."

Steve saw Gabriel's expression turn from triumphant to confused to worried—and finally to pained as Steve began squeezing his arm. On instinct, he swung his right fist into Gabriel's face; it exploded in a red spurt. Gasps erupted from the gathering crowd.

Steve let go of Gabriel, and he fell backward, unconscious. It all felt unreal, like the day Raymond had come calling. Katie looked horrified.

People mulled around, confused. Someone was crouched over Gabriel, asking if he was OK.

"We have to go," Steve said to Katie. He didn't want to end up spread eagle on the floor, explaining to mall cops what just happened. He was worried that Katie would not want to come with him, but she grabbed his hand and they moved swiftly out of the mall.

Outside, Steve could tell a rainstorm was on its way. The smell of the desert and the smell of humidity were in the air—and those two didn't belong together. The upcoming storm would settle the score.

"That Gabriel seems like a nice guy," Steve said as they neared his car.

"I'm so sorry. Are you OK?"

They were now in his car. He half-expected burly cops to come running out of the mall, but he saw no movement near the exits.

"Oh, you're bleeding," Katie said.

He looked in his rearview mirror as he pulled out of the mall parking lot; there was a small dribble of blood coming out of his right nostril. After the punch he took, his nose should have been flattened on his face. He should have been knocked out. But he was fine, despite this small trickle. Katie dabbed his nose with a tissue, but there was no need: the bleeding had already stopped.

"He was my boyfriend for five years. We met in college and moved out here together. We were going to get married, for God's sake. The only problem was, he had another girlfriend the last three years."

"That sucks," Steve offered mildly.

"Yeah it does! It's amazing how little you can end up knowing about someone who you think you know everything about."

Steve sat silent, not knowing what to say. He was just glad he was there. He had enjoyed punching the male-model ex in the face, something he would never have done a few weeks ago. Katie continued on about Gabriel: "And now he turns into super stalker . . . I'm going to have to call the police! I can't take it anymore."

She stopped talking for a moment and then said, "His father is really rich, like *Forbes* top-ten rich."

"Oh." Steve wanted to know who Gabriel's father was, but he decided not to ask.

They sat in silence for a few moments as rain began pounding on his windshield. While they were stopped at a red light, Steve looked over at Katie. She was staring absently out the window. He couldn't help himself; she was so beautiful. He leaned over, tenderly moved her chin toward him, and kissed her gently on the mouth. The intensity of the kiss increased, and although she seemed surprised at first, she quickly answered his intensity.

Her smell, the way she felt—Steve drank it all in. It was everything he had dreamt of, hoped for.

The blast of a horn awoke them from their kiss; the light was now green. Steve drove on, Katie resting against him, not moving from his side after their interrupted kiss.

They arrived at her home much faster than Steve would have liked. Neither spoke as Steve got out of the car, walked around to Katie's side, and opened her door. It was raining hard again. Katie grabbed his hand and led him up her walkway. She opened the door, took his hand again, and led him into her house.

As soon as they entered they fell into each other's arms, wordlessly. They meshed together, becoming one, falling to the floor of her foyer, twisting and pulling on each other's clothes while they continued their kiss. They made love there, in the foyer of her house. When they were finished, Steve lay on her cold tile floor, and Katie rested her head on his naked chest. He felt a peace and contentment he had never felt before. He didn't want to move or speak, fearing he might lose that feeling.

CHAPTER 12

Tec walked up the steep mountain pathway. The jungle's canopy blocked the sun, leaving the path as dark as night, but he felt no fear. He could feel the jungle around him; no threats loomed. The thirty men who wound down the path behind him had no idea what surrounded them in the jungle, but they too felt no fear, not with Tec leading them.

It had been five full years since he and his brother had brought the rock to their father and the priests—the rock that changed their lives. They were now men, the two best warriors in their tribe and among all of the tribes they had conquered. The power of their tribe had spread tenfold in the last five years. Tec and Que were now seen as gods. Even their father treated them differently since the great day of change, when they returned to the village seeming much more powerful than they had when they left. They were brought to their father and the priests, to whom they recounted their story many times. They amazed the assembly with feats of strength and speed. The lesser priests all agreed the boys' transformations were a gift from one of the gods for their father's fidelity. The main priest had walked up to Tec and told him to hold out his arm. When he complied, the priest gashed his arm with a knife. Tec howled in pain and anger as the blood poured out of the wound. The priest muttered as he walked away—he had been worried that Tec and Que were evil spirits, no longer of flesh and blood.

The night after they discovered the rock, the two brothers could not sleep for excitement over what had happened. They had run through the jungle at speeds they never would have imagined, while the night animals—predators that should have posed mortal threats to the young princes—ran from them.

This had been the greatest day of the brothers' lives; they shared a closeness they had never felt before. The only time Que seemed like his old self was when they talked to each other about what had happened. "The power of the god rock was mine. It called to me, but you pulled me away," Que said darkly.

"I think I saved you, brother. I think it was meant for both of us," Tec responded, looking directly into Que's eyes, no longer feeling any fear of his brother.

Maybe Que felt the change also; he had just grunted a sound of disbelief. When they woke in the morning, Tec had checked the gash on his arm. It was now a mere scratch. A wound that should have taken at least a week, or maybe even weeks, to heal had healed in less than a day. That was when he knew for sure that he was blessed by the gods, no matter what his brother thought.

Tec and his warriors reached the summit of the pathway and emerged from the dark jungle. Below them, the city, their home, was illuminated by bright sunshine. They could see the great temple and the king's palace rising well above the rest of the structures. Tec knew his brother had returned to the city. He could feel his presence, and he was sure Que could feel him as well.

Tec wished they could have stayed as they had been after the great event, happy in the wondrous mystery of their new existence. But things changed for the worse soon after that; his brother had grown darker in the soul. The seed of Que's anger was their father's failure thus far to name an heir to his throne. In the days prior to the miraculous event, Que was the natural choice, even though he had been born after Tec. But now Tec was a warrior feared by everyone, even his brother.

Tec and Que had not fought directly since the day they found the rock, and Tec knew his brother could most likely still best him. But among the rest of his people and the people of other tribes, no man was his match in speed, strength, and cunning. Their father would often send them out separately to lead raiding parties. They almost always returned victorious with the spoils of capture, and with the people they left behind swearing their loyalty. Sometimes the king sent Tec out alone as an emissary. "Sometimes being a good king requires talk as well as action," their father explained.

But because only Tec was sent on these missions, Que became more withdrawn, more bloodthirsty, more brutal. He and Tec had not spoken more than a few words to each other for a long time. Que lived on the outskirts of the city with a handpicked group of twenty of the tribe's most brutal and feared warriors. It was said that when they conquered a city, they painted it in the blood of their sacrificed enemies. There were even stories of Que eating the hearts of his captives.

When Tec and his warriors descended the path and entered the city, they were surrounded by chanting and cheering people, all reaching out and trying to touch him or ask for his blessing.

Tec climbed the palace temple stairs alone; his warriors and the rest of the tribe knew that entering without an invitation was an offense punishable by death. As Tec entered the main chamber, he heard his father talking loudly, but when his father saw him, his voice became suddenly quiet. The king, Que, and the ever-present priest were in the throne room. His father and brother looked agitated. The priest, as always, looked subdued, gazing off in the distance as if he were uninterested in the happenings of this world.

"Father, don't stop. I have no fear of my brother hearing what I have to say," Que boomed.

Tec had not seen Que for a while. His appearance startled him. Que was greasy, like the wings of a bird, and his hair was missing in patches, his muscles throbbing; he looked like a wild animal.

"What is that, brother?" Tec boomed back, not wanting to appear weak.

"I am asking why our father favors you, why he sends you out instead of me. Surely I would bring favor to our people!" Que screamed.

"I favor no one! Your accusations anger me. Test me no more!" the king yelled at an even louder volume.

The sound of his father's angry voice still sent a shiver down Tec's back. He was surprised to hear his brother answer back.

"Test you no more? What would you do, Father? What could you do?" Que asked with an evil smile on his face.

Tec instinctively stepped toward their father. Que, seeing this, focused his anger on Tec.

"Brother, why do you move to protect our father? Do you think I mean harm to him? Is this how you see me?" Que asked. He sounded hurt.

"No, brother. Let us end this discussion," Tec said quietly. "With Father's blessing, we should go together in the future," he added, looking hopefully to their father, who remained calm, but whose eyes showed contempt for Que.

Que now seemed intimidated by their father's stare. He started toward the door, but before leaving said, "Father, I should be king. You told me when we were younger that

I was to be king. I am the better warrior. I am feared by our enemies and our friends. I, too, have been touched by the gods. I will no longer stand for this disrespect. Hear my words, old man."

Tec thought he saw a stream of dark liquid leaking from his brother's nostril. But before he could tell for sure, Que marched out of the room.

The priest laughed quietly, to Tec's surprise. He looked at Tec and said, "Leave now. We have much to discuss."

The king sat silent, staring intently at the spot where Que had stood.

Tec left the room without a sound. He thought of his brother's words as he walked to his house. Had his father really promised Que that he would be king?

His dropped those thoughts when he saw his home. It was a small, two-room stone structure near the jungle's edge. A person of his stature could demand a much better home, but he enjoyed being near the jungle, living next to its life force.

He often thought about escaping into the jungle, leaving behind the pressures of his future. He stared longingly into the thick trees, studying its mysterious darkness.

Tec thought of going toward the sun, the forbidden direction in which people went and didn't return. He was imagining what he would find there when a noise from the village brought him back and reminded him that he had reason to stay here in the village.

He hoped Isla, his new love, was waiting for him inside the house. They had been courting for many days, but it was still forbidden for them to be alone together. Not until many months had passed were they allowed to meet without a member of her family present. However, they had been breaking that rule for many nights. She would slip out of her family's hut after everyone was asleep, stay the night with him, and then slip back into her home before dawn.

Tec loved her, and he knew they would marry as soon as the required time had passed.

When he entered his house, Isla was sitting cross-legged on the floor. A smile filled her face when she saw him. "You have returned!" she said as she jumped up into his arms.

"I have, my love," Tec said as he breathed in her familiar and lovely smell. "I have."

CHAPTER 13

Jim scurried around the office, passing out copies of his Friday flyer. His new find was a place called Nacho Mama's: free buffet 5 p.m. to 6 p.m. and, for the ladies, a free shot with the first beer. Steve was dumbfounded by Jim's giddiness and by his enthusiasm for a dive bar in a strip mall. Odds were that only a third of their coworkers would attend, the food would be cold, and the clientele frightening, but Jim was acting like he had found Shangri-la.

Steve had his arms behind his head and was looking through the window of his new office, which had a view of the cubicle he once occupied. He scanned the office, amused by Jim and wishing that big-headed Manny in accounting would move his sizable noggin to the left so that he could have a clear view of Katie. Manny worked in his team, and Steve had considered moving him to a new cubicle so he could look at Katie whenever he wanted rather than waiting for Manny to go to the bathroom or tilt his head just right. Steve was surprised that even though he and Katie had been seeing each other for a few weeks now, they had so far been able to keep their romance a secret from the rest of the office. But they had been smart, not arriving together and keeping their small talk to a minimum. His favorite moment of the last few weeks was when he'd been in the supply closet by himself when she had walked in. He played it cool, mostly because the secrecy was more important to her than to him; she was afraid of gossip, but mostly she thought it would look inappropriate, especially since his promotion. But that didn't stop her from planting a passionate kiss on his lips and then leaving the closet without saying a word.

They had been inseparable since their first date. Most nights he stayed at her house, where they took turns cooking each other dinner and talked for hours. These were probably the happiest few weeks of his life so far. He was beginning to feel the "L word," but wasn't ready to say it out loud. He didn't want to scare her away.

"Bro, you're going, right?" Jim asked with a goofy smile, and then turned his head to see what Steve was looking at. "That Manny has a huge cranium," he said.

"Yeah, I'm going, but I think your new place is in a bad neighborhood," Steve said, now paying full attention to Jim.

"No, man, it's all right. That's a Korean neighborhood, you racist. Why you always bangin' on my homies?"

"OK, but explain the whole block of boarded-up houses before the strip mall."

"OK, you're right. The neighborhood sucks. But the hot wings are awesome there; make your ass burn the next day." Jim walked off laughing at his own humor, but then he quickly returned with a serious expression on his face. "Dude, I forgot. You're gonna love this."

"What?" Steve asked, interested.

"Miss Landry will be gracing us with her presence!"

Steve already knew. Katie and he had discussed this the night before as they lounged on her patio, drinking homemade margaritas. They planned to slip out early; no one would be any the wiser.

"She is?" Steve feigned surprise. "That's awesome!"

"Maybe you can make a move, you puss! Shit, you saved her life. You should at least get to second base for that."

Steve kept a straight face. "Probably get to third if it was your mom," he replied.

"Dude, that's cold!" Jim said in mock anger, and then, as he walked away, added, "Probably get to home with my mom!"

* * *

Nacho Mama's looked like a dump. The strip mall it was set in was only half-filled with businesses; paint was flaking off the exterior walls; the parking lot was covered in cracks. Appropriately enough, an actual tumbleweed rolled past the entrance as Steve approached it.

The early fall air was warm but pleasant. The sun, which usually produced a painful glare at this time of day, instead offered a nice warm glow. Steve entered the bar area of Nacho Mama's, which was empty and smelled of stale beer. His first thought was to turn around, but he noticed an open double door at the back of the bar. He walked toward the door as a bartender came out from a back room, eyeing Steve suspiciously. The door led to an open-air beer garden where Jim, smiling and wearing a horrible Hawaiian shirt, and a few other Hubbel employees greeted him.

"All right, you're here. Let's party! Dude, shots!" Jim said, as he put his arm around Steve and led him to the outside bar. After a shot, Steve ordered a beer, hopped on a seat, and settled in. Jim didn't stop talking from the moment Steve arrived. He must have been Jim's only friend.

Jim was incensed about the new version of some video game. Steve barely paid attention to him, only occasionally adding a few words to the conversation. He was mostly keeping an eye on the door, looking for Katie. After his first beer, the effect of the alcohol kicked in, and he began to feel that fine, warm sensation in his belly. The beer garden was getting crowded, mostly with Hubbel employees.

"Man, you're getting more ripped every day! What's your secret?" Jim was leaning in toward Steve, breaking him from his buzzed trance.

"I don't know. It must be this shake I'm drinking," he answered, a little embarrassed.

"I've *got* to start working out," Jim said, making a muscle with one of his thin arms. Judging from Jim's tone and slight slur, Steve figured that Jim had gotten a good head start on him at the bar.

"I went to the doctor, actually," Steve said.

"Why?" Jim asked, sounding slightly more serious.

"I gained twenty pounds of muscle without doing anything different. I can see better and hear better. I'm sweating all the time. I was worried I had a thyroid problem or something."

"What did the doctor say?" Jim asked.

"He said I was fine. They did blood work, an ultrasound. I even had a CAT scan. All good. The doctor said sometimes people just have weird growth spurts. But he told me to stop taking the powder."

"Well if it's a disease, I want some!" Jim laughed, leaning in on Steve a little too close for Steve's comfort, his sweet alcohol-tinged breath hitting Steve full force in the face.

"Sorry, dude, not getting gay on you or anything. I need to slow down," Jim said through a belch. "I'm getting some wings. Want any?"

"Yeah, I'll get some in a little bit."

"OK." Jim walked off with the slight lurch of a drunk man trying to appear sober.

Steve sat back, took a slug of his beer, and then took a deep breath of the dry, warm air of a beautiful fall evening. A few people from the office noticed him alone and cornered him, asking him the questions he had been asked a dozen times before in the office over the past few weeks—questions about what happened with Raymond. He answered the questions good-naturedly while continuing to look at the entrance to the beer garden, waiting to see Katie's face. He was about to slip away and call her when his phone vibrated in his pocket. It was her.

"Hey, where are you?"

"I'm sorry. Greg dragged me into a conference call. Sorry I haven't called."

"That's OK." He didn't try to hide his disappointment.

"By the way, I spoke to my father. He's coming to Vegas in a few days. He wants to meet you." She said the last part in a singsong voice.

"You told him about us?" he asked. His heart raced, another sign that he and Katie were more than just a short-term thing.

"Well, he wants to meet the man who saved his daughter." Her tone had changed slightly.

"When?" Steve tried to play off his nervousness.

"He's still finalizing his plans; he'll let me know for sure tonight or tomorrow."

"OK. I guess you can let me know when tomorrow, I guess."

"I think I'm going home. I am exhausted," Katie said.

Nervous thoughts raced through Steve's mind. *Is she avoiding me?* he thought. That fear was soon dispelled.

"Am I going to see you tonight?" she asked. "I was thinking you could stop by after you have fun with the boys."

In a moment he had gone from dejection and worry to elation.

"Yeah, sounds great. No later than midnight. OK?"

"Sure, wake me if I'm asleep."

"Sure." He smiled; there was no way he wouldn't wake her.

"See you then," she said as she hung up.

Jim stumbled over. "Your dream girl didn't show," he said as he looked around, slightly unsteady.

"Nope, maybe next time." Steve smiled as he said it; Jim was too drunk to notice.

"Dude, can you drive me home after the casino?" Jim asked, forcing his keys into Steve's hand.

"Casino?"

"Yeah, we're all going." Jim spread his arms as he turned to the beer garden crowd. Steve usually stayed out of casinos; he hadn't won a dime in his life. But Katie wasn't expecting him for a few hours, and it was a Friday night so the casino was sure to be a fun scene. "Why not? Sure," Steve said, patting Jim on the back and nearly knocking him over.

* * *

Steve wandered aimlessly through the bustling casino at the Del Rio hotel, the newest hotel on the strip. In fact, because of the seemingly endless recession, the Del Rio was the only casino that had been constructed in many years. It was packed tonight with a vibrant crowd of people drinking, smoking, and gambling. Steve had tried to find a low-dollar blackjack table where he could sit with Jim and some other Hubbel workers, but there weren't many open seats. Eventually, one by one, they sat at tables scattered throughout the casino. Steve never found a spot, so he just walked around, enjoying the atmosphere.

He passed a craps table where a woman in a sequined dress was jumping up and down, delighted by her date's roll. Steve couldn't help but watch with amazement as her ample breasts defied gravity and remained perfectly still while the rest of her bounced all over. She looked up when she stopped bouncing and met his eyes with a look of disgust.

It was ten o'clock. He wanted to get Jim, drive his drunken ass home, and go to Katie's, but he couldn't find him. He wondered if he had stumbled off into a taxi for adventures at other casinos. He pictured Jim waking up tomorrow wearing a pirate's hat and with one hell of a hangover.

He decided to make one more pass through the casino and call it a night. The place was so big he had lost all sense of direction, but he figured if he followed the walls he would find the exit sooner or later. He entered a quieter area of the casino, populated mostly by older women. Then he saw why: nickel slots. Between two ladies with different shades of blue hair sat Jim, squinting at a slot screen, holding a tropical-looking drink.

"Jim," said Steve.

"Hey, dude." Jim sounded far less enthusiastic than he had earlier that night. "We should play this. It's the progressive." His voice trailed off. He sounded like he was on the edge of sleep. In the hand without the drink, Jim held a crumbled five-dollar bill.

"I think you're cooked, my man. Time for bed," Steve said.

Jim sat still, staring at the screen for a few more seconds, and then turned and answered. "OK, but I need to piss first." Jim jumped out of his seat, spilling some of his drink on his shirt. "Which way to the pisser?" he asked.

Steve assumed he was talking about a bathroom, so he pointed him in the right direction. "I'll wait for you here."

"OK." Jim started off, still clutching his five-dollar bill in one hand and his now half-filled drink in the other.

Steve sat down between the two ladies, and each gave him

a dirty look at the same time. The one on his right adjusted her oxygen tank and got back to busily feeding nickels into her machine.

The game in front of Steve was called Pharaoh's Treasure, and the rolling numbers let him know the accumulated jackpot was up to $9,100,103.25. The 5 on the end rolled to 6, then to 7. Steve had never tried slots, but it seemed fairly easy: stick his money in and press the button to spin the reels. He got out a dollar, stuck it into the machine, and hit the button. The display showed a sphinx, a pyramid, and a cactus; he'd won nothing. *This* was supposed to be fun?

He was about to hit the button again when he noticed a small flash of light behind the reels. He was looking to see where it came from when he saw another flash. He then put his hand on the button and pressed it just as the light flashed a third time.

A colorful profile of Cleopatra stopped in the first window, then the same image stopped in the second, and then the third. He figured he had won something, but nothing happened immediately. A few seconds went by before a siren wailed. Steve thought it was a fire alarm until the blue-hairs on either side of him screamed simultaneously.

They must have won too.

But theirs weren't screams of joy. The old woman without the oxygen tank looked at Steve menacingly and said, "You son of a bitch. I have sat here all day, and you win after sitting here for what, five seconds!"

He was stunned. A crowd of people gathered around Steve. He looked above his machine and saw that the tally was frozen at $9,100,103.45. Had he won that? Had he *fucking* won that?

A dark-suited man approached Steve and said, "Congratulations, son! You won!" before using his walkie-talkie to call for security.

Some people were patting Steve on the back; others were jumping up and down. Steve waited patiently for a casino employee to tell him the machine had malfunctioned. What were those flashing lights? Were they normal? Was the machine broken?

"Dude, did I win?" Jim said, looking disoriented and now wearing the entire contents of his drink on his shirt.

"I think I won, but you get a cut," Steve told him. "I never would have sat down here if I wasn't looking for your ugly ass!"

Jim looked up at the number on the screen. "Ah, screw that. You only won nine hundred dollars," Jim said, dropping heavily to a nearby seat.

"I think you're missing some decimals, dude," Steve said, but Jim, his chin resting solidly on his chest, was nearly comatose.

A number of casino employees descended upon Steve, asking him questions, giving him forms to fill out, and eventually taking his driver's license to prepare some other forms for him. The original dark-suited casino employee came back with a man wearing a tool belt. He was a slot technician, according to the title on his blue work shirt. He opened the machine and the horrible bell stopped ringing. He pulled out some mechanical gizmos, poked around with his flashlight for a few seconds, and turned around and said to the suited man, "Pay him."

Steve looked at the man in the suit with a puzzled look.

"We had to make sure there was no funny business with the machine," he explained.

It wasn't a malfunction? He almost brought up the flashes of light but caught his tongue.

The dark-suited man spoke into his walkie-talkie again.

"It will just be a moment," he told Steve. That's when it hit him full force. A warm sensation washed over his body; he felt a little nauseous. He'd just won nine million dollars. *He'd just won nine million dollars!*

He could think of only one person to share the news with. He called Katie on his cell phone but got her voicemail. *How do you leave this message on a voicemail?* he thought. He said simply, "Call me. I have great news!"

The siren was back; the maintenance man had closed the machine and was walking away. More people passing by stopped to see what the commotion was. When they figured out that Steve had won so much money, they congratulated him: "Great job!" "Nice hit!"

The suit guy returned, followed by another group of casino employees. Their name tags indicated that they were managers. One of them gave Steve a giant check and took a picture of him holding it in front of the machine while onlookers cheered.

The siren stopped. Suit guy stuck a key in the slot machine and turned it, and then a squat, grumpy-looking man also dressed in a suit did the same. They were resetting the machine back to zero dollars.

Suit guy gave Steve a receipt showing his winnings and also gave him back his driver's license. "Follow me please," the grumpy guy said.

Steve followed him across the room to a door that said CASINO SERVICES. They entered a nondescript office, where Grumpy introduced himself as Chip Carter, vice president of casino services. He didn't look like a Chip. The only personal item on Chip's desk was a plaque that read: THE HOUSE ALWAYS WINS!" Steve sat in the only available chair.

"So, the way this works is this," Chip started. "I'm required by law and casino policy to withhold thirty percent for the IRS. That will leave you north of six million. We can either directly wire it to an account of your choice within the next thirty days, or you can pick up a check at the cage on Monday, after one.

Steve said, "Check."

"Most people do that."

They filled out several forms and Chip gave Steve a handful of papers.

"OK, son, don't blow it all in one place. Unless it's here."

Steve thanked him and returned to the casino floor. Jim— where was he? Steve did a lap around the casino but found no trace of his friend.

He thought about Katie, about sharing his news with her, and tried her phone number again. Once more, he got her voicemail.

* * *

On his way to Katie's house, Steve noticed the light on his cell phone was blinking, indicating he had a message. Katie had called, telling him that she was waiting up for him. In the noise of the casino he must not have heard his phone ring. Steve thought of calling her back, but he was only a few minutes away from her house.

As he drove, he wondered how he would tell her about the jackpot—and about what he could go buy tomorrow: cars, houses, trips. Would he keep his job? Where would he put the money? Would he invest it? Did he need a lawyer?

As Steve drove slowly down Katie's street, he caught a whiff of fresh cigarette smoke. He looked through his passenger window and into the parked car he was passing. The driver held a pair of binoculars trained in the direction of Katie's house.

As he passed, the driver slouched down, but not before Steve recognized him. It was Katie's ex, Gabriel. What the hell was he doing here?

Steve glided around the block, hoping Gabriel didn't see him, and found a parking spot on the next street. He walked through the neighbor's backyard and then across Katie's yard to the sliding glass door that opened into her family room. Katie was on the couch watching television. Steve knocked lightly on the door, and she jumped up, looking startled and then annoyed. She yanked open the door.

"What are you doing?" she asked in a tone that surprised Steve; he had never heard her angry before.

"Gabriel's sitting out front. With binoculars!"

"You're kidding me! I'm calling the police." Katie was wearing an oversized T-shirt and nothing else.

Steve walked up to the front window on the second-floor landing and peered down to the street. Gabriel was still there, his binoculars trained on the window below Steve. "OK, thank you," Katie said before hanging up the phone. "Someone will be here within ten minutes," she told Steve as she returned to the couch.

Within five minutes a police car had arrived, driving slowly and shining a searchlight into each car along the street. Gabriel pulled slowly out of his spot. Almost immediately, the police car flashed its lights and Gabriel's car stopped. One of the cops got out of the cruiser and approached the car.

"They got him," Steve announced from the window.

Katie jumped up to go to the front door.

"Maybe you should put some clothes on . . ." Steve said.

She looked down and smiled. "But I thought you'd like this look," she said coyly.

"Believe me, I do! And I am sure the cops will too."

"Yeah, I'll go change."

There was a knock at the door as she ran up the stairs.

"I'll get it," Steve called up.

A large black officer stood at the doorway. "Katherine Landry?" he asked.

"She's getting changed. Be down in a minute."

Steve looked over the cop's shoulder and saw Gabriel standing with his palms against the cruiser, while the other officer frisked him. It looked like Gabriel was arguing with him.

"Need to talk to Ms. Landry," the cop at the door said seriously.

"That's me," Katie said as she came to the door from behind Steve.

"You stay here," the cop said to Steve. "You come with me."

Katie followed the cop toward the now-handcuffed Gabriel.

Steve couldn't hear the conversation, but it looked like the cops were asking Katie and Gabriel questions. Gabriel gave one-word answers, while Katie was more animated. The cop who had frisked Gabriel rummaged through his car, and when Gabriel was presented with the binoculars he slumped slightly and looked into the distance, directly at Steve. Then he turned back to the cops. "Bitch," Steve heard him say.

That seemed to do it. One cop nudged Gabriel into the back of the cruiser while the other escorted Katie back toward the house. He gave Katie a copy of a report he had filled out and then returned to the cruiser. His partner turned off the twirling lights and they drove away. Steve noticed a few curious neighbors retreating back into their homes.

Katie seemed excited when she came through the front door. "He was arrested for being a Peeping Tom, basically," she explained breathlessly. "I was getting worried until they found the binoculars. I guess, legally, he could have sat there as long as he wanted to. But the binoculars did him in. The good news is I can get a restraining order against him now."

The words "good news" reminded Steve that he had something to tell Katie. He pulled out the cashier's receipt from his pocket. "Remember how I said I had some good news when I called you?" he asked.

Katie looked at him. "Oh yeah. What is it?"

He put the receipt in her hand. She turned on the hall light and asked, "What's this?" She looked at the receipt and again asked, "What's this? Is this a joke?"

Steve grinned as widely as he ever had and shook his head. She screamed so loudly Steve was afraid the police might return.

CHAPTER 14

Ted waited patiently in the lobby of Mr. Vega's office. Mr. Vega usually wouldn't keep anyone waiting; he was meticulous with his time management.

Nellie, Mr. Vega's assistant, sat at her desk, looking toward the lobby entrance with a slight smile. An occasional beep from her computer or buzz from her phone interrupted her for a few seconds, but then she would return her attention to the door.

Ted tried a few times to see what she was looking at, thinking he was missing some hidden screen or something, but as far as he could tell there was nothing there but a large, stone, glyph-filled wall hanging. He was going to ask Nellie a question about the wall hanging when a group of employees, all wearing lab coats, exited the area where Mr. Vega's office was located. They were engaged in a hushed but heated conversation. The only words Ted made out clearly were, "It is clear. I can't change . . ."

Nellie put her hand to her earpiece, continuing to smile slightly as she looked directly at Ted, and said, "Mr. Baron, Mr. Vega will now see you."

Her look sent a shiver down Ted's spine. He had with him an ornate wooden box containing papers that were sealed individually in plastic. They looked to be hundreds, if not thousands, of years old and were inscribed with glyphs familiar to Ted, symbols from some ancient language. In fact, they were similar to the symbols on the wall hanging that Mr. Vega's secretary spent her days staring at.

As he raised his hand to knock on Mr. Vega's door, Ted had flashes of his mother staring at a television screen, looking like Nellie did. It was the look she had after she took her medicine. The thought of his mother caused Ted's stomach to turn. He hadn't had a thought like that for years; he kept his past dead and buried. As Ted knocked on the door, he composed himself by taking a deep breath.

"Enter," Mr. Vega's voice boomed, sounding slightly strange and containing too much emotion.

When Ted opened the door, he found Mr. Vega facing away from him, looking at a painting on the wall behind his desk. To Ted's shock, Mr. Vega's always-perfect hair was slightly mussed near the top of his head, as if he had just run his hand through it. Mr. Vega flattened his hair to his head, as thought he had heard Ted's thoughts, and turned around. His complexion was pale; he looked frightened.

"I have retrieved the item you asked for, Mr. Vega."

"Yes, yes, put it on my desk. Excellent timing as always," he said, motioning toward his desk with his hand. He walked over to a wall and pressed what must have been a hidden button. A small panel slid open, revealing several bottles of alcohol. Mr. Vega poured himself a drink, not offering Ted one, and downed it as quickly as he had poured. Ted had never before seen his boss take a drink. He poured another and turned toward Ted as Ted put the box of papers on the desk.

"Is there anything else, sir?"

Mr. Vega stared through Ted, not answering.

Ted stood for a few minutes in silence and was going to turn and leave when Mr. Vega spoke. "Ted, my whole life I have believed that I was something special. Today I found out that might not be the case."

"Sir?"

"I thought I had found my legacy, my birthright. But today I found out I might be wrong, my father might have been wrong, his father . . ." His voiced trailed off.

Ted stood at attention, silent, his military training taking over while his mind whirled.

"I have discovered one of the greatest secrets of all time, Ted. I have decoded both the Popol Vuh and the Mayan calendar." He became silent.

Ted suspected the papers in the wooden box were pages from this text, the Popol Vuh. The man in Spain Ted bought the pages from, for $80,000, had said it was like the Mayan genesis story. Ted was pretty sure that over the years he had bought different versions of this text for Mr. Vega.

"My family is old, Ted. I am a descendent of kings, part of the origin of Mexico. I thought everything in my life had led to this point, this pinnacle, the end of the Mayan calendar in December . . ." He trailed off again.

"Is there anything I can do?" Ted asked, wishing he could take it back almost immediately. The question seemed inappropriate. Ted was glad Mr. Vega ignored it.

"Ted, don't worry. I will take care of you and your family."

"I don't have family, sir," Ted blurted out as he pictured his mother in their home in Montana, in the living room that was always freezing cold in winter, lying on the couch, in front of the TV, dead from an overdose.

"I will, Ted. I will." Mr. Vega said, apparently not hearing Ted. He finished his drink and said, "I need you to find my son. He has gotten into trouble in Vegas. Bring him to me. He needs to be close to me. I will forward you information about his location."

Ted knew Mr. Vega had a son with his ex-wife. He also knew that Mr. V didn't see his son often, if at all. "Yes, sir," said Ted. "It will be my priority."

Mr. Vega laughed at that. "Priorities," he said.

"OK, Mr. Vega." Ted turned and left the office.

He felt panicked as he entered the elevator. What the hell was happening with Mr. V? He was someone whose words you did not ignore. But what was he saying—a great secret, the Mayan calendar, taking care of Ted? All Ted knew is that Mr. V had put the fear of God in him.

He needed to see the sun, to feel it on his face.

When he reached the ground-floor lobby, he walked toward the exit so fast that he nearly crashed into the automatic doors before they opened.

Outside the temperature was in the low eighties, but it felt much hotter compared to the chill in Mr. Vega's office, the chill that had him thinking about Montana and his mother and trying to plug a crack in the window pane with his sock as the winter wind blew through, numbing his fingers.

After taking a few deep breaths of air that smelled of car exhaust and the geraniums planted throughout the Next Industries grounds, he felt more like himself, more in control.

Ted continued walking down the sidewalk, past the security post at the front gate. The guard there recognized him but looked surprised. Ted had never walked off the campus like this. He always left by car.

Ted decided he needed to look into what Mr. Vega was saying about the Mayan calendar and then question him about it. That would be his plan of action. Ted could handle anything if he had a plan.

Feeling fully composed now, he turned around and approached the front gate. He pulled off his badge to show the security guard, but the guard waved him through without looking at it.

"Are you letting me in?" Ted asked in an even tone.

Seemingly unsure of how to answer, the guard said, "Yes?"

"Is that policy, son?"

"No, sir," he answered firmly. "Sorry, sir." He scrutinized Ted's badge and then Ted's face before opening the gate.

"Don't let it happen again," Ted said as he walked through the gate.

He took out his phone and called Ken. "Ken, there is a gentleman working at the front gate whose performance I am not impressed with. This is his last day."

"I'm on it, sir. Sir, Mr. Vega sent a packet to you. It's on your desk."

Ted closed his cell phone without a good-bye. He figured the packet was the information about Mr. Vega's son. He was good now, ready to go back to work.

CHAPTER 15

Steve woke early on Monday morning, very early. His head pounded from the celebrating he and Katie had done all weekend. Their lunches ran so long that they turned into dinners, and they consumed way too many cocktails. But it had been the best forty-eight hours of his life.

Katie's alarm clock, glowing next to him, read 4:43 a.m. From the other side of the bed he heard Katie's slow, even breathing. He had a busy day ahead of him. He was going to pick up a check for over $6 million, and then he was going to meet with an investment advisor that Katie's father recommended. That evening, he would have dinner with Katie and her father, at the same restaurant where Katie and he had had their first date.

Katie's father decided to change his plans and come to Vegas today, after Katie's late-night call telling him about the events of the previous night. Steve lay in bed, picturing how the day would play out. What if the casino doesn't give him the money? What if Katie's father hates him?

He tried to put these thoughts out of his head. There was no reason to think the day wouldn't go as planned. Early as it was, he got out of bed, knowing there was no chance he was going to fall back asleep before 7 a.m., when the alarm was set to go off. His body needed more rest, but his mind was off to the races.

In the kitchen, he'd planned to make himself a cup of coffee, but the metal can was sealed and he didn't know where Katie kept her can opener. He opened a drawer and was greeted with a picture of Katie in a swimming pool, smiling and in the arms of Gabriel. Gabriel's smile highlighted his perfect cheekbones. Under that photo there were others featuring Katie and Gabriel—skiing, in New York, in the backseat of a car. A pang of jealousy hit Steve, but he reminded himself that this was the guy she was getting a restraining order against today.

Still, his mind ran wild. He pictured Gabriel and Katie making up at the courthouse: perhaps it was all a misunderstanding. She loved Gabriel! How could Gabriel think she would really be interested in him. She always loved Gabriel. Didn't Gabriel remember their trip to New York?

Steve actually shook his head to get these visions out of it, and that made his head pound even harder. He needed coffee. He finally found the can opener behind the coffee pot and made himself a strong pot of the stuff.

Sitting on a bar stool in Katie's kitchen, sipping his coffee, Steve looked around the apartment. The furnishings and décor had a 1970s look to them, everything very square and uncomfortable looking. But everything was very tasteful— not exactly *his* taste, but nice just the same.

He wondered if Katie and he would go on. He hoped so, but he wasn't naive enough to think their infatuation would last forever. What about a year from now, when his quirks weren't so endearing anymore? Would her taste in '70s style drive him nuts? Obviously, things change. Look at the happy couple in the photos in the kitchen drawer.

"What're you doing? It's 5 a.m.," Katie said groggily as she came down the stairs.

"Couldn't sleep."

One thing was for sure, he wouldn't get sick of the way Katie looked. Even at 5 a.m., just rolling out of bed, she was beautiful. Did she realize how stunning she was? Why was she with him?

"Couldn't wait to be a millionaire, huh?" she asked teasingly as she hugged him.

"Maybe not."

After a few seconds of silence Steve said, "I am quitting my job at Hubbel today."

"I figured you would. Could you call Greg an A-hole when you do?" she asked, laughing.

"You don't need to ask. That's a given. I think I'm going to go work out and meet you back here at seven or eight. OK?"

"OK, muscle man," Katie said as she went to the refrigerator.

"Why don't you go back to sleep?"

"I can't now. You got me all awake," she said, grabbing a bottle of orange juice.

"Maybe we can go back to bed and I can tire you out," Steve said hesitantly.

"You want it all today, don't you?"

"I guess I do."

She finished her juice, looked at Steve, and said, "OK, Mr. Soto. I'll race ya!"

Katie bolted around the corner and up the stairs. Steve followed quickly, his doubts now quieted.

* * *

Steve pulled up to the front of Katie's house. He was coming from his apartment, where, after a great workout at the gym, he had pounded a muscle shake, showered, and dressed in his best shirt and pants. He didn't know if he would have time after his busy day to get back home to change for dinner with Katie's dad, and he didn't want to be underdressed when he met him for the first time.

Katie was waiting for him outside, in the cool, cloudy morning, a welcome reprieve from the hot weather they had faced all year long. She jumped into his car, slid over, and gave him a big kiss.

"Are you going to have a fancy red sports car by the end of day?" she teased.

"Hey, I like my Prius!" he said, with fake outrage.

Steve really did love his car, especially the way it drove so quietly at low speeds. But he did enjoy knowing he could buy almost anything he wanted: a new car, a beautiful house. The thought sent a surge of warmth through his body.

What was he going to do, besides quitting his job? He could do just about anything. He had the girl of his dreams, the body he wanted, and more money than he had ever hoped he would have. He also had doubts, the kind he felt earlier that morning in Katie's kitchen. He was pretty sure he wouldn't change his life that much—maybe he'd buy a house and invest the rest of the money. But he did need to figure out what to with the rest of his life.

"My, you look nice," Katie said as they pulled away from the house, noticing the clothes he had picked out for the day. Their first stop was the Del Rio hotel and casino.

"So do you," he added, and he wasn't lying. She was wearing a sundress—long, aqua blue, and snug in the right places—with a white sweater resting on her shoulders.

On their drive to the Del Rio, Steve worried that somehow the casino wouldn't honor his wrinkled receipt for more than nine million dollars. He distracted himself by asking questions about Katie's father. He learned that Mr. Landry was a loving, flawless father who had never approved of any boyfriend, except Gabriel Vega.

"It wasn't like they were best friends," Katie said of her father and Gabriel. "But Dad really liked him, and he came from a really important family."

"How does he feel about him now?" Steve asked as they pulled up to the valet at the Del Rio.

"He can't believe he's turned into a stalker. He can't believe he had a girlfriend in New York. He's shocked."

Steve tipped the valet five dollars. This was the first time he had ever used a valet, so he wasn't sure if that was low or high, but he saw the driver of the car in front of him give a tip and felt he needed to as well, especially in front of Katie. Unfortunately, Katie was looking the other way, but judging by the smile on the young valet's face, five dollars was a satisfactory amount.

In the casino, they walked toward the main cage and passed a wall hung with photos of the Del Rio's biggest winners. There was Steve, holding the giant check. A plaque underneath his photo claimed that his jackpot was largest in Las Vegas in the last ten years.

Katie noticed the photo. "I hate to say it, but you look kind of drunk."

He looked at his picture; she was right. His eyes were glassy and looking away from the camera.

Suddenly it hit him: *Jim! Shit! Did he get home?* Steve hadn't even thought about his friend since that night. He owed him a cut, didn't he?

Steve punched Jim's number into his cell phone and got his voicemail.

"Who are you calling?" Katie asked.

"Jim. I forgot about him."

"Hmm," she said.

Steve knew Katie didn't think much of Jim, and he could see why. Jim was a pig, but he still felt horrible that he had forgotten about him. He tried his work extension and again got voicemail. Steve left a message, asking Jim to call him back.

They reached the casino cage, where Steve could hear screaming from a winner at the craps table. Even at this time of the morning, the games were still going strong, which struck him as funny.

"Hi, I'm here to collect my check," Steve said at the counter, pushing the crumpled receipt over to the cashier, a stocky older woman with white hair. Over bifocals balanced on the edge of her nose, she looked at him incredulously. "I won that Friday night, Sally," Steve said cheerfully, looking at the woman's name tag. "They told me to come back on Monday morning, 9 a.m."

She looked at her wristwatch. "Nine-o-three, a little anxious, are we?" she asked, flatly.

"Tony!" Sally called over her shoulder before Steve could answer. "Please move to the side, over there. Tony will be right with you," she said, looking over his shoulder at the line of customers behind him.

Tony, who was the casino manager according to his name tag, came up behind Sally. She slid the receipt to him as she counted out cash for the next customer, bobbing her head toward Steve. Tony, who looked like a young Wayne Newton and was wearing a dark suit, checked the receipt and approached Steve from behind the cage.

"Mr. Soto, I'm ready for you. Please." Tony pointed to a side door that led to casino services. "Congratulations again," Tony said, shaking Steve's hand as he and Katie passed through the door and entered the same hallway he had been in Friday night.

This time they went farther down the hall, to Tony's office. As they sat down Steve caught Tony trying to glance down Katie's dress. Tony, unfazed, opened a drawer in his desk and pulled out a file with a check paper-clipped to the front it. The check was for $6,006,067.98.

"So here you are, your check. Unfortunately Uncle Sam took his piece already," Tony said with a smile.

"That doesn't seem fair," Katie said, not too seriously.

"You would be surprised how quick people blow all their money and then don't have anything to pay the tax man," Tony answered as he signed some forms.

He pushed the forms toward Steve along with a plastic card bearing the Del Rio logo and Steve's name. "This is your premier club membership card," Tony explained. "You get free food and drinks and, of course, private play."

"Thanks," Steve said. He wasn't sure what "private play" meant, and he really didn't care, since he didn't see himself coming back here or to any casino in the near future. Steve knew it was rare to walk away on top from the Vegas casinos, and he intended to be one of the few who do it.

Tony stood up and offered his hand. "Well done and hope to see you again at the Del Rio soon."

"Sure, thank you very much," Steve said. As he shook his hand he wondered if Tony was one of those old-school Vegas casino managers, the kind who busted kneecaps every now and then. The glint in Tony's eyes suggested that this might be the case.

"Thank you," Katie said sweetly as they turned and left.

Steve was sure Tony was taking in a view of her backside as they left; he thought of turning to see if that was the case but instead chose to just get out of there with his money. When they return to the casino floor, Katie grabbed his hand and squeezed. "I am so happy for you!" she said, giving him a peck on his cheek.

He squeezed her hand back. He still couldn't believe he was leaving the casino with this check. He expected to hear Tony's voice: "Stop them! There's been a mistake!" When they made it outside, into the cool Vegas air, Steve's cell phone started vibrating. It was Jim.

"Hello?"

"Dude, why aren't you at work?"

"I'm quitting today," Steve answered. "What happened to you Friday night?"

"Oh, dude, I'm not sure. I woke up on my kitchen floor at like two o'clock."

"Yeah, you were definitely messed up. I was going to get you a cab or drive you home from the casino, but you disappeared."

"Casino? I was at the casino? Wait . . . yeah I was. Now I remember, I think."

"You don't remember the casino?" Steve asked.

"Not really. But wait, you're quitting?"

The valet arrived with Steve's car.

"Jim, I won nine million dollars. You don't remember that?"

"Yeah right! I'd remember that."

"I did. That's why I'm quitting."

There was only silence on the line.

"Jim?"

"Yeah, shut up. You're messing with me.'

"And you're getting a cut. I was thinking five hundred grand. Your drunken brilliance is the reason I played the machine I played."

"Dude, this is just *mean*. Don't do this to your bro."

"Meet me in the Hubbel parking lot in fifteen minutes. I'll show you the check!"

The valet was waiting with the car now.

Katie had a surprised look on her face. "You're giving him a cut?" she whispered.

"It was because of him I won," he whispered back, covering the cell phone.

"I have to say, if you're fucking with me that would be just cold, way cold," said Jim.

"I'll see you in fifteen minutes!"

Steve pocketed his phone and handed the valet a twenty.

"You're one good friend, Mr. Soto," Katie said, shaking her head as they got into the car.

"Maybe," Steve said as they drove away.

* * *

Steve had been in the Vegas police station's domestic violence department for only an hour, but it seemed like five. Katie had answered all the basic questions: what, when, where. She told the officer how she had asked Gabriel to stop following her many times, in person and on the phone. Witnesses could verify her statement.

Because of the complaint she filed the previous night, Gabriel had been held at the station for a few hours before making bail. The police charged him with invasion of privacy, and at worst he would have to pay a fine. Still, the officer assured Katie and Steve that the arrest left a good paper trail leading up to the restraining order Katie could file later today in front of a judge.

As the officer ran through where and how she was to file the papers, Steve had to turn his head for some fresh air— evidently, the officer had eaten a fine, garlicky meal the night before. Steve could tell from the way Katie winced each time the officer breathily began a sentence that she too was suffering.

"OK . . . thank you," Katie said as she snatched the papers from the cop. She gave Steve a look of relief and grabbed his hand as they left.

"Maybe you should drop me off at home," she said as they walked to his car. "I know you have some more chores, and I need to pick up Dad and his lawyer." Her father was flying in with a lawyer who would help her get the restraining order.

"Am I picking you up before dinner, or should I meet you at the restaurant?"

"I'd rather go with you, but I don't know how long the court stuff will take. Let's play it by ear, OK?"

"Sure," Steve said.

He was exhausted by the time he'd dropped her off, but he still had to meet Jim. When he pulled into the Hubbel parking lot, Jim was pacing back and forth, looking crazed. Steve walked toward him, holding the check carefully in front of him. Jim approached quickly but slowed down and squinted when he got close enough to read the numbers on the check.

"You're giving me five hundred grand of that?" Jim asked. He seemed dumbfounded, almost disappointed.

"Yeah," Steve said.

Jim's bear hug nearly tore the check.

"Stop . . ." was all Steve could get out.

"I don't know what I did, or why you would do this, but we are brothers for life!" Jim said, his face buried in Steve's chest.

"OK, big guy. You're welcome."

"No one has ever done anything like this for me. I'll always have your back, man, always."

"OK, OK, but really, you deserve it. If I hadn't been looking for you, I wouldn't have played that machine," Steve said, hoping Jim would let go soon.

"Yeah, but I can't even remember it. I was so shitfaced. Dude, I have to stop the tequila shots."

After a few more awkward hugs, Jim ran—skipped, really—back into the Hubbel building.

* * *

Steve's new broker was named John Riland, and he worked in a giant glass cube of a building in downtown Las Vegas, in the main branch of the Grand National Bank. He was large, good-looking, well mannered, and intelligent, and he was a manager in the bank's wealth management division.

John had spent an hour explaining Steve's investment options for the casino check. Charming as John was, he did mention that Steve's check put him at the bottom of John's portfolio range. Or as he smilingly put it, "I never deal with anyone who has less than five million liquid." That initially made Steve feel like a poor man invited to the ball, but John quickly got into all of the investment plans, at which point Steve struggled to keep up.

To John's chagrin, Steve wanted to put his money in a simple money market account rather than the hedge funds, municipal bonds, corporate bonds, and portfolio indexes John

was touting. Steve knew what his 401(k) looked like after it
went through two market crashes, and he didn't want to take
any risks with his casino winnings; he could live comfortably
off the money's interest alone. John sighed in frustration and
left the office to retrieve some paperwork. Steve had a feeling
he would be ushered out soon so that he didn't waste any
more of John's precious time.

While John was gone, an impeccably dressed gentleman
with bright white hair came into the office and introduced
himself as Charlie Bivens, John's boss, the wealth management
vice president. "John tells me you're hesitant about some of
our investment products," Bivens said.

"Not hesitant. I just want to see how things shake out."
Steve tried to sound casual.

"You know, a sum this size could grow quickly with the
right investments," Bivens said.

Steve knew that his money could shrink quickly too.

"I'll think about it." He just wanted to deposit his money
and get out of there.

Bivens nodded. "If you change your mind, let us know."
Without a handshake, he left the office.

John returned with Steve's deposit documentation and
ushered him out of the office with a quick good-bye. As he left
the building, Steve didn't quite believe he had the millions of
dollars deposited in his account. He was afraid someone was
going to jump out of one of the offices he passed and tell him
there was a problem with the check.

It was 3:00 p.m., and Steve had more than enough time
to get home and shower before dinner. He pulled out his cell
phone to call Katie and saw that she left a message half an
hour earlier; apparently the glass-cube design of the bank
wasn't conducive to cell phone service. Katie's message said
that the restraining order was signed and that she was on her

way home. She suggested they all meet outside the restaurant at six. Steve was relieved: he'd been dreading picking up Katie and her dad for the awkward drive to the restaurant. Now he could get to the restaurant early and have a cocktail to relax before meeting Mr. Landry.

* * *

At the restaurant bar Steve, wearing a shirt and tie, ordered a beer and shot of tequila. He had debated with himself over whether to go with a tie, finally deciding that it was better to be safe than sorry.

When his drinks arrived he slammed the shot and drank almost the entire beer in one swig. Then he sat back and let the alcohol's comforting warmth spread through him. He had a view of the restaurant's entrance from his barstool, so he'd be able to see when Katie and her dad arrived. The bartender asked if he wanted another round. He shook his head and paid the tab, adding a tip that equaled the cost of the two drinks. *Why not?* he thought.

He popped in a piece of gum and walked to the restaurant entrance as soon as he saw Katie arrive with a stocky older gentleman. She looked glorious in a blue dress that was conservative but nevertheless made his heart race. Her father looked exactly as Steve had pictured him. He was dressed in a suit and tie, and Steve was happy he'd gone with the tie himself.

Steve stuck out his hand and said with a smile, "Hello. Mr. Landry, I presume." For a second Mr. Landry didn't react. Wasn't this Katie's dad?

To his relief, Mr. Landry met his handshake after the brief pause. "Hello to you, Steve," he said, hesitating slightly before saying Steve's name. Mr. Landry glanced at Katie, and she smiled back. "Call me Fred, by the way," he added, patting Steve on the back.

Katie went to tell the maître d' they were ready to be seated. After a few seconds of awkward silence, Katie's father said, "Steve, I have to thank you for saving my daughter." His eyes teared up as he spoke.

Steve almost answered, "It was nothing," but he caught himself. Instead he said, "I am just glad I was at the right place at the right time."

Dinner flew by, with the help of two bottles of wine. Steve's winning the casino jackpot was a major topic of conversation. The only uncomfortable moment came when Katie mentioned the restraining order. "I really liked Gabriel," Katie's father said. "I can't believe he resorted to such . . . such a state. I never saw him as this type of person. Hell, I thought you and he would marry. Shocking." He looked down at the time, as if he had said more than he meant to.

Stevie and Katie glanced at each other, and then her father continued. "You know, I am friends with his father. That's how you two met, isn't it, sweetheart?"

"No," she said, looking uncomfortable. "We met on our own, at school."

"Oh, yes, small world. Anyway, I know his father. He owns Next, you know."

"The software company?" Steve asked. "He's *that* Vega?" Steve couldn't believe it. In all of their conversations about Gabriel, Katie had never mentioned that. He knew Gabriel was from a rich family, but not that rich.

"You didn't tell him, honey?" Mr. Landry asked, downing the last of his wine.

"Didn't I? I thought I did. But who cares? It doesn't matter, right?"

"No," said Steve.

He thought back to everything Katie had shared with him about Gabriel, how he had cheated on her with at least two different women, one in New York and one in L.A., and how she had found out about these women when she saw some incriminating e-mails in Gabriel's inbox. He never tried to explain; he just called the relationships mistakes. When Katie broke up with him, Gabriel began following her, trying to get her back. He even sent her copies of the e-mails he had sent to these women, telling him he was breaking up with them.

Katie finally changed the subject by asking her dad about a crazy aunt of hers. The rest of dinner was uneventful.

At the restaurant door, Steve gave Katie a peck on the cheek and a promise of phone call, then shook her father's hand and left. Katie had said earlier that it was best if they stayed at their own places tonight, because her father was old-fashioned. Steve was glad he was going home alone; he was exhausted and looked forward to the comfort of his empty bed.

CHAPTER 16

Steve awoke to the phone ringing. He lay staring at the ceiling, trying to will the phone into stopping the noise. The face of his alarm clock showed 10:32 a.m, and he knew the call wasn't from Katie; she called only his cell phone now. Steve knew better than to answer—one of the many lessons he'd learned in the few weeks since he had won a fortune. There was a very good chance an old acquaintance, a second cousin, or, worst of all, a person with no hope was leaving him a voicemail right now.

As he lay in bed, he thought about what he would do that day. He'd been feeling lazy and bit down the last few days; Katie had said he was living the life of the idle rich: one boring day after another.

He grabbed the phone next to his bed and played his three voicemail messages. One was a raspy breath followed by a hang-up; the second was his investment broker "just touching base"; the third was a courtesy call from the cable company to see if he was satisfied with his recent service upgrade. He had splurged on all the premium channels.

That's how his life had changed since winning six million dollars: he had a better cable package, went out to dinner more frequently, and spent most of his mind-numbingly boring days waiting like a puppy for Katie to return from work.

After the initial euphoria of winning the money and quitting his job, he'd gone house hunting and car shopping. But after a long Saturday of looking at luxury apartments and country club houses with Katie, he decided to keep his apartment, even though he wasn't there very often. He spent most days and nights at Katie's, so spending money on a luxury condo seemed like a waste. Last night was an exception: he slept at his apartment because Katie had to wake up extra early on Monday.

He got out of bed and went to the kitchen to brew some coffee, preparing himself for another day of the three Ws: working out, watching cable, and waiting for Katie. He needed to find a hobby or a job he really liked.

He had enjoyed only a few days of anonymity after winning the jackpot. First came the phone calls from local television stations and newspapers, and then they came from cities farther away, in Texas and California. Apparently, the hero who hits the jackpot a few weeks after stopping an office madman was a great story. Eventually the media moved on to other stories, but that's when the letters began arriving, followed by the phone calls. People down on their luck begged him for money: parents whose kids had cancer, families losing their homes.

At first he read the letters. He even looked into one of them, the most honest-sounding one. A little girl named Edna from Salt Lake City asked for $20,000 so her mama could get a surgery to help her breathe better. She listed her return address, and Steve used it to find her phone number. When he called, a gruff-sounding man answered.

When Steve had asked to speak to Edna, the man said, "Edna? Dude, you got the wrong num—" At that point, he heard a woman speaking animatedly in the background.

"Uh . . . hold on," the man had said.

"Hello, sir?" Edna was on the line now. She sounded about forty, maybe fifty.

Steve had hung up the phone without a word. A few seconds passed before it rang again, the caller ID showing the number he had just called. He unplugged the phone.

He followed up on some of the other heartbreaking letters, and all of them turned out to be scams.

There were now two piles of letters on his kitchen counter, a tall one from people asking for help—monetary help, of course—and a shorter one from people claiming to be relatives who hoped to be reunited with him. He swept the tall pile into the garbage and left the family pile on the counter. Even though he was sure most were bogus, a part of him yearned for a family connection.

He'd decided he had to change his life, although that thought almost made him laugh. Most people would be completely satisfied with his life: plenty of money, a beautiful girlfriend, and lots of leisure time. But he had too much leisure time. He was sleeping ten to twelve hours a night, getting up later and later and then doing nothing but going to the gym and watching television until Katie got home.

Today was the day he would change things. He resolved to either find a great job or donate his time to a charity. He loved animals.

This sudden burst of ambition excited him. He would skip the workout today and instead make a list of jobs to go after or charities to work for.

Steve imagined telling Katie of his plans; he thought she would be happy. Things were going great with them, besides the issue of Gabriel. She still thought she saw him at times—a face in a crowd or in a passing car. Steve had to keep reassuring her that since being served the warrant he had most likely left town. He figured that if someone took out a restraining order on him, he'd be too embarrassed to stick around.

After he showered and ate a bowl of cereal, Steve sorted through the mail. His pile of bills was growing tall. There were a few pieces of junk mail, and then a very thin, almost transparent envelope with red and blue striping on the edges. It was addressed to Master Steven Soto, and showed a return address in El Paso, Texas.

Inside were a letter and a faded Polaroid photo. Steve read the letter:

> *Dear Steven,*
> *My name is Esteban Soto. I live in El Paso, Texas. If the man in the picture is your father, then I am your grandfather.*

Steve looked at the picture again. Anything he remembered about his father was from the photos his mom had of him. The guy in this photo looked like a younger version of his father—in fact, he looked a lot like Steve. He compared the photo to his mother and father's wedding picture, which he kept in a drawer. There was certainly a resemblance between the two men. Steve continued reading:

> *I would very much like to meet you. I saw your story on the news, about you being a hero and having won a large amount of money. I hope that you are my grandson because of the great luck you have and what a fine young man you seem to be. If you are my grandson, my phone number and address are included. I hope you will contact me. If you are not, thank you for your time.*
>
> *Sincerely,*
> *Esteban Soto*

Steve knew his father and grandfather had been estranged for a long while before his father died. From what he understood, his father had run away from home, in Mexico, while he was in his teens, and never returned.

The photo suggested that Esteban Soto was who he said he was, but Steve felt in his gut that this man was his grandfather.

He picked up the phone and dialed the number in the letter.

The phone rang many times before an older man picked up. "Bueno?" He sounded out of breath, like he had run to the phone.

"Um, hi," said Steve. "Can I speak to Esteban, Esteban Soto?"

"This is he," the man answered in a Mexican accent.

"Hi, this is Steve Soto. I received your letter."

"Steven? Is that you?"

"Yes. You are Michael Soto's father?"

"I am. He was Miguel to me. He changed his name, after he left."

"So that makes you my grandfather," Steve said with a little laugh, because it sounded so funny.

"I am, I am, son. I am very glad you called. I have always wondered what became of you and your mother."

"Well, she died several years back. I live in Las Vegas, and I am a system analyst at a large company," Steve replied eagerly. He realized he should have said he used to be a system analyst, but he didn't correct himself.

"Sorry to hear about your mother. I saw you also won a lot of money."

Steve waited for it to come, the big hit up. "Sure did," he said.

"That is great," his grandfather replied. "I would have liked to have introduced you to your grandmother, but she passed two years ago."

"Oh, I'm sorry to hear that."

A few seconds of silence followed.

"It's a shame what happened between your father and me. I always thought we would reconcile, but it didn't work out that way." The old man trailed off, his voice filled with emotion.

"When was the last time you saw my father?" Steve asked.

"At his funeral. Before that, when he was fifteen or sixteen, before he ran off. The funeral was the only time I met you. You were a baby. Then your mother moved to I don't know where."

Steve wanted to ask more questions: Why had his father run away? What was he like? Why hadn't his mother ever talked about his father?

"I would like to see you again," his grandfather said.

"Sure, that would be great."

"I could come see you," his grandfather said, tentatively.

"Why don't I come see you?" Steve offered. He certainly had time to make the trip.

"That would be great."

"I'll check flights and call you back . . . Grandpa."

"Great."

"OK then. I look forward to seeing you."

"Me too."

Steve hung up and walked around his apartment, still holding the phone in his hand. He stopped in front of a window and looked out at the street. Traffic moved slowly by, and the basketball courts across the street were empty. Near the courts, a guy wearing a baseball cap was leaning against a light pole and looking up at his building. What was he doing there? He didn't have a basketball, and he wasn't at a bus stop.

Steve looked at the guy more closely, and when he looked up at the building again, Steve got a good look at his face under the brim of the baseball cap. It was Gabriel, or at least someone who looked like him.

Steve thought of calling the police, but then realized that the restraining order kept Gabriel away from Katie, not him.

Gabriel most likely had every legal right to be on that corner. But Steve was angry, and he was going to take care of this himself.

He stormed out of his apartment and bolted down the stairs instead of waiting for the elevator. When he hit the ground floor, he realized he wasn't wearing shoes. No problem. He'd kick this guy's ass without them.

"Hey!" Steve screamed from across the street as a car passed.

Gabriel looked startled when he saw Steve.

"What the hell is wrong with you?" Steve yelled.

As Steve marched shoeless into the street, Gabriel ran away, down the street.

"Hey! Come back here!" Steve started running after him. But in his stockinged feet he couldn't keep up with Gabriel, who had disappeared around a corner. Steve stopped running and noticed a few people on the sidewalk looking at him like he was a madman. He turned around and headed back to his apartment.

How long had Gabriel been watching him? Why?

He had to warn Katie, have her call the police. This guy needed to be stopped. He felt a pang of guilt—maybe Katie really had been seeing Gabriel in crowds and he'd just been too dense to see him too.

CHAPTER 17

A drop of sweat fell into Ted's eyes as he tried to pick the lock to Gabriel Vega's door. For three days, Ted had waited for Gabriel to return to his apartment, and now he half-expected to find the kid's dead body inside.

This wasn't the first time Mr. Vega had asked him to help Gabriel with a problem, or to bring him home. There had been a DUI in Los Angeles, a problem with a girl in Miami. The most memorable incident was when Gabriel assaulted a kid and put him in the hospital.

Ted couldn't figure out what Gabriel was thinking. He was good-looking and rich; the world was his oyster. But instead of taking advantage of his opportunities, he lived off of a trust fund, had no job and no common sense, and constantly had to be rescued by his father.

Ted heard the familiar click of the picked lock, turned the knob, and opened the door. He put away his tools and wiped the sweat out of his eyes. It was after midnight, and there was no movement or sound in the hallway outside Gabriel's apartment. Ted figured a swanky apartment building like this would have better security, but he had entered undisturbed.

Gabriel's apartment was pitch black. Before he turned on the light, Ted called out a warning. "Gabriel, it's Ted Baron. Your father sent me."

No response.

"I'm turning on the lights."

Again, no response.

Ted felt along the wall and found a switch that illuminated a long entrance hallway tiled with stone. Gabriel's good taste was immediately apparent.

Ted listened intently, but there was still no sound—and no smell of a decomposing body, just the musty scent of dirty laundry.

He walked to the end of the hallway.

"Gabriel, it's Ted Baron."

Nothing.

He felt around and found another light switch. Flicking it revealed a large room filled with high-end furnishings and strewn with dirty laundry, newspapers, pizza boxes, and plastic takeout containers. Ted moved to the kitchen, where the sink and counters were stacked high with dirty dishes. The food on the top plates was dried but not moldy. Ted guessed that they had been sitting there for about a week.

The bedroom was also messy, and the guest room contained mostly workout equipment and more piles of clothes, paper, and trash. Gabriel's closets and dressers seemed intact; there were no signs that he'd gone on a trip. Finally, Ted checked the bathroom in the master bedroom, which turned out to be the neatest room in the apartment. Gabriel's toothbrush sat on the counter.

Ted checked the medicine cabinet and found several vials of prescription pills, all in Gabriel's name. The only prescription he recognized was for Alecta, a popular antidepressant. He wanted to write down the names of the drugs he didn't recognize: Fluoxanol, Apenime, and others.

Ted remembered the time he'd had to visit Gabriel's high school to, as Mr. Vega put it, "clean up" after the boy. A teenage Gabriel had accused one of his former best friends of trying to kill him and steal his identity. As ridiculous as it sounded, Gabriel was convinced this boy was slowly poisoning him, so Gabriel attacked him in the hallway of the school, beating him until he fractured the skull.

Ted had been able to convince the schoolmaster not to contact the police. He promised the headmaster that Mr. Vega would be grateful, and that he would express his gratitude with a very large contribution to the school's endowment. Soothing the parents of the beaten boy took a little more finesse. Ted got the father alone and first promised a large government contract for his business. When that didn't work, he mentioned a few details about the father's hobby of cruising for male prostitutes during business trips.

Ted remembered driving Gabriel home a few days afterward. The boy seemed different from the one he remembered. He had become more withdrawn, vacant, and non-responsive to the simplest of questions.

Ted didn't see Gabriel much after that. The boy went away to college until the Miami incident, at which point Gabriel was sent away for several months. When he came back to San Francisco, he again seemed like a different person, much more sedated than before. Ted knew Gabriel had finished college somewhere in California, closer to home, but the one time he had asked Mr. Vega how Gabriel was doing, Mr. Vega looked up from the documents he was reading, examined Ted through slightly squinted eyes, and said, "Fine, thank you for asking," before returning his attention to the page in his hand.

With no trace of Gabriel in the apartment, Ted wasn't sure what to do next. He figured the most logical thing to do was to follow the girl Gabriel was following. Odds were, if he wasn't coming home, he wasn't taking his medications. And without them, he most likely wasn't thinking straight.

Ted decided to hire a private detective to watch Gabriel's apartment while he covered other ground.

He left the apartment as he found it, turning off the lights and wiping down the switches as he backtracked out the door. *No reason to spook the kid*, he thought. He exited into the brisk night air and ran across the street to his rental car. He knew he had to call Mr. Vega tomorrow at the latest, and he hated calling with no information.

In the car Ted reached for one of several books he had picked up recently on the Mayan calendar and 2012. The best-seller lists were full of them. The books had been his companions as he sat outside Gabriel's apartment, and he'd just finished one detailing several theories on what the calendar meant: an asteroid might crash into Earth, the sun could go nova, or, his personal favorite, Mercury may fall out of its orbit and crash into Earth. One book described the hippies' interpretation of the calendar—that December 21, 2012, was the day a great spiritual leader was going to rise up and unite the world, ushering in an era of peace, love, and harmony. The thought of this made Ted laugh.

In a way, Ted found these books reassuring. He no longer felt the cold dread he had experienced in Mr. Vega's office when the subject first came up. He knew Mr. V was a brilliant and powerful man, but if he believed this crap, he was nuts.

Ted watched the passing street signs as he drove. His mind almost went to that dark place, the place of his childhood, his mother, the pain.

But he would not dwell on the past. He then did something out of character: he turned on the radio, and to his luck it was set on a station that played country, the only music he could stand. He cleared his mind by humming along with a song he didn't know.

CHAPTER 18

S teve looked out the window during his descent to El Paso International Airport. The landscape of El Paso might look desolate to most visitors, but to someone from Las Vegas it seemed lush. This was Steve's first flight, and he had been terrified since takeoff; his hands ached from gripping the armrests. The speed of the plane as it rushed down the tarmac was far greater than he had imagined, and he'd searched the faces of the other passengers for signs of panic. The plane shook dramatically after takeoff and then banked left. Steve thought they were going to flip over. Halfway through the flight he had turned to the passenger next to him, a large man wedged into his seat, and asked if this was a bad flight. The guy looked at him as though he was crazy, saying it was one of the smoothest flights he had been on in a long time. As the plane drew closer to the ground, Steve's confidence grew, but he was already considering renting a car and driving back to Vegas.

They landed with a bump and the screeching sound of the thrust reversers, and then a force pushed Steve back into his seat. He was glad Katie wasn't there to see his fear. At least now he had a flight under his belt if they ever flew anywhere together.

Steve was anxious to meet his grandfather, but he was worried about Katie being alone in Las Vegas with Gabriel possibly around. There had been no sign of him since Steve chased him down the street. The police had gone to Gabriel's apartment but, not finding anyone there, said he'd probably left town. They'd agreed to send a patrol car past Katie's house at least once a night, and Katie promised not to leave work alone and not to go out by herself while Steve was gone.

When he got off the plane, Steve dialed his grandfather's cell phone number.

"Hello?" he answered.

"Hi . . . Grandpa." Steve stumbled over the word. "I'm in the terminal."

"Good. Walk out and to the left. I'm parked at the end of the middle island. I'm in a red Chevy truck."

Steve walked out into the bright sunshine. The El Paso air was a bit more fragrant than that of Las Vegas. He saw the red truck and next to it a short, older man with a belly protruding over his belt buckle. He was wearing a worn white hat, with yellow stains where he imagined his grandfather's hands had touched it many times.

"Hello," Steve said as he approached.

His grandfather turned quickly. The first thing Steve noticed was the twinkle in his eyes; he looked ten years younger than his seventy-five years. He had white hair and a salt-and-pepper beard, and he teared up a little as he looked Steve up and down.

"Son," he said and then gave Steve a huge hug.

Steve now noticed that his grandfather was more than a foot shorter than he was. A feeling rushed over Steve, something he hadn't expected. He choked up, his eyes filled with tears.

He returned the hug with the same intensity, surprised at the love he felt for this man he had just met. They separated.

"OK, get in, before I get a ticket," his grandfather said as he stepped into the truck on the driver's side.

Steve threw his bag into the back of the truck and hopped into the front seat. As they moved through El Paso, Steve noticed that adobe style architecture was very popular here; most buildings, including the airport, which looked like a giant adobe tent, had a similar beige exterior. Steve realized he needed to travel more.

"Good flight?" his grandfather asked.

"Sure, I guess. My first time. I hate flying."

"Me too."

As they drove, his grandfather mentioned all the people he wanted Steve to meet, cousins from his grandmother's side, uncles, friends, and neighbors. Steve found out his grandfather had owned a group of convenience stores that he had sold off a short time ago. Before that, he had spent more than twenty years as the foreman of a large, corporate-owned chicken ranch.

"I will never eat chicken again," he said with a laugh.

They pulled into a neighborhood of small homes. A few were in good shape, with manicured lawns, but others, their yards overgrown with weeds, looked like they had been abandoned.

They pulled into the driveway of a small but neat ranch house. "Here we are," his grandfather said with pride.

Inside the house, there were pictures of Steve's family on every wall. Most of the photos were of his grandmother, and a few were of his father as a little boy. Many showed people who Steve had never seen before, but his grandfather pointed to each person, explaining who he or she was.

"But don't you worry. By the end of today, you'll know all these people. I'm throwing a welcome-home party for you."

"Sounds great." Steve paused before adding, "Grandpa?" Finally, he just asked the question: "What should I call you?"

"Can you call me *abuelo*?"

"Sure. Abuelo it is."

They both smiled.

CHAPTER 19

Ted sat in his rental car, ten houses down the street from Katie's residence. He had been waiting here for two days and felt like he'd done enough sitting on his butt to last a lifetime. In fact, he had a raging case of sciatica down his left leg.

Ted had seen Katie come and go several times, but no one had been following her. He had tailed her a few times to see if Gabriel was stealthier than he gave him credit for, but no such luck. He was impressed with Gabriel's taste: Katie was a beautiful girl.

All the sitting and waiting did give Ted time to continue reading his stack of books on the Mayan calendar. He now knew enough about the subject to form an opinion, and his opinion was that while the topic might sell a lot of books, anybody who believed in this crap wasn't the brightest of bulbs. It was just a three-thousand-year-old calendar that happened to end on December 21 of 2012. The calendar might prove the Mayans had been good astronomers, but so were the ancient

Chinese and countless other civilizations—and there's nothing sinister about studying the stars.

Having reached this conclusion, Ted remained concerned about Mr. Vega. How could such an intelligent man buy into this stuff? Then he remembered Gabriel's medicine cabinet and another thought occurred to him: maybe Mr. V wasn't as stable as Ted thought he was. Aren't mental problems often hereditary?

Ted decided to call Mr. Vega and give him an update. Maybe he would tell Ted to come home. There was no evidence Gabriel was still in town.

He flipped up his cell phone, adjusted his position to minimize the dull pain shooting through his leg, and called Mr. Vega's direct line. He was greeted by Nellie's robotic voice.

"Nellie, it's Ted Baron for Mr. Vega."

"Please hold." Her disconnected, unemotional tone irritated him more than usual. A few seconds later she was on the line again. "Hold for Mr. Vega."

Ted did not reply.

"Ted, have you found my son?" Mr. Vega sounded tired.

"No, sir. He hasn't been to his apartment for a few days. No sign of him at the girl's place, either."

Mr. Vega liked to let the silence hang for a few seconds when he was especially disappointed. When it had gone on so long that Ted feared the connection had been lost, Mr. Vega spoke again. "What's your next step?"

"I've hired outside help to watch Gabriel's apartment. I could have someone watch the girl's home, too."

"No, Ted. You need to find my son and bring him home as soon as possible. I need him home and safe."

Ted tried to let the silence hang on his side, too. "I can continue the surveillance, but I really don't think he's in town."

"Have you checked your e-mail? I had someone forward you some banking info." Mr. Vega sounded impatient.

"Um, no, I haven't checked."

"Gabriel withdrew cash yesterday from an ATM in Las Vegas."

"Do you still have the address?" Ted felt his face flush with embarrassment.

"I can forward it again," Mr. Vega answered tersely.

"Can you read it to me? I'm not getting many messages here. Bad reception."

It was a weak lie, but one that would get him off this call.

Mr. Vega read the address as Ted popped it into the GPS unit in the rental car. The place was a block away, two-tenths of a mile from where he was.

"OK, I'll check it out, sir."

"You do that," said Mr. Vega, and the line went dead.

Ted rubbed his face with his hands. He knew he wasn't taking this task seriously enough.

He went around the block to a small kiosk on the side of a strip mall. Gabriel had been here less than twenty-four hours ago.

Ted had watched the girl's house himself and knew that no suspicious cars had parked anywhere near the place. He hadn't seen anyone who looked anything like Gabriel in the vicinity, and yet the guy had been just around the block, getting cash. Maybe Gabriel was wearing one hell of a disguise.

Ted decided to start from the cash machine and work backward through all the scenarios he could think of. He parked his car and walked to the machine. From there, he looked in every direction: at the strip mall, the car dealership, and the side streets leading to the girl's neighborhood.

Behind the strip mall was a row of houses facing the girl's house. He walked to the back of the strip mall, checking out the small backyards of the homes, and then around the block to walk down Katie's street. Maybe Gabriel was hiding in one of the parked cars and Ted had missed him. Then Ted noticed the "For Sale" sign on the house across the street from Katie's. The house appeared to be vacant, and if Gabriel were hiding in the neighborhood, this would be the perfect spot.

Ted got in his car and trained his binoculars on the front of the empty house. He watched each of its three front-facing windows for over a minute but saw no movement.

As the day wore on, he alternated between surveilling the girl's house and the vacant house. He saw nothing for several hours. But then, just as he was thinking of taking a break, maybe to make a quick drive to a fast-food joint, he saw motion in the vacant house.

His heart rate surged. Could it have been just the reflection of the setting sun on the window?

Ted got out of his car, quickly crossed the street, and went into the alley between the strip mall and the back of the vacant house. His knees and hips were stiff from prolonged sitting, making it hard for him to walk without a pronounced limp. When he finally stood completely straight, pain shot through his back. The alley was empty, except for a group of cacti near a small patio, and there was no sign of forced entry at the back of the house. Ted thought about going in through the backyard right then, but instead decided to wait until dark.

In the meantime, he could get some dinner. He walked around the block to a burger joint he had seen earlier, ordered a cheeseburger and ate it quickly, and then ordered another. *This is not how we keep in shape*, he thought.

When he had finished eating, Ted looked at his watch and glanced outside; he figured he had, at most, an hour to kill before it would be dark enough for his purposes. He went to the burger joint's bathroom, holding his breath at the none-too-fresh smell, and scrubbed his hands, washing them of the grease from the burgers. Satisfied that his hands were as clean as they were going to get, he splashed water on his face and saw in the mirror how haggard he looked. *How long can I keep doing this job?* he wondered.

He pushed some water through his hair, slicking it back in the fashion he liked, and returned to his car. There, he opened the windows and sat listening to the sounds of the city around him.

He picked up one of his books, *The Mayan Prophecy: The End of Time*, and selected a chapter at random.

Among their other accomplishments, the ancient Mayans invented a calendar of remarkable accuracy and complexity. The ancient Mayan pyramid, Chichen Itza, located on the Yucatán Peninsula of present-day Mexico, was constructed circa 1050, during the late Mayan period, when Toltecs from Tula became politically powerful. The pyramid was used as a calendar. Each of its four stairways consisted of ninety-one steps topped by a platform, making a total of three hundred and sixty-four steps, nearly equivalent to the number of days in a calendar year.

The Mayan calendar was adopted by other Mesoamerican nations, such as the Aztecs and the Toltecs, who adopted the mechanics of the calendar unaltered but changed the names of the days and months.

The Mayan calendar uses three different dating systems in parallel: the Long Count, the Tzolkin (divine calendar), and the Haab (civil calendar). Of these, only the Haab has a direct relationship to the length of the year.

A typical Mayan date looks like this: 12.18.16.2.6, 3 Cimi 4 Zotz.

Ted flipped through other pages. He read on:

Logically, the first date in the Long Count should be 0.0.0.0.0, but as the baktun (the first component) is numbered from 1 to 13, rather than from 0 to 12, the first date is actually written 13.0.0.0.0.

Assuming one of the first two equivalences, the Long Count will again reach 13.0.0.0.0 on 21 or 23 December, 2012 AD.

The date 13.0.0.0.0 may have been the Mayans' idea of the date of the creation of the world and the date when time would begin again, or end completely.

Ted skimmed most of the numbers stuff. It made his head hurt. He found it intriguing that a primitive civilization could invent or comprehend such a complicated system, one that he didn't quite understand.

He flipped through the index, looking for interesting chapter titles. He found one that sounded good: "World's End." It included an illustration of planets and suns exploding. Ted skimmed through the pages until he came to a particularly disturbing passage:

December 21, 2012 AD, (13.0.0.0.0 in the Long Count) represents an extremely close conjunction of the Winter Solstice sun with the crossing point of the Galactic Equator (the equator of the Milky Way), and the Ecliptic (the path of the sun). This was what that ancient Mayans recognized as the Sacred Tree. This is an event that has been coming to resonance very slowly, over thousands and thousands of years. It will come to resolution at exactly 11:11 a.m. GMT on that day.

There were illustrations of a tidal wave hitting New York City and of the Golden Gate Bridge dangling into the ocean. Ted closed the book.

So what? Some guy thinks the planets will align. Does that mean anything? Probably not. Wouldn't the government warn its citizens? He looked at the picture of the author on the back cover; he looked like a nut job, with crazy large glasses and wild-looking hair.

Ted decided he was going to flat-out ask Mr. Vega what the hell he thought was going to happen. He threw the book to the passenger seat, and it fell to the floorboard. He swept the rest of the books off the seat to further prove his point.

He was suddenly disgusted with himself. What had gotten into him—reading these dumb books, slacking off on his job, eating two cheeseburgers? "Goddamn it!" he said to himself.

He took a deep breath and got out of his car. He tucked in his shirt and smoothed his hair again. He was beginning to feel better until he saw a spot of grease on his shirt. It was his scarlet letter for this evening.

Ted got back in his car and sat there until it was dark enough to provide cover, yet light enough for him to see without a flashlight. The evening air was losing its heat quickly. It was going to be a cold desert night.

He easily hopped the chain-link fence and silently walked to the back of the house. He tried the back door, but it was locked. He pushed up on the first floor's back windows, but they didn't budge. He walked each side of the house and found everything locked tight.

Ted was about to check the front of the house when he nearly tripped over a well cover for a basement window. He pulled on the handle and the cover opened with a loud squeak, revealing a sliding window that led into the pitch-black basement. Ted groaned from the pain that shot up his leg and

into his back as he jumped down into the window well. He
was going to pay for that tomorrow.

He slid the window open, remembering how, when he was
a kid working for a contractor who built houses, he would
leave a window unlocked at the end of the day so he and his
pals could come back later in the evening and drink beer they
had taken from their parents' refrigerators.

Sitting in the bottom of the window well, Ted dropped his
feet through the opening and squinted into the darkness; he
couldn't even see the floor in front of him.

He slid gently down the wall, feeling for the ground with his
feet. By now his eyes had adjusted to the dark, and he could
make out the outline of stairs leading up out of the basement.
On his way to the stairs he kicked a stray two-by-four, sending
it rattling across the floor. Ted stood frozen, listening for any
movement above him. The only noise he could hear was the
beating of his own heart.

Ted climbed the stairs slowly, cringing at every creak they
made. The door opened to the kitchen, where the real estate
agent had left a stack of brochures that included the house's
floor plan. He could see most of the first floor from where he
stood, and there was no sign of Gabriel. In fact, the place was
empty except for the brochures.

He made his way to the second floor, which contained three
bedrooms, including the master suite, which faced the house
across the street—Katie's house.

As Ted approached the master bedroom, he stopped to
listen for any sound and heard the air whistle in front of him,
right before something hard crashed into his face, shattering
his nose and knocking him on to his back. A wave of pain
coursed through Ted's head, and he felt the warmth of the
blood that was flowing from his nose and covering his face.

A man's face appeared in front of Ted, and it took him

a few seconds to recognize it as Gabriel's. He was holding a bloody two-by-four and looked so much older than Ted remembered. His hair was much longer. He was leering at Ted and saying something, and Ted had to listen closely to make out the words.

"You're trying to stop me," Gabriel muttered like a madman. "But I know, I know. You're trying to put controls in my brain, make me a zombie."

"Gabriel?" Ted said.

Gabriel kicked Ted in the stomach, which didn't hurt nearly as much as the waves of pain that hit his head. He tried to roll over and get up, but the even smallest movement doubled the pain in his head.

"You already got to her," Gabriel said. His face, unshaven, was inches away from Ted's. His breath smelled like rotten meat.

Gabriel continued to babble and then faded into the fog as Ted passed out.

* * *

He awoke to the sound of a drumbeat coming from his temples. He was aware of bright blue and red lights flashing from behind his eyelids. He rolled to his side and, suddenly feeling nauseous, threw up the remains of the two cheeseburgers. Getting to his hands and knees, he saw that the flashing lights were outside. He looked around the room with his right eye— he couldn't open his left—and saw no sign of Gabriel.

When he got to his feet he almost fell over, but he managed to keep his balance. Outside were three police cars. People were standing in the front yards of the houses across the street, all looking at the girl's house.

He walked slowly, almost stumbling down the back stairs to the backyard. Pain shot through his head with every step.

He reached the fence he had jumped earlier that evening, but now he walked to the gate, praying that it was unlocked; there was no way he could hop this fence now. *If this gate is locked*, he thought, *I will lie down and die, and that will be that.* He pictured his mother, dead and cold, her eyes open and vomit on her cheek. *I'll be just like her*, he thought, *just like her.*

He flipped up the gate latch and walked out into the alley and toward the strip mall where his car was parked. Each step brought more and more agony to his head. He felt another wave of nausea. It came on so quickly that most of the vomit splashed on his clothes.

Ted gathered himself and continued walking. When he finally made it to his car, he opened the passenger-side door and collapsed onto the seat, the center console under his chest and his feet hanging out the door.

CHAPTER 20

Tec waited with a group of ten warriors. Across the small valley, his brother waited with ten other men. Seven more raiding parties, each made up of ten men, were positioned in the hills. Below them was Oxtab, a rival village. If Tec and Que conquered Oxtab, their tribe would control all of the land between the two great mountain ranges.

But Oxtab was said to be different from the other tribes Tec and Que had vanquished. There were stories of magic and of a place somewhere near the village where the gods had left gifts that gave the people this power. Tec didn't believe these stories; he had never encountered anyone who had seen these gifts. But he knew Oxtab's ruler, Xlab, was a fierce warrior.

Tec and Que were waiting until sunrise to attack. Their force of ninety men would be outnumbered by the Oxtab warriors, but they had the element of surprise and superior battle skills in their favor.

He pictured returning home to his wife and newborn baby, the joy in her face. He pictured the look of pride on his father's face as he and Que marched the captured slaves into the city's main square, as they had many times before. He imagined the people cheering while the priests selected slaves for sacrifice.

A signal that sounded like a birdcall from across the valley brought him back to the task at hand. One of his brother's warriors was marking the advance.

Que had become more and more reclusive, separating himself from his family and from the rest of the tribe. He also had undergone startling physical changes; most noticeably, he seemed to be aging rapidly. He was hunched over, and his skin had become loose and full of blotches. His face was gaunt. Nearly all of his hair had fallen out. He was still a ferocious warrior, but he wasn't the man Tec once feared.

Que often missed the tribal counsel meetings, and when he did come, he sat silently, usually glaring at the assembly and at Tec. He spoke only when questions were directed at him, and occasionally he would respond to something Tec said with a snort. Sometimes he suffered coughing fits that caused him to leave the meetings.

Meanwhile, the king had grown increasingly distant from Tec. He had heard whispers from the priests that his father was worried about Tec trying to supplant him. The king even seemed to explicitly favor Que now, directing questions at him during the council meetings and ignoring Tec. He guessed Que's deteriorating physical condition made him less of a threat.

Tec looked to either side and saw that the warriors flanking him, their bodies painted black and red, had also heard the birdcall signal. With his men in a tight line behind him, he slowly and quietly proceeded down the hill. As he approached the tree line, he scanned the village for signs of movement but saw none.

On the far side of the village, Que's warriors advanced with burning torches and began setting the straw-and-wood houses aflame. Tec waited to hear the screams from the people inside and to see them rush out of their houses. But nothing happened; the houses just continued burning. Tec figured the villagers must have already fled. *So much for the gods protecting this village*, he thought. Tec wasn't surprised; legends were usually exaggerated. He'd heard that some people though he and his brother were twice the size of other men, ate babies, and could fly.

Tec had by now reached the village, and he looked inside a few of the burning homes. They were empty, of people and possessions.

All the warriors met in the center of the village. When Que approached, his appearance shocked Tec. His skin appeared to be melting off his bones.

"Brother," Que croaked, laboring to breathe, "it looks like they have fled."

"Search!" Tec barked to the warriors as he pulled Que aside, out of earshot from everyone.

"Que, is there something wrong? Are you sick?"

"Hah," Que sputtered. A dark liquid oozed from his mouth, and he quickly wiped it away. "I am strong. I can still pin you to the ground."

"What happened? We need to have the priests look at you."

"I think it may be too late for that, brother," Que said, offering a nearly toothless smile. The teeth he *did* have were black. "I feel the life force leaving me. The gods picked you."

As he spoke, Que put his hand on Tec's shoulder. His fingernails were as black as his teeth.

"Brother, we will go home now," Tec said with tears in his eyes. "We will go see the priests. Surely they can fix this."

"How can the priests fix what the gods have done? This started with the rock in that cave. From that day, I have felt the weakness growing, the changes happening—but only to me, not to you. How could men fix that?" Que began coughing. "The gods picked you," he repeated. He tried to continue, but his coughing became too intense. The fit stopped only after he spit up a black chunk of phlegm.

A warrior approached the brothers and said, "I think I know where they are." Tec signaled for the rest of the men to return, and they followed the warrior who had found the missing villagers to the foot of a cliff. The wall towering above them was made of smooth, black rock that reflected the rising sun like a mirror. At its base was a jagged opening that led into darkness.

The mud in front of the cave was filled with fresh footprints. The villagers must have been alerted to their arrival, thought Tec. They must have moved during the night, but they had to have known that he and his men would follow them.

"It's a trap," Que declared.

"I think you are right," Tec said.

Tec walked to the cave's opening and looked in, but he couldn't see anything.

An instant after he felt something slice through the air next to his face, he heard a scream behind him. He turned and saw Pedvo, one of the younger warriors, fall back onto the ground. Pedvo lay with his eyes wide open and a small black hole in his forehead. He was dead.

Tec ordered everyone back and asked if anyone had seen what happened.

"I saw a ray of the sun come down and strike him lifeless," one of the warriors said. "It was the sun god. It is true; the Oxtab are protected by the gods!"

"I did not see that," Que replied. "He just fell."

Tec looked at Que and was reassured to see that his brother showed no signs of fear.

"They have village priests, just like us," Tec said. "You

know the sleight of hand they pull, the tricks. They make you see things that aren't there."

"But Pedvo is dead," said another of the warriors. "That isn't a trick."

"I know he is dead," said Tec. "But it is witchcraft, not the gods."

The men looked to Tec for direction, and he offered a plan. They would burn the rest of their homes and fields and slaughter their animals. "Clearly we are at a disadvantage entering the dark cave," said Tec. "If destroying their village doesn't draw them out of the cave, we will wait until night, when we all will be in darkness."

The village and the fields burned, but no one emerged from the cave.

When night arrived, Tec gathered his men. "We now avenge Pedvo," he said. "We will take no prisoners as a lesson to others. But I need to know what we face and how they are positioned before we attack."

Luxe and Zarco, two of his best men, volunteered to enter the cave.

The entire group approached the entrance, and the two warriors ran into the darkness. Seconds later, Tec and the others outside the cave heard screams that faded fast, as though Luxe and Zarco were being pulled deeper into the cave at a great speed.

"Fall back to the village!" Tec ordered his men, who were already backing away from the cave. "What do you think we should do?" Tec asked Que.

"We should charge in with torches. Surely we can overwhelm them. They fight like cowards." Que's eyes were gleaming, full of life.

"I knew you would recommend the bravest option," Tec said, patting Que on the shoulder.

As Tec stared at the black hole that had brought death to three of his warriors, he heard grumbling from his other men. They were talking about the stories of Oxtab, saying that they were true, that the tribe was protected by the gods.

Despite his brother's advice, Tec decided that the best plan of attack was to wait them out. He imagined they had limited supplies in the cave. As Tec and his warriors made camp outside the still-smoldering village, Tec noticed that the stream near the village came from a nearby underground spring and appeared to run into the cave. If it did, it would provide an unlimited water supply for the people hiding there.

Tec ordered his men to fill any container they could find with water from the stream and then throw the decaying corpses of the animals they had slaughtered into the stream near the spring, to poison the water. If the villagers were drinking from the stream, they would become sick. And if the stream wasn't flowing into the cave, they soon would run out of drinking water. Either way, the villagers would have to come out of the cave soon.

For five days they waited outside the cave, but no one came out. They were running out of water themselves, and the closest supply was more than a half-day's travel away. After a long discussion with his most senior warriors and Que, Tec decided it was time to go back to their own village. They would be returning for the first time without victory. Tec looked at the poisoned stream, the burned village, the ruined fields, and the slaughtered animals and was convinced that the Oxtab wouldn't see this as a victory either. He felt a twinge of guilt, but ignored it as he prepared to march his men home.

CHAPTER 21

Steve woke up to the aroma of coffee. He didn't know what his grandfather had in store for him today, let alone for the following three days he would spend here in El Paso. Last night, after learning a little about his father's family, Steve shared a pizza with his abuelo and went to bed. Tonight there was going to be a party in his honor, with his grandfather's friends and family—cousins, aunts, and uncles Steve had never met. It promised to be the type of big family party that Steve had longed for as a child.

Steve's grandfather had the TV tuned to a Spanish-language station and was trying to fry eggs.

"Good morning," his grandfather said, peering at the burning eggs as though he was diffusing a bomb.

"Good morning. Do you need help with that?"

The smoke from the frying pan was starting to fill the room. Steve reached over the stove and turned on the exhaust fan.

"Oh, *gracias*," his grandfather said, flipping the eggs, which were now blackened on both sides. "I don't usually cook.

Your abuela did most of the cooking, but a boy your age needs nourishment." Sweat beads were forming on his brow.

"What do you normally eat for breakfast?" Steve asked.

"Oh, I go down the street to a little *carniceria*. It's like a butcher shop that serves meals." A drop of sweat fell from his forehead and into the frying pan, sizzling on impact.

"Why don't we go there?" suggested Steve. "I don't want you to go out of your way, Abuelo." His grandfather smiled at the name.

"Yes, let's do that." His grandfather turned off the stove and dumped the eggs into the sink. "Let me get my hat."

By the time his grandfather had returned, Steve had matted down his hair, brushed his teeth, and slipped on his shoes.

"OK, let's go!" his grandfather said.

They walked out the door, across his finely trimmed front yard, and down the block. Most of the houses were well kept, but a couple had broken-down cars parked in their driveways and lawns with waist-high grass. As they made their way to the restaurant, they were occasionally greeted by an *"Hola"* from someone sitting on a front porch or doing yard work. Speaking Spanish, his grandfather introduced Steve to these neighbors, who greeted him with smiles and hearty handshakes. Steve learned that all of them had been invited to his party.

As they neared the restaurant, Steve noticed that half the storefronts lining the street were vacant, and the businesses that were open—an auto shop, a lawyer's office, and a dentist's office—seemed to cater only to Spanish-speaking customers.

Under a sign showing a big chicken, Steve and his grandfather entered La Gallinita. There was a meat counter on one side of the room, and chairs and tables occupied about half the floor space.

Several men, their cowboy hats resting on seats next to

them, greeted his grandfather loudly in Spanish. He introduced Steve to the group, and a series of handshakes followed. Steve was a good foot taller than all of the men, which made him feel awkward.

Steve and his abuelo took a seat at one of the tables where his grandfather's friends were sitting. He noticed that the place had a distinct and not particularly appetizing odor, like a mix of pepper and brine. A line of people ordered meat at the counter, and a chubby young waitress took orders at the tables and refilled coffee cups. Some floor tiles were missing or cracked, and duct tape covered holes in the leather-upholstered seats.

Steve picked up one of the single-sheet placard menus and reviewed its contents. He was famished. Everything was listed in Spanish, but he had enough experience in Las Vegas's Mexican restaurants to steer himself through the menu. Steve's grandfather was engaged in an animated conversation with his friends, most of whom looked about his age. He was obviously happy, smiling and telling stories, and occasionally pointing at Steve. There was no doubt that he was the center of attention this morning.

Occasionally he turned to Steve and said a few words, just so he wouldn't feel ignored:

"Order what you want."

"The meat is great here."

"José over there is from my village and remembers your father."

"*La Gallinita* means 'little hen.'"

Steve didn't mind that he couldn't understand their conversation; he was content just taking in the scene.

"Can I help you?" the waitress asked Steve, in English, without an accent and with a disinterested tone.

"I'll have the eggs with chorizo, please, and coffee."

"Oh, good choice," his grandfather turned and said when he heard his order. "I'll just have coffee," he said to the waitress, adding, "You know, this is your second cousin."

Looking unimpressed, she left to fill the orders.

Steve's food came quickly; his second cousin practically threw it in front of him and then asked if he wanted his coffee refilled. His plate was heaped with eggs and chorizo and peppers. He filled a tortilla with the mixture, sprinkled some hot sauce on it, and devoured the first taco. When his plate was empty, Steve sat back with a protruding belly and a burning mouth.

"My God, you're done already? I wanted some," Steve's grandfather said loudly.

"I didn't know. Sorry." Steve's answer prompted laughs from the other men at the table.

"I'm kidding. I never eat breakfast. You want more?"

Steve contemplated ordering a second helping, but he didn't want to look like a glutton. "No, I'm good. That was great!"

The chatter continued around Steve, punctuated by occasional eruptions of laughter. After the bills were paid, everyone got up to go at the same time. On the sidewalk outside, Steve shook hands and said good-bye to the men as they left, most walking, some getting into beat-up cars and trucks.

"Much better than my cooking," his grandfather said as they walked back to his house. "We meet there every day except Sunday and gossip like old women."

Steve wanted to ask questions about his father but wasn't sure how. He was hoping his grandfather would broach the subject, but so far he had mentioned him only in passing. Steve wondered, as they walked and his grandfather made small talk, what this kindly old man could have done to drive away his teenage son? Or what could a teenage son have done that forced him to leave? Whatever had happened, Steve was sure it wasn't a pleasant memory for his grandfather, and so he was reluctant to ask him about it.

"We have a lot to do," his grandfather announced. "We have to go to the food store, back to the butcher, get beer. Are you up for helping an old man?"

"Of course, anything you need."

His grandfather slapped him on the back, his hand lingering on his shoulder, patting it a few times. "OK, great."

The old man beamed at Steve with that proud look he was quickly getting used to.

* * *

Steve had endured the awkward greetings from the fifty or so people who filled his grandfather's backyard, and now the party was in full swing. He recognized some faces from breakfast, and most of the other people were related to him in some way or another. Even the waitress, his second cousin, was there. And she was actually smiling.

His grandfather had been grilling since the first guests arrived, and now he was finally sitting and helping himself to his own dinner and a well-deserved beer. At the beginning of the party, when Steve had offered to help cook, his grandfather looked at him as if he had just punched him in the face. "The guest of honor does not cook at his own party!" he exclaimed as he pushed Steve away.

Steve made small talk with a few people but spent the most of the party sitting at the end of a table, eating and drinking. The beer left him feeling relaxed, almost sleepy.

After a while, the waitress came up to him and said, "What up, cuz?"

"Oh, hi."

"I'm Connie," she said with a smile.

"Hi." Steve shook her outstretched hand and asked, "So how are we cousins?"

"You know, some of our relatives had kids," she said, looking at him as if he were slow. Then she burst into laughter. "Just fucking with ya. Your grandmother is my grandmother's sister. Say that three times fast."

"Well, then, good to meet you, cuz."

"I can't believe I have a white cousin." She covered her mouth with her hand and almost spit out her beer as she laughed. "I'm sorry. That sounded racist." This made her laugh even harder.

"You sure seem happier than this morning," Steve said with a smile.

"I was so hung over, and I have to put up with those blowhards every morning. It makes a girl cranky. My dad makes me work there in exchange for room and board at our house. And I get to keep the tips. It's temporary, until I go to community college. What about you?" She sat down in the chair next to him.

"I live in Vegas, had a job . . ."

"Won the lottery or something," she said. "Everybody knows. I am amazed that half these drunks haven't hit you up for money yet."

"No, no loan requests yet. And it wasn't the lottery. It was a slot machine."

"Must be nice." She nodded her head.

"So far nothing has changed, but who knows."

"Dude, I would be traveling the world."

Her "dude" made him think of Jim. Steve wondered if he had already blown the money that he gave him. He pictured

Jim smoking a stogie, lying in bed in a trashed hotel room, a prostitute under each arm.

"You know your grandpops is a big deal in this family. He is like the partridge, or whatever."

"You mean the patriarch?" Steve asked.

"Yeah, he's the leader."

On an impulse Steve asked, "Do you know what happened between my grandfather and my father?"

"Kinda. Most of our family was born in Mexico, you and me being exceptions. Your dad didn't want to stay on the family farm. He wanted to come to the U.S., and that's what he did. Then he married a white girl." She paused and finished the last of her beer. "It was a big deal at the time, now, not so much. Your grandfather and my grandfather both lost their farms in Mexico soon after this happened with your dad, and they had to move here. They've been here ever since. Thank God, or else I would be stuck in Mexico."

"So that's it?" Steve asked.

"Yeah, from what I know. Your dad broke from tradition when he married your mother. I think the last argument your father and grandfather had might have gotten physical—not too serious, but serious enough to have them not speaking to each other. The rest is history."

Steve was shocked. He couldn't believe his mother was the cause of the rift between his father and grandfather. He couldn't believe that the nice old man would disown his son for marrying a white girl.

"I need another beer. Later, cuz," Connie said as she got up and slapped his knee.

Steve looked up and saw his grandfather standing over him. "I see you're getting to know your cousin better," he said, pointing toward Connie.

"Yeah, she's nice."

"Bit of a gossip, huh?"

"No, I was the one asking questions, mostly about my father." His grandfather pursed his lips and said, "I figured you would be curious. It's not something I am proud of. You know, I was raised a certain way. You treated your parents a certain way and listened to them, no matter how stupid they were. Your father rebelled against that, and probably rightly so. Things happened, and we had a huge fight. We both went too far, and he ran away."

Steve remained silent, not sure what to say.

His grandfather continued. "It is the thing I regret the most in life. But by the time I realized what was more important, he was gone."

His grandfather's eyes teared up.

Steve's cell phone began to vibrate in his pocket. It was Katie. He hadn't called her all day, and it looked like his grandfather would appreciate a few minutes to collect himself.

"Take it," his grandfather said, turning his head and pulling out a handkerchief.

"Hello Katie, I've been—"

"Steve, oh my God. He's outside, trying to get in!"

Steve heard a boom in the background followed by Katie's scream.

"Katie, what the hell is going on?"

"Gabriel is outside my house. He's trying to get in!"

"Call the police!" he shouted. A few of the party guests looked at him quizzically.

"I did! Oh my God! Where is he?"

Steve heard glass breaking and then Katie screaming again. He shouted her name, but she didn't answer.

Finally, she spoke in a hushed tone. "I think he's in the house. I'm so scared."

"Where are you now?" Steve's eyes had filled with tears.

"I'm locked in my bathroom," she whispered.

Steve pictured her bathroom. It had a small window that no one could fit through and a pretty sturdy door. It was probably the safest room for her to be in. "Get something sharp from the medicine cabinet, anything."

"I got scissors."

"Great. How long ago did you call the police?"

"A few minutes before I called you."

"OK, you need to hang up with me and call 911 again. Tell them he's in the house, and tell them where you are. OK?"

"But—"

"Do it now!" Steve shouted. "OK?"

"OK."

The line went dead.

Steve decided to call the LVPD himself, but he needed the number, and a pen and paper to write it down.

He looked up and saw that the party had ground to a halt. Everyone was staring silently at him.

"I need a pen and paper," he said to his grandfather. "I'll explain in a minute."

"This way," he replied, turning and leading Steve through the crowd and into the house.

CHAPTER 22

Ted was walking through snow in a leafless forest. His feet were numb from the cold, his head was pounding, and each blink was torture. He had no idea where he was, but he had to keep going. Someone was following him. He came to a clearing, a frozen expanse that went on farther than he could see. In the sky, a light was growing brighter, becoming larger. He realized it was speeding toward him.

He stood in terror and looked back to the forest. Whoever was chasing him was still in pursuit. He turned back around and looked at the sky. It was now filled with a fiery rock ten times the size of the moon bearing down on where he stood.

When he turned to run back to the forest, his mother emerged from the trees. A black liquid was oozing from her eyes and mouth. Then the world exploded around Ted.

He woke up to a female voice: "Are you OK?"

Ted pushed himself up and saw a pool of blood in the car seat where his face had just been. He eased himself out of the car.

"Are you OK?" Ted recognized the girl but couldn't figure out from where.

"I'm going to call 911," she said.

"No, no, I'm fine. Don't," Ted croaked.

"I really think I should."

Now Ted remembered her. She had taken his order at the burger joint, the one around the corner. He looked into his rearview mirror and didn't recognize his reflection. *That little shit sure did a number on me*, he thought. His nose was swollen and pointing to the right. His left eye was swollen shut. Blood covered his cheeks and chin. Ted felt another wave of pain in his head and nearly dry-heaved. His whole body was shaking.

"How far is a hospital?" he asked the girl.

"Right down the street, maybe a mile or two."

"I can't call the police. It's complicated. Can you help me out and drive me there?"

Without waiting for an answer, Ted sat straight up in the passenger seat, in the sticky puddle of blood. He felt for his keys, realized they were still hanging in the door, and motioned to them.

The girl stood looking at him.

"Please, I'll give you a hundred bucks for your time," Ted whispered, as he moved his head to rest it sideways on the seatback. He added a groan for good measure.

That did the trick.

"OK, OK," she said as she grabbed the keys, closed his door, and got in on the driver's side.

Ted must have fallen asleep; when he came to, the girl was saying "Mister! Mister!" and the car was stopped in front of the emergency-room entrance. He took out his wallet, grabbed a handful of bills, and gave them to the girl.

"OK, disappear. You've never seen me," Ted said, turning his head so that he could look in the girl's face with his right eye.

She grabbed the money and jumped out if the car, leaving her door open and the engine running. Ted opened his door and pushed himself up and out of the car. He steadied himself on the door, stood up straight, and walked toward the automatic doors under the EMERGENCY sign.

A man in blue scrubs met Ted at the door and said, "OK, buddy, take it easy. We got you."

Ted collapsed into the man's arms.

"I fell down, in my bathroom. Hit my face on the sink," Ted said as he was moved into a wheelchair.

* * *

"Mr. Baron?"

A bright light was shining on Ted's eyelids, making his head hurt even more. He tried to open his eyes, but only his right eye cooperated.

"Mr. Baron, can you hear me?"

He wanted to answer yes, but instead all he could manage was an "Arggh."

"Mr. Baron, do you know your first name?"

Of course he knew his name. Who was this dumb ass? "Ted," he answered.

"Good, good. Do you know what day it is?"

"Wednesday. No, Thursday."

"OK, good, good."

The light was removed, and now Ted saw the face of a young Indian or Pakistani man, Dr. Pashma, according to his name tag. Ted tried hard to open his left eye, with only minimal success.

"OK, so you said you fell?" the doctor asked.

"Yeah, fell, in my hotel bathroom."

"Why didn't you call for help? Did you drive yourself?"

"I didn't realize how bad it was. I must have been dazed."

Ted saw that there was a tube stuck in his arm and that his bloody clothes, cell phone, watch, and wallet were in a bag on a chair next to the bed he was lying in. His cell phone was vibrating. The doctor looked over at the phone. "Is there anyone you want us to call?" he asked.

"No, that's fine." The truth was he had no one who would care that he was in an emergency room. He did owe Mr. Vega a call, but he wasn't looking forward to that.

"OK, Mr. Baron, we need to do some tests—X-rays, an MRI—and we need to perform a minor surgery on your nose."

Ted now remembered seeing his face in the rearview mirror. "How long will I be laid up?"

"Barring any surprises, we'll watch you for one night and fix up your nose tomorrow. So maybe the day after that."

Ted realized the headache he'd had was gone. As though reading Ted's mind, the doctor pointed to the IV and said, "We have you on some pain management."

"Can you hand me my cell before you go?" Ted asked.

Ted saw that he had missed a call from Mr. Vega. In fact, he had missed six calls from his boss in the last six hours. Ted hit the dial button.

"Hello, Ted?" said Mr. Vega after the second ring, sounding irritated.

"Yes, it's me. I'm in the hospital. That's why I missed your calls." Ted hoped this information would diffuse some of Mr. Vega's anger.

"Yes, well, I have heard from Gabriel," Mr. Vega said.

"He's the reason I'm here," Ted answered, a little perturbed. He wasn't expecting tears from his boss, but he could have at least asked why he was in the hospital.

"The reason you're there?" Mr. Vega sounded accusatory, almost menacing.

"Yeah, I found him in a vacant house, across from the ex-girlfriend's place. It looked like he'd been squatting there for several days at least. And, anyways, he surprised me and the—" Ted nearly said "little shit," but he caught himself. "He hit me with something across my face. My nose is busted . . ."

Mr. Vega interrupted him. "Yes, he called me tonight. He was talking gibberish. He said he killed you, that he was going to kill everyone. Just gibberish." Mr. Vega sounded upset. "I had a feeling his hold on reality wasn't, well, sound right now."

"Well, I am going to be laid up for a few days."

"Ted, I need you to find my son now, before he hurts someone else, or himself. If you can't, I'll send someone else."

"I need surgery Mr. Vega. Plus, I have no idea where he could be. I have associates here in Vegas. Let me put them on the streets."

"OK, you start that. I'll be sending help also. I need him home *now*, Ted. I cannot stress that enough. If you have to tie him up and throw him in your trunk—you can use any force necessary."

"I'll call you as soon as I find out where he is."

"And, Ted, have them check on the girl first. I am worried Gabriel did something."

"OK, Mr. Vega. I'm on it."

Mr. Vega hung up without asking what happened to Ted, how bad his condition was, what kind of surgery he needed. Ted was angry. He knew he wasn't family, but apparently he didn't even rank with the family dog. Nevertheless, Ted called the PI firm in Vegas he was using to watch Gabriel's house and set up what he needed.

* * *

Against doctor's orders, Ted checked out of the hospital six hours after they fixed his nose. He left with enough pain medication to last him a few days.

He got his rental car out of the parking lot, where someone had parked it for him, and headed to his hotel. He needed to change his clothes. He was wearing a hospital-supplied T-shirt—his dress shirt was caked in blood, and his pants had bloodstains on them. He didn't want to spend any time in public looking like this.

After the hotel, he had to meet with Tom Baker, the private investigator he had hired. Tom ran a top-notch operation; his company wasn't in the business of catching cheating spouses. Tom had offices in a half dozen major cities across the country and catered to clients who paid well to have their problems solved discreetly.

The girl's house was on the way to his hotel, so he drove by to see if one of Tom's men was there, though he hoped he wouldn't be able to spot him.

When he got to the street, which had been filled with police cruisers the last time he was there, he saw a slab of plywood covering the front window of the girl's house. *What had Gabriel done?* he wondered.

CHAPTER 23

Steve didn't want to wake Katie, so he walked quietly through the hallway of Mr. Landry's guesthouse. A few days before, Katie and Steve had flown to Los Angeles on Mr. Landry's private jet and were then driven up the coast to Malibu, to his estate overlooking the Pacific. Steve had just peeked in on Katie as she slept. He still felt guilty about leaving her alone while Gabriel was on the loose.

A neighbor had scared Gabriel off after he broke Katie's front window in an attempt to get into her house, and the cops arrived minutes later. Katie wasn't hurt, but Gabriel was still out there.

The plan was for Katie and Steve to remain in Malibu indefinitely. Mr. Landry had hired full-time security, and besides, Thanksgiving was next week, so it made sense to stay.

Steve was going to let Katie sleep for a couple more hours before he woke her for lunch. He thought of visiting the Landry's extensive fitness room, but he would have felt strange walking into the main house without Katie. And the truth was, he didn't feel motivated to work out, even though it had been a week since he had been to a gym or had one of his powder shakes. He chalked up his lack of motivation to the emotional strain of the last week.

He plopped down on the couch, turned on the giant flat-screen TV, and flipped through the channels, looking for something interesting. Noticing that his belly was pushing uncomfortably against the front of his jeans, he unbuttoned the top button of his pants. He hated to admit it, but he was getting fat, or at least his belly was. In the mirror that morning he'd looked frumpy, his muscles saggy. He also noticed that his senses didn't seem as sharp as they had been. At least he could stop worrying about thyroid tumors.

"What are you watching?" Katie asked, coming up behind Steve and hugging him.

"Not sure. Flipping around," Steve said as he turned to her. "I think you broke your record. You slept for twelve hours."

"Yeah, I know. I feel good, though, like something is healing."

"You want breakfast before we take our walk on the beach?" Steve asked. They had developed a routine the few days they had been at Mr. Landry's. She slept much later than he did, and when she awoke, they had breakfast, went for a long walk on the beach, came home and had a light lunch, spent the afternoon by the pool, had dinner, watched a movie, and went to bed. They had yet to deviate from that itinerary, except that Katie's father would sometimes join them for one of their meals.

"OK," she said, slipping away from him. "But I just want juice."

"Sounds good." Steve looked down at his belly. He was glad she didn't ask for pancakes like she had the past few mornings.

Steve continued channel surfing until she returned, sipping an orange juice and dressed in a powder blue sweat suit, her hair pulled back in a ponytail.

"Ready?" she asked.

"Let's hit it." Steve popped up off the couched. He grabbed a couple of bottled waters—another part of their ritual—gave Katie one, and they left the guesthouse hand in hand.

"Let's say good morning to Daddy," Katie said as they walked.

They entered the main house through the back doorway, which was unlocked.

"Hello?" Katie called out as they stepped into the kitchen.

Maria, a member of Mr. Landry's domestic staff, appeared from around the corner. "Mister in study," she said with a smile and continued into the kitchen. "May I make you lunch?" she called over her shoulder.

"No, thank you," Katie answered.

They passed under a stone archway and down the hall to the study. The French doors were closed, but through the smoked glass Steve could see Mr. Landry leaning back in his chair, arms folded behind his head, talking to someone. It appeared, however, that he was the only person in the room.

Katie knocked on the door, and opened it partially. She stuck her head through the opening, and Mr. Landry waved them in.

"OK then, gentlemen, let's get the report out, and we'll deal with the fallout next week." Mr. Landry had his hand in the air, signaling Katie and Steve to remain silent.

After listening to a round of "Yes, sir's" and "Very good's," Mr. Landry punched a button on the phone and it went dead.

"Good morning, sweetie." He got up from his chair, smiling.

"Good morning to you," Steve said before Katie answered. Katie giggled. Mr. Landry looked at Steve with a questioning glare. Steve made a mental note to himself: Mr. Landry does not like jokes.

"How are you feeling?" Mr. Landry asked as he hugged his daughter.

"Great, really great."

Mr. Landry pulled her close and hugged her again. Steve's face reddened. He wasn't used to parental affection.

"I called the Las Vegas Police Department again and spoke to that Detective Goosling or Gosling or whatever it is," said Mr. Landry. "They haven't found Gabriel yet. They think he may have left Vegas. They've issued an arrest warrant. So we'll see."

He smiled at Katie and added, "Don't worry, honey. They'll find him, and you won't have to see that creep ever again."

"OK, Daddy."

"Did you know he was institutionalized for nearly two years, Kate?" her father asked.

"I knew he had some problems, as a kid. He got into trouble. I didn't know he had been sent away."

"Well, anyway, you're safe here, honey. You have me, Steve, and a security guard to protect you." He gave a nod to Steve.

"OK, Daddy. We're going for our walk."

"You kids have fun," he said, getting up and showing off a pair of golf pants with more plaid per square inch than seemed possible.

Steve suppressed a snicker when he saw the pants and quickly turned to leave the room. When they were out of earshot, Katie whispered, "I know what I'm going to buy you for Christmas."

CHAPTER 24

Que screamed in pain as the village priests huddled around him. Tec couldn't see what they were doing, but they all backed away at the same time. One of them, a bald, heavy-set man who Tec had privately nicknamed the Pig, lit a bundle of dried plants.

Tec had seen most of these plants before; most did nothing but leave a foul odor, although some could make you feel light-headed.

Tec now had a good view of his brother, who was lying on the temple altar. His body was marked with spots of some kind. The priest holding the burning plants circled Que several times before stopping. Then, without a word, he and the rest of the priests departed, leaving Que and Tec alone in the chamber.

Tec approached his brother, who was raising himself off the dais, and he saw that the marks on Que's body were small gashes.

"They say I have an evil spirit in me, taking my strength," said Que. "They let it out."

"How do you feel?"

"Like I did before, but with a bunch of little cuts all over my body." Que managed a slight smile.

Together they left the temple and walked through the village. Que was oblivious to the surprised and concerned looks he received—from people who customarily would have looked at the ground in the presence of the princes. Que was mostly skin and bones now, and very pale. Tec wondered how much longer he would be able to hunt, or go on raiding parties. Their father, displeased with their failure, was sending them back to Oxtab, but Tec didn't see how his brother could accompany him.

Tec had hoped the priests would be able to determine the cause of Que's malady, not only for his brother, but also for himself. He too was losing hair by the handful, even though it seemed to grow back within a day.

He and Que parted company at Que's house, which looked dark and foreboding even in the bright sunshine. Tec walked to the other side of the village, toward his own house. He had moved into a more opulent home near the palace after Isla bore him his first child, a beautiful daughter.

It was midday, and the streets were bustling with activity. Tec was proud of their thriving city. It was a jewel, especially compared to the other cities he had conquered, or planned to conquer.

He would be returning to Oxtab soon, with more warriors, and with priests to counter whatever magic powers the villagers had. This time they would crush Oxtab.

The people on the streets parted for him like the water of a river as a boat sails through. Some dropped to their knees; others made a shrill sound from their throats, a customary show of devotion. Tec still wasn't used to the amount of respect he received. He was going to be king—there was no question of that anymore. His brother might not even outlive his father.

Out of the corner of his eye, Tec noticed a young man he didn't recognize glaring in his direction. Tec turned to see who he could be looking at with such disdain, but there was no one behind him. When he turned back to where he'd seen the young man in the crowd, he was gone.

Tec felt a chill. Had he imagined that man?

Tec pushed through the crowd of admirers, which was continuing to grow. He finally broke free and continued to look around for the man, but he still didn't see him. He picked up his pace and arrived at the entrance to the royal compound, where a guard stood watch, staring straight ahead and standing as rigid as a statue.

A priest greeted him at the entrance and said, "Prince, I have something to tell you."

"What is it?"

The priest looked around before he spoke. "A plot exists to harm you."

"A plot?"

"The king fears you. Your brother plots. You have been warned."

"What do you say?" Tec demanded.

"I have heard the whispers. Be vigilant. That is all I will say." The priest threw his hood over his head and started to leave the compound.

Tec grabbed his arm. "Do not make accusations, priest, unless you are willing to face scrutiny."

"You must be vigilant. Say anything and we both will die. I see the power and goodness in you. The gods are with you, my king." He finished his sentence in a whisper, pulled away from Tec, and disappeared around a corner.

The recent happenings in court, his brother's sudden

friendliness—it made sense now. Did he really think his brother had changed? Tec would heed the priest's advice.

* * *

Tec lay back, floating on the current. He swam alone in the ocean almost every morning. He swam to cleanse himself and to be near the cave where he had been touched by the gods.

As he started swimming back to shore, he noticed something moving near the tree line, something large, maybe a jungle cat. He wrapped himself in his clothes when he reached the shore and walked through the surf as he neared the jungle and the path that led through it to the village. Was the plot against him happening already? Tec was about halfway along the jungle trail when he saw a blur coming toward him, and then two other blurs from either side.

He spun out of the way of his first attacker's spear and planted his fist in his face, knocking him onto his backside. From his left came the young man he had seen in the crowd the previous day. He too charged with a spear. To his right, a man he didn't recognize was leaping from a tree with a dagger in his hand.

Tec used the momentum of the knife attacker's jump to toss him into the jungle. Then Tec crouched down, bracing for the attack of the remaining spearman. The tip of the spear tore into Tec's side, but the wound was not deep. As the attacker charged him, Tec delivered an elbow to his face that collapsed him almost immediately.

Two of his attackers were disabled, but the man with the knife pounced out of the jungle.

He wore his hair much longer than Tec's people did, and he was tall and muscular, with a strange medallion around his neck. The man feigned several thrusts. His knife's blade was shiny, its edges like the teeth of a shark. There were no knives like that in Tec's village.

The man jumped at Tec, emitting an ear-splitting scream as he flew into the air. Tec twisted his body so that he could grab the man's arm and pull the knife from his hand. But his attacker, anticipating Tec's maneuver, flipped in midair and slashed Tec deeply in the back. Tec screamed in agony and anger. They now faced each other, and Tec's attacker had a look of confidence the prince had never before seen from an opponent.

While the man with the knife again feigned several thrusts, Tec circled right, toward one of the man's fallen comrades. When the attacker lunged again at Tec, he rolled across the ground, grabbed one of the fallen men's spears, and impaled the knife-wielding man with it. He landed on top of Tec, the spear piercing him through the chest. Tec felt warm blood spilling onto his chest and threw the body off him. The man's dead eyes stared into the distance; the look of confidence was still on his face.

Tec dragged one of the unconscious attackers next to the other, collected some tough vines, and tied them up before going back to the village for help. He needed to know who these men were. They bore the body art markings of Oxtab, but was this just a ruse? Could these men have been sent by someone close to him?

* * *

The screams echoed through the halls of the palace as the king's guard tortured one of Tec's attackers. His companion was being forced to listen in an adjacent chamber.

Tec's instincts told him that neither his father nor his

brother were involved in the attack, and the treatment of the prisoners seemed to prove that these men did not report to either the king or the prince. In fact, his father and brother seemed more concerned about the attack than Tec did. Maybe the king was worried that the attack represented a larger threat to his kingdom.

"Why do you look at me with such hatred?" Tec asked the prisoner who, at the moment at least, was not being tortured. It was the young man he had seen glaring at him in the village. He'd waved the guard out of the room and was now alone with the prisoner.

"Why?" Tec asked again. "In the end, you or your friend will speak." A scream from the other room punctuated his threat. "They are probably ripping off his fingernails," Tec said as he grabbed the captive's hand. "We will find out who you are, and I will personally kill all of your family, every man, woman—"

Before Tec could finish, the captive spoke. "You already did!" he said, still glaring Tec.

One of the priests entered the room. "You are from Oxtab," the priest said. "Your friend has told us. What magic of the gods do you possess there?"

The prisoner did not respond.

"The one who answers our questions first will live." The priest bowed his head to Tec as he left the room.

When the priest had gone, Tec approached the prisoner. "Oxtab," he said. "We did not kill anyone at Oxtab."

The prisoner looked at Tec with fury in his eyes, but said nothing.

The only casualties at Oxtab had been Tec's warriors, but clearly this man thought otherwise. Tec and his men had killed the Oxtab people's animals and burned their fields. And they had poisoned their drinking water.

"Was it the water?" Tec asked.

The prisoner's look of hatred gave Tec his answer.

Tec examined the rock pendant around the prisoner's neck and took it in his hand. It was an odd color and weighed much less than any stone he had ever felt.

"What is this?" Tec asked, but he received no response. "And how did you make this?" he asked, holding up the sharp and shiny blade used in the attack.

The king entered the room, followed by a group of priests and warriors. "Has he said anything?" the king asked gruffly. This was the first time in many days that Tec's father had spoken directly to him.

"I killed his family. They must have drunk from the stream we poisoned."

"His friend said something similar."

The king and the priest had learned from the tortured prisoner that the Oxtab people had remained in the cave for many days after Tec and his warriors invaded their village. They didn't realize their water was poisoned until everyone became sick. Many people had died.

Que entered the room, his hands bloody from leading the torture, one of his special talents. The small wounds on his body were still visible, but he appeared more vibrant than he had in a long time.

"They had to move into the jungle, abandoning their precious land of the gods, because we destroyed their water supply," Que said.

"You are cursed," the captive shouted at Que.

Que walked over and hit him across the face with the back of his hand. The prisoner turned his face with the slap. When he turned back to Que he was smiling. "The gods will make you pay for defiling their home!" he said to Que, laughing.

Que pounced on the young man, punching with all his might. But the prisoner continued to laugh during the beating.

"Enough!" the king roared. "The priests need information. We'll see what more we can learn from the other prisoner."

As he was leading the priests and Que out of the chamber, the king turned to Tec.

"Tec, I want you to see your brother's skill. Come with us."

In the adjoining chamber, Que's handiwork was on display. The prisoner was sobbing. His eyes were swollen shut, his upper body looked like it had been dipped in blood, and his mangled fingers were tied to a board. Tec found it hard to breathe; he wanted to run from the room. Que raised his hand as if to strike the prisoner, prompting him to scream in anticipation of the pain. Que laughed, and the king smiled. Then the priests moved in like vultures.

"What do your people say of Oxtab, this place where the gods left their gifts?" the head priest asked.

Fearing another beating, the prisoner answered without hesitation. "It is the city of gods. It is where they created man. We emerged from that birthplace. It is a place of power and healing. It contains gifts from the gods only the priests may handle."

"Where is this place?"

"Only our priests can go there. It is sacred," the prisoner said eagerly, just before Que struck him across the face with the back of his hand.

"Please, please," the prisoner screamed. "I have never been there. I know where the priests go, but we are not allowed past the statue."

The priests glanced at each other.

"Before you destroyed our village, our king was going to try to steal your god rock. There is a place for it in the city of the gods!" the prisoner offered hurriedly, still fearing more torture.

"But you can lead us there?" the king asked.

"Yes, yes. There is a great cave near our village. The priests enter the cave and descend into the birthplace of man. But only priests go there, or—"

"Or what?" the king demanded.

"Or slaves. They are brought down there, but they never return."

"Where is your tribe now?" Tec asked.

"In the jungle, many days from our village, hiding, waiting."

"Waiting for what?" Tec asked.

"Our return with your gift from the gods. We were told to kill the king's sons and bring the rock back to our village so that we would once again be in the favor of the gods."

"Remove him," the king ordered. "Bring in the other one. Let us see if their stories match."

While the king huddled with the priests, Que walked over to his brother and asked, "Do you want to take care of this one?"

Tec knew Que was trying to embarrass him in front of the others, but before he could answer, Que started coughing and then violently hacking.

While Que was doubled over, trying to clear his throat, Tec interrupted the king's discussion with the priests. "Father, I am going to rest. My wounds are bothering me," he said.

The king, looking irritated, just waved him away.

As he passed Que, who was still bent over, trying to catch his breath, Tec said, "Brother, you should rest."

Tec could feel his brother's angry glare as he left the room.

CHAPTER 25

Steve and Katie were planning to go out for dinner for the first time since taking up residence in the guesthouse of the Landry estate. In fact, this would be the first time they had left the property, except for their walks on the beach, which ran only a mile in either direction and was bordered on both ends by large rocks "to keep the riffraff out," as Mr. Landry had put it.

Ten houses shared this stretch of the beach, but it was deserted most of the time. Still, Mr. Landry had a security guard posted at the beach entrance. In addition to the guard at the beach, there was one at the driveway entrance to the estate and another who patrolled the grounds. Gabriel would be no match for any of these muscle-bound, serious-looking men.

"God, I can't wait to eat at Aurelio's. I'm starving. Can we go early?" Katie asked as they entered the guesthouse.

Steve looked at the clock. It was 2 p.m. It seemed like every day they were eating dinner earlier, going to bed earlier, and sleeping longer. Steve had joked that they were turning into senior citizens, but the truth was that he was a little worried. Wasn't that type of behavior a sign of depression?

"Sure, let's shower and go," Steve said.

Before they left, Steve turned on his laptop to order more of his protein powder. He had been struggling through his workouts since coming to Malibu, and he felt his muscles becoming flabby and his belly growing bigger. Even Katie noticed. By the pool earlier in the day, she had slapped his gut and said teasingly, "The beach life is starting to show!"

Katie went into the bedroom and called back, "Maybe you can join me in the shower?" Steve hurried to find the website he ordered the P80 powder from. Their sex life had been nonexistent in Malibu—not that Steve blamed Katie. She had been through a lot, and Steve was content to wait for her to show some interest. It sounded like she was interested now.

The website didn't come up on his screen instantly, and after a few seconds he got the bad-website message. He hoped the manufacturers of P80 hadn't gone out of business. When he went to the website of a chain of stores that sold nutrition supplements and searched for the P80 powder, this message appeared on his screen:

> "The USDA and FDA have announced the immediate ban of P80 protein powder and all other products manufactured by the Mega Muscle Corporation. The powder was found to have high levels of anabolic steroids as well as other dangerous and banned substances. Users are advised to immediately stop using all products from Mega Muscle Corporation until further notice."

The site went on to say that the product was manufactured in China, and that the company claimed it was unaware of the Chinese manufacturer's practices. It also described various symptoms users might experience. Steve was familiar with most of them. The notice advised anyone experiencing these symptoms to seek medical help.

Steve was stunned. He searched news websites and found a number of articles on the ban. Apparently this was a big national story a few days ago, but because he'd been cocooned in the Landry guesthouse, he had missed it. He felt like someone had punched him in the gut. He felt embarrassed and even a little guilty. What was he going to do now?

Steve nearly jumped out of his seat when Katie's warm, moist hands massaged his shoulders.

"Didn't accept my invitation?" Katie had a towel wrapped around her body and another around her hair. "Is something wrong?" she asked as Steve closed his laptop.

"Nah, I just got lost on the Internet."

"I guess the magic is already gone," she said as she plopped into his lap.

"No, I'm sorry. I just . . ." He was about to tell her about the powder when she planted a passionate kiss on his lips. Soon his problems were lost in a tumble of towels.

* * *

Steve and Katie sat in an uncomfortable silence in the back seat of the Jaguar, one of her dad's cars. The burly security guard who was usually stationed at the beach entrance was driving. Steve felt awkward carrying on a conversation in front of him.

Finally, Katie broke the silence. "Can you turn on the radio?" she asked the driver. The sounds of light rock filled the car. The music wasn't bad enough to ask the driver to change the station, but it wasn't good enough to enjoy.

Steve and Katie chatted about the weather, and then about

the news stories they had seen on television. The big story was about a cult in Mexico; 160 members—men, women, and children—had killed themselves. Apparently, they felt it was better to die in this manner rather than on Earth's last day, which they believed to be December 21, 2012, less than a month away.

"I'm going to an end-of-the-world party on the twenty-first," the bodyguard said, looking into the rearview mirror.

"Yeah, I heard that's the big thing this year," Steve answered.

The date, 12/21/12, had become a massive part of pop culture. It was constantly referenced in songs, television shows, and commercials. The closer the date drew, the more frenzied the hype became. Few people actually believed anything cataclysmic was going to happen; it was just a good reason to throw a blowout party. It was like having another New Year's Eve.

"Can we go to one?" Katie asked.

"Sure, but we need to get friends first," Steve joked.

They soon arrived at Aurelio's, a quaint restaurant housed in a building that looked like a small Italian villa. The driver pulled up to the front of the restaurant, quickly getting out to open Katie's door for her. Steve opened his own door.

"I'll be out here, watching the front door," the driver said. "Any problems, or if you see anything funny, call my cell." He handed Steve a business card with his name—Nathanial "Nate" Becker—and his cell phone number.

"Thanks, Nate. You want us to bring you out anything?" Steve asked.

"No, I'm good. Thanks. You kids have fun."

In the restaurant they ordered a bottle of wine, and then Katie went through the menu and described almost every item on it.

"Have you ordered everything?" Steve asked.

"I've been coming here since I was like five," she said.

Steve ordered the lasagna and Katie ordered the tilapia. It was the best lasagna—if not the best pasta dish—he had ever eaten. He could finish only half the dish, yet he still felt some remorse as he looked down at his belly. He asked to take the rest of the meal home in a doggie bag. It was dark when they left the restaurant; they had been there longer than Steve thought.

"Good dinner?" Nate asked as they approached the car.

Steve handed him the bag containing his lasagna. "Best lasagna ever, but you be the judge."

"Hey man, thanks. This will be better than the sub sandwich I was going to pick up at a gas station."

When they reached the Landry estate after the short ride from the restaurant, Nate pulled up to the entrance and reached out to enter the security code into the keypad at the gate. One of the other security guards, standing a few feet inside the gate, gave him a wave.

Looking out his window, Steve thought he saw something or someone moving in the shadows beside the main house.

"Do you see that?" he asked Nate.

"What?" he asked, interrupting his attempt to enter the code.

Steve pointed in the direction of the movement he'd seen. Nate peered out the open window. "Hey, what the hell is that?" he said as he got out of the car. "Terry!" he called out to the security guard on the other side of the gate.

Terry flashed a light at the spot Nate pointed to. Katie, who was leaning forward in her seat, gave a short scream when she saw Gabriel looking back at them like a startled raccoon.

"Katie!" Gabriel shouted, and then walked—almost lurching—toward the car.

"Hey buddy, drop what's in your hand!" Terry shouted.

Gabriel kept walking toward the flashlight, like a moth toward a flame, holding something black in his right hand.

"Stop!" Terry screamed. He had his pistol drawn.

"Down!" commanded Nate. "He has a gun! He has a gun!"

Pop, Pop, Pop.

The gunfire wasn't loud. It sounded like firecrackers exploding in the distance.

Nate looked stunned. Terry ran over to Gabriel, knelt down, and checked his pulse. Katie's screaming snapped Nate out of his trance. He jumped back into the car, punched the code into the keypad, and sped the car toward the house.

As they passed Gabriel, Steve saw Terry, with a horrified look on his face, picking a pair of binoculars up off the ground.

CHAPTER 26

She was passed out again on the couch, facing the ceiling, saliva running out of the corner of her mouth. Her bruised arms were folded on her lap in a prayer-like pose. A needle and bag containing powder sat on the coffee table in front of her, and an eleven-year-old boy stood over her, holding a pillow in his hands.

Go ahead and do it, the boy thought. He was cold; the house offered little protection from the gusting wind that swirled the snow outside. They had no heat in the house. The gas had been shut off for the second time in a year.

The boy's pants were too small and his T-shirt was dirty. He hadn't owned a pair of underwear or socks in months; she'd said to him, "You're growing too fast. They're a waste of money."

He was hungry. He was always hungry. Sometimes, after a man visited their house, they would have groceries for a few days, but then he'd have to beg the neighbors again for food.

This woman wasn't his mom anymore. He knew that she

cared more about her "medicine" than about him, and that her need for it would soon kill her—or him.

He had a plan. He would put her out of her misery, and then a friendly family member or neighbor would adopt him. He pictured himself playing catch on a warm day with his new father.

She started coughing, and then she vomited. She was still unconscious and gagging. She was going to choke to death on her own puke. Her breathing seemed to be fading already.

He stood over her, watching with fascination as her body convulsed, planning what to do next. He would dab some hot sauce in his eyes to cause tears and then run next door to the neighbors, crying like a baby. "My mama ain't breathing!"

Suddenly her eyes shot open. When she tried to flip over, her choking became more violent. She looked at him, full of fear, her eyes begging for help.

He placed the pillow over her face and pushed down with all his might. She fought a lot less than he thought she would. For the first time in his life he felt strong.

His mother had stopped struggling, but he still pushed down as hard as he could. A minute went by, and he slowly released the pillow. His arms were shaking from the exertion. If she moved at all, he was ready to slam the pillow right back on her face.

But she didn't move. He pulled the pillow away and saw a look of terror frozen on her face.

He didn't have to fake tears because he was sobbing, sobbing loudly. The sound of his crying seemed to surround him.

Ted awoke in a stuffy hotel room in Los Angeles, sweat and tears streaming down his face.

What the fuck was that? He tried to shake the sight of his dead mother's face out of his mind. Yeah, his mom had died on their couch, but he hadn't done it. He'd just found her dead.

He lay in bed, breathing heavily. His sheets were soaked with sweat, but he felt cold, like he had in the dream. He had arrived in L.A. on a late-night flight and thought it best to crash at the airport Hilton before continuing his quest for the elusive Gabriel.

Gabriel had bought a ticket to Los Angeles on his credit card three days before. Ted also found out, through a neighbor of the girl, that she had gone to stay with her father in Malibu for a few weeks. Ted now had a pretty good idea where Gabriel was.

His cell phone, sitting on the nightstand, vibrated. It was a call from Mr. Vega's mobile number.

"Good morning, Mr. V." Ted winced as soon as he finished the greeting. *Mr. Vega, dumbass*, he told himself, *not Mr. V.*

"Ted, you have to bring my son home." There was no emotion in Mr. Vega's voice. Ted had never heard him speak like this.

"I'm on it, Mr. Vega. I think I'm getting close—"

Mr. Vega interrupted him. "No, Ted, you have failed. Gabriel is dead."

"Dead? How? Where?"

"Malibu, shot by Landry's security guards as he tried to attack the girl, or so I've been told."

"I am so sorry, Mr. Vega."

"Bring his body home, Ted. I have texted you the information."

"I am so sorry. Is there anything else I can do for you?"

"You could have prevented this, Ted, but he is dead."

Ted remained silent, hoping Mr. Vega would soften his last words. Finally Ted said, "Mr. Vega, I cannot apologize enough . . ." He stopped when he realized Mr. Vega had hung up.

Ted felt nauseous. He paced around his room. What did Mr. Vega mean? How could he have stopped this?

He picked up the pain pills the hospital had given him for his nose, popped the top, swallowed three, and waited for them to kick in. He just needed his medicine. That thought made him laugh, as he slid along the side of the bed and onto the floor.

* * *

Ted slept for a few hours and awoke clearheaded, despite the pills. He got up off the floor, showered quickly, put on a fine suit, and was out of the room in fifteen minutes flat.

He checked the information Mr. Vega had texted to him. His boss had sent him the address of the hospital morgue holding Gabriel's body, the contact information for the police investigating the shooting, and a copy of the police report. Ted looked at the report on his phone display. He had some questions about it.

Los Angeles in the daylight was a depressing sight; the weather was cold and misty. He picked up a rental Cadillac near the airport and drove toward the morgue. On the way he called the detective in charge of the case, a Ms. Monica Ruiz. He got her voicemail and left a detailed message.

It seemed he could keep the madness he felt in the hotel room at bay as long as he occupied his mind with something else. He tried to focus on the road, on the houses and businesses he passed. He turned on the radio and frantically changed the station, looking for something to steady his mind.

His phone vibrated as soon as he found a news station.

"Hello?"

"Hello, this is Detective Ruiz returning your call."

"Thank you, detective, for being so prompt." Ted was surprised at how rational he sounded.

"How can I help you?" she asked.

"Well, my employer's son was Gabriel Vega, as I said in my message, and I was wondering what the status of the case is?"

"Pending review, it's been ruled a justifiable homicide."

"I see. Could I—"

Detective Ruiz interrupted him. "Look, Mr. Vega was wanted by the Vegas police for attacking Ms. Landry. He had a restraining order against him by Ms. Landry. Mr. Vega's residence was in Las Vegas. Mr. Vega was found on the Landry property and refused to surrender himself. The bodyguards involved all had proper registrations for their firearms."

"I understand all of that, but Gabriel had no weapon, from what I read. Security guards can't just go around shooting unarmed people."

"I agree, Mr. . . . ." She paused.

"Baron."

"Right, Mr. Baron. But the guards thought he had a gun, and they were hired to protect Ms. Landry from this person, who had a history of attacks against her."

"I understand, but my employer's son is now dead for holding what, a pair of binoculars?"

"We are just going to go round and round. Like I said, pending review by my superiors, I am going with self-defense. I really have to go, Mr. . . . ." Another pause.

"Baron!" Ted replied, letting his frustration seep into his voice.

"Sorry, Mr. Baron, but that's all I have to say."

"I guess you'll be hearing from our lawyers," Ted said before hanging up. He didn't really think they would be hearing from Mr. Vega's lawyers, but who knew?

Ted pulled into the hospital parking lot. He called the airline that had flown him to Los Angeles and made plans for Gabriel's body to be taken to San Francisco. Then, in the hospital, he arranged to have Gabriel brought to the airport and put on the flight. He wanted to get this business out of the way as soon as possible, so he could get out of town today, get back to normalcy.

You have failed. Mr. Vega's words echoed in his head. But how could he blame him for his son's death? He had done his job.

CHAPTER 27

Que lay unconscious in his house, surrounded by priests burning plants and animal remains while they chanted. He had passed out three days earlier, after beating to death one of the prisoners from Oxtab, the prisoner who had refused to speak and only glared with hatred. Tec had not been present for the interrogation, but he saw the aftermath: Que lying on his back, covered in blood; the prisoner, chained to a chair, his body beaten nearly beyond recognition as a human.

Tec had spent these last three days either by his brother's side or wandering around the village in the middle of the night, as he was doing now. In his heart he wanted to do whatever was needed to save his brother, but he hadn't forgotten the priest's warning about the plot against him.

Instead of returning to his brother, Tec went to the priest's compound, where the other captive was being held. The man now spoke freely of everything he knew about Oxtab and the city of the gods. His name was Toxco, and when Tec arrived he was sitting at a table, talking to one of the priests. His face was still swollen and around his neck was a collar that was tethered to the wall.

Toxco bowed his head when he saw Tec. The priest motioned for Tec to follow him into the next room.

"Our new friend has shared much, much about the city of the gods, as they call it." The priest practically purred as he spoke.

"Do you believe he is telling the truth?" Tec asked.

"He knows we will be bringing him with us when we leave in two days. He will be the first to die if it is a lie or a trap."

"In two days?"

"The king has so decreed. He believes the power that is there must be retrieved before the people of Oxtab know their assassins have failed. I am sure he is going to let you know tomorrow."

"What is the power?" Tec asked.

"Our friend has never been in the city itself, but he has heard that there are gifts from the gods and riches beyond description in it. He also says they too have rocks from the sky."

"It might be a trap," Tec said flatly.

"He says the city has great healing powers, that many dying people were brought there, and that they returned in a few days in perfect health."

"Why didn't he say this a few days ago?"

"You can dangle a treat in front of an ox, or you can push it. Sometimes the treat works better," the priest said with a smile. "Maybe the power of that place could help your brother, if that is what you want." The priest paused for a moment. "We also believe we should bring the god rock with us. If this is what the priests of Oxtab wanted, maybe it would also be to our benefit."

"I have a feeling this is already decided."

"That it is," the priest said.

"I will speak to my father," Tec said as he left the room.

Toxco was greedily eating a piece of fruit, but when Tec walked by, he buried his head in his hands.

Tec headed toward his house to rest and spend time with his family before the upcoming journey.

CHAPTER 28

S teve watched the service from a safe distance. Katie stood silently next to him. He still thought coming to Gabriel's burial was a mistake, but she felt she needed to; she felt she was somehow responsible for his death.

Katie had been taking it well, almost too well. The morning after Gabriel's death, it was as if it had never happened. That's why he was surprised when she had announced the day before that she would be flying to San Francisco to attend the burial service. Steve had agreed to accompany her, but suggested that they stay toward the back of the crowd, which would no doubt be huge, and she agreed.

It was a pleasant late-fall day, and they stood under the shade of a tree. The Vega family wouldn't recognize her at this distance. Katie was dressed in black and was wearing large sunglasses. She hadn't said a word since they arrived.

Steve wore the darkest clothing he had: jeans and a navy blue shirt.

They were on slightly higher ground than the burial plot and had a clear view of the Vega family. Mr. Vega wore an elegant black suit, and dark sunglasses covered his eyes. One by one people approached him and paid their respects; he didn't seem to acknowledge any of the people shaking his hand. He just stared straight ahead.

As the crowd of mourners thinned, Mr. Vega walked over to a thickset, clean-cut man dressed in a well-tailored suit.

Mr. Vega spoke into the man's ear for a few seconds, pulled a piece of paper out of his pocket, and handed it to the big guy, who slipped it into his pocket without looking at it. Mr. Vega then returned to his chair and continued to sit in silence.

"So, are you OK?" Steve asked Katie.

"Yeah, a few more minutes."

Steve heard Mrs. Vega crying. She looked younger than Mr. Vega, tall and very attractive. Steve figured they must be divorced; she sat several chairs away from Mr. Vega and was now being consoled by another man.

"OK," Katie said simply.

"Ready?" Steve asked.

"Yeah, I think so."

She grabbed his hand and gave it a squeeze. "Thank you for coming with me. You're a good man, Steve Soto."

"You a want few minutes more? I can pull up the car, away from the crowd?" He pointed to the empty street behind them.

"OK," she replied.

He gave her a kiss on the cheek and walked toward the main parking lot.

Steve felt like a weight had been lifted off of Katie and him: no more Gabriel drama. They could move forward, in Vegas or any other city they chose to move to.

What if he wanted to move to Miami—would Katie go with him? They hadn't been dating that long, but they had been through a lot together. He was sure he loved this girl. Did she feel the same?

He followed a path to the bottom of the hill, where he nearly collided with the big, well-dressed man Mr. Vega had spoken to moments earlier. Up close, Steve could se that he had terrible bruising around his nose and a look in his eyes that screamed danger.

The guy didn't even acknowledge Steve, passing right by as though he owned the path. Steve reached the parking lot, got into his car, and drove it slowly up the hill to where Katie was waiting.

"Thank you again," Katie said after she got in the car. She leaned over and grabbed his free hand.

Everything is going to be OK, he thought as they drove away.

CHAPTER 29

For the first time in his long career with Mr. Vega, Ted did not want to follow orders. He did not want to kill Katie Landry. He sat in a rental car, watching her house, trying to figure out what he was going to do. He had completed every task Mr. Vega had asked him to do without asking any questions. He had stolen; he had uncovered information that destroyed people's lives; he had killed—men and women. But now he was questioning his whole way of life.

Here he was at forty years old with nothing: no wife, no family, no friends. He had a fat bank account he would never enjoy, and a boss who he would take a bullet for, but who now blamed him for his son's death.

Mr. Vega had called him to his office on the day of Gabriel's wake. He kept Ted waiting for an hour while he conducted a meeting with Next Industries division heads. Ted used to be invited to meetings of this level.

When the conference room doors finally opened, the company's twenty or so division heads emerged. As they filed out, Nellie handed each one a sealed packet, which they accepted wordlessly.

Rebecca Barnes—the toughest bitch in the world, as Mr. Vega described her—wiped tears from her eyes as she passed Ted. He noticed that all of the executives appeared shaken. Some looked like death-row inmates heading to the gas chamber.

Mr. Vega must have torn each of them a new one, Ted thought. He was one tough son of a bitch doing business like this on the morning of his son's funeral.

"He will be with you in a moment," Nellie said to Ted, meaning that he should sit his ass back down again. He looked closer at Nellie and noticed that she looked like she had been crying too. *Must be the kid's death,* Ted thought.

After a few moments, a stream of Apollo scientists and that odd priest Ted had encountered before filed out of the conference room. They looked better than the department heads, but not by much.

"You may go in," Nellie said.

Mr. Vega was at the front of the now-empty room, standing before a giant video screen.

"Ted." Ted didn't know one word could contain so much resentment. "I have a job for you to do, as soon as possible, definitely in the next week."

"Yes, sir!"

Ted had wanted to apologize again to Mr. Vega, but he figured it would just add to his boss's contempt for him. He had hoped that as the days passed Mr. Vega's anger would pass, but it just seemed to have grown stronger.

"I want Katie Landry dead, any way you want."

"Sir, why?" That was the first time he had ever asked any such question of Mr. Vega.

"Why?" Mr. Vega said, shaking his head, holding in his anger. "Because I want that son of a bitch Landry to feel this pain. He also could have stopped this. But he hired goons to protect his daughter; I want him to know what it's like to have his child taken away from him!"

If Mr. Vega was planning this kind of punishment for someone who "also could have stopped" Gabriel's death, what did he have in store for Ted? He tried not to think about that.

"Aren't you worried that if she dies so soon after Gabriel, someone might think it was revenge?" Ted asked, trying to delicately talk Mr. Vega out of this plan.

"There isn't enough time to wait," Mr. Vega said quietly. "It has to be now."

"There isn't enough time?"

"Are you going to do it, or are you going to fail me again?" Mr. Vega screamed at Ted, marching to within a few feet of him.

For the first time, Ted didn't see Mr. Vega as a visionary. No—he was evil, pure evil, and Ted was his right-hand man.

"OK, Mr. Vega."

"When you get back I will have another project for you, in Russia. You will have to be there on December nineteenth."

"Yes, sir."

Sitting in the rental car outside the girl's house, Ted realized he would have to do the job very soon if he was to get back home, get his stuff together, and get on a plane to Russia. He had wasted a week watching the girl and her boyfriend coming and going, bringing in food, taking out garbage. They were two kids, wasting their youth by eating fast food and sitting on their asses. Although, Katie was a hot piece of ass, and maybe the boyfriend wasn't such a dimwit to stay home with her.

Ted considered just disappearing into the night, leaving behind his job and Mr. Vega. But the prospect of a life with no work and no Mr. Vega made him think of his childhood:

desolate, dark, and cold. No, he had already resigned himself to completing this assignment. Maybe, as time went on, Mr. Vega would forgive him. If not . . . he didn't want to think of what would happen if not.

It was 6 p.m., and the boyfriend had just left the house. These two kids were like an old married couple. Every day, he left around the same time, either by car or by foot. He would be gone an hour or so, return with takeout food or groceries, and not stick his nose out again until the following day. The girl never left the house. Ted wasn't sure she was even there until he caught a glimpse of her face in the freshly repaired front window earlier that day.

Ted slipped on a pair of leather gloves and got out of the car. It was a cold evening; he could see his breath in the air. He quickly walked a couple of houses down the block and cut through a darkened yard to the alley that ran behind Katie's home. He was hoping her back door was unlocked; if not, he would ring the front doorbell and ask to use her phone. He'd be in the house before she could say yes or no.

He slowly twisted the knob on the back door, and it turned easily. Silently he entered the darkened kitchen. He planned to make the girl's death look like an accident, regardless of his vague directive. He imagined Mr. Vega would thank him for this at some point in the future. *Ted, you always have my best interest at heart,* he would say.

If the girl discovered him, he had his gun, and he would make it look like a robbery.

One lamp dimly lit a corner of the family room, where the television played an annoyingly loud game show. Ted could see Katie lying on the couch, covered in a blanket. He drew close enough to see her sleeping, looking like an angel.

Her beauty was breathtaking even in the gray light of the television. He moved to the front of the couch, grabbed a pillow, and kneeled down in front of her. His body began to tremble, and tears ran down his face. Was he really going to do this? He usually felt like a spectator of his own actions, like he was not in control of his body—but not this time.

The girl's eyes popped open and her face contorted into a look of horror. She screamed, and Ted, as a reflex, put the pillow to her face, muffling the scream. When she tried to get up, he threw his body on hers. He wanted to say "stop screaming" to explain that it was all a mistake. But he was beyond that point now. His instincts and training took over.

He spun her over, burying her face into the couch, and got his arms around her head and neck. Her scream had been audible for a second when he flipped her. She wriggled beneath him as he held her head in what looked like wrestler's headlock, forcing it into the couch pillow.

Please no, please no, Ted said to himself over and over. But he moved his arms in opposite directions, twisting her neck and creating a snapping sound. Her body immediately went limp.

Ted could hear himself sobbing as he held the girl's dead body in his arms. The job was done; he had done what he had to do.

He carried Katie up the stairs and into the master bathroom, laying her gently on the floor. He turned on the faucet in the bathtub, making sure to run warm water—a cold bath would make investigators suspicious. He gently took off her clothes and put them in a pile in the corner of the room. He lifted her naked body, slammed her head into the faucet, and laid her in the tub at an awkward angle. He looked over his work. It met his satisfaction.

He closed the shower curtain, grabbed a small towel, wiped the excess water from the floor, and replaced the towel. He walked downstairs not thinking about what he had left upstairs in the tub, instead focusing on getting to his car, leaving, and getting home.

He put the pillows on the couch and let himself out the back door, locking it as he closed it. He followed the same route back to his car that he had taken to the house, looking for any signs of witnesses and finding none.

"That was my last kill," he said aloud as he took one final look around before driving away. He wasn't going to do this anymore, for Mr. Vega or anyone else.

As he drove away and passed under a streetlight, he saw the boyfriend returning with a bag of what he figured was takeout food. Ted looked ahead, trying not to draw attention to himself. Out of the corner of his eye he saw the boyfriend look in his direction. Once he passed, he glanced in the rearview mirror and saw the boyfriend stop momentarily and then continue on his way.

By the time the boyfriend called the police, Ted would be at the airport, and he'd probably be in the air when the detectives got to the house. But he had nothing to worry about anyway. He had done a good job. The scene looked like the girl had accidentally fallen in the shower and banged her head. Case closed.

Ted thought about going back. The boyfriend probably wasn't a threat, but he might have seen his face.

He drove on. Letting the boy live felt liberating. Maybe he could change.

CHAPTER 30

Steve sat in a dark hotel room, staring at an infomercial for a workout DVD. He didn't know what time it was. He wouldn't look at the clock next to his bed, and if there was daylight outside, the heavy shades blocked it. This is how his last few days had gone.

He was a public enemy, a media sensation, and his lawyer had booked him a room under a false name in a hotel he had never heard of. He waited for only one phone call, the one from his private investigator. For the first time since Katie's death he didn't feel numb. He felt angry, and it led him to turn his head and look at the time. It was nearly 8 p.m. He exhaled loudly and stood up.

He had found Katie lying unconscious in her bathtub. When he had lifted her, her head flopped back farther than it should have. In a panic, he called 911. The cops questioned him and politely invited him to the police station for more questioning. He kept telling them how he had seen a man, an acquaintance of Edgar Vega, driving away as he returned to Katie's with dinner.

"The Vega who owns half the world?" a Detective Taylor asked in a tone that announced his disbelief. Steve explained everything, about Katie and Gabriel and Gabriel's death. Surely that was a motive.

But the cops were more interested in Steve. Where had he gone that night? What time did he leave the house? What time did he return? What had he touched in the bathroom? Why did he turn off the water? Were he and Katie fighting? The questioning went on for hours, until Steve asked for an attorney. It was many hours before a public defender arrived. He explained to Steve that the police always suspected the husband or boyfriend when someone died under questionable circumstances.

After a few more hours Steve was released with the warning not to leave town. By now he had hired his own lawyer—and the media had learned of Katie's death. A beautiful dead girl and her jackpot-winning hero boyfriend as the suspect. They couldn't have asked for a juicier story. His apartment building was soon overrun with reporters and cameramen.

His lawyer got him into this hotel, and then Steve hired the private investigator to track down the man he saw driving away from Katie's house. If the police weren't going to do their job, he would do it for them.

As he stood up and stretched, his cell phone rang. It was his lawyer, Mort Stern. Steve had been referred to Mort by his investment broker, the only person in Vegas he could think of who would know of a respectable law firm.

"Hello?" Steve was surprised by how rough his voice sounded.

"Did I wake you?" Mort asked.

"No, I'm good. What's up?"

"I have good news. They're ruling Katie's death an accident. The autopsy findings came back yesterday, and they informed me a few minutes ago."

"Accident? What about what I saw?"

"The police said they're closing the case, unless more information comes up."

"More information? Maybe they should actually dig into what I told them about the guy I saw at Gabriel's funeral."

"I think they meant more information concerning you, Steve."

"Me?"

"They don't believe the mystery-man-connected-to-the-world's-richest-man thing. Actually, they said that story makes you look more guilty."

"What if I bring them the name of the guy, will they look into it?"

"I don't know. But I do know that you, personally, should do nothing. Lay low for a few more days."

"If I find anything out I'll call you. Maybe you can bring the information to the police?"

"Sure, we'll see, kid. I'll call tomorrow." Mort hung up.

Steve felt a little better until he thought of Katie. He squeezed his eyes closed as if that would blot her from his mind. He never should have left her alone.

He had left the house while they were in the middle of an argument. He walked instead of driving because he needed a break from her. She had hardly left the couch since they returned from Gabriel's funeral, and because she spent all her time obsessing over being the cause of Gabriel's death, she was falling into a deeper depression every day. The strain on their relationship was reaching a breaking point. *If only I had driven that night to pick up dinner*, Steve thought, *she might be alive.*

He settled on the floor in front of the bed and watched the hard bodies on the TV screen. Maybe he would buy this DVD.

He wanted to go to Katie's funeral, but he hadn't heard

from Mr. Landry. No doubt Mr. Landry was devastated, and he probably didn't know Steve well enough to disregard the suspicion that he had killed his daughter.

His cell phone vibrated again, this time from a private number.

"Hello?"

"Mr. Soto?"

"Yes."

"It's me, Ralph Corner." Ralph was the private detective Steve had hired.

"Yeah, Ralph. You got anything?"

"I have a listing with photo IDs of all of Next Industry's employees. If he works for Vega, he should be in this file."

"How did you get that?" Steve asked.

"I'd like to tell you about how hard it was, but Next is a public company. Most of this is public information, if you know where to look. And I know where to look."

They agreed to meet in a half hour, at the diner next to the Del Rio casino. It was a five-minute walk from Steve's hotel. Steve thought about having Ralph come to his hotel, but he knew he needed to get out and smell some fresh air, even if it was Las Vegas air.

Steve gave himself a quick smell test and decided to rinse off and brush his teeth before heading out.

* * *

Steve arrived at Bethyl's Diner fifteen minutes early. It was small, dark, and nearly empty. He took a seat that had a good view of the door. He had never met Ralph, but he figured he'd be able to pick him out of the crowd, especially one this sparse. The smells of the diner reminded him that he hadn't eaten in about two days. He ordered a Gut-Buster Cheeseburger from the waitress, a red-haired, middle-aged woman. He hoped the burger tasted half as good as it looked in the picture in the menu.

He was down to his last bite of the burger when a gawky, balding man carrying a briefcase walked into the diner and looked around.

"Ralph?" Steve asked, loud enough for him to hear.

"Mr. Soto?"

Steve didn't feel right being called Mr. anything by a man twenty-plus years his senior, but he didn't correct him. He rose from his seat and extended his hand, after wiping the grease from his burger on his jeans.

"Want anything?" the waitress asked Ralph as he sat down and popped open his briefcase.

"No, thank you," he replied amiably, holding the half-open briefcase to his chest and patiently waiting for her to leave. "Some of these photos are grainy," Ralph said as he placed a thick manila folder in front of Steve.

Steve pushed his plate aside and opened the folder. The top sheet of paper showed Edgar Vega. He flipped through a few more sheets of paper and stopped at the fifth one: Ted Baron. He was listed as Head of Corporate Security. The sheet included his Next Industry address and a home address.

Steve stared at the photo.

"Is that him?" Ralph asked.

"Without a doubt."

"What's next?" Ralph asked. "Giving the information to the police?"

"Yes, sir. Great job, by the way."

"Thank you."

Seeing Ted Baron's face again gave Steve a purpose, and his purpose was to see this guy behind bars.

CHAPTER 31

Ted drove into the Next Industries parking lot. Getting back into his element and his routine was doing wonders for him mentally. He parked his BMW in the spot marked with the RESERVED FOR T. BARON sign and turned off the car. He checked himself out in his rearview mirror; the bruising was fading on his nose, although it still looked slightly swollen. Wondering if that swelling would ever go away, he got out of the car, straightened his shirt and tie, put on his Armani jacket, and entered the building as he had so many times before.

This is just what the doctor ordered, he thought. He just needed some everyday routine, and the past few weeks would fade from his memory. No more bad dreams. No more emotional breakdowns.

He passed through security silently, taking pleasure from the surprised expressions on the faces of the guards. *I must be a mysterious figure to these people*, he thought, allowing himself a slight smile. He pushed back his shoulders and exaggerated his posture to look even more imposing to his staff as he passed by.

He expected to see Ken's eager face when he got to his office, but Ken's desk was empty and his computer was not even turned on.

Had Ken been slacking off in his absence? He pictured Ken in bed, still sleeping.

He had exchanged e-mails with Ken frequently during his travels, but there hadn't been any emergencies.

He turned on his office light and waved his hand over the desk to light up the computer screens on the wall.

His e-mail folder was filled. Many of the messages were marked urgent, and most were from Ken, who had condensed reports or given his impressions of reports.

Ted liked to work backward through e-mails, starting with the most recent messages. The majority of his e-mails involved Dale Thorn, the guy whose activities Ted had been monitoring before he started looking for Gabriel. *Him again*, Ted thought.

Thorn had tripped several of the alerts Ted had set up to keep tabs on Next employees. He had moved large amounts of money in and out of bank accounts. He had several unexplained absences from work. He had entered the Next campus multiple times after hours. And he had strange activity on his personal workstation, at strange hours.

Any one of these alerts should have prompted his department to take some action. But apparently nothing had been done. What the hell had Ken been doing while he was gone? The anger felt good to Ted. It felt really good.

"Action: Call Ken." Another benefit of working for Next Industries was the phoneless office.

"Hello?" Ken answered.

Ted could hear machinery in the background. It sounded like a car race was taking place behind him.

"Ken, it's Ted. What's going on?"

"Good morning, Mr. Baron. Are you back?"

"Yes, I am, and I'm surprised to not be seeing you right now."

"Didn't Mr. Vega tell you or leave you a message?" Ken asked, sounding confused.

"No, he didn't." Ted was equally confused.

"He's had me in charge of a project here at Apollo day and night for the past week."

"What project?"

Ken explained that he was in charge of security for trucks arriving at the Apollo loading dock. He told Ted there had been hundreds of trucks. They arrived full and left empty.

"There are uniformed men in the dock," said Ken. "They unload the skids, and the truck leaves. I'm to keep the flow going and not let anyone in or out."

"Or out?"

"Yeah, after they closed down Apollo last week—"

"They closed down Apollo?" Ted asked.

"Yeah, without notice. Only a few people were let in. The rest were turned away at the door, sent home with a year's severance."

Ted's head was spinning. "You're at the Apollo docks right now? I'm coming over," Ted said, and, without waiting for Ken's answer, added, "Action: End call."

Ted called Mr. Vega's office.

"Hello, Mr. Vega's office. May I help you?" said a pleasant-sounding female voice.

"Where's Nellie?" Ted asked.

"She no longer works here. How may I help you?"

"I need to speak to Mr. Vega. It's Ted Baron calling." He closed his eyes, waiting for the stupid questions a new receptionist might ask.

"Mr. Vega instructed me to tell you he is 'incommunicado' for the next few days and will answer only e-mails."

Incommunicado? What the fuck does that mean? "I really need to speak to him." Ted hated the way he sounded, like a jilted girlfriend.

"That is all the information I have. Feel free to e-mail him. Have a nice day." The line went dead.

* * *

The main Apollo building stood eleven stories tall and the exterior was all glass. It was attached to a squat building that covered twice as much ground as the glass structure and had no windows. Ted had never ventured to the loading docks. As he neared the back of the windowless building, a large, unmarked semi truck barreled past him in the opposite direction. As he rounded the corner of the building, he saw people rushing around and several forklifts moving back and forth. Armed men in black uniforms guarded the ten loading docks at the back of the windowless building. Trucks were backed up to eight of the docks.

Ken, wearing a suit, stood out from the crowd of dockworkers and guards. He was giving instructions to the driver of a forklift.

Ted stopped, drew in several deep breaths, pushed back his shoulders, and walked toward Ken.

"Hey, chief," Ken said when he saw him.

Ken looked ragged. His hair was a mess, his suit stained, and he even had a few days' stubble on his ordinarily clean-shaven face.

"Ken, what the hell is going on?"

"You don't know, sir?" Ken said to Ted and then shouted at one of the forklift drivers. "No, dock *six*!"

"I've been gone, and I can't get a hold of Mr. Vega," Ted said.

"Tell you the truth, I was hoping you could enlighten me," Ken said, looking directly at Ted for the first time. "Mr. Vega gave me a schedule of trucks and docks. I'm here directing traffic. I haven't had more than three hours of sleep in the last two days. The trucks don't stop coming."

"What's in the trucks?" Ted asked.

"As best as I can tell, it's army supplies, medicine, food, stuff like that. It's like Mr. Vega is stocking a small army."

"It's going into Apollo's warehouse, or whatever that is?" Ted asked.

"I don't know, sir. I have security clearance for the dock only." He flipped up the orange laminated card that was around his neck, and Ted grabbed it. It read, NEXT INDUSTRIES: GROUP ORANGE.

"Who are those guys guarding the dock?" Ted asked.

"I don't know. They don't talk. Very serious dudes. I've never seen any of them before. They have black ID cards— like mine, but black. They can go into the dock area proper. I haven't seen what's beyond that."

Did this have to do with Gabriel's death? Did this have to do with that damn Mayan calendar? Did Vega have secret information from the government? Were we going to war? Had Vega lost his marbles? The possibilities spun through his head.

"What do you think is going on, chief?" Ken asked, as if he knew what Ted was thinking.

Ted didn't answer.

"Do you think Vega got word of a terrorist attack or something?"

"Maybe," Ted said.

They both watched the bustling scene—trucks, forklifts, dockworkers, security guards—until an arriving truck caught Ken's attention. "Hey! No! Over here! I gotta go, boss," Ken said as he marched off toward the truck.

Ted walked toward one of the armed guards. He could tell by the man's demeanor and build that he was no rent-a-cop. Calmly, the guard said to Ted, "Credentials, please."

Ted showed him his Next badge.

"Sorry, sir. That's improper identification." The guard had barely glanced at the badge.

Ted looked him up and down. "Son, I don't know you, so I assume you don't know me. I'm in charge of security here and have been out of town doing . . . doing something for Mr. Vega."

The guard didn't appear to be impressed.

"Ken over there works for me, you see," Ted continued. "I want to know what the hell is going on here."

Still speaking in a calm tone, the guard said, "Sir, you need to step back unless you can provide me with proper identification."

Ted tried to control his anger. He stepped up to the stair directly below the guard and came almost nose-to-nose with him.

"Son, you will get your superior out here right fucking now or so help me, your next job will be at Walmart!"

The guard looked to his colleagues for help, but none of the other guards came to his aid. He reached down to his belt, pulled out his walkie-talkie, and called for Mr. Bell to come to the dock.

Ted stepped down one stair. "Thank you," he said, pushing back his hair.

After a five-minute wait, the door behind the guard opened and Frank Bell walked out. He was dressed in the same fashion as the guard and had the same black ID card around his neck.

"I heard some asshole was making a ruckus out here. I guessed that would be you," Frank said, cracking a big smile at Ted.

"What the hell are you doing here?" Ted asked.

It had been a long time since he had seen Frank, an old army buddy who had worked for him some years back.

"Vega hired my company for security."

"Your company? Very impressive."

"I learned from the best. Come on in." Frank motioned him past the guard.

The warehouse was dimly lit. Skids upon skids filled what had to be nearly a 200,000-square-foot building.

"Hell that's not even half of it," Frank said as Ted looked around the building. "There's another warehouse below here, twice this size, filled with similar stuff."

"What is all this?" Ted asked.

Frank looked surprised. "I thought you would be knee-deep into this shit."

"I've been out of town for Vega for weeks. I still haven't seen him. I'm sure he'll—"

"Yeah, yeah. Secret stuff. I get it. Nothing changes. Well, brother, I really can't give you the dime tour unless you have the badge." Frank flipped up his black placard.

Ted noticed that most of the skids near him were marked as canned pineapple and canned tuna.

"I know a little of what's going on. It must be nice to be paid to babysit food," Ted said, trying to prolong the conversation while he took in more of the contents of the warehouse.

"Yeah, I have to deal with truck drivers and guard crates

of food—not too shabby. The orange-badge guys below are dicks though."

Ted remembered Vega's hidden floors and the old military bunker under the Apollo and Next buildings. Whatever was going on here had to be related to all of the scientists and engineers who roamed the hallways of the hidden floors.

"Yeah, those eggheads are hard to deal with," Ted said, on a hunch.

"Damn right, brother. Those guys suck," said Frank.

"Well, I'm sure I'll be seeing you soon."

"Yeah, I hope," Frank replied.

"Have they let you go underground yet?" Ted asked conspiratorially, moving closer to Frank as he asked.

Frank looked around and whispered, "No, I've only been to the blast doors. But from what I hear from those eggheads, there's a city under there."

Ted nodded his head knowingly. "It is like a city. Maybe when I get my badge I can take you down there."

"Sounds great. Listen, brother, I got to get back at it." Frank offered Ted his hand.

"Yeah, we've gossiped like women long enough," Ted said, smiling and shaking Frank's hand.

Ted left the building and walked wordlessly past the guard. His right hand was shaking. He started thinking of the girl lying dead in the bathtub. No, he was not going to go down that path! He walked more briskly and tried to fill his mind with other thoughts, but now images of all the people he had killed over the years flashed through his mind. He didn't notice right away, but he was emitting a soft whine. He took a deep breath and tried to steady himself.

He continued to walk along the side of the building. When a truck came speeding around the corner, he imagined throwing himself in front of the truck and ending the pain, the guilt. Something had to give.

Only one thing mattered to him now, and that was talking to Vega and finding out what was going on. It seemed things, whatever they were, were coming together at rapid speed. He wanted answers and had to figure out a way to get them.

He pulled out his phone and sent a text to Mr. Vega: "Need to speak. Urgent."

CHAPTER 32

Ted pulled up to the curb in front of Dale Thorn's house, a drab-looking structure fronted by landscaping that looked like a jungle. Ted had twenty-four hours until his trip to Moscow. He had tried a number of times to get ahold of Mr. Vega but hadn't heard back from him. He did, however, receive a file from Vega containing the information for his trip, including the flights.

Chasing down Dale Thorn was part of his plan to get an audience with Mr. Vega. Figuratively speaking, Thorn had tripped many of the Next Industries security alarms. He looked like he was up to no good, at least from his recent activities, and catching Thorn red-handed as he stole from the company would at least merit a conversation with Mr. Vega.

Ted no longer cared whether Mr. Vega forgave him for his son's death. He wanted to change his job and his life, but he needed to know what was going on at Apollo. It looked like Mr. Vega knew something big was about to happen, and Ted worried that it was connected to that damn Mayan calendar thing, that on December twenty-first something was going to happen. He didn't believe in any of the end-of-the-world crap on television or on the radio or in the books he read. But maybe it was something man-made, maybe by the government or Vega himself.

Most of the world, particularly the United States, was going to treat December twenty-first as a holiday, a reason to celebrate with parties and other events. Ted wouldn't be going to any parties. Most likely he'd be flying back from Russia that day.

Ted saw a man leave the house carrying a suitcase. He recognized Thorn from the photo in his employment file. He looked like an aging hippie, his long white hair pulled back into a ponytail.

Ted slowly got out of his car. He had his gun in a side holster under his suit jacket. He'd decided to arm himself for this chore; rats backed against a wall can be unpredictable. Ted walked up behind Thorn as he was tossing his suitcase in the trunk, which, Ted noticed, was filled with other bags.

"Excuse me," Ted said calmly.

Thorn turned around. He had a wild look in his eyes.

"Yeah?" he replied, shutting the trunk behind him.

"I'm Ted Baron, with Next Industries security."

Thorn's expression didn't change. He didn't get the look of dread that Ted had anticipated.

"Fuck you. I have to go."

Ted pushed Thorn lightly against the car. He had a good fifty pounds and at least six inches on Thorn.

"I would like to speak to you in private, please." Ted opened his jacket, showing Thorn his sidearm.

Thorn threw his head around wildly, muttering, "Fucking perfect. Goddamn it!"

He then tried to break free of Ted, who easily pushed him back against the car.

"Look, I have to catch a plane, I have to—" Thorn was almost begging.

"Just a few minutes, a few questions, Mr. Thorn. How about in the garage?" Ted said calmly.

Thorn must have realized he didn't have a choice. "OK, a few minutes."

Ted grabbed his arm and they walked through a side door and into the garage, which was cluttered and smelled of gasoline.

Thorn spoke first. "You work for Vega, right? I've seen you before."

"Yes," said Ted.

"You know what's going on, then. I know I am not supposed to know. I won't tell anyone, OK?"

Ted just nodded his head. "Where are you going?"

"To the fucking equator, man. Bioko, off the coast of Africa. I already bought a house there. Listen, your secret is safe with me. I just want to live."

Ted tried to play along. "How did you find out?" he asked.

"I knew Vega kept us working separate for a reason. But I was the telemetry guy. It didn't take a genius to figure it out. I did some digging and saw that the government knew. I'm surprised none of my coworkers figured it out."

Ted gave up. "Listen, I have no fucking idea what you're talking about. I just stumbled onto you. But one thing is for sure, if you don't tell me exactly what the hell is going on, I'm going to put a bullet in your leg, and you ain't going anywhere."

He grabbed Thorn's arm to make sure he couldn't run and pulled him close.

Thorn pulled away and began swearing again at Ted. Ted swept out his leg, knocked him down, and rolled him over so that he was facedown on the dirty garage floor. Ted planted his knee in Thorn's back and bent his arms up toward his shoulders, causing him to scream in pain.

"Let's try again. You tell me what's going on, you can leave. You fuck with me, you stay here. Got it?" Ted spoke in a calm voice, easing the pressure on Thorn's arm.

"OK, OK. Vega had us working in many teams. My job was to watch a certain patch of space."

"Space? Like outer space?"

"Yeah, outer space. I saw it a month ago, an unnamed asteroid. At first I thought it was cool. I would get to name it, or whatever. I watched it for the last several weeks, passing the information on to another guy. Bottom line is, that asteroid, actually that group of asteroids, have a very good chance of hitting us, Earth."

"Doesn't that happen all the time?" Ted asked.

"Yeah, little shit hits us all the time. Not anything this size. I stumbled upon the work of the guy I passed the information to. I put it together and saw that the asteroid I spotted was going to pass close to Earth, very close. The more I looked, the clearer it became that it wasn't just one; it was many. And the biggest is huge. I mean, end-of-the-world huge."

"You said it has a chance of hitting us. So maybe it won't?" Ted asked, trying to process the information.

"Yeah, when I first saw it I thought it had a chance. But as it got closer I kept checking my info versus others'—which we weren't supposed to do, but I did. Every day the probability of a strike increased. First it was like two percent, and it went up each day from there."

"What's the probability now?"

"89.7 percent chance. That was a few days ago."

"OK, so the earth gets hit by an asteroid. Isn't there a pretty good chance it will land in the ocean, or where people don't live? Why the panic?"

"This thing is like over fifty miles long, and there are a few of them. It's unheard of. You know the asteroid that wiped out the dinosaurs? That was five miles long. Nowhere is safe. The dirt and shit that it will knock into the air will block the sun. We'll be in an ice age for years, hundreds of years, man. No sun, no plants. No plants, no food. You need to find the warmest place on Earth, and buy as much food and as many weapons as you can. Maybe you'll survive . . ." He trailed off.

Mr. Vega's underground city now made sense.

"Won't the government do anything?" Ted remembered that Thorn had mentioned the government.

"They would if they'd had a year or two to try to stop it. They can't stop it, man. Vega must have notified them. I saw memos and shit. They were talking about it, man."

"Why haven't they announced it?" Ted asked, trying to punch holes in Thorn's story.

"Can you imagine what would have happened? We'd all have killed each other by now. Imagine the riots. But they are going to announce it. I saw they're going to announce it on the twentieth, just in time for our government to be sealed safely in underground bunkers. Imagine what's going to happen, man, when they announce that an extinction-level asteroid is going to hit on the next day, the twenty-first." Thorn was laughing maniacally.

The twenty-first. Ted's stomach dropped.

"You mean like that fucking calendar?" Ted asked.

"Yeah, isn't that nuts? How did the Incas know that?"

"Mayans," Ted corrected him.

"Mayans, Incans, Martians—who gives a shit? When God's hammer comes down in Russia on the twenty-first, we're all screwed."

"Russia?" Ted asked, his insides going cold.

"Yeah, that's the most likely strike zone. At least those people won't have to worry about starving to death. That whole part of the world will be caught up in an explosion that will look like all of the nuclear bombs in the world going off at the same time."

"I'm supposed to leave for Russia in a day."

"You'll be in ground zero. I suggest instead you get to a friendly country in the warmest place on Earth and buy all the food and guns you can, man."

Thorn giggled and added, "Man, you would have had the worst luck in the world if you went to Russia. When they announced the end of the world, you'd be stuck in the bull's-eye."

Ted released Thorn and sat back. Vega was sending him to his death. He suddenly became nauseous, leaning over and throwing up on Thorn's grease-covered floor.

Thorn hopped up and fled the garage. His Camry started up and screeched away.

When Ted finally got up off the floor, dusk had fallen. He stumbled to his car, tore off his suit jacket, and let it fall to the ground. Part of him wanted to make plans to flee like Thorn. The rest of him just wanted to get home and go to sleep. Instead he drove toward Next Industries. He had no plan; he just wanted to hurt Vega, to make him pay for his betrayal.

* * *

The Next Industries parking lot was dark when Ted arrived. He entered in his normal manner and made his way directly to Vega's floor, which also was dark. He banged on the locked doors to Vega's office, but no one answered.

Ted figured Vega was probably already in his bunker under

the building, and he would need the master keys to get into the secret elevator behind the wall panel. Ted and Vega had setup a master key system so that if the boss were ever incapacitated, or if he died, Ted could pass on the codes and keys to the next officer or estate trustee. In Ted's office was a safe that held the codes to Vega's safe and a master swipe card that opened every office door and elevator at Next Industries. In Vega's safe was a transparent piece of plastic that displayed Vega's handprint to hand recognition sensors.

Ted retrieved Vega's safe code from the safe in his own office and then returned to Vega's floor. Using the master swipe card, he opened the door, and his heart leapt in his chest: the lights were on. Then Ted realized they were activated by the door— no one was in the office. Why did he care if Vega caught him anyway? Vega should be afraid of *him*.

The combination to the safe was a twenty-digit number that had no rhyme or reason to Ted, but he was sure it meant something to Vega; he had seen him enter it many times from memory.

The safe contained rows of folders, most involving Vega's estate. Ted also found several badges like the ones he had seen at the loading dock: black, orange, and gold.

When Ted grabbed the badges, he noticed a metallic keycard. He grabbed that too, along with the plastic handprint sheet.

Ted's plan, which he was making on the fly, was to kill Vega without anyone knowing and then get to the underground bunker so that he could survive the asteroid strike and its aftermath.

But did he want to survive? What kind of life would it be, living like a rat underground until he ran out of food at the ripe old age of seventy?

What had Thorn said, an 89.7 percent chance of the asteroid hitting? *Maybe it will miss*, he thought as he walked toward Vega's secret elevator. He opened the wall panel, pulling on the rock as Vega had done, and then scanned the plastic handprint. Inside the elevator, Ted put one of the orange badges around his neck and pressed the X button.

As rush of cold air entered the elevator when the doors opened. Ted was surprised to see a group of men and women rushing about, carrying boxes and pushing carts. All of them had the orange badges hanging from their necks. Ted moved into the flow of people and saw that a number of rooms were being cleared out and filled with rows of bunk beds. Most of the people were wearing green khaki uniforms. A few men in black military garb were directing traffic.

Ted stood out in his dress shirt and pants, and people were starting to look at him. He retreated into the elevator, and as he did a very attractive woman turned and looked at him suspiciously. The doors closed, cutting off her view.

Ted pushed the Z button, hoping there would be fewer people there, and that maybe he could find one of those green or black uniforms, so that he could blend in with the crowd.

The doors opened to a brightly lit and empty hallway. Ted exited the elevator and walked down the hallway, which led to a catwalk that rimmed a vast cavern. Dim blue lights lit the cavern floor, which had been divided into many rooms containing what looked like generators—some running and some idle—and huge metal containers labeled FUEL, WATER, or FERTILIZER.

The cavern also contained a subterranean lake. Water flowed down the wall of the cavern, and mechanical pumps were operating on the edge of the lake. Ted saw some people working on the cavern floor, and he saw rows and rows of skids, most likely the same ones he had seen being loaded onto the Apollo dock.

Judging from the massive amounts of supplies, Ted could

envision people surviving for decades down here. *This is really happening*, he thought. *The world is going to end. Maybe that's not so bad.*

Ted felt slight tremors throughout his body. At first he thought it was an earthquake, but then he realized it was just his own shaking. A wave of weariness swept over him—he just wanted to sleep. He walked back to the elevator, returned to Vega's hallway, and then went back to his own office. He wished he had a couch. He just needed a little shut-eye, and he was far too tired to drive home. He decided he'd catch a catnap and then figure things out, and collapsed on the couch in the conference room near his office.

Ted awoke with a start. He'd had a dream that he was standing in a large room, Mr. Vega behind him. In front of him were the pale, ghostly figures of every person he had killed. Gabriel's girlfriend, the picture of beauty, stood at the front of the crowd. She looked at him and smiled. A bright light drowned out the scene, and that's when he awoke.

He felt an odd sense of peace, like a huge weight had been lifted off his shoulders. He was going to die. Everyone was going to die. Instead of feeling horror, he felt relief.

He sat up with a groan. Daylight was streaming into the hallway. He stood up, pushed his hair back, and tucked in his shirt. He hoped it was still early and that Next Industries was empty. He took his phone out and saw it was nearly 7 a.m. He also noticed that Vega had texted him: "Have a good trip. Notify me on your arrival." Ted laughed out loud.

His lack of fear and willingness to die continued to grow. He wanted to atone for his sins. He was almost giddy. This was the best he had felt in years, maybe decades. He considered calling people he had harmed and calling the families of people he had killed to apologize.

But he still needed to make Vega answer for *his* sins. He didn't know where his boss was now, but he knew where he would be on the twenty-first.

* * *

The woman who had taken Nellie's place as Vega's receptionist looked nothing like her put-together predecessor. She was large and messy-looking, with hair dyed a shockingly bright red. Perhaps Vega had tucked Nellie into the safe city beneath them.

"Hello, is Mr. Vega in?" Ted asked pleasantly. He was freshly showered and wearing a clean suit.

"No, Mr. Baron," she said, her eyes scanning his security tag.

"I'm head of security, and I'm doing my monthly security sweep. I need access to Mr. Vega's office."

She looked concerned.

"Don't worry," said Ted. "I have a key and identification. You don't have to do anything." He gave her his biggest smile. His cheek twittered; his face was uncomfortable with this expression.

"If you say so, Mr. Baron. I'll note this."

"Fair enough. You'll get used to this. I practically live on this floor."

She mumbled a reply.

Ted entered Mr. Vega's office, turned on his computer manually, and used his code keys to log on. He went through his logs, e-mails, and expense records. It seemed Vega had been traveling on his private jet, mostly in Mexico. From several recent e-mails, Ted gathered that he was rounding up family members, probably to bring them to his underground bunker. His schedule showed that he was due back that evening, a day before they announced the pending disaster.

Ted turned off everything and left Vega's office. He would stake out the airport later that evening, follow Vega, and when the moment was right, have his reunion. Mr. Vega would not be joining the underground city.

CHAPTER 33

S teve didn't want anyone to witness what he had planned. He looked out the front door of his apartment complex. Two cars that he knew held reporters were parked in the street, and there was no way he could pull his car out and not be seen by them.

If the previous day's events were any indication, once the reporters saw him, they would follow. The day before, he had called a taxi and run out of his apartment building in a hooded sweatshirt. To his dismay, the two cars, each carrying a reporter and a cameraman, followed immediately. He'd offered the cabbie an extra hundred to lose them, but he wasn't game. The driver returned him to the apartment, and Steve hadn't been fast enough to get in the building before the vultures descended on him. "Steve, why did you kill her?" one of the reporters had screamed. "Steve, are you innocent?"

His new plan was simple. He bolted out the apartment door with his hood up, made it to the street, and then ran to an alley next to the building before the reporters' cars even started. He sprinted to the next street and turned out of their view. Instead of continuing, he stepped into the vestibule of a nearby building and stood against the wall for several minutes before running back toward his apartment. Both cars were gone. He figured they were driving up and down the side streets, trying to catch him as he looked for a cab. He grabbed his bag, which he'd left in the apartment building's lobby, ran to his car, and screeched off.

* * *

Steve walked out of the North Las Vegas pawnshop with a new Beretta Tomcat pistol. He was surprised at how easy it had been to buy a gun. After filling out a few forms, showing some identification, going through a background check on the store's computer, and paying $500, he was the proud owner of a stubby firearm. Steve had never held a gun, let alone owned one, but he knew he needed one now: his girlfriend had been murdered by an employee of one of the richest men in the world.

He put the gun case and ammo in his trunk and got into his well-supplied car. He had a suitcase with clothes and enough caffeine products and protein bars to drive coast to coast, although he was driving only to San Jose, a little over eight hours away.

It was foggy—rare weather for Vegas—when he got onto the I-15 and headed out of town. The only sound in his car was the intermittent squeak of the wipers across his windshield. He turned on the radio and tuned it to a light jazz station—not usually his cup of tea, but it seemed to fit the situation.

His bag contained his new Beretta, a video camera, a

tape recorder, some rope and duct tape, and few changes of clothes. His plan seemed better when he had come up with it while sitting in his underwear in a hotel room. Actually, it seemed brilliant at the time: get Baron to admit on tape that he killed Katie and then take the tape to the Vegas police. Baron would turn on Vega, and Katie's murder would be avenged. The gun was for Steve's protection, but he might also need it to be more persuasive with Baron. The police in Vegas had barely concealed their laughter when he brought them Baron's picture. They'd said they would look into it, but Steve knew that wouldn't happen, that he had to take things into his own hands.

Steve pictured Edgar Vega, that stupid smiling file photo they showed on TV whenever they ran a story about him. He had to be the cause of Katie's death. It couldn't be a coincidence that his son died chasing her, and then he sees Vega with the man who murdered her.

Before long, Steve was in California. The fog had lifted, and a dim sun shone through high, thin clouds. Steve loved when the light looked this way, in early winter; it was so peaceful.

He stopped at a gas station near his exit, filled his tank, and bought a cup of coffee and a doughnut. *Get fat*, he thought. *It doesn't matter.*

Steve had talked on the phone with his grandfather a few hours before leaving Vegas. The old man sounded devastated by the news that Katie was dead; he'd even offered to come visit. Steve told him it was OK, that maybe he would come for a visit at Christmas instead and spend some time in El Paso. That pleased his grandfather. As they hung up, Steve had the feeling he would never speak to his grandfather again.

The hours and miles flew by, and soon he was on the final leg of his trip, speeding down U.S. highway 101. Baron lived in Cupertino, on the outskirts of San Jose. It was getting dark when Steve reached Bark Lane, and he drove slowly down the street until he found Baron's address, a ranch house that was completely dark. He pulled into a spot across the street from the house.

Was he really sitting outside this guy's house—*with a gun?* His resolve was quickly fading. Just as he was about to drive off, a BMW pulled into the driveway of Baron's house.

Baron's shoulders were slumped when he got out of the car, his shirt partially untucked. He looked disheveled, not at all how Steve remembered him from the cemetery.

Now that Katie's murderer was in front of him, Steve gave no more thought to leaving. He took the gun out of the bag next to him and felt its weight. He considered walking straight up to Baron and shooting him in the back.

When Baron walked under a light near the street, his face surprised Steve. He didn't look like the menacing character Steve remembered. He looked scared, and tired. Steve didn't let that faze him. He grabbed the bag next to him and waited until Baron entered his front door. Then Steve got out of the car and tucked the gun in his back waistband, like he'd seen on TV and in the movies. He was smiling at the insanity of what he was doing as he walked up to Baron's house.

CHAPTER 34

S teve crept up behind Ted as he was unlocking his front
door, stuck his gun into the small of Ted's back, and said,
"Get in."

Ted froze. Steve was afraid he was going to turn around and
smash him, but instead he turned just his head and looked into
Steve's eyes. "It's you," Ted said, and started laughing.

It wasn't the reaction Steve had expected. He jammed the
gun more forcefully into Ted's back.

"OK, OK," Ted said. He opened the door.

Steve ordered him to turn on the lights, which illuminated
a sparsely decorated house. They stood in a small foyer that
looked into a living room, a dining room, and the entrance to
the kitchen.

"Sit." Steve motioned to one of the wooden chairs around
the dining room table.

Steve tried to control his breathing, but his heart felt like it
was going to jump out of his chest. A drop of sweat ran down

his forehead and into his eye. He wiped it away quickly. "Sit, now!" Steve said again, pointing the gun menacingly at Ted.

"Take it easy, buddy." Ted spoke in a friendly voice while beaming a smile at Steve. He turned a chair toward Steve. "Like this?" he asked.

"Just sit," Steve said, moving closer to Ted.

When Ted sat down, Steve stepped behind him and dropped his bag on the floor. Watching his captive closely, he opened the bag and got out the rope. Steve now realized he had no idea how he was going to tie him up with one very long piece of rope. He paused for a moment before looping the rope around Ted's feet, under the chair, around his chest, around his neck, and back behind the chair. He then tied it to the legs of the chair. Steve was impressed with his rope job, but Ted started laughing again.

"What's so fucking funny?"

"Nothing, pal, nothing."

Steve took another look at the rope and pulled on it to make sure it was secure. Then he put his digital camera on the table facing Ted and set it to pause.

"You're probably wondering who I am." Steve had played out this scene in his head many times.

"I know, kid. I know. You're the boyfriend, and I am truly sorry about your beautiful woman. I really am."

Ted sounded sincerely remorseful, and Steve was caught off guard. "You're admitting you killed Katie?"

"Yeah. It's Steve, right? I did it for Edgar Vega. You know, Gabriel's father. It was a revenge thing. I am sorry."

Steve was staring at Ted with his mouth open. He fumbled with the digital camera to start recording. Ted saw this and laughed again.

"Let me guess, you're going to take that to the police? You got balls, kid. You got balls." Ted was shaking his head approvingly.

A man in his situation shouldn't be acting this way, like he wasn't worried at all, Steve thought. He looked around quickly. Maybe there was someone else in the house. "Don't move," Steve ordered. He proceeded to go through the house, turning on the lights as he looked into each room. All of the rooms were barely furnished and had no art or other decorations on the walls. It looked like Ted had just moved in, or didn't spend a lot of time here.

After checking out the whole house, Steve returned to Ted.

"What, you worried we aren't alone? I haven't had a houseguest in . . . shit, ever."

Steve went back to the camera, focused it on Ted, and asked, "So you admit to killing Katie Landry?"

"Yeah, kid. I already said that. But it doesn't matter. The world ends in two days."

"What—you're trying to look crazy for the police?" Steve asked.

"No, really, a huge asteroid is going to hit this planet on the twenty-first. Trust me. I work for one of the world's most—"

"Are you kidding me? You killed my girlfriend and you're giving me a crazy act?"

"No, they're going to announce it on TV tomorrow. Listen, I owe you. You need to get to the equator, far from here."

"Shut up!" Steve yelled. His temples pounded from the blood rushing through his head. He wanted to smack this clown in the face. He was making a mockery of the crime he had committed by talking crazy like this. Steve's head was swimming. He didn't know what to do.

"Listen, it's all coming together. I am meant to help you. I saw your girlfriend a few nights ago. She was smiling at me. She wants me to help you."

Steve snapped. He struck Baron across the face with his gun and then whacked him again and again. When he caught hold of himself, blood was running from several cuts on Ted's face, and his head had drooped forward.

"Don't pretend you're unconscious."

Steve pushed Ted's head back. Ted's mouth dropped open, and Steve could feel his pulse as he held his chin up. He let go of his head, and it fell forward. Steve saw the red light on the camera, indicating that it was still recording. He picked it up and played back the last few minutes, horrified by the look of rage on his face as he beat Ted. Steve sat down on the floor.

His plan was falling apart. The recording made him look like the criminal, beating up a crazy man.

He had to figure out what to do. He turned off all the lights, except one near Baron, and closed all the drapes and blinds. In the living room, he moved the couch—one of the house's few pieces of furniture—and positioned it so that he could watch TV and keep an eye on Ted. He turned on the news and waited for Ted to wake up.

* * *

Steve was asleep on the couch when Ted came to. Ted had no idea how long he had been passed out, but he could hear an infomercial on the television, so he figured it was the middle of the night.

"Two more days for humanity," a female voice said in his head. It must have been Katie—he had dreamed of her again.

He didn't remember the details of the dream, but he knew they spent time together, and that she wanted him to save Steve. She was like his guardian angel. The thought made him smile; she must have forgiven him.

But how would he save the boyfriend? Steve wouldn't listen to anything he said, and it was probably too late now to get him somewhere safe. Money wouldn't be a problem, but time would. If Thorn was to be believed, the government was going to announce the asteroid today.

Then, out of nowhere, an idea came to Ted. He smiled as he thought about his plan's simple brilliance.

But first he needed to get free. The kid obviously didn't have much experience tying up people. He started working the rope, loosening the part around his chest and arms so that when he had the opportunity he could strike.

CHAPTER 35

The television was on and sunlight was streaming through the gaps in Ted's curtains when Steve woke up. It took him a moment to get his bearings, and when he remembered where he was, he got a sick feeling in his stomach. What the hell was he doing? The morning sun seemed to have illuminated his stupidity.

Ted was still slumped over in the chair. He had an urge to run. Maybe if he left now, this all could be forgotten.

He couldn't show the tape to police, and he didn't think he could get Ted to confess again. So his plan now was to try convincing Ted to turn himself in to the police. This seemed like his only viable option.

He decided to make some breakfast for the both of them; it was easier to catch a fly with honey wasn't it?

On the TV was a morning financial news show, but Steve couldn't have cared less about what was happening with the world markets; he had more pressing matters to worry about.

When he passed Ted and saw the dried blood on his temple, Steve winced. The rage and anger that had filled him the day before were gone. He felt more like himself this morning, more so than any time since Katie had been killed.

Steve didn't find much to eat in the kitchen. He brewed a pot of coffee and spread peanut butter on some graham crackers. As the coffee was brewing, he checked Ted's medicine cabinet and found a first aid kit. When he returned to the dining room where Ted was tied up, something was strange; something seemed off in the room. The TV was still on, and Ted was still tied up with his head slumped down, but something was wrong.

He smacked Ted in the arm. "Hey, wake up."

Ted raised his head, blinked, and looked at Steve. "Are you gonna hit me more?"

"No, I'm going to fix you up."

He pulled a chair up in front of Ted and opened the first-aid kit. Using an alcohol rub, he cleaned the biggest wound, a quarter-sized abrasion over his eye. Without the blood surrounding it, it didn't look that bad. A large yellow pattern had formed around the wound, reaching almost to the middle of Ted's forehead.

"I made breakfast," Steve announced as he got up and went into the kitchen. He poured a cup of coffee for himself, diluted it with cold water from the sink, drank it, and then repeated that process two more times. He wanted the caffeine quickly.

He brought Ted a cup of coffee and several graham crackers.

"Mmmm, coffee," Ted said.

Steve gently brought the cup to Ted's mouth and tipped it up until the coffee rolled into his mouth.

"I'm sorry about what happened yesterday, but we both know what you did," Steve said. He could feel his anger rising again, but if he wanted to get this guy to turn himself in, he had to try a different tack. He lowered the cup and took it from Ted's mouth.

"Kid, I'm not crazy. A rock four times the size of Manhattan is coming toward Earth, and you need to try to save yourself. I'll turn myself in, but you have to get south."

"You'll turn yourself in?" Steve tried not to sound too surprised.

"Yeah, but I gotta piss like a racehorse, and I don't want to piss all over myself." Ted looked down at the rope that bound him.

"OK." Steve looked at the rope, trying to figure out how they could accomplish this while Ted remained tied up.

"Loosen my hands a little and bring me a bucket," Ted said, squirming in his chair for effect.

"Where's a bucket?"

"There's one in the closet in the hall, I think."

Steve went to the kitchen hallway, returned with a bucket, and placed it on the floor next to Ted. Steve loosened the rope around his wrists, but left the rest of it in place. When he felt Ted's hands were free enough to handle his business, he put the bucket in his captive's free fingers so that he could position it.

"OK?" Steve asked.

"Yep."

Steve didn't want to leave the room, but he did turn around to give Ted a little privacy.

After a few seconds Steve realized he wasn't hearing the sound of Ted relieving himself into the bucket. He snapped his head around to see Ted half-standing, with the rope loosened and one hand free. The blow to Steve's throat felt light, but it caused his throat to close reflectively, and now he couldn't breath. He bent and grasped at his neck. Ted threw his body into him, smashing Steve against the wall and breaking the chair that had held him.

Steve fell to his knees. He felt Ted's arms around his face, like he had him in a wrestler's sleeper hold. Was this how he was going to die?

* * *

Steve's head was pounding when he woke up. He blinked a few times to clear his vision. Ted was sitting in front of him with his legs crossed—cleaned up, wearing a fresh suit, and sipping a cup of coffee. An overnight bag sat on the table next to Ted.

Steve looked down and saw that he was now tied to a dining room chair, with his own rope. He also noticed that Ted knew how to properly restrain someone; there was no way Steve was going to wiggle out of the rope.

"Hello again, sleeping beauty. You've been out for three hours." Ted took another sip of his coffee and turned his attention back to the TV.

"So what now?" Steve asked.

Ted looked at him and put his coffee down on the table.

"Son, a giant-ass rock is going to hit Earth tomorrow. I'm going to save you. I need you to do what I say, OK?"

"OK." What else could Steve say?

"It will be on the news," Ted said, motioning to the TV. "When they announce it, we'll make our move, when there's complete chaos at Next Industries."

"OK," Steve said again.

Ted saw that Steve still didn't believe him. "You'll see, you'll see," he said as he got up and turned up the volume on the TV, which was turned to a twenty-four-hour news channel;

the host and commentators were discussing world economic data. "Want something to eat?" Ted asked, walking into the kitchen.

"No, I have to piss like a racehorse. Get me a bucket."

Ted broke out in a loud laugh. "I knew I would like you, kid. I just knew it."

A high-pitched screech came from the TV as it displayed the emergency broadcast logo. "The emergency broadcast system has been initiated," a voice announced. "This is not a drill."

Steve looked toward Ted, who turned and looked as shocked as Steve. Their eyes locked.

"It's happening. See? I told you." Ted turned the volume up.

The president of the United States was now on the screen. "My fellow Americans, we have discovered that an asteroid is heading toward Earth and may impact the surface in the next forty-eight hours. To minimize damage and casualties, we are ordering people to remain in their homes until this threat passes. We do not have much more information about the asteroid other than the window of time for a possible strike. When the threat is over, we will give the all-clear signal through these same methods. Effective 9 p.m. Eastern time, martial law will be enacted across the country. Keep watching and listening for further instructions on how to safeguard yourself and your loved ones during this crisis. May God watch over you in this time, and may God bless America."

The screen went back to the emergency broadcast logo.

Steve stared at Ted, dumbfounded.

"He isn't telling the whole truth. He's already in a bunker, and this sucker is going to hit and pretty much wipe us off the face of the Earth." Ted said.

"Then why are you saying that we're going somewhere warm?" Steve asked.

"It's too late for that. We're going to an underground city, right here, under Next Industries, built by Vega."

"Why are you helping me?"

"It seems it's meant to be. I know what I did . . ." Ted's voice trailed off.

On the TV now a young woman was giving instructions on what to do, which amounted to go home, stay home, and get into your basement. The stationed continued to play this segment in a loop. Apparently she and the rest of the broadcast crew were heeding those instructions.

"Don't worry, kid, I have a plan," Ted said.

"Can it start with untying me?"

* * *

It was dark now as Steve sat in the back of Ted's BMW, on his way with Ted to Next Industries. Martial law may have been imposed, but as Ted had predicted, there were no police around to enforce the law.

Buildings were ablaze and the sound of gunshots was frequent along their route. Like the rest of the drivers on the road, Ted was ignoring stoplights. Steve's hands were still restrained, now in handcuffs. "Just a precaution," Ted had told him.

Steve still wasn't sure whether to trust Ted, but he had been right about the asteroid, and he could have killed Steve already and hadn't. He hadn't told Steve the details of his plan, just that Steve was going to be safe, and that he wanted revenge on Vega. *Revenge for what?* Steve didn't know.

Ted, who was humming a song as he drove, turned the car down an alley to avoid a gang of looters and then slowed it to a crawl.

"This doesn't look good," he said. A Dumpster was blocking the alley. Ted opened his window, pulled out a handgun, and fired it at the Dumpster, sending the people who were hiding in the shadows scurrying away.

"Go move the Dumpster," Ted said.

"Are you kidding? They still might be out there."

"Don't worry. They ran away. And I'll cover you."

Steve heard the door lock pop next to him, and he begrudgingly got out of the car. With his cuffed hands he pushed the Dumpster to the side, giving the car enough room to pass. He had the urge to run, but knew he wouldn't get far with handcuffs on. He'd be easy-pickings for the roving mobs. He got back into the car.

"Good choice," Ted said.

As they drove on, Steve thought of his grandfather. Ted had let him try to call him, but just as he predicted, the phone lines were jammed. He tried dozens of times and kept getting a recorded message that the circuits were busy.

The Next Industries parking lot was nearly empty. Ted pulled up to the front of the main building and turned off the car.

"Aren't you afraid people will see us?" Steve asked.

"Nobody's here. They're all home with their families, or they're prowling the streets, burning buildings and stealing shit. Besides, the people we're interested in are below us."

Steve still didn't quite believe there was a bunker city under Next Industries, but at this point it really didn't matter what he believed or didn't believe.

"Let's go," Ted said. He got his overnight bag out of the car and led Steve through the building's front doors. Just as Ted had predicted, the lobby was empty. Steve followed him to the elevator, which took them to another empty floor. Ted led him into his office, closed the door behind them, and dropped his bag on the floor.

"Now we wait," Ted said, motioning for Steve to take a seat.

"Wait for what?"

"Wait for the middle of the night, and then I'll do some reconnaissance. You might as well try to take a nap, so you're ready to move when it's time."

Finally grasping what was going to happen to the world in the next day or so—and decades or even centuries after that—Steve was terrified. He wanted to live, but he couldn't see how this guy could save him. He still didn't trust him.

Steve curled up in the chair, doubting there was any way he could nap. But within minutes he was dreaming—of running from fires and from zombies.

"Hey." Ted's voice startled Steve out of his slumber. Ted, covered in sweat, was pulling Steve's chair toward the middle of the room.

He freed one of Steve's wrists and told him to sit on the floor. Steve sat next to a desk that was attached to the floor, and Ted locked the open cuff to one of the legs.

"I'm going to recon the situation," Ted said. "I'm leaving you here. If you're thinking about escaping, don't bother. First, you won't be able to move the desk. Second, I'm locking you in. And third, I'm your only chance to live beyond today." Ted's tone was matter-of-fact; he could have been talking about the weather.

Steve had no idea how long he had been asleep. He looked at the clock on the wall and saw that it was nearly two in the morning.

"Today's December twenty-first," Steve said, remembering the crazies on TV and the radio talking about the end of the world. "That Mayan calendar thing."

"Yeah, the Mayans were right, and Vega knew. That's why

he's so prepared." Ted had changed into a black uniform and had a gold badge hanging from his neck.

"Be good, kid," Ted said as he left the room.

Steve heard the door lock after it closed. He pulled against the desk; it didn't budge.

CHAPTER 36

Ted took the secret elevator outside Vega's office to floor X. It was dark and quiet now. He walked down the hallway, looking into dimly lit rooms filled with people sleeping on bunk beds. He figured Vega was somewhere on this floor, secluded from the rest of the people. He turned a corner and almost walked into a guard dressed similarly to him.

"Sorry," the guard said. Then he looked at Ted, squinting his eyes, trying to recognize him.

"Hi, I'm Ted Baron, Mr. Vega's right-hand man. I just got in." Ted stuck out his hand.

The guard, whose hand hovered over his sidearm, looked Ted up and down and saw his gold badge. Just as he moved his hand from his gun to meet Ted's, Ted grabbed his hand, pulled him forward, and thrust his knee into the guard's face. Then Ted stood him up, spun him around, grabbed the guard's gun out of his holster, and held it to his temple.

"Say a word, and you'll die before it leaves your lips," Ted said quietly. "OK?"

The guard, whose nose was bleeding a steady stream, nodded his head in the affirmative.

"Now quietly answer: How many guards on this floor?"

"Just me, for another hour."

Ted noticed the guard had a two-way radio.

"Is Vega here?"

"Yeah, he got here in the afternoon. He made a big speech to everyone."

"Where is he?"

"I . . . I . . . don't know."

Ted hit the guard hard in the forehead with the butt of his gun and then quickly pressed it back against his temple.

"I don't know where he is," the guard said. "He's somewhere in the compound, but I don't know where."

"Can I call him?" Ted said, pulling the radio from the guard's belt.

The guard's eyes moved wildly from side to side.

"Listen, you answer my questions, I leave, you live," Ted said calmly. "You don't answer, I put a bullet in your head and leave. This is your last warning."

"His frequency is zero-zero-zero. But we aren't supposed to use that frequency. We use two-two-two."

"Good boy. One last chore and you're a free man. Get up."

He escorted the guard to the elevator. They took it to the floor where Vega's office was located, and Ted brought him into the boss's office. He moved Vega's chair into the middle of the room and made the guard sit in it. Then, with the rope that was in his bag, Ted tied the guard to the chair.

"I am going to need you to do one more thing," Ted repeated, looking the guard directly in the eyes, inches away from his face. "You do it, you go back down. You don't, you die."

"OK, but if we stay up here too long, we're going to die. The asteroid—"

"Shhhh, don't worry, my friend. You do what I need and you'll be back in safety before you know it."

The guard looked around nervously without answering.

"Who's in charge of security down there?" Ted asked.

"Mike Belmont."

"Who's Vega's second in command?"

"Same guy, I guess. It's not like there's an org chart."

"I'm going to have you call Vega, on his frequency. I'm going to tell you what to say, and you'll say every word to the letter, or I'll put a bullet in your head. OK?"

"OK," the guard said softly.

Ted went over the few sentences he wanted the guard to say and made him repeat them a few times. Then he picked up the radio, set the frequency to zero-zero-zero, and pressed the connect button. With his other hand Ted held the gun to the guard's head.

"Mr. Vega," the guard said. After a few seconds of silence, Ted motioned for the guard to try again. "Mr. Vega."

"Who is this?" Vega sounded sleepy and irritated.

Ted felt that chill again, the one he hadn't felt in a couple of days.

"This is Phil Huffington, guard on level X. I just caught a man getting onto the elevator. I followed him back to your office and disabled him."

"What are you saying?" Vega sounded confused.

"I've restrained him, and I checked his wallet. His name is Ted Baron."

Ted signaled for the guard to stop.

"Baron, here?" Vega asked.

Ted motioned for the guard to continue.

"I think you should come up here and see what he had on him. It looked like he was using a handprint to make the elevator work. I assume it's your handprint?"

"Is he alive?" Vega asked.

The guard looked at Ted questioningly. They hadn't practiced a Q and A session. Ted motioned for him to continue, hoping he would follow along.

"Yeah, but he's hurt. I've restrained him, just in case."

Ted nodded his head in approval.

After a few seconds, Vega responded. "I'll be right there."

Ted shut off the radio.

"Very good, Phil. This will be over soon, and you'll be safe and sound. One last thing: you will not say a word when Vega enters the room. Absolute silence. Or this will not end well for you. We're almost there, pal."

Ted smashed all the lights in the room—the ones that turned on automatically when the door opened—except for the one directly above the entrance. He positioned the guard's chair so that he was facing away from the door. Then Ted took his place off to the side of the doorway.

After what seemed like an eternity, the door opened and two men entered the office. Ted couldn't see their faces from where he was standing. One of them tried to turn on the lights while the other called the guard's name.

Following Ted's instructions, the guard said nothing.

The men cautiously moved into the room. The guy in front had his sidearm drawn. Ted raised his gun and squeezed the trigger. His target fired a response shot as he dropped to the floor.

Ted jumped from his hiding spot and tackled the other man. As he'd guessed, it was Vega.

Ted punched him in the face several times, until he was unconscious. Then he looked over his shoulder and saw that neither the man he shot nor the guard in the chair was moving.

"Phil?" Ted called out. There was no reply.

Ted took a pair of handcuffs from his bag, cuffed Vega's

wrist to his ankle, and then walked over to Phil. There he saw
the results of that second gunshot: Phil had a gaping hole in
the back of his head. Ted felt a momentary pang of guilt. He
flipped over Vega's companion and saw that he had a bullet
hole in the middle of his forehead. Ted took a piece of cloth
out of his bag and gagged Vega, then grabbed everyone's radios
and guns and put them in his bag. He moved the bodies out
of sight, in case anyone came looking. He picked up his bag,
wrapped his arms around Vega in a bear hug, and dragged the
limp body out of his office.

* * *

"OK, Mr. V, I'm going to take the gag off. But first, the ground
rules: you will answer my questions, and if you don't, this will
be the last room you ever see."

Ted removed the gag. Vega was handcuffed to a chair next
to Steve, his face bloodied.

"Ted, we can work this—"

Ted interrupted him. "Mr. V, please, let me ask some
questions. Then we can talk."

"OK, Ted. OK."

"So a big rock has a chance of hitting the Earth today?"

"Yes, Ted, today, around noon. And it may be several
asteroids, but the biggest asteroid will almost certainly hit."

Steve was watching and listening to the conversation. Ted
seemed calm, and Vega sounded friendly. But then, Vega didn't
have much of a choice.

"My men will come looking for me. You know that, Ted.
Just let me go, and we can work it out. You can join us."
Vega smiled.

"Mr. V, I was your closest aid for years, and during most

of that time I had no idea where you were or what you were doing. You wanted it that way. I'm guessing you have the same arrangement with your new friends, no? I think if anyone other than the guard who was with you knew where you were going, we would have already seen them. I don't think anyone has a clue where you are." Ted was smiling slightly.

Vega's expression turned sinister. "Ted, I can save you. Enough of the bullshit! What do you think, you can just show up down there and be welcomed? No, no, you need me, my friend."

"OK, Mr. V. Is this rock going to hit for sure? I heard if it did, it would be in Russia."

Vega's face sank. "Ted, I'm sorry. I wasn't thinking. You know, my son. I . . ."

"I served you for most of my life, and you send me to die! Because your psycho son is out of control! That's my fault? *My* fault?" Ted was screaming. Hatred twisted his face. This was the first time Steve saw him as the cold-blooded killer he'd imagined, but as quickly as the storm had risen, it ended. Ted dropped his head, took a deep breath, and smoothed back his hair. When he looked up, his pleasant expression had returned.

"Ted, I am sorry. Please, we must get underground . . ."

Ted, who was smiling now, interrupted Vega. "I know, Mr. V, I know. So this thing is hitting, right?"

"Yes, it is. At last check, there was a 99.8 percent chance of at least one strike, 76.4 percent of multiple. But the big one is an extinction event, and it's most likely going to hit in North America, not in Russia. We don't know exactly where. Any little thing can change its course. We won't know until it hits."

"One thing has bothered me about this whole thing," Ted said. "How did you know this was going to happen before anyone else did? You knew long ago, didn't you?" He sounded like a talk show host asking a question of a guest.

"My family has studied the Popol Vuh and the Mayan calendar for generations," Vega replied. "My family's bloodlines go back to royalty, Mexican royalty. Our family legends inspired me to further the research of my father and of his father. The researchers I funded years ago found a code in the Popol Vuh, a very old collection of Mayan myths, thousands of years old. The code explained the Mayan calendar, that it foresaw the return of the same band of asteroids that circled our solar system thousands of years ago. The Mayans were the first to chart the asteroids. Their civilization saw them light up the sky three thousand years ago and then again fifteen hundred years later. They thought the asteroids were the goddess Ixtab, their goddess of death. So they sacrificed many people to placate her."

Ted looked unconvinced. "So if these asteroids have flown by before, why are we here? I don't think there were mass extinctions fifteen hundred or three thousand years ago."

"The asteroids the Mayans saw didn't strike Earth. They believed Ixtab spared them because of the sacrifices they made to her. They predicted that there would be another pass-by now, because it's fifteen hundred years since the last one. But this time there will be a direct hit. My scientists believe that the asteroids that hit and wiped out the dinosaurs came from this same group, that this swarm of rocks has visited every fifteen hundred years for millions of years. Sometimes a few asteroids hit, sometimes not."

"Why were you so excited at one point about this? I remember you thought you were going to be king of the world." Ted was laughing at Vega as he asked the question.

"I expected another close call, not a strike. Imagine the panic when it was leaked that an asteroid the size of a mountain was coming in a few weeks. The world would panic; the market would crash. Imagine if a man knew this ahead of time and shorted the markets with his billions. He would make trillions. Then, just before the crisis passed, this same man would take his trillions and invest it in the now-crashed markets. Those trillions would become, well, let's just say he would be richer than any country in the world. He would be the most powerful person in the world. When I found out it wasn't going to be a near-miss, we moved to plan B: survival."

Steve finally spoke. "Do you think you're going to survive in your hole in the ground? It sounds like nothing will be left."

"Who are you?" Vega asked.

"He was Katie Landry's boyfriend," Ted said.

"Why is he in cuffs?"

"Long story, and I'll get to that in a minute. Answer his question."

"The people on the surface of the Earth are doomed," Vega said. "The explosion alone will incinerate half the planet. The people remaining will be faced with a decade of nuclear winter, most likely triggering another ice age. Between the explosion, starvation, and disease, no one on the surface will survive. Within ten years only the people in bunkers like this will survive, and even they will run out of food sooner or later. There's a chance humanity will be extinct in twenty years."

Steve and Ted remained silent.

"Ted, this is silly," Vega said. "We are family, and families fight. Let's all go down below."

"First I want you to do something for me. If you do it, then we can go together to the bunker," said Ted.

"Anything, Ted. What is it?" Vega was turning on the charm now.

"I want you to call down to Mike Belmont and announce that your nephew is coming down to the bunker. And that he is to be treated with the utmost respect."

"What is this all about?" Vega asked.

"I have the gun. If you don't do it, you're dead, and I'll take my chances with your people down there without you. I have a feeling I'll fit right in." Ted picked one of the stolen badges off his desk. "You have five seconds to agree," Ted said, lifting his gun to Vega's temple and clicking the safety off. "One . . . two . . . three . . ."

"Fine, fine, Ted. Stop." Vega's eyes were closed as he spoke, as if he wasn't sure whether Ted would stop before he got to five.

"Great. Any funny stuff and pop-pop." Ted mimicked his gun firing.

Ted set the radio to Mike Belmont's frequency and put it in front of Vega.

"Mike."

"Yes, sir?"

"It's Edgar Vega. We will be having a new arrival today, my nephew. I want him to be given full access and clearance, and put him near my quarters. He is like a son to me." Vega glared at Ted.

"Yes, sir, Mr. Vega. Sir, I was going to call you. Two guards are missing."

Ted waved bye-bye to Vega.

"Mike, I will have to call you back."

Ted cut the connection.

CHAPTER 37

Steve followed Ted through the hallways of Next Industries. He didn't know why this man wanted to save him, but he knew it was his only chance to live.

Ted opened the panel that hid the secret elevator and turned to Steve. "OK, kid, you're going to press X. When you get there, tell the security people that you're Vega's nephew and tell them to check with Mike Belmont."

"OK," Steve responded.

"And whatever you do, don't tell them what's happened, nothing about me or Vega."

"What if they ask me where Vega is?"

Ted thought for a second before replying. "Say he's returning to his house to get something, that he'll be back shortly." He glanced down the hallway in both directions. "Vega won't be coming."

Ted removed a plastic handprint card and several badges from his bag. He put an orange badge around Steve's neck. "This plastic thing is Vega's handprint. It will operate the elevator. Place it on the control inside the elevator to activate it."

Baron looked through the bag, removed a gun, and then handed the bag to Steve.

"There's a gun in there for you as well as other cards I stole from Vega. I imagine they open his private quarters and things like that down there. Hopefully they'll be useful."

"What about you?" He wasn't sure he wanted Ted to come with him, but he would feel safer with him.

"I won't be joining you either," Ted said, looking down.

Steve just nodded.

"OK, off with you. Good luck." Ted pressed the button and the elevator doors opened instantly.

Steve stepped in and almost said thank you, but caught himself before he did.

As Steve pressed the button for floor X he heard Ted say, "I'm sorry kid, sorry for everything."

The doors closed, and he began his descent. Twenty seconds later, the doors opened to a bright hallway. When he stepped out of the elevator, a large guard with a shaved head and black uniform drew his gun and shouted, "Freeze!"

Steve raised his hands and spoke as fast as he could. "I'm Edgar Vega's nephew. Call Mike Belmont. He's expecting me."

The guard looked him over and, with his free hand, pulled out his walkie-talkie. "Mr. Belmont, I have an intruder. He says you're expecting him, that he's Vega's nephew."

"Bring him to Ops," an angry voice on the other end commanded.

"Let's go." The guard didn't holster his gun, but he wasn't pointing it directly at Steve any longer. He pointed forward and followed behind Steve. When they came to an intersection of hallways, the guard barked, "Left."

Steve saw people milling about, all looking busy, and almost all of them doing double-takes at him, probably because he was the only person not wearing a uniform. They came upon double doors bearing the word OPERATIONS. The guard opened the doors, and Steve stepped into a room filled with television screens showing different news channels and other screens showing sloping trajectory lines around Earth that looked like something out of a science fiction novel.

"Mike Belmont." A large man who looked like a younger version of Ted extended his hand.

"Steve Soto," Steve answered and then flinched. Was he supposed to use his real name?

Belmont was too busy looking at the screens to see Steve's hesitation.

"Great, we'll get you settled in. Laurie, can you take Mr. Soto to the Vega family residences?"

"Sure." A beautiful woman around Steve's age turned away from the screens.

She got out of her chair and extended her hand. "Hi, I'm Laurie," she said with what seemed like a forced smile.

As they turned to leave, Belmont called out to Steve, "By the way, where is Mr. Vega?"

Steve felt his face flush, even though he had been expecting this question. "He said he needed to return to his home. He needed to get something very important."

"I hope he's safe," said Belmont. "We should have sent a few guards with him. By the look of things, we've destroyed the world before Ixtab got a chance to." He pointed to the TV screens, which showed scenes of destruction and rioting.

"Ixtab?" Steve asked.

"Yeah, that's what the asteroid has been named. Vega named it after some myth or something."

Belmont went back to his work, and Laurie led Steve out of the Operations room.

"Well, it's three hours and counting," Laurie said as they walked through the halls of the complex.

"Three hours, oh."

"So you're part of Mr. Vega's family?" She didn't sound completely convinced.

"Yeah."

"He's a great man. You're lucky."

Steve was looking at the rooms they passed. Most were filled with bunk beds.

"It will be nice for you to be with your family in a time like this," she continued.

Steve thought of his grandfather and felt a strong pang of sadness. "Yeah," was the only response he could muster before his eyes teared up.

"There are twelve people in the family residences. Do you know if any of your immediate family is here?" she asked.

Steve could tell now she was challenging him. He stopped Laurie, looked her in the eyes and said, "Vega came to me today. I'd never met him before. I thought I was an orphan, but he claims I am blood, that he's been looking for me."

Laurie looked confused.

"I'm his illegitimate son. Apparently, my mom and him, well, you know. I'm a secret. I think he wants it kept that way."

He looked around for an exit so he could run when she called for security. But she just looked at him and said, "Oh, I get it. No worries. We don't have to say anything. I'll give you a room. Mr. Vega's secret is safe with me." She made a motion like she was locking her mouth shut.

"Thanks." He could feel the sweat beading up on his forehead. When she turned and continued walking, he quickly wiped away the sweat.

"Everyone seems pretty calm down here considering what's about to happen," Steve said, trying not to give her the opportunity to ask any questions about his lie.

"Well, we have jobs to do. And quite frankly, I think most everyone is hoping we hit the lottery, and that the .20 percent chance happens."

They entered a stairway and descended several flights, passing the Y level.

"What's on the Y level?" Steve asked.

"More of the same: bunks, the mess hall, and medical. We're going to the Z level. Only people of our security clearance level are allowed there. Wait until you see it. It's the storage area, the Vega personal compound, and our water supply."

"Water supply?" Steve asked.

"Yeah, there's an underground aquifer that has been diverted to here. We have all the clean water we could want."

"Where did this place come from?" Steve asked.

"Well your father—I mean, Mr. Vega—bought this area some years back from the government. It was a government facility in the 1950s."

"How many people are in here?" Steve asked, as they came to the Z-level door.

"About three hundred, give or take. Mostly families that Mr. Vega knew, as well as scientists, doctors. We have enough food for thirty years, and water, like I said, is unlimited. They even planted a farm on Z. They're hoping for the first harvest next year."

A few beats went by. "I would think your father would have filled you in more," she said.

Her gaze once again betrayed her disbelief. Steve watched her hand, worried it would go to her radio.

"I was only with him for a few hours. He said Belmont would fill me in. And to tell you the truth, I don't appreciate your tone. I'm pretty much blown away right now. A few hours ago, I had no father, and the world wasn't ending. And now . . ." He rubbed his face, showing his frustration.

She looked directly at him. He had no idea which way this was going to go. "I'm sorry," she said, putting her hand on his arm. "I mean, this is a pretty stressful situation. It's getting the better of me."

Steve smiled and nodded his head. "Yeah, you got that right. I'm sorry too, for being snippy. We're getting off on the wrong foot, aren't we?"

"Yeah, not the best first impressions," she said with a slight laugh.

They continued down the hallway until she opened a door that led to a catwalk above the cavernous level Z. Directly below him was the farm Laurie had just mentioned, inside a glass enclosure, with bright blue lights shining down on the budding growth. The rest of the cavern was filled with stored supplies—skids and skids of them. A guard stood on the catwalk. He continued to stand at attention when he saw Laurie.

To the right was a stairway down to the cavern floor, but Laurie led him left, into another hallway that was painted a pale blue and trimmed with dark wood. It opened into a room with a large stone wall decorated in black-and-white photos of men in military uniforms and a row of photos of United States presidents, starting with FDR and ending in JFK.

Laurie noticed Steve looking at the pictures. "Lyndon Johnson shut this place down. It was vacant until Mr. Vega bought it years ago."

She led him to a small room containing a bed and desk.

"What about power?" Steve asked when she flipped on the light.

"We have a large supply of oil and other fuel, and I hear we'll run some generators off our waste," she said, making a funny face. "I'll have someone bring you some clothes and your badge." She indicated the gold badge around her neck. "You can get settled in, and I'll come back later and give you the dollar tour."

When she had left, Steve surveyed his new room and then lay down on his bed.

Three hours until the end of the world, he thought. He suddenly felt exhausted, the frenzy of his recent days catching up with him. Within a few seconds he was asleep.

A light tap on his arm woke him. It was Laurie, holding a stack of olive-colored clothes. A bright, gold-colored badge sat on top of the pile.

"It's nearing the time. Would you like to join us?" she said solemnly.

"Time for what? Oh, time for . . ." He didn't need to finish his sentence.

"Why don't you get changed?" Laurie suggested. "We're monitoring it on TV as a group in the mess."

He changed into the loose-fitting military uniform, put his badge around his neck, and joined Laurie in the hallway.

"The last report was the biggest one, Ixtab, would hit in North America, probably the Midwest somewhere," she said softly.

"Will we be OK here?"

"Yes, unless it hits within forty miles."

"Is it still going to be as bad as they were saying?" he asked.

"If it hits Chicago, the crater will be five times the size of the city. The world as we know it will end. The people in the U.S. will be . . ." A tear ran down her cheek. "Well, they'll die instantly, incinerated, no suffering . . ."

Steve, on instinct, put his arm around her. After a second she pulled away. They shared an uncomfortable few seconds as they left the room and began walking down the hall.

Then Laurie stopped. "Steve, I have more bad news. Your father, Mr. Vega, he hasn't returned." Tears filled her eyes.

He didn't reply.

"I'm sorry. Maybe he'll get here under the wire, like you did," she said.

They began walking again. "I also told Mr. Belmont about your secret. I'm sorry. I blurted it out when he told me Mr. Vega hadn't returned yet. But he won't tell anybody. He has Mr. Vega's best interests at heart." She looked sincerely pained.

"Um, it's OK," Steve said as they entered the stairwell and began climbing to the Y level.

The Y level looked a lot like the X level. He followed Laurie into a large room filled with people dressed in colored uniforms: red, black, yellow. A few were wearing green, like his, including Belmont, who was at the head of the room. Several TVs were tuned to news stations around the world. A large screen showed the number 0.00 and a countdown: 10:16, 10:15, 10:14 . . .

"There's ten minutes left?" Steve asked, pointing at the countdown.

Laurie nodded her head.

She pointed to the 0.00. "That's a digital readout of a seismograph. We should be able to figure out how far away it hits by reading that."

Belmont noticed Steve and walked over to him. Steve tried to appear calm.

"Laurie told me about you and Mr. Vega. I'm sorry to say he has not arrived yet," he said in a hushed tone.

Steve remained silent, not knowing what to say.

"We're sealed up down here, but he can still get in by his personal elevator. So let's keep our fingers crossed." He patted Steve on the shoulder and went back to the head of the room.

Laurie gave Steve a sympathetic look.

The mood in the room was somber and tense. Laurie talked quietly with the people around her and introduced a few of them to Steve. He didn't register their names. He kept his eyes on the countdown. Everyone he knew—his grandfather, Jim, his stupid neighbors—everyone was going to die. The clock kept ticking down. Only four minutes to go. The room became silent. They watched the TV screens that showed brave reporters standing by familiar monuments, masses of people rioting, some crying. People in the room began to huddle together. Some embraced. A few cried. Laurie moved close to Steve. He put his arm around her, and this time she accepted it.

Steve heard prayers being uttered. A few feet from him, a couple embraced and the husband whispered over and over to his wife, "I love you. I love you. I love you."

The clock now showed less than a minute. Steve almost expected a New Year's Eve–style countdown when it reached ten seconds. But there was none.

The four digits all hit zero.

* * *

Ted and Vega sat side by side on the Next Industries rooftop.

For three hours Vega had offered Ted deals, apologies, and explanations, until Ted gagged him again. Now he had the gag over his mouth and his hands cuffed around a piece of mechanical equipment.

Ted was at peace with himself and with the world. Maybe the asteroid would strike. Maybe it wouldn't. It was in God's hands. He and Vega would face their judgments together.

Vega had told Ted that the impact would happen around noon, and now it was minutes away. At this point, he felt that taking the gag off Vega was the right thing to do.

"Ted, there is still time. I can save both of us."

"Who are you kidding? You'd have one of your lackeys put a bullet in me as soon as we got down there."

"No, Ted, no." Vega looked nervously around the roof and then screamed, "*Help! Help!*" until Ted punched him in the gut.

"Shhhh," Ted said quietly.

Vega was sucking air in hard, trying to get his breath back.

"People like you and me should not be the seeds of another era of the human race. We sit here," Ted said.

"That is not fair. Things need to happen. The strong survive. You and I are lions of the Earth."

"No, Mr. Vega. We are the evil of the earth." He looked at his watch. "I thought you said 11:57 a.m.?" He showed Vega his watch. It showed 12:04 p.m.

"Ted, how accurate is your watch?" Vega sounded excited.

Ted stood up and looked around. The world seemed to be at a standstill. It was absolutely quiet—no cars, no planes. It was beautifully peaceful.

"Did it miss us?" Vega whispered. "Oh my God, it would be a one-in-a-million shot."

Ted had never seen him look so happy. He looked like a child. It didn't last long. He and Ted both looked to the east when they heard what sounded like thunder. Ted saw a dim light in the distance, and then the building began to shake, mildly at first and then more intense by the second.

Ted dropped to his knees and laughed. The building was shaking violently now, swaying slightly back and forth.

"Why are you laughing?" Vega asked through clenched teeth.

"My watch runs fast."

The tremors stopped.

"Maybe it hit Europe, or the Atlantic. Maybe we still have time to get below." Vega sounded hopeful.

Ted looked back to the east. The dim glow was now a bright wave coming toward them rapidly. "I don't think so."

Ted stared into the oncoming orange wave. He could see it hitting buildings in the distance. It was a fiery orange wall, a tidal wave of fire. It was the most beautiful thing he had ever seen.

The building started to shake violently again, just before the orange wave crashed into the Next Industries campus. Ted extended his arms, embracing the fire as it incinerated him.

CHAPTER 38

With a shrieking explosion the rock crashed into the Earth's surface near the Texas coastline. The Gulf of Mexico evaporated in seconds.

A blast of energy spread from the rock in every direction at the speed of light, bringing death in waves.

The energy contracted as quickly as it had spread, returning to its source, back to the remains of the once great asteroid, transforming the rock at an atomic level. The ancient material briefly experienced a mingling of its existence and the destruction it had caused.

The rock lay cooling, its glow dimming but never dying out completely. Time covered and uncovered it. It waited, hidden, incomplete. Calling. Waiting.

CHAPTER 39

Steve stared at the zeros on the countdown clock. Nothing happened. The screens still showed the reporters and the masses of people. He was about to say to Laurie that maybe they hit the .20 percent when, all at once, every screen went to static. The seismograph readout climbed to one, then two. The room shook lightly, and as the seismograph reading increased—to three, four, five, and still higher—so too did the shaking. Steve and the others fell to their knees. It was a reflexive action. The lights were blinking, dust started to fill the air, and people screamed out, including one who shouted, "It's too close! We're going to die!"

When the seismograph hit six, it slowed down, and so did the shaking. The people in the room looked at each other with relief and disbelief.

Steve was hugging Laurie when the shaking began again. It was more violent this time, sending the seismograph past seven. Again, the shaking slowed and stopped. People picked themselves up off the floor and again hugged each other, but more cautiously than enthusiastically. "I think impact was around one thousand to two thousand miles away, southeast of here," Steve heard one of the scientists in the front of the room say.

"What does that mean?" Steve asked Laurie.

"That means . . ." She stopped.

"That means what?"

"That means there is nothing left up there. Most of the U.S. has been wiped out."

Belmont shouted above the din, "OK, people, we all have our jobs. Let's get to them, just like we practiced."

People quickly moved out of the room.

"We have to check for damage now. That's what he means," Laurie said.

"What should I do?" Steve asked.

She looked around. "I guess you can help me."

"OK." Steve was relieved to have a job.

Steve felt someone grab his arm. He turned and saw it was Belmont.

"Your dad isn't responding. I don't think he made it back," he said, holding up his walkie-talkie.

Steve tried to look sad.

Belmont put a hand on his shoulder. "When we're done with the damage review, we're having our council meeting. I think you should be there, if you're up to it."

"Um, OK." Steve didn't want to arouse suspicion.

"Great," Belmont replied, and walked off.

Steve followed Laurie out of the room, ready to begin his new life.

CHAPTER 40

Tec and his group of warriors regrouped at the edge of the jungle. They had spread out and searched Oxtab and found that it was still deserted, as their prisoner had said it was. They returned to the others from their village: Tec's father, the village priests, their prisoner, and Tec's brother, who was still unconscious and was being carried by two warriors.

"No one is there," Tec reported to his father.

"If this is a trap, you are the first to die," the king said to the prisoner, speaking to him directly for the first time. The prisoner, who was tied to a warrior, looked down and did not speak.

When Tec heard his father speak of traps, he wondered whether there was one waiting for him. He had left the village with great apprehension, but the people of Oxtab seemed a greater threat than the plot that the priest had warned him of. They had entered the village bracing themselves for an ambush, but they found only the homes they had burned and the bones of the animals they had slaughtered the last time they were here.

They were nearing the cave—the supposed entryway to the city of the gods—when Tec spoke. "We should stop here. This was where the first warrior died."

The king ordered the prisoner to walk toward the cave entrance, out in front of the warrior he was tied to. The prisoner took only half steps in the direction of the cave, the warrior walking a good distance behind him. They reached the opening and stopped.

"Go in," the king called out.

When the prisoner stood frozen, the king ordered a warrior to ready his bow. Seeing this, the prisoner entered the cave, sliding along one of the walls.

"We need torches," the warrior attached to the prisoner called back to the group, after his charge disappeared into the darkness.

The king ordered two warriors to bring them torches.

Tec moved closer. "Careful. Not too close," the king said to him. "I do not want to lose a son today."

Tec nodded and moved closer cautiously. He got to the opening just as the warriors were illuminating the cave. In front of Tec was a tremendous drop. He grabbed a torch from the warrior next to him and dropped it down the shaft. It fell until he could not see it anymore.

The prisoner and the warrior tied to him were against the cave wall to the left, holding a rope attached to the wall. The rope led down a narrow walkway that descended into the drop.

"That is the way to the city," the prisoner said, pointing down the twisting path.

Tec returned to his father and told him what he had seen.

"Let us proceed," the king announced.

They left Que and two warriors at the mouth of the cave; the path was too treacherous for them to carry him. If the prisoner was telling the truth about the city's healing powers, they would find a way to get Que down the path later.

The warriors and priests descended single file down the pathway. It sloped down at a dangerous angle, forcing everyone to hold tightly to the rope as they moved forward. The priest carrying the god rock walked behind Tec.

They eventually came to a landing that led to a hallway carved into the rock. Following the hallway for several feet, they found that it opened to a room dominated by a stone wall. The prisoner dropped to his knees when he saw the wall.

Tec approached the wall with his torch. It displayed the strangest drawings he had ever seen. They had no color, and the images were so clear they looked real. They were drawings of men, dressed in a type of clothing he had never before seen. Beneath each drawing were words he didn't recognize.

The king kicked the prisoner. "What is this?" he demanded.

"Pictures of the creators."

The king looked closely at the drawings and snorted in disgust. "Take us to the city," he said, kicking the prisoner again.

The prisoner got up off his knees and led them on, down another hallway carved out of the rock. When they passed through an entry onto a surface made out of a substance Tec had never seen before, the prisoner stopped. The warrior attached to the prisoner held his torch near his feet, illuminating a narrow ledge riddled with holes. Tec felt the ledge. It was hard and shiny, like his knife. He stomped his foot on it to see if it would give way, but it didn't move.

Below him, through the holes in the ledge, Tec could see the floor of the cave, far enough below them that a fall to it would be deadly. He looked back to his father for direction.

"Send the prisoner first," the king commanded.

The prisoner did not seem to fear that the ledge would not hold him. He walked out onto it until he reached a set of stairs that descended to the cave's floor. The rest of the group followed hesitantly, but grew bolder with every step. When they all reached the floor, the king asked the prisoner, "Where is the city?"

"This is the city." The prisoner spoke forcefully for the first time. "Only men who are pure of heart can come here and survive, to see where men were made by the creators and then released into the world."

"You will not survive another breath if you—" A piercing scream interrupted the king. Flashes of light popped in the darkness, spears flew through the air. One struck the chest of the warrior next to the king.

Men rushed out of the darkness, screaming as they attacked Tec's warriors. Most of his men were already down when Tec drew his dagger and dropped his torch. He backed away from the fray and picked off attackers one after another, jumping in and out of the darkness.

Tec saw his father and ran to him, plunging his dagger into an enemy on the way. He joined two other warriors who were guarding his father. He grabbed his father's torch and threw it forward, illuminating four approaching enemies.

Tec ran toward them, picking a spear up off the floor. He launched it at the closest attacker, piercing his torso and dropping him to the ground. Tec danced in and out of the light. He could now see fear on his enemies' faces. One by one he killed them, and their screams filled the room.

Tec turned back toward his father. He was surrounded by

four enemy warriors, each armed with a spear. They were moving closer, tightening the circle around the king, who had his dagger drawn. The two guards who had been with him lay dead on the floor.

Tec, screaming a fierce battle cry, made up half the ground between him and his father before two of the enemy warriors plunged their weapons into the king. The king bellowed and fell to the ground, slashing one of his attacker's jugulars on his way down. Tec pounced on the back of the closest enemy, running his blade across his neck. One of the remaining attackers pushed his spear forward, impaling the man who Tec had just killed and tearing into Tec's leg.

Tec cried out in pain but then launched himself through the air and drove his dagger through the open mouth of his attacker. He felt a swoosh of air pass by him as a spear meant for his midsection missed its target. He lunged forward, stabbing the enemy who had thrown the spear. The last warrior screamed and then fell silent.

All Tec could hear now was his own breathing. Torches littered the floor, illuminating small pockets of the cavern. Tec scanned the room and saw no movement.

He moved quietly through the cavern, staying out of the light. He stayed alert, preparing himself for an attack, but nothing came. He climbed slowly up the stairway, backtracked down the hallway, and climbed the steep slope that led to the bright light and the entrance to the cave.

When the guards saw him emerge, bloodied, they ran to his aid.

"We were attacked," said Tec. "It was a trap."

Que's gurney was empty. Tec looked around and saw his brother lying facedown a short distance away. Another body lay next to him, and a few more bodies were scattered nearby.

"They came at us from all directions," one of the warriors explained. "We guarded your brother as best we could. We killed them all, but one of the enemies hit your brother with a spear. Your brother rose from his slumber and pulled the spear out of his body to join the fight. He even killed a man." The warrior pointed to the body next to his brother's.

Tec walked over to his brother's body and turned him over. The wound in his stomach was still bleeding. His eyes were closed, and although his skin was a sickly shade of gray, Que's mouth formed a peaceful smile. Tec touched the skin; it was as cold as the ocean. He leaned in close to his brother's mouth and heard no breath. He touched the chest and felt no heartbeat.

Tec fell back. "The king also is dead," he said.

He sat next to his brother for a long time. The warriors remained silent.

Finally he got up, his leg aching from where the spear struck him. "We need to retrieve the god rock and my father's body," he told the two warriors.

They followed him into the cave and down the path to the chamber where the fight had occurred. Torches were still burning on the floor. They found the body of the king and began to carry it out of the cavern.

Tec found the body of the head priest. Waving a torch in front of his prone body, he saw a large hole where the priest's nose had been. He could see almost through his head. What type of magic had done this?

A strange device lay on the floor next to a dead enemy warrior. Tec picked it up. It felt very light. He put his finger in a ring-like piece of the device, felt a moveable part and squeezed it. The device produced a loud bang and a burst of light. He dropped the device, and it tumbled across the floor and into a pool of water he hadn't noticed before. He considered trying to retrieve the strange device, but chose not to.

This is an evil place, he thought. He grabbed the bag containing the god rock from around the priest's waist and left the cavern. On his way up the path, he met the two warriors and helped them carry his father's body out into the daylight.

Tec knew they wouldn't be able to carry his father and brother back to the village, so he ordered the warriors to dig two graves in the jungle, where no one would be able to find their bodies. They buried them at nightfall, a great king and great warrior prince laid to rest side by side. Tec looked the other way when the dirt hit their faces.

They left Oxtab at night—better to march in the darkness than to face another attack. The prisoner's words rang in his mind: *Only men pure of heart can come here and survive.* Was he pure of heart?

He realized he was now king, and as he marched through the dark jungle, he wondered what type of king he would be.